The New Age of
American Foreign Policy

THE *New Age* OF
American Foreign Policy

FREDERICK H. HARTMANN

THE MACMILLAN COMPANY
Collier-Macmillan Limited · London

The New Ag
American Foreig

THE *New Age* OF
American Foreign Policy

FREDERICK H. HARTMANN

THE MACMILLAN COMPANY
Collier-Macmillan Limited · London

THE MACMILLAN COMPANY
866 Third Avenue, New York, New York 10022

COLLIER-MACMILLAN CANADA, LTD., Toronto, Ontario

Library of Congress catalog card number: 74–99492

First Printing

To Peter

whose generation will prove or disprove
the wisdom of our decisions and, hopefully,
create a more stable world.

Preface

WHEN I accepted my present position at the Naval War College I already had in mind writing a book about American foreign policy. In fact, I had even written a short, experimental draft (to which the present text has only a slight resemblance). That is another way of saying that my thoughts have undergone considerable refinement in the last three years, for three reasons.

First, events of great impact, forcing a reappraisal of American policy, have evoked much significant analysis in print and in public debate. Second, I have had to lecture to (and hold seminars with) a mature student body of officials and officers of the United States who normally have been involved professionally with these problems. Third, I have had the rare privilege of exposure to the views of a very large number of distinguished academic colleagues and senior officials of our government within a setting which permits and encourages the frankest exchange of views. While this book is written in awareness of those views, it does not attempt to reflect any of them, for there are enormous differences of opinion, and it is the deliberate policy of the Naval War College to seek out contrasting approaches to problems. Moreover, the opinions of lecturers at Newport are privileged and not for attribution—a policy which, by conferring anonymity, also encourages the shelving of platitudes.

My overall theme in this book is that the United States, once it had dealt rationally and realistically with its early problems (which, being close at hand and fairly obvious, were widely and easily understood), benefited almost without effort from a world made secure for reasons that Americans largely did not understand. When we then encountered a period (1914–1939) of grave stresses and strains, we made little effort to understand their true source and reacted largely by an attitude of avoidance, "going it alone." When Pearl Harbor nonetheless brought unwanted war to our very door, we determined to play a "proper" part in the world. Yet our concept of what was "proper" was deduced largely by the avoidance of (or opposite of) pre-Pearl Harbor attitudes or actions (acceptance of membership in the UN compared with rejection of membership in the League; entering into alliances such as NATO and SEATO and the Rio Pact instead of shunning "entanglement"; having a foreign policy reaction to virtually everything versus having none to speak of).

Today, it is increasingly clear that such a new approach contains many of the defects of the old. This time it attempts too much rather than too little. But, as before, it is characterized by two failures: (1) to ask the right questions in the right sequence, and (2) to make *distinctions* in the relative effects and values of what is done. The record indicates that we still badly need to evolve more precise methods of thinking that will avoid the simple formulas of anticommunism and the like. To achieve more effectiveness involves encouraging thinking in terms of national interests and devising an appropriate foreign policy strategy which will *limit* our commitments to what other nations will not in the nature of things have to do for us anyhow—if we let them.

My organizational approach (by Parts) is first to show the difficulties that impede any foreign policy, and to sketch the particular nature of the American approach, relating it to the background conditions under which our attitudes were formed. Second, I show how the American governmental apparatus for handling national security questions has evolved and the overall effects of the political system on strategic choices. Third, I analyze, more or less chronologically, the development and implementation of our policy, clarifying both the sequence of events and their evolving psychological impact. Fourth, I give a functional-analytical treatment of the major contemporary problems of United States foreign policy. And my fifth objective, in the conclusions, is to indicate an overall perspective.

Thus Part Three and Part Four both cover the major problems of the last decades; Part Three does it chronologically and in detail, whereas Part Four does it analytically and more succinctly. Hopefully, this dual approach will prove more effective than merely the one or the other, since I believe it is difficult for the student to grasp the sequence if the treatment is only functional or to grasp the whole analysis if the treatment is essentially chronological.

I wish to express my thanks to my students at the Naval War College, particularly for the charming manner in which they combine the utmost personal courtesy with an utter lack of awe at "professorial wisdom." My 1968–1969 seminar group deserves special thanks, for they read and criticized the entire manuscript—to my great profit. The detailed comments of Col. L. C. Hutchins, USAF, and Cmdr. D. J. Ellison, USN, were especially helpful. Col. Murray Marks, USAF, brought to my attention the Chinese map shown as Map 5. My appreciation is also extended to my students at Brown University and Wheaton College who helped me smooth the edges of some ragged thoughts presented to them in lectures and discussions. Mrs. Lucille C. Rotchford, senior reference librarian at the Naval War College, gave her skillful attention to the bibliography; and Miss Ann Hardy, reference librarian, was of much help in clarifying certain obscure details.

A number of my academic colleagues here at the War College have been kind enough to read parts of this book. I acknowledge their help while absolving them of any responsibilities for its errors or defects. Particularly, I want to thank Harry L. Coles (Ohio State), Richard H. Cox (SUNY at Buffalo), Ambassador Thomas S. Estes (U.S. State Department), and Raymond G. O'Connor (University of Miami). Burton M. Sapin (George Washington University) read the entire manuscript and gave me wise counsel, which I deeply appreciate. Harry R. Warfel (University of Florida) made welcome suggestions on English style. Finally, I want to thank the many military colleagues on the Naval War College faculty who in numerous conversations helped me clarify the thinking behind this book—whether they agreed with it or disagreed. Rear Admiral John Chase, USN, deserves special thanks, as do Vice Admiral John T. Hayward (now retired but formerly President of the Naval War College) and Rear Admirals Joseph Wylie and Henry Eccles. The precision and breadth of their thinking on strategic questions has been a constant source of stimulus to me.

The title of this book was first suggested to me some five years ago by Howard H. Symonds (Spring Hill College). The book does not necessarily represent the views of the Navy Department or any other unit of the United States Government. It does represent my thinking on United States foreign policy.

F. H. H.

Newport, R.I.

Contents

List of Tables   xv

List of Maps   xv

PART ONE
Perspectives

INTRODUCTION Concept and Approach to American Foreign Policy   3

CHAPTER 1 The Dimensions of the Problem   8

    The Importance of American Policy   10
    American Handicaps   12
    From Isolationism to Globalism   18

CHAPTER 2 The Unusualness of the American Experience   23

    The Effects of Geographic Isolation   23
    The Effects of Historical Experience   26
    The Effects of the Domestic Environment   37
    An Assessment   43

CHAPTER 3 The Impact of American Attitudes   46

    Attitudes about Government and Politics   47
    Attitudes about Human Relationships   54
    An Assessment   59

PART TWO
Foreign Policy-Making:
Politics, People, and Organization

CHAPTER 4 National Security Coordination and Foreign Affairs   67

    The Revolution in the U.S. Foreign Policy System:
    Primitive Beginnings   71

The Revolution in the U.S. Foreign Policy System:
World War II and After   74
Coordinating Devices and Presidential Style   78
An Assessment   82

CHAPTER 5   The Department of State   84

Personnel Problems   85
Organizational Problems   90
The State Department in Operation   97
An Assessment   102

CHAPTER 6   People, Politics, and Foreign Policy   104

Three Qualifications to a Model of Political
Group Interaction   106
Group Pressures   110
The Consequences for Foreign Policy Change   113

CHAPTER 7   Congress, President, and Foreign Policy   119

Congress vs. President: An Overview   119
The Decline in the Congressional Role of Debate   125
The President's Role   131
An Assessment   135

PART THREE
Foreign Policy in Operation

CHAPTER 8   The Formative Years   141

Three Long-Range Trends   141
An Empire in the Pacific   144
Toward Increasing Global Awareness (1899–1917)   147

CHAPTER 9   America, the Great Power   153

The Versailles Settlement   153
Far Eastern Affairs and the Washington Conference   156
Retreat into Isolationism   161
War Draws Near   164
World War II   166
An Assessment   171

CHAPTER 10   The New Age: Initial Disillusionments   173

Preconceptions   173
The Cold War Begins   175
The Fall of Czechoslovakia and Blockade of Berlin   181
The Fall of China and the Korean War   187
An Assessment   192

CHAPTER 11   The New Age: Liberation vs. Containment   194

    Korea, Indo-China, and SEATO   195
    The German Problem After Stalin's Death   200
    The Summit Conference—Interlude Between Storms   205
    The Crises of 1956: Poland and Hungary   207
    The Crises of 1956: The Middle East   210
    An Assessment   214

CHAPTER 12   The New Age: Soviet Challenge   216

    Squeeze Play on Berlin   217
    The U-2 Incident and the Berlin Wall   222
    The Cuban Missile Crisis   225
    The Congo Crisis   230
    An Assessment   233

CHAPTER 13   The New Age: Polycentrism and Fragmentation   235

    Khrushchev's Revisionism   236
    The Sino-Soviet Dispute   240
    Communism, Post-Schism   246
    De Gaulle and the Change in NATO   250
    An Assessment   255

PART FOUR
The Problems of Foreign Policy

CHAPTER 14   Alternative Strategies for U.S. Policy   259

    The Strategic Questions Debated   259
    Perceptions   263
    Foreign Policy Objectives   267
    Alternative Strategies for U.S. Policy   270
    A Better Alternative   275

CHAPTER 15   Military Problems   282

    Sophistication, Game Theory, and Other Ideas
      or Models   283
    Systems Analysis and Military Management   287
    Effects of Advances in Military Technology   290
    Effects of Arms Control and Disarmament   293
    Effects of Military Developments on U.S. Policies   295
    An Assessment   297

CHAPTER 16   Socioeconomic Problems   299

    The Widening Gulf Between Rich and Poor   300
    Prospects for World Economic Development   305
    Technical Factors Affecting Development   309
    Implications for U.S. Policy   314

CHAPTER 17   Political Problems: I   318
             The United Nations   318
             Political Problems: Soviet Troops in Central Europe   324
             Soviet Weaknesses   327
             The Crisis in NATO   331

CHAPTER 18   Political Problems: II   339
             Asian Developments   339
             The U.S. Role in Asia   343
             The Middle East   349
             Africa and Latin America   354
             Progress and Reform in Latin America   355
             The African Dilemma   358

PART FIVE

Conclusions

CHAPTER 19   One Foot in the Future   363
             An Overview of the Argument   364
             Reality and Image: Geography and Strategy   368
             Reality and Image: Counterbalancing Interests   371
             The Strategic Implications   374

BIBLIOGRAPHY   379

INDEX   389

List of Tables

2–1. Secretaries of State Become Presidents   29

2–2. Regular Army Strength: 1817–1901   30

5–1. Department of State Personnel   85

16–1. U.S.–Latin American Trade   303

16–2. Major U.S. Trading Partners   304

List of Maps

1. NATO Military Commands   206

2. Chinese Losses to Russia   247

3. U.S. Forces in Asia   276

4. Southern Africa: White Minority Rule   323

5. A Chinese View of China   340

6. Israel After the "Third Round"   350

7. Latin America: A Continent in Transition   356

PART ONE

Perspectives

INTRODUCTION

Concept and Approach to American Foreign Policy

TODAY the foreign policy problems confronting the American people are large in number and intricate in their interrelationships. Any compact book dealing with these problems must inevitably emphasize certain trends, developments, and details at the expense of others. Given the highly desirable contemporary emphasis in political science on a much more rigorous attention to conceptual framework than was fashionable earlier, it is useful to begin this book by stating the point of view and assumptions that determined its structure and content.

The first assumption is that the American people have come to a critical point in their post-World War II foreign policy. Primarily as a reaction to the Viet-Nam War, many Americans have begun a re-examination of the thrust of U.S. foreign policy. Specifically, the policy of global commitments that has characterized so much of what we have done since 1945 (i.e., in the "new age" of American foreign policy) is under attack and undergoing review. Consequently this book attempts to provide an intellectual framework that will make this re-evaluation more meaningful.

The second assumption is that the main external affairs concern of most Americans in this new age of nuclear weapons is and has to be with security-related problems. Consequently this book gives primary attention to these problems, with only secondary emphasis on other aspects (and even then essentially within the perspective of the primary concern).

The third assumption is that the nature of the American historical experience constituted a poor preparation for developing a sophisticated awareness of the international system as it actually functions. We were long insulated from the storm centers of European (or Asian) power politics by virtue of geographical location in the New World. Only recently has technological progress altered the significance of this location.

Even here, as we shall see, the extent of the alteration needs careful assessment. In colonial times we confronted Europe's great powers on our own periphery; today we confront the world powers on their peripheries. In between, and for much of the nineteenth century, we stood aloof and untroubled. Rather than analyze the operation of the political phenomena loosely known as the "balance of power," we consciously rejected this study as irrelevant to our own concerns and counterproductive to our true interests. Consequently this book continually emphasizes the principles of international relations and such phenomena of the world system of nation-states as a meaningful and essential perspective against which to weigh American foreign policy. For that reason the discussion devotes careful attention to the history of that policy.

The fourth assumption is that although the instruments for U.S. foreign policy-making and execution are worth studying for their own sake, they are important within the present framework primarily from the point of view of whether they enable the U.S. to create and implement a coordinated and sophisticated policy suitable to our needs and interests, especially our security interests. Specifically, do these instruments provide an efficient governmental machinery for strategic planning in the broadest sense, and for coordination in carrying out agreed operations? Consequently this book emphasizes the bureaucratic problems implicit in overall planning and coordination, while giving much less attention to myriad minor changes in bureaucratic nomenclature and organization. It is of minor importance, for example, that the Operations Coordinating Board (OCB) was established early in President Eisenhower's administration and abolished equally early in President Kennedy's. But it is of major importance to understand the problem both Presidents were trying to solve—which still exists. In the same way this book examines whether the Congress today is fulfilling its essential role of examining foreign policy alternatives through debate—thus also illuminating the issues for the American people.

The fifth assumption is that the thrust of U.S. attention to major geographical areas of the world has not been balanced: specifically, that we have been primarily concerned with Europe and Asia, then with the Middle East, and only lastly with Africa and Latin America. In the author's view, this division of attention roughly reflects American security interests in the outside world and is, in turn, reflected in the treatment of events and U.S. policies in this book.

The sixth assumption is that although it is unwarranted on the basis of the available empirical data to offer generalizations about the political behavior of the entire American nation as scientific fact, tentative hypotheses are inescapable unless we wish to shut our eyes to an important part of the total problem. Although such hypotheses are offered in Part One and must be considered tentative, it would hardly do to assume that the American people as a whole do not share certain attitudes that strongly influence their style in conducting foreign policy and the goals and content of that policy. What is legitimately in dispute is which attitudes and to what extent. If what is said on these points must be considered tentative, the reader will still need to make a judgment as to the degree of their truth, bearing in mind that the larger the generality, the more it risks departing from reality. Consequently this book explicitly examines these points.

The seventh assumption derives from the third and sixth and assumes that the combination of the rather truncated and peculiar American experience in world affairs with typical American attitudes about life in general and political phenomena in particular has produced a marked tendency in American political analysis toward two extremes: either a rather abstract point of view (which may do violence to the real-life variety) or a concern with the concrete details of problems at the expense of their more general meaning. Specifically, American deterrence theory tends to be abstract and ignore the question of whether Americans, Chinese, and Russians would all react to a nuclear confrontation with precisely the same logic and come out with the same decision. Specifically, American analyses of U.S. foreign policy organization and implementation often fail to shed light on such fundamental questions as why Americans so frequently assume that if something needs to be done, the U.S. is the one to do it. Consequently this book attempts to sketch out a perspective avoiding these pitfalls.

The eighth and ninth assumptions are the most important and are foreshadowed in the foregoing. The eighth assumption is that the formulation and conduct of U.S. foreign policy has proceeded in the new age with little systematic examination of alternative strategic solutions to the problems of U.S. security in the broadest sense. Specifically, the general concept of containment has led to a massive U.S. involvement in world affairs, complete with whole hosts of commitments, without any great consideration as to whether the overall policy goals might alternatively be achieved at less expense in blood and money. Noteworthy is the contrast with Soviet behavior which, although vigorous, has avoided direct commitment of Soviet troops in battle. It is not necessarily contended that the same economy in the use of force was open to the United States. It is contended that the United States has not rigorously examined alternatives that might lead to that result. Consequently this book devotes much emphasis to the conceptual problems of U.S. foreign policy as they relate to grand strategy.

It is here that a book on U.S. foreign policy simultaneously meets its greatest test and encounters its most important conceptual problems. For the ninth assumption is that the procedural explanation of our failure to examine strategic policy alternatives lies in our failure to ask the right questions in the right order. Specifically, the nomenclature and terminology customary in the field reflect this failure. The recent and highly useful Institute for Defense Analyses Study of *The President and the Management of National Security* contains a glossary of terms that is representative of current usage.[1] Foreign policy (general) is defined as comprising "the aggregate of the activities of a government conducted for the purpose of achieving its international objectives." By contrast, a foreign policy (specific) is "a course of action for accomplishing a specific purpose in international relations, and includes an objective(s) and the ways and means of attaining it." So general foreign policy is all the activities conducted to achieve objectives, whereas a specific policy includes objectives and ways and means to reach them. Note "ways and means" is included in the definition for specific policies and presumably has a tactical connotation. If we want Peru to cease expropriating American oil, we consider how to pressure or persuade or cajole her into more acceptable behavior. But general foreign policy is an "aggregate of . . . activities" and "ways and means" do not receive mention unless we subsume them as part of the "aggregate." Activities may here denote thought about alternative ways and means, but it is not specifically singled out. In practice, in U.S. policy formulation it tends to be left out, whereas in policy implementation it is given great consideration—precisely as these definitions imply. The point here is not to question whether the definitions are accurate representations of current thinking, for they are. The point is rather that the most important questions about foreign policies should cluster around what we would like to see happen and who might do it for us. In an action-oriented United States, "activities" are likely to add up to a program outlining what the United States should do rather than consider what we might not have to do at all.

The same Defense Analyses Study defines "national security policy" as consisting of "the objectives and the ways and means of attaining and maintaining national security." Here "ways and means" reappear, as they should, which makes the contrast even more marked. Of course, if one conceptualizes national security policy as a term subsuming general foreign policy in its security aspects, as normal usage does, then the problem begins to lessen, and indeed the actual study does do this from the point of view of appropriate governmental organization.[2] But even so, investigation of "national security policy" and of "national security policy planning," as these terms are generally used (and as this study uses them), tends to focus on organizational matters, "contingency planning" in the armed forces, and coordination between State Department,

---

[1] *The President and the Management of National Security*, Institute for Defense Analyses, edited by Keith C. Clark and Laurence J. Legere (New York: Praeger, 1969), p. 266.

[2] The *content* of policy was not within the scope of the Defense Analyses Study.

Defense Department, and the White House, and students of these problems in fact are not likely to place much emphasis on the overall strategic policy choices. Because we fail to ask the right questions in the right order, the national security apparatus does not actually concern itself much with these choices—as a close study of these arrangements will show. Rather recently (spring, 1969), President Nixon took the step of having a broad review of military posture options prepared, with more than nominal State Department inputs. But this has been the exception in the new age, rather than the rule. Since 1950, large armed forces and worldwide commitments have been more accepted as inevitable than questioned in terms of first principles. Yet the most fundamental questions about our policies can only be answered in terms of first principles. The extent and size of the armed forces and the utility and/or necessity for U.S. commitments turn not just on what needs to be done for U.S. security interests to prosper. They turn more precisely on what is left for us to do if others act in their own interests and we, in our impatience, do not preempt them.

Thus the most meaningful problems of foreign policy are security related, and their solution turns initially on the adequacy of our conceptual approach. This is the realm of grand strategy, a term that for too long has been connected in the popular mind too exclusively with military affairs. This defect in our approach needs remedying. The belief that this is true is why this book emphasizes the strategic alternatives and provides a frame of reference and a set of criteria for assessing and choosing among the grand alternative foreign policy choices open to the United States.

CHAPTER 1

The Dimensions of the Problem

N O NATION can, by an act of will, wish away the world out-side its frontiers. It must deal with that real world of violence and change, by attempting to control its tensions and make inevitable change serve constructive ends. How the American people solve these problems is the subject matter of American foreign policy. In its essence, foreign policy must be an overall program for action, including both a viable strategic conception and related tactical plans for dealing with other nation-states.

If foreign policy is both well conceived and successfully implemented, the American nation will avoid excessive costs in attaining objectives. Conversely, there are seven ways in which policy can fail: first, if alternative strategic conceptions are not explored; second, if the plan is no real plan but simply a jumble of incompatible hopes; third, if the plan departs from the fundamental values of the American people and eventually fails to be supported; fourth, if the plan is frustrated by lack of coordination or mechanical defects in the apparatus of the American government; fifth, if there is not adequate national power backing (military or nonmilitary) for the policy attempted; sixth, if the plan is designed to deal with an imaginary world rather than the one which really exists, or reality itself changes and the plan is not flexible enough to adjust; seventh, if the plan runs into important or even overwhelming opposition by other nations. Failures are possible in conceptualization, organization, and application.

These seven tests of foreign policy success or failure have determined the form and organization of this book. Since it is *America's* foreign policy, we must first gain perspective on our own background, experience, and resulting attitudes. Second, we must examine the internal pressures on, and arrangements for, foreign policy—noting the changes in the governmental apparatus that make possible the infrastructure necessary to staff our present great involvement in world affairs. Third, we must achieve an acquaintance with the detailed events and crises that have been the content of American foreign policy, seeing them both in an historical and evolving psychological context. Fourth, we must examine the policy approach made to the world and its problems in the most hardheaded way possible, looking analytically at the military, socio-economic, and political problems that confront the American nation. And, fifth, we must attempt some useful overview and conclusions about these problems. These five areas of concern are, in sequence, the five parts of this book.

Where failures are possible in conceptualization, organization, and application, failures in organization and application will be very important but failures in conceptualization will be critical. If our government does not deal with the real world, if we attempt more than we need to attempt, if one goes at it through a strategy involving excessive and needless costs, elaborate organization and meticulous application will merely carry the nation more efficiently in the wrong direction. That is why foreign policy, as an overall program for action in world affairs, must indeed reflect a strategic concept.

To arrive at that strategic concept we must continually ask ourselves three questions: (1) What is the objective? (2) Who can realistically oppose it (and who may have to assist with it)? (3) How can we in this context succeed at minimum cost? Moreover, it is critical to ask the third question in the light of the first two, for it is not who opposes the United States in general that counts, but who opposes our particular objectives in handling a specific, concrete problem. (The Soviets, for example, while opposing us generally, may be forced to serve our objective in Asia vis-à-vis China.) The third question, "How can we succeed?" cannot be answered usefully until we see it within the perspective of answers to the two prior questions, for those who wish us failure may be unable in a particular case to act against our interests without doing even more damage to their own, and our conviction that this is so may be the very key to success.

One may ask first, "Who are, abstractly, the enemies of the United States?" but it is better to ask what nation or nations can afford to act contrary to our interests in a particular situation. The world is, after all, not bilateral. Every nation confronts many problems and "politics makes strange bedfellows." In a specific problem area one may ask first, "What should the United States do?" But it is far wiser to ask, "What is it that the United States would like to see done?" and then, "Who might have to do it?"

Because Americans are both impatient as a people and inclined toward direct action, many of us tend almost automatically to ask at the outset *what we should do* rather than *what we want done* and who might do it. Specifying the objective must be the beginning of analysis; answering what we should do should come only after a careful consideration of what, if anything, will be left undone after all those who are also under compulsion to do something do it. It cannot be overstressed that this simple transposition in the order of the questions we ask ourselves about American foreign policy is the single greatest procedural source of our difficulties and failures. Once we learn to ask the right questions in the right order we will find ourselves with a whole host of interlocking considerations that require subtlety and skill to unravel. Greater amounts of thought can often be substituted for greater amounts of American blood and agony. The effort is worthwhile.

In thinking through our problems we must keep thoroughly in mind a principle we are prone to neglect: the principle of *counterbalancing interests*. Just as the allocation of budget resources represents both a positive and a negative choice (something bought means also something not bought), so, too, the choice of a national policy or strategy involves the rejection of alternatives. No one choice is ever completely satisfactory, although it may on balance be—or appear to be—more desirable at the time the choice is made. Since conditions change and every nation must and does continually re-evaluate its choices, a previously rejected course of action may well become more appealing later. At all times, however, there are minor or major disadvantages to any particular choice. As policies shift, the calculus of relative advantage shifts with it, but one can never completely "have one's cake and eat it too." The strategic point of the continual reappraisal should be to collect as few formidable enemies as possible. While this advice might appear idealistic, it is well to remember that potential enemies have the same problem. (It is no accident that Soviet gestures toward détente with the United States occur in a time of worsened Soviet relations with China.) Consequently, each state is engaged (if it is wise and alert) in a continuing quest to maximize the realization of its important interests while amassing the least possible total resistance.

To formulate and execute a successful foreign policy is no easy task. In a nation such as the United States, highly literate, bombarded daily with large quantities of information and misinformation, very articulate and given to public debate, and very important to the rest of the world, the process is certain to be noisy, confused, and full of dispute. While that debate proceeds and the pros and cons are argued out, the whole of the American political process remains under close and continuous scrutiny around the world by many peoples whose destinies may well be affected by the decision.

The Importance of American Policy

WHY the American people have become so foreign-policy conscious is apparent. Since 1941 Americans in uniform have been dying in action in some foreign land almost continuously, whether in a "war," or a "police action," or as "advisers" or combatants in Viet-Nam. Why the policy of the United States is so important to non-Americans is somewhat less obvious. There is, of course, the clear impact of the substantial military power of the United States, whether we use that power or not. Beyond the stocks of H-bombs, the fleets of Polaris submarines and the like, there are other tangible reasons. The United States consumes approximately half the raw materials produced in the world. We are enormously important as a market, especially to "one-crop" or "one-product" countries. American support of the United Nations is so important to its functioning that the UN could not conceivably continue with its present program if that aid were curtailed or withdrawn. It is not just the direct, annual U.S. budget contribution that counts here (although a 37 per cent share —as of 1965—is the largest single contribution of any nation). There are also the "extra" contributions made to such special activities as the refugee program. There are the logistical supports so frequently offered for UN peace-keeping operations: airlift, sealift, and worldwide communications. To the poorer and weaker half of the nations of the earth, whose UN mission is their most important diplomatic effort, U.S. support of the UN takes on great significance. Without the UN many nations' voices would be extinguished simply through a lack of funds and trained personnel necessary for representation in more than 130 foreign capitals. For all these reasons, U.S. actions are critical to most other nations.

A position so powerful and influential in the affairs of mankind easily produces mixed feelings and reactions. Self-conscious American feelings of responsibility compete with resentment over the invective that America's actions and inactions inspire abroad. Governor Rockefeller's curtailed "good will" tour of Latin America in 1969 illustrates this predicament.

America's role is played in a world with greater problems than ever before. Even discounting the multiplier effect of the revolution in communications, which makes the American people daily aware of coups and unrest everywhere, there are more and greater problems to be handled.

First, the danger of a nuclear war has increased as such weapons have proliferated and spread into a larger number of national arsenals. At least some of the newer nuclear states have a list of grievances that imply tension and danger. Communist China is a notable example. Any further spread, too, has its own internal dynamics: in a relationship such as that between Israel and the United Arab Republic, if either one acquires nuclear weapons, the other must.

Second, the proliferation of nation-states has an important negative consequence. Whatever the theoretical or actual benefits to these newly independent states, it is not possible to multiply the number of "actors" in the state system without increasing the probability of armed conflicts among states. Being unstable, many of these newer nations are faced with chronic problems that defy easy solutions, and want redress for real or imagined grievances. Too many are "mini-states" of doubtful economic or political stability. Industrialization is simply not feasible to cure all ills everywhere—even assuming that it would. The base of many of these new units is too small, all other considerations apart.[1] Even in the larger, newer units the problems are quite obvious, as illustrated by the unhappy recent history of supposedly stable Nigeria.

Yet the very existence of so many newer units has multiplied the demands made on the older states, compounding the problems in formulating and executing a viable American foreign policy. It is frequently not possible to reconcile the demands and claims of new states with old, or one with another. The inevitable consequence is that some nations will be pleased by what we do or fail to do, but others will resent our intervention or abstention. As the other super power, the Soviet Union is caught in much the same dilemma, which is a consolation but not a solution.

In today's complex world American foreign policy has a highly important effect on international relations, but the world's complexity makes both the conception and attainment of appropriate foreign-policy goals difficult.

American Handicaps

CONFRONTED with the necessity of formulating and executing a sensible policy to deal with world problems, the people of the United States have attempted to do so—but with two great handicaps so far as many Americans are concerned. The enormous power of the U.S. has not made these handicaps less important; indeed, the very vigor of the American approach is multiplied by the power at its disposal and carries with it the result that any defects in U.S. policy are magnified in their effects. What are those handicaps?

The first handicap is the self-image widely prevalent in the American people—the belief that we typify the aspirations and hopes of the whole world. Many believe that in the management of its own internal affairs the U.S. has conducted a living laboratory experiment directly relevant to the hopes and fears of all other peoples. Those who share this self-image reject the dilemma in the preceding paragraph that an active foreign policy may well create hostility and friendship in fairly equal degree. They repudiate this thought on the grounds that America's policy *must* win a net friendship as long as it remains faithful to "humanity's goals." In turn they argue that our faithfulness to universal goals is amply demonstrated by the recurrent American pronouncements in favor of self-determination of nations, the rule of law, and a high

---

[1] In discussing the "two China question" in 1965, the U.S. Ambassador to the UN, Arthur J. Goldberg, pointed out that Formosa with its 12 million people contained a larger population than 85 of the then 117 members of the UN.

standard of living, plus the many concrete moves the United States has unquestionably made toward the implementation of such principles.

Simple arithmetic tells us that it is not possible for more than a minor part of the world to have the material abundance that the U.S. enjoys, since we do so by consuming more than our per capita share of the world's raw materials. Even assuming abundant technological advance and the achievement of a much greater degree of universal political stability, like most dreams, this particular dream is unreal. Not only can the greater part of the world not realize the American dream in the discernible future, but even today there is relatively little equivalence outside U.S. frontiers to what exists inside them. Much of the world is emphatically *unlike* the United States. If the political stability of the American system is not quite as unusual as United States material abundance, it too finds only relatively few equivalencies abroad. Although the American Constitution dates back only to 1788, it is already something of a world record. Few documents have lasted as long as popularly supported basic descriptions of the allocation of political power. Some stable political systems are older (such as the English have enjoyed), but most are much newer, and the majority of the older nation-states have experienced far more instability than the United States. The patterns revealed by French and Chinese experiences are much more typical.

Very few people in the world have lived, do live, or can live in the material and political environment that the American nation takes more or less for granted. Yet to many Americans this observation simply means that the other peoples have not yet been successful in finding their way to the right formulas. Foreign peoples are thought to be attempting to follow the same general path of development with less success. They are thought to be innately disposed to acknowledge American leadership and example in the pursuit of the "common" goals except where they are tempted by the false allures of communism.

A basic ambivalence is built into such views. The United States is the only large nation-state of first class power in the world whose population is almost exclusively composed of immigrants from across the ocean and their descendants. Many of its settlers came to the New World to realize goals and dreams whose fruition was denied them in the political-economic system left behind. Americans often even take satisfaction in this thought. But if it is assumed that the latest generations in these older societies can now achieve there what our own forefathers could not, on what grounds will it be done? Essentially it must reflect a belief that the American experience has "proved" the "rightness" of these dreams and aspirations, that the old barriers in the older nations will now fall and they too will follow our path. This belief sheds light on the incredulity with which an influential segment of American opinion, while applauding the French Fifth Republic's greater economic stability, denounced those "backward" policies of de Gaulle which led away from

American-espoused "common" goals of European integration and a stronger NATO.

To the extent that such an American attitude prevails, it leads also to many unwarranted assumptions about the newer nations. The people of the United States greeted the formation of the many new African states with prevailing optimism, which fact testifies to the strength of these assumptions. The launching in Latin America of the "Alliance for Progress" was accompanied with the same sort of acclaim and expectations. The point is not whether the new African states can eventually accommodate themselves to life in the contemporary state system on a basis far short of the initial dreams, or whether needed reforms in Latin America can be accomplished short of social revolution. Nor is it the point that the United States is wrong to encourage progress and reform. The point is rather that developments in these other lands so frequently are seen against the background of an American experience, which does not translate at all well for the purpose of appraising developments and forces abroad, but is widely believed in principle to do so. Actually it would be astonishing if the American experience were relevant elsewhere, since conditions in the United States have so little parallel to conditions abroad. There are no limits to the degree to which other peoples may envy us our stability and abundance and wish they had it, too, but there are quite harsh and severe limits that circumscribe how much success they can hope for in imitating our results.

These nations are aware of this difference, or are coming to suspect it, even if we do not. They may welcome our good wishes on their behalf, they may welcome certain tangible projects for development; but they cannot help but resent any assumption on our part that we have a patented solution for the cure of the world's ills. Even a casual look at the reaction of many of these newer nations in the last decade reveals that they are suspicious of too great an American influence in their affairs, and that few of them believe the American model can be simply followed. The very widespread public approval in these nations for varying forms and degrees of "socialism" is one indication. It is not enough to dismiss this as a yielding to the temptation of a shortcut.

Any self-image of the American people as pioneers along humanity's preferred paths to progress thus is a handicap to an effective foreign policy; it encourages a distorted conception of the value goals in a multitude of foreign societies. It is a handicap if and when it leads to judgments that another people's concern is to become more like us in fundamental ways. It is a handicap if and when it leads to assumptions that others will follow our leadership because they want to achieve the same objectives in the same way. It is a handicap if and when it tempts us to look out on the world and visualize each nation as occupying a position along a single spectrum of development, with some of them nearer our lead position, some of them still far behind, and some of them wandering off the main road into the dead end of socialism-communism. Far more useful is a very different assumption: that the world is quite diverse and will remain so, although each part of it will constantly be changing into something else which may resemble us or may not.

The second handicap of the American people stems from the particular way many of us view our own history and the history of the rest of the world. Even discounting Fourth of July oratory, we frequently tend to ascribe our historical good fortune and unparalleled security to our own efforts more than sound scholarship would substantiate. The inevitable obverse of this habit is to distort and minimize what was occurring outside our own frontiers. This distortion, to the extent that it prevails, encourages a relatively shallow appreciation for the roots of problems and the complex interplay of cause and effect in world affairs.

Our own attention turned inward for much of the nineteenth century; as a people we did not concern ourselves with what was going on far from our shores. Our perception of these events was often inaccurate. Later, when we became very much involved in world affairs, we were to this extent poorly prepared to handle them. We lacked substantive knowledge, for one thing.[2] We frequently did not know the background of what we faced, the real sequence of cause and effect. Since as a people we are not much given to looking backward but prefer to face problems in the here and now, we were not always aware that a little knowledge of history, too, can be a dangerous thing. We have shown a tendency to want to move on to solutions in unwarranted confidence that we know what the problems are—when in fact we have often failed to master the historical roots of what we are facing.

Illustrations of these points are not difficult (although we shall delay until later a conclusive treatment). Even our usual views as to the circumstances in which American independence was achieved leave a great deal to be desired in terms of teaching us our own history. One readily gains the impression from many public school textbooks that our own sense of outrage at Great Britain's consistent disregard of our rights as free men led the colonies to a reluctant defiance. The subsequent war, fought on a shoestring, was then won by men who knew they were right and who persisted until victory—with some incidental assistance by the French (who were, of course, motivated by jealousy of the British). The very substantial and critical French contribution to American freedom tends to be underrated, as does the widespread Tory resistance to the "rebel" point of view *in America*. On the other hand,

[2] Former Secretary of State Dean Rusk at the outset of World War II served as an Army officer in intelligence. He tells the story that the total background data he found in the files for his new section, covering from Afghanistan through southeast Asia and Australia, was a tourist handbook on India and Ceylon, a 1924 military attaché's report from London on the Indian Army, and a drawer full of old *New York Times* clippings.

the logistics complications for the British alone would have crippled their efforts, had it not been for willing aid from Tory elements in major American seaports, which also tends to be downgraded. Looked at in this fashion, the American Revolution assumes more complex dimensions.

Once independence was achieved (except in the War of 1812 and during the American Civil War), the United States was fairly immune to European threat. This immunity continued for balance of power reasons even after the great technological-military revolution, which began about 1855 and for the first time created the physical and logistical conditions for forceful and large-scale interventions from Europe—even against determined opposition on American shores. Although it remains a moot question how successful such an invasion might have been,[3] it did not come. It was hardly deterred by the miniature American land and sea forces of that period. Many Americans tended to ascribe their immunity to a prudent regard to Jefferson's counsel to stay out of Europe's problems plus the timely pronunciation of the Monroe Doctrine. Americans gave little thought to the intricate balance of power on the Continent contrived by Bismarck or to Britain's general refusal to see any alteration in the *status quo* of the New World. Indeed, in the twentieth century when the United States at last began to play a key role in world affairs, American Secretaries of State (and Presidents) frequently spoke of ending the balance of power and doing away with the very rivalries and "power politics" that had played such an important role in buttressing America's own security.

Once America's attention was focused on Europe as a consequence of World War I, the United States (in the person of Woodrow Wilson) quickly enunciated a program for the reform of international relations (the Fourteen Points); and then it backed an action program to achieve the desired results (the League of Nations). But on second thought we abandoned the whole project and retreated to an uneasy "isolationism."

The consequences of both American policy decisions were ultimately to have far-reaching effects on the way Americans viewed world affairs. America more than anyone else had founded the League of Nations. Yet the League failed, and that failure coincided with the advent of World War II. Two events or series of events during the post World-War-I era made a lasting impression on the American people and led to widely and strongly held assumptions about proper policy after World War II.[4]

---

[3] The War of 1812 does not contradict but demonstrates the point, for although the British landed both near Washington and New Orleans, lack of native American support denied them an exploitable foothold.

[4] See, for example, the extensive quotation from Secretary of State Rusk near the end of this chapter and in Chapter 14. Rusk's views illustrate well what is said here and in the next paragraphs.

The first of these events was the failure of the League to oppose what is commonly called Japan's aggression in Manchuria in 1931. This inaction is supposed to have undermined the League's ability to deal adequately with Mussolini at the time of Italy's aggression against Ethiopia in 1935. This weakness in turn is supposed to have both encouraged Hitler's aggression and led to the failure to restrain him. The second occasion was the aftermath of the Munich Agreement (1938), when Neville Chamberlain, British Prime Minister, returned to his people with the triumphant but fatuous conviction that he had achieved "peace in our time." What he had actually achieved was the weakening of the coalition against Hitler, the sacrifice of Czechoslovakia, and the loss of the large Czech armaments industry to Hitler's use. Truly, that last year of peace (1938–1939) was dearly bought.

Leaving aside the complexity of these historical issues, the point here is that many Americans were beset by guilt feelings that their nonsupport had undermined the League and were convinced that unrestrained aggression leads to further aggressions. As a result they enthusiastically endorsed the UN and unhesitantly backed our going to war over Korea (1950). The belief that appeasement did not pay (as Munich showed) was translated for them into a general axiom of American foreign policy. The real importance of the Munich episode stemmed from Czechoslovakia's strategic location, but it came to be identified in America with the abstract proposition that *any* aggression anywhere could have disastrous results. This simplification was widely shared by policy-makers and led the United States not only to the Korean intervention but also to a whole philosophy on how to handle communist bids for expansion, fairly indiscriminately applied. Jolted out of her unparalleled security America suddenly became aware of the world and its dangers. In the League and Munich experiences America saw object lessons in how not to do things and then more or less literally began to apply these new prescriptions, under circumstances that, from a shallow perspective, they seemed to fit.

One of the problems with such an approach is that it focuses attention on the last stages of a controversy, when violence is imminent. A related problem is that it polarizes the controversy into a contest of good and evil. Another problem is that it encourages applying the principle out of context. Still a fourth problem is that the assumed remedy is utilized whenever the principle seems to apply. In a complicated world where much violence always exists, more violence may be added. It becomes difficult to distinguish what one ought to do—when, with whom, and to whom—except on the basis of certain formulas. Looked at this way, one ought to be against aggression (since failure to resist simply leads to even bigger wars). One ought to oppose communism (since it is seen as subversive and aggressive, humanity would never freely choose it over democracy). One ought to fight for freedom anywhere and everywhere (since it is our duty). These three formulas actually came in the new age to constitute the central ideological thrust of American foreign policy.

This second handicap in the predominant American perspective, arising out of what might be called historical innocence, has its greatest effect when we confront situations in which our own interests are difficult to discern other than via these formulas. For example, there is a curious lack of historical awe in our dealing with the 38th parallel in Korea. It is as though Korea had never been divided near that line until it happened in our own day. Also, there is little awareness that Viet-Nam has had troubles over many centuries in its attempts to be independent. It is as though China never was a problem (or Russia or Germany either) until *we* encountered it. It is as though the United States believes that what it did or did not do is decisive in world affairs without any real corresponding feeling for how these problems were handled a hundred years ago or more, or who handled them then. Thus a Sino-Soviet tension with much past precedent in Chinese-Russian relations is thought unlikely until its existence cannot be denied. Many Americans tend to look on these events and forces as though they were brand new, had no roots, and only now exist when we are there to perceive them and formulate some policy toward them. Much of our present uncertainty and confusion stems from our previous unparalleled tranquillity and security; its effects are compounded by our tendency to see it all as full-grown, newly existing problems, to be resolved via a few newly discovered rules of thumb.

When one takes into account the interacting nature of these two handicaps, much of the reason for recent American difficulties stands revealed. Sound guidelines were lacking. A very powerful America became predominantly convinced that it "represented" not only the "free world" but the peoples elsewhere who would be free if they could. Inadequately armed with any deep historical sense of cause and effect in world affairs, she plunged into a vigorous role of leadership with very little in the way of solid concepts as to what ought to have been attempted. The widespread conviction that America represented the "conscience of mankind," coupled with our disposition toward a foreign policy conceptualized in universal abstract formulas, led toward ever-extending world-wide commitments. It led to the situation of the late 1960's.

From Isolationism to Globalism

THE vigorous American policy of full participation in world affairs after World War II represented an abrupt reversal of earlier actions. Because what was done from 1919 to 1939 was considered essentially wrong, it was assumed that doing the reverse after 1945 would be essentially right.

If before 1939 we refrained from membership in the League, from making alliances, from sending troops outside the hemisphere, from offering elaborate and continuing foreign and military aid to other nations far from our own shores, after 1945 we did all those things.

We became a founding member of the United Nations. Its very Charter was adopted in a conference at San Francisco on our West Coast. Thus called into existence, the organization was then established on our East Coast, at New York. From the beginning we played a great role in its affairs. Quite contrary to our suspicious attitude toward the League in the 1920's, we took the UN onto our own soil and determined to make it a principal part of our foreign policy. When outright aggression in Korea challenged the UN in 1950, we furnished the greatest single armed support to the UN effort (in contrast to our actions during Mussolini's assault on Ethiopia when we actually sent augmented supplies of oil and war matériel to Italian Africa during the League efforts at economic sanctions). At the height of the U.S. involvement we had 250,000 troops in Korea. Not content with the limited ability of the veto-ridden Security Council to cope with such problems, we also led the way toward an enlarged security role for the General Assembly.

We proceeded to elaborate alliance commitments linking us to dozens of states in defensive arrangements. Not only did we accept such major commitments as the Rio Pact, the North Atlantic Alliance, and SEATO, but we supplemented these with bilateral commitments to such nations as Australia and New Zealand, Nationalist China, and Japan. Less formal links were made via the military assistance program to many other nations. While we did not formally join CENTO, we furnished the money and arms without which it would have had no significance. American arms and military training units were widely distributed; it became inevitable that there would be clashes among nations each substantially armed and equipped from American sources. The India-Pakistan clash (1965) was an example. All these actions represented substantial policy reversals compared to what America did before World War II.

The most controversial fruit of these new policies was undoubtedly the American commitment in Viet-Nam. It is true that the Korean War sometimes aroused bitter debate in the U.S., after China's entry and before the armistice. But since the initial action of the U.S. in deploying troops in Korea to defend the UN Charter had virtually unanimous popular support in America, the Korean debate did not turn on the commitment but over how to discharge it—a substantial minority argued for a more aggressive military policy against China, demanding a "victory." The decisions in early and mid-1965 to abandon the advisory role in Viet-Nam and participate directly as a combatant, did not even initially command the same virtually unanimous American popular support as did the early stages in Korea. A more complex and vehement debate began. Again, as in Korea, some people favored an escalation of the military effort. But a substantial second group opposed the "unnecessary" war and protested vigorously against the civilian slaughter which the frontless war in Viet-Nam made inevitable. Other views were also strongly held.

The Viet-Nam War came to mark a real watershed in the development of postwar American foreign policy. The ensuing debate made it unlikely that the post-1945 policy of pyramiding commitments in the name of the three aforementioned formulas would be carried further without searching re-examination of the strategic concepts behind them. Especially after the Korean War and until the Viet-Nam War, sheer momentum accounted in large part for what was done: having decided on a new path of involvement, we went quickly down it to a marked extent wherever it led. The Viet-Nam debate, although obscured in the public press by much meaningless contrasting of the changing views of "hawks" and "doves," of "moralists-pacifists" versus "realists-escalators," inevitably was penetrating as it went on to the more fundamental strategic problems.

The basic debate over the *strategy* of U.S. involvements began (1969) to focus on the issue of how much the U.S. should attempt to determine results in world affairs, especially in Asia, and particularly through primary reliance on its own military efforts. Great differences of opinion over the prior strategic questions as to objectives and the identity of the real opposition, made it both inevitable and desirable that the military deployment necessary for success would be hotly argued as well.

There was disagreement over *where* to hold the line. Was, for example, the U.S. policy between 1945 and 1950 of avoiding involvement in land warfare on the continent of Asia shown by later events to have been inadequate? Was the Korean War an exception made reluctantly because of the UN principles involved? Or was the Korean War fought essentially to hold an anticommunist bastion on the periphery of a Communist Asia? Was Korea the exception, made for exceptional reasons, or was it the logical extension of a strategy of Communist bloc containment which properly could and should be further extended through the use of American military power elsewhere? One could hardly answer these questions in isolation from other strategic considerations.

Intertwined in the controversy was a second complicated strategic question. If the U.S. conceived of events on the Asian mainland as having vital effects on its own security, necessitating paying high costs in blood and treasure if required, was this payment then required in Viet-Nam? *Who* is the enemy against which the line should be held? Expressed another way, if the expansion of Communist China is considered dangerous to the security interests of the U.S., was this what was at stake in Viet-Nam? The answer to this question varies directly with the way the question is posed. Are the Viet-Cong a satellite instrument of North Viet-Nam, and North Viet-Nam in turn a satellite of China? Are all extensions of communism into Southeast Asia extensions de facto of Chinese power and influence? Or is the contrary argument more valid: is a strong Viet-Nam, whether Communist or not, acting as a strong container of Chinese ambitions because it reflects local nationalism? Is the enemy communism (in which case we should lump together the Soviet Union, Communist China, North Viet-Nam, and the Viet-Cong), or is it China (an expanding China, to be precise)? Also, was China actually attempting to expand, or was expansion merely considered probable?

Yet a third strategic question was involved: *how* should the line be held? Could the U.S. rely upon the greater powers of Asia, with some help from the less important, to do the job of stabilizing the Asian balance if the U.S. conceptualized the problem along somewhat different lines? Rather than assuming the primary and virtually unilateral military role, could the U.S. become a reserve force in Asia arrayed *in support of* the efforts of Asian nations to bring their own part of the world into some greater semblance of security? Can Soviet needs for stability in Asia serve U.S. interests? Can Japan, India, and Indonesia play a greater role and accept a larger share of the burden? Is the argument that these three nations are beset with overwhelming domestic problems and a disinclination toward a more active role a rationalization or a circumstance that could be altered? Given Japan's great industrial power and past military achievements, how likely is a continuation of her present minor and passive role? What U.S. actions might alter that role?

Indonesia's economic difficulties did not deter Sukarno from "confrontation" with Malaysia. India, too, showed an ability to use force when attacked or involved with Pakistani and Chinese military power. What accounts today for the curious circumstance that a power such as the U.S., geographically far remote from Viet-Nam, seems greatly concerned about potentially adverse developments in Asia while major Asian nations show very little concern—or at least do very little about any concern which they may have?

On January 4, 1967, Secretary of State Dean Rusk, responding to these kinds of questions and doubts, wrote an eloquent defense of American foreign policy, which he ended as follows:

Meantime, we shall continue to do what is necessary—to protect the vital interests of the United States, to stand by our allies in Asia, and to work with all our energy for a peaceful, secure and prosperous Southeast Asia. Only by meeting these commitments can we keep on this small and vulnerable planet the minimum conditions for peace and order.

Only history will be able to judge the wisdom and the full meaning of our present course—in all its dimensions.

But I would close by sharing with you a hope and a belief. I believe that we are coming towards the end of an era when men can believe it is profitable and, even, possible to change the *status quo* by applying external force. I believe those in Hanoi who persist in their aggressive adventure—and those who support them—represent ideas and methods from the past, not the future. Elsewhere in the world those committed to such concepts have faded or are fading from the scene. . . .

The overriding question for all of mankind in this last third of the Twentieth Century is how to organize a durable peace. Much of the experience which has gone into answers to that question has been largely forgotten—perhaps some of it should be. But the question remains—and remains to be answered.

Former Secretary Rusk's answers are as clear as those of his opponents. The question is, who is right? Are we nearly there, nearly to a secure world if we persist a little longer and fight aggression, oppose Communist expansion, defend freedom—everywhere? Or does such an approach carry within it, through its too simplified vision of the world, the seeds of even greater bloodshed and trouble? If the correct sequel to a prewar policy of shunning obligations is a policy of carrying a proper share of the world's load, how does one determine what that share is, and what are the best means to utilize in handling the burden? How do we decide on proper objectives, realistically assess the true obstacles, and implement a successful strategy at minimum costs?

In later chapters we shall seek for meaningful answers to these questions. To start us on our way we must next turn to the unusualness of the American experience that has so largely produced the two handicaps to an effective policy discussed in this chapter.

CHAPTER 2

The Unusualness of the American Experience

C OMPARED to the experiences of any other contemporary great power, the total "mix" of American environmental conditions was highly unusual, if not unique. This highly unusual background experience furnishes important clues as to why the United States has conducted its foreign policy as it has. Let us begin with the effects of geographic isolation upon American security problems.

The Effects of Geographic Isolation

THE fact of *where* the American nation is physically located has had a profound and continuing effect, for the United States is the sole great power in the world without great power neighbors nearby. True, Soviet and American frontiers are close in the northern Pacific, but this particular proximity has very limited effects.

In a nuclear missile age this factor of distance does not imply the same degree of absolute security benefits as it frequently has in the past; but even today the effect of America's distance from other powers confers distinct benefits lacking for the rest. Without entering fully into the complex questions of what course a major nuclear war might follow and whether a missile exchange would both begin and end a war without the former need for an ensuing conventional occupation of the loser's territory, it is still clear that a grievously wounded America—unwilling to surrender—would be difficult to subdue merely because of the distance factor. By contrast, if Germany were devastated by nuclear attack, she would be more vulnerable to final defeat, merely because of the proximity of Soviet forces confronted by no formidable geographic obstacles. In a Soviet-American conflict, if the seas were highways of invasion, they also would offer secure hiding places for the harassment of those who would invade. Assuming an American defensive role, it would be a task of enormous dimensions for the Soviet Union (even with its expanding naval

capability) to bring its power to bear upon the American continental
land mass other than via the air.

If a missile exchange might be both the beginning and the end of a
war, distance may no longer play a significant role—but such an assumption is very doubtful. If we assume both an initial rough parity in power
and a fair degree of *mutual* destruction in such a war, the inability of the
one nation to rouse itself to parry a further attack may be roughly
counterbalanced by the inability of the attacker to readily mount his
assault. This factor would be of greatest importance if the would-be
attacker must proceed by sea. Although relatively formidable land forces
might still proceed under fairly primitive logistical conditions to invade
against a weaker opponent, an overseas movement is infinitely more
sophisticated and technically complicated. The United States, which has
twice deployed great forces across the Atlantic, has done so each time
with friendly bases on the European end of the operation.[1] In its deployments in the Pacific to theaters of large-scale land fighting the U.S. has
consistently enjoyed friendly bases at the far end—as in Korea and South
Viet-Nam.[2]

Distance—especially sea distance—still seems likely to confer some degree of security from physical invasion. It is by no means obvious that
nations would consciously choose to fight a missile war predicated upon
the assumption that a nuclear exchange would be the sole significant
military activity. To do so might well repeat Hitler's great error after
Dunkirk, when he assumed that no invasion of Great Britain would be
necessary to force the British to acknowledge defeat. Distance cannot
confer immunity from physical destruction. It may well confer some immunity from the likelihood of a decision to engage in a nuclear exchange
that cannot easily be followed up by a more conventional assault—if
such an assault proves necessary to achieve a surrender. Such politico-
psychological imponderables, directly related to the effects of distance,
are today still quite uncertain parts of the total strategic equation.

We have deliberately begun with one extreme of this question, where
the security advantages today of distance may be most validly questioned. At the opposite extreme is the effect of distance in the prenuclear
age, especially before the first great military-technological revolution,
which began around 1855.

A comparison of two early wars, in both of which America fought
England, is instructive: the American Revolution and the War of 1812.
In the first the fighting extended over eight years. The British occupied

[1] In the North African invasion a part of the U.S. forces was deployed directly
from the continental U.S. The very comparison of this case with the use of Britain
as an advance base in the Normandy invasion illustrates the point. North Africa was
a comparatively small operation; the Normandy assault was on a grand scale.

[2] The Pacific island war (1942–1945) by its seeming exception proves the point,
for these island invasions were relatively small scale and against enemy land forces
which could not be substantially reinforced.

Boston, New York, Charleston, and other American seaports virtually at will, launching land forces from these bases in marches calculated to destroy rebel resistance. At first glance the British military operations in the American Revolution seem to show the reverse of the point made that distance conferred a certain immunity on America. However, these British forces were not only small in size; they were consistently augmented by American Loyalist volunteers and drew much logistical support from native American sources. Without the indispensable Loyalist support of food, shelter and supplies—let alone men—the British war effort in America would have quickly collapsed. The Battle of King's Mountain, to cite one illustration, was largely an American battle on both sides, even though British troops also participated. If all the Americans there had fought together against the British, the British would have been overwhelmed.

King's Mountain may not be typical, but consider the small size of the British forces. When the American Revolution reached a climax in 1781, with the crucial surrender of General Cornwallis to Washington, only 7,000 British troops were involved. This is an eloquent testimonial to the conditions of the day. Even though the French contribution to Cornwallis' defeat—in the form of a naval blockade and troops on shore—was an essential element in the American victory, the reason that France's assistance was so crucial was not because of Britain's ability to muster overwhelming military power in the American colonies 3,000 miles from London, but because the Loyalist support in the colonies gave the British such important local resources.

Contrast this first American civil war, the American Revolution, with the course of the War of 1812. In the second war the important actions were at sea. The land campaign initiated on the American side involved a little-remembered attack against Ontario, Canada, which soon was frustrated by British forces. For their part, the British landed in Chesapeake Bay, marched on Washington and burned the White House. That completed, they left to bombard Fort McHenry—an event that inspired Francis Scott Key to write "The Star Spangled Banner," but which did the British no good. Landing later at New Orleans, they assaulted Jackson's troops, who from behind their cotton bales decimated the orderly British ranks—ironically with the war already over, although the news had not yet reached the United States. Altogether, even allowing for British distractions with the situation in Europe (then at a pause in the Napoleonic Wars), the War of 1812 illustrates the military futility of the British attempt to exercise power under hostile circumstances and at a distance. This time, since the Loyalists had left the colonies or were largely reconciled to an independent America, the British efforts were fruitless. Frustration of the British was accomplished by a weak American army, this time unsupported by any French forces.

In this early period the military story elsewhere is again and again the same. Large-scale movement of forces to battle at distant points was frustrated by mere distance and its ensuing complications. Napoleon's campaign in Egypt and Syria (1798–1799) with 35,000 men proves the same point. The difficulties that defeated him there were sanitary and logistical, not military. Nor was Clive's conquest of India the accomplishment of large British forces but the result of Indian princes fighting one another to British benefit. The average army in Frederick the Great's time was 47,000 men; in Napoleon's wars the average size was still only 84,000 (but not for overseas campaigns). British victory over China in the First Opium War (1841–1842) was accomplished by the seizure of several coastal ports and was a testimony to China's weakness rather than to British war-making power far from home. Even in 1860, when the technological innovations in warfare were beginning, the British and French expedition that seized Peking numbered only 17,000 troops. Today we chiefly remember the Crimean War (which broke out in 1854), for the charge of the Light Brigade, the introduction of systematic battle area hospital care, and the fact that the British and French transported large combat forces by sea and maintained them relatively effectively at a significant distance from home.

Distance in the first half of the nineteenth century in itself conferred substantial military security. Of all the nations who were subsequently to play a great role upon the international stage, the United States was most fortunately endowed by geography in this respect. We were not only far removed physically from the great powers, but as we grew in strength we also became the only significant power in all this part of the world. The corollary of Europe's limited ability to bring the U.S. readily to heel via military coercion became our own ultimate ability to dominate affairs in the Americas. After technological progress made it possible to exert real force at a distance, the great powers of Europe and Asia were no longer sufficiently secure in their home areas to entertain thoughts of adventures in the Americas. Throughout, as our power expanded, distance from danger was an important ingredient in our ability to act as an ultimately decisive, untouched, and reserve force on the world balance of power. This was the role we played successfully in two world wars.

Today, the linkage between distance and security is no longer so simple; yet the fact that the United States remains the sole great power in the world without cheek-by-jowl, indigenous great power neighbors continues to permit her a wider range of strategic choice on foreign policy problems—as we shall see in later chapters.

The Effects of Historical Experience

NEXT for consideration is the fact of *when* the United States came to exist as a sovereign nation. The character of international relations in our formative years was very significant in its effects. The United States is the sole great power in the world whose historical experience occurred so predominantly in the rather unusual—even peculiar—century between 1815–1914. Compare other powers in this respect. Whether one takes Prussia-Germany, England, France, Russia, China, Japan, or India, each had lengthy experience before 1815—as we did not.

The people of the United States did not begin their corporate background with the coming into force of the American Constitution (June 1788), or with George Washington's inauguration as first President (April 30, 1789). The American Revolution had already taught important lessons in diplomacy, on the significance of allies, on the need to pay prudent heed to how the affairs of nations greater in power could affect the destiny of the United States. These lessons were reflected in Washington's Farewell Address, in Jefferson's advice, and in the general outlook of the Founding Fathers. Even earlier, in colonial days, lessons were learned when the colonies were outposts of the British Empire and took limited part in the American branch-wars of Europe's powers. Yet since colonial concern at that time was primarily oriented toward the two-fold problem of hostile Indians and white foes, these lessons were not quite so meaningful as those from the Revolution.

The early period of American national existence has frequently and correctly been characterized as one of realism. A relatively weak United States had of necessity to brush aside illusion, to see the problems candidly. Very revealing is the action of Jefferson in acquiring the Louisiana Territory (April 30, 1803), doubling the area of the United States fourteen years to the day after Washington was sworn in as President. Despite Jefferson's principles about a modest and proper role for the Federal government, the opportunity was too good to be missed. The roll-call of continental expansion continued with its notable landmarks: the area west of Lake Superior (1818), Florida from Spain (1819), the Maine boundary and Lake of the Woods area (1842), Texas (1845), Oregon (1846), California and the Mexican cession (1848), the Gadsden Purchase (1853); all in all a remarkable expansion from coast to coast in just 64 years.

United States foreign policy was concentrated essentially on things close to home and well understood. The first of a number of foreign policy "doctrines" was announced by President Monroe (December 2, 1823) after British foreign secretary Canning had suggested a joint warning against European intervention in the Western Hemisphere to restore Spain's possessions. The Monroe Doctrine, although rather grandiose for the small American nation if one forgets the large British fleet ready to enforce it by closing the exits from European waters, was nonetheless realistic in addressing a pressing American concern: to expand continentally while seeking freedom from effective European power bases in the Americas. Accordingly, the Monroe Doctrine addressed both ends of the problem, claiming a special role for the United States and denying it for Europe's powers. Although Britain's continued presence in Canada was unwelcome, the effects of that presence were counterbalanced by Britain's de facto underwriting of the basic Monroe policy and the fledgling development in Canada of separatist sentiments.

Gradually, one by one, European possessions in the New World began to disappear. Still literally encircled by European powers (1789), the U.S. broke out of its "containment." Only during the American Civil War (1861–1865) was new European military power introduced into the Western Hemisphere on any significant scale; Maximilian tried to conquer Mexico with the backing of French troops. When American unity was restored (1865), the French efforts were quickly abandoned, for it was clear that the U.S. both would and could expel the French expeditionary force.

The American Civil War represented a watershed in U.S. affairs and circumstances in several significant ways. First, as we shall soon see, the European balance of power changed at this time, although not to America's disadvantage. Second, the great military-technological revolution was begun, making it possible for large-scale military efforts, such as Napoleon III's Mexican adventure, to be carried out if the balance of power permitted—which fortunately for the United States was *not* the case. Third, the virtual insulation of the United States from military danger led to a lessened concern with and involvement in world affairs. Since Europe now largely remained aloof from New World commitments, U.S. foreign policy in turn became of modest dimensions and lessened importance. The very success of the Monroe Doctrine policy and continental acquisition turned much of America's attention and energies to domestic tasks: settlement of the West and industrialization in the East. It is not that American foreign policy became less realistic but rather that we attempted less because we felt less need. It was simpler than in Washington's day, less daring, and involved fewer risks. Outside the Americas it amounted to the proposition: Stay out of others' affairs.

The distinct change in American politics and foreign policy even before Lincoln's time can be seen in terms of the background experience deemed desirable in a President. In our early history, being Secretary of State was considered an important way station on the road to the Presidency. Such active experience in foreign affairs, at first considered fairly essential for presidential prospects, later became relatively unimportant. The trend is quite clear from Table 2–1.

The tendency, and its gradual falling off, is unmistakable. Moreover, after the American Civil War the reverse was uniformly true: No Secretary of State *ever* became President.[3] One might argue that the increased complexity of the American political process after the early decades brought with it a further division of political labor, but it still seems significant that by Lincoln's time the presidential aspirant was cultivating other fields than foreign affairs. William H. Seward, our twenty-fourth Secretary of State, a member of Lincoln's cabinet, once remarked

TABLE 2–1

SECRETARIES OF STATE BECOME PRESIDENTS

Secretary of State	Years	Under President	Became President
Thomas Jefferson	1790–93	Washington	1801–09
James Madison	1801–09	Jefferson	1809–17
James Monroe	1811–14	Madison	1817–25
John Q. Adams	1817–25	Monroe	1825–29
Martin Van Buren	1829–31	A. Jackson	1837–41
James Buchanan	1845–49	Polk	1857–61

on how American senior diplomats and ambassadors were chosen: "Sir, some persons are sent abroad because they are needed abroad, and some are sent because they are not wanted at home."[4] Even allowing for the temptation to utter a *bon mot* for its own sake, it is unquestionably true that by Seward's day it was not Benjamin Franklin or John Jay who was representing this country abroad. The practice of choosing ambassadors primarily for their party fidelity and financial generosity, so notorious until well into the twentieth century, had already taken root. Able American diplomats were few and far between in major posts abroad until the 1930's or 1940's. It is difficult to avoid concluding that relatively small importance was attached to the job from the standpoint of the national security. If we tackle the point from another direction, the conclusion is reinforced. Consider how few important international relations or great power crises involved the U.S. outside the Caribbean area between the Civil War and World War I, aside from the Spanish-American War and the annexation of Hawaii.

[3] One might argue that the reason that the Secretary of State tended to become President is that in early decades he was also the chief party organizer. One is still left with the observation that the chief party organizer was given the foreign affairs seat in the cabinet. Unless one wants to argue that the Secretary of State had so little to do in foreign affairs that this title was essentially a sinecure to support him in his party work, this combination can only mean that it had the significance here attributed to it.

[4] Quoted by Roy R. Rubottom, Jr., Assistant Secretary of State for Inter-American Affairs, *Department of State Bulletin,* May 12, 1958.

Although U.S. foreign policy was realistic enough in this period in confining itself largely to the affairs of this hemisphere, the inevitable corollary was that we paid less attention to what was occurring elsewhere. Gradually our judgments of affairs abroad became somewhat abstract—it was all very far away and involved us only slightly. The exciting things were happening right here at home.

The unparalleled security of the U.S. was sustained by Britain's role and the balance of power after technological change no longer conferred almost automatic security, and was naturally reflected in the size and condition of our armed forces. No one today can look at the figures for the size of the United States Army (regular forces) between 1817 and 1902 without a sense of awe or shock. They are given in Table 2–2.

TABLE 2–2
REGULAR ARMY STRENGTH: 1817–1901

1817	8,220	1847	21,686	1874	30,520
1820	8,942	1850	10,763	1877	24,854
1823	5,949	1853	10,417	1880	26,509
1826	5,809	1856	15,562	1883	25,547
1829	6,169	1859	16,435	1886	26,254
1832	6,102	1862	25,480	1889	27,544
1835	7,151	1865	22,310	1892	26,900
1838	8,653	1868	50,916	1895	27,172
1841	11,169	1871	28,953	1898	47,867
1844	8,573	1872	29,214	1901	81,586

SOURCES: House of Representatives, 57th Congress, 2nd Session, Volume 97, Document 446; Heitman, Francis B., *Historical Register and Dictionary of the United States Army* (Washington: Government Printing Office, 1903), p. 626.

In the last decade before World War I the picture does not change significantly. At a time when European standing armies were on the order of 600,000 (in 1914), the U.S. Army was 97,760. The utter neglect in which the U.S. Navy existed for most of the same period tells the same story. Although improvement came sooner in the sea forces, the long gap between the era of the *U.S.S. Constitution* (end of the eighteenth century) and the renewed forces of the Spanish-American War (end of the nineteenth) is an eloquent reminder of long decades when there was no fleet at all but only a gunboat navy, parceled out for pork-barrel purposes to the various naval yards which dotted the Eastern seaboard of the United States.

Indeed, the instruments of national power, from the nonexistent career diplomatic service to the virtually nonexistent armed forces (especially in view of the persistent use of the army for fighting Indians in the Far

West) eloquently testify to a nation not actively concerned for its national security. The picture is completed if we add the fact that neither army nor navy was organized for effective fighting against foreign foes, either at the level of fleets and armies or in the Washington organization, and that no attention was paid at all to intelligence operations. The departments of the government dealing with the armed forces had no general staff or other such devices and were organized exclusively for routine administrative purposes.

These highly nominal gestures in the field of national security were not unrealistic; in all of this period the U.S. was confronted with no formidable military or foreign affairs threat. It is time to consider why not.

In all of modern history since the nation-state system emerged, there has never been so prolonged a period of general peace as between 1815 and 1914. Before 1815 Europe's great powers were repeatedly embroiled in conflict. The savage Thirty Years' War (1618–1648) is one illustration; the Peace of Westphalia did not usher in a period of prolonged general peace. New fighting broke out over the Lowlands; the Treaties of Nimwegen (1678–1679) were unable to bring a permanent settlement. The War of the League of Augsburg (1688–1697) was the third war in a series that began in 1667. Close after it came the War of the Spanish Succession (1701–1714). The Treaties of Utrecht (1713) and Rastadt and Baden (1714) did not entirely end the widespread conflict. Next came the War of the Austrian Succession (1740–1748) and the Seven Years' War (1756–1763). Relative peace was then restored until the French Revolution (1789) was followed by a series of European wars lasting to 1815.

After 1815 the picture was substantially, even radically, different. From 1815 until 1848, while there were a number of revolutions in Europe, there were no great power wars at all—not even bilateral ones. In this curious era the monarchs of Europe were far too busy attempting to stay on their thrones and retain their heads (literally) on their shoulders to afford the luxury of war. Between 1848 and 1870 there was a series of limited wars, but these each involved only two or—at the most—three great powers. The six wars which occurred during this period, with the exception of the Crimean War, were concerned with Italian and German unification. Next, after 1871, came a period when wars between great powers again ceased. Of the six great powers in 1871 (Germany, Austria, Russia, France, Italy, and England) not one fought a war with another in Europe until the actual outbreak of World War I in 1914. This cessation of war is a highly remarkable fact.

Minor wars—especially colonial wars—continued to occur; but the great powers did not fight one another. The single exception was in Asia —the Russo-Japanese War (1904–1905), marking the emergence of Japan into great power status. Although sometimes bloody enough, the colonial wars did not bring the wholesale destruction that comes when two or more powers, each well armed and modernly equipped, fight.

In this perspective, the twentieth century, even taking into account only World War I and World War II, stands in great contrast. The contemporary age resembles far more the period before 1815; with the important change that today's mechanization of warfare and harnessing of scientific knowledge to weapon improvements, has resulted in a completely new magnitude of bloodshed.

The unusually peaceful hundred years between 1815 and 1914, with its lack of general war, was a great but unearned boon to the United States. Although we accepted it with little thought, what actually caused so long a period of peace?

We have indicated one important clue for the initial phase (1815–1848), when Europe's monarchs cooperated internationally to preserve their thrones domestically. After 1848, especially during the next phase involving Italian and German unification, how was general war avoided? Unifying these nations represented a far more fundamental alteration in the map of Europe than even the Napoleonic Wars produced.

Two answers may be advanced. On the philosophical level, the first is that the unification of these states was not contrary to the long-run historical tendencies of the age. Even though the creation of a united Italy and a united Germany radically altered the map of Europe, the process involved an amalgamation of states predisposed toward union. The effects were not directed outward in the form of designs on the territories of non-Italian and non-German states. As such the amalgamations could be tolerated. Of course, in the process, neighboring great powers such as France and Austria had to be persuaded (by force) to relinquish special claims and positions in these territories. That is why the unifications did involve (limited) war.

The second answer to why the wars were limited involves observing the principle used by Otto von Bismarck, then Chancellor of Prussia, and the prime mover in what happened. His essential technique was to proceed against one foe at a time, ensuring through clever and patient diplomacy that that foe for the moment had no military allies. When he fought Austria, Austria stood alone. And when he fought France, France in her turn was isolated.[5]

Once Germany was successfully unified, Bismarck focused his attention on maintaining a stable peace in Europe—because German unity, while now formally achieved, had to grow real roots. Since France was the prime dissatisfied great power in Europe, the one nation who was disposed to challenge the new *status quo*, Bismarck proceeded to use the

---

[5] The detail of these maneuvers can be found in Frederick H. Hartmann, *The Relations of Nations* (3rd ed.) (New York: The Macmillan Company, 1967), pp. 329–330.

same technique in peace that he had already used so well in war. He isolated his primary potential enemy by an intricate alliance system centering on Germany, with intimate ties to Austria and looser ties to Russia (France's most important potential ally). Since Austria-Hungary was at odds with Russia and the temptation was strong, given Germany's alliance with Austria, for Russia to seek an alliance with France, the result Bismarck attained was not the most likely. Bismarck avoided the "natural" expectation by a clear but complicated policy. Even while allying with Austria, whose "natural" enemy was Russia, he refused to support any and all Austrian interests. He remained determined to serve certain Russian interests which the Russians could not achieve by a policy of treating Germany as an enemy. (Russia, for example, also feared and distrusted the British Empire.) He applied this "counterbalancing interest" concept, protecting Austria from Russian attack but "reinsuring" Russia against Austrian attack. He guaranteed Austria help if Russia attacked her but guaranteed Russia his neutrality if Austria attacked Russia. This protection was what Russia needed if she was not to ally with France. Her desire for a French alliance was motivated solely by a need to feel secure against a combined Austro-German assault. Bismarck, taking into account the entire range of interests and concerns of France's potential allies, thus utilized the counterbalancing interests involved for Germany's benefit. His goal was not alliance of all those other states *with* Germany, but to prevent their allying *against* Germany. If he had instead attempted as impressive an alliance group as possible he would have driven other nations into France's arms as a counterweight to German power. Although Britain was not an integral part of Bismarck's elaborate network, the persistent and perennial friction between Britain and France (who were colonial rivals) banished any serious likelihood of an Anglo-French entente, provided Germany did not arouse British concern by challenging important British interests.

When Kaiser Wilhelm retired Bismarck (1890), this intricate system was dismantled. Wilhelm refused Russian offers to continue the Bismarckian arrangements. The consequence was that by 1894 Russia had made a firm military alliance with France. In building a large German Navy Wilhelm next aroused serious concern in Britain—so much so that by 1904 Britain and France had agreed to settle outstanding colonial rivalries. By 1907 the British had reached a similar understanding with Russia (with whom colonial antagonisms had previously kept relations tense). By 1914, after a series of crises, war came, and Germany found herself fighting not only France but Britain and Russia as well.

Consider the meaning of all of this maneuvering to the United States, for it is what made possible the small military forces and the inadequate diplomatic and security organization maintained by America. While the U.S. was concerned with acquiring coast-to-coast continental territories (until 1853), the American policy benefited from two important circumstances: (1) the technological difficulties of Europe's mounting an effective expedition to the New World; (2) the determination of Great Britain to prevent any important alteration in the *status quo* in the Americas. After 1853, on the other hand, although the technological difficulties in European expeditions to the New World were rapidly overcome, the British policy remained substantially as before. The invasion of Mexico by French troops under Maximilian (1861–1867) showed the importance of both of these effects. It showed that European troops could be sent and maintained. And it showed that this deviation from British policy (for Britain had originally sent troops, too, to collect debts from Mexico) was a vital part of making such expeditions feasible.[6] In this later period a new circumstance was added that had not existed before 1853: the Germans appropriated control of the European balance of power. It was Bismarck's actions as much as American hostility that led Napoleon III to abandon the Mexican venture. After 1871, when Bismarck encouraged France to new imperialism overseas, the British barred the way across the Atlantic. As a consequence Africa and Asia became the theater of Europe's new imperialism.

It is startling to note that in the thirty years after 1873, in this new era of colonial imperialism, England alone added more than three million square miles to her empire (all but one-half million in Africa) and that France took an additional four million square miles (mostly in Africa too). Between 1884 and 1890, Germany acquired nearly a million square miles in Africa plus scattered areas in the Pacific (including a large part of New Guinea). Italy took Eritrea, Italian Somaliland, and Libya in Africa; Belgium took the nearly million square miles of the Congo. Japan took Korea from China; and in 1898 Britain, Germany, Russia, and France forced spheres-of-interest concessions from China which, if they had endured, would have destroyed China's independent future.[7] Even Chinese customs money was collected under British supervision.

These tremendous overseas activities of the European powers are remarkable in that they essentially did *not* involve the Americas. While German-maintained stability in the European balance between 1870 and 1890 permitted and encouraged imperialism abroad, the British prescribed the areas where it would be allowed. After 1890 and until 1914, as the European theater became increasingly tense, the European powers became steadily more inclined to concentrate their attention close to home. In addition, with so much of the colonial world now appropriated,

---

[6] Becoming belatedly aware of the unlimited aims of Napoleon III in Mexico, Britain soon terminated her intervention. Maximilian was subsequently deserted by Napoleon III because of Napoleon's need for troops at home.

[7] All these "leases" were for 99 years except for Russia's lease on the southern Liaotung Peninsula which was for 25 years.

significant gains began to be possible only at each other's expense: namely, one colonial power would have to take what another had already claimed.

Viewing American foreign policy during this same period, one is struck by the paucity of developments of much significance, especially if one excludes such strictly inter-American conflicts as the Mexican War (1846–1848). There was the Clayton-Bulwer Treaty (1850) with Great Britain over Central America, in which Britain retained ambitions bound up with a future interoceanic canal. There was the isolated incident of Commodore Perry's visit to Japan (1854), which was designed primarily to open up commercial relations with Japan. There was the Ostend Manifesto (1854), in which the American ministers to England, France, and Spain proclaimed that the U.S. would be justified in acquiring Cuba by force, if Spain refused to sell. There was the purchase of Alaska from Russia (1867). There was the Treaty of Washington (1871), by which the U.S. and Great Britain agreed to settle peacefully all outstanding issues. In 1889 came the first Pan-American Conference, followed by the Bering Sea Seal Fisheries Treaty with Great Britain (1892). The Venezuelan boundary dispute erupted between the U.S. and Britain (1895), but serious trouble was avoided. In 1898 Hawaii was annexed and the Spanish-American War broke out. The acquisition of part of Samoa came in 1899, and the Philippine insurrection (1899–1902). The Open Door Note (1899) asked for equal U.S. commercial access to China. In 1901 came the Hay-Pauncefote Treaty with Great Britain, which abrogated the Clayton-Bulwer Treaty and permitted U.S. construction of a Central American canal, and which was soon followed by U.S. intervention in the Panama revolt against Colombia. The Alaska boundary question was settled (1903). In 1904 came the Roosevelt corollary to the Monroe Doctrine and intervention in Santo Domingo. Other Caribbean issues arose between 1909 and 1912, and in 1914 new trouble came with Mexico.

When one considers that the above listing is virtually a complete catalogue of important U.S. foreign involvements for two-thirds of a century, one is amazed from today's perspective at the modest dimensions of U.S. foreign affairs and the fairly complete absence of issues having no roots in the Americas. If one excludes issues connected with U.S. acquisitions of territories outside the Americas, there is almost nothing left. At a time when the political complexion of most of the world was being radically altered, American foreign policy, the Philippine involvement aside, was limited to issues in our immediate area and to minor overseas acquisitions.

A cataloguing of American military involvements is also revealing. After the War of 1812, United States troops did not fight the troops of a major power for over a hundred years. There were a number of minor military involvements such as: the Undeclared War with France (1798–

1800), the naval expedition against the Barbary Pirates (1801–1805), and a later expedition against Vera Cruz and pursuit of the Mexican bandit Pancho Villa (1916–1917) by General Pershing. Otherwise, the entire list of American wars during this whole time comprised two: the Mexican War (1846–1848) and the Spanish-American War (1898). Each of these wars was against a second-rate power, compared even to the then limited power of the United States. The U.S. won each war with comparative ease. Each, for that matter, could have been avoided if the United States had not chosen in favor of a larger sphere of interest and/ or territorial expansion. We engaged in very little war, in a century distinguished by its world-wide great power peacefulness, and what little we chose to fight we won hands down. Eventually, we shall return to these observations, for they were to have distinct and important effects on subsequent American attitudes. Largely, the ability of the United States to "choose" its wars was intimately related both to the self-limits of American foreign policy and to the operation of the nineteenth-century balance of power, already described.

In 1917 when President Woodrow Wilson led the American nation into the "war to end all war," he was responding with perhaps pardonable naiveté to a very unusual hundred years' experience of general peace. World War I burst like a thunderclap on a psychologically unprepared world. Americans, even more than Europeans, had accustomed themselves with a certain smugness to the assumption that technological progress had overcome and made obsolete older "power politics." The mechanisms of statecraft were not understood; the significance was missed of the pre-Wilhelmian balance of power that had preserved the peace and the role of British seapower in underwriting American security. Little overt attention was paid by American officials (and even less by the American people) to how and why peace had been so long preserved. When American attention did finally focus on the recurrent crises which preoccupied the European great powers between 1905 and 1914, the reaction was essentially one of distaste and a spirit of thankfulness that America was above this sordid game. As crisis followed crisis without actual war, there was also a feeling that each would somehow be resolved—an expectation fulfilled until the aftermath of the assassination of Austrian Archduke Franz Ferdinand. The bottom fell out with sickening suddenness. Yet even then the whole truth of what lay ahead was not perceived. Europe's conscript armies mobilized with a pervasive air of enthusiasm—shortly to evaporate before the grim reality of trench warfare and the implacable machine gun.

When Wilson spoke of a "war to end all war," he meant putting an end to what he thought had caused World War I and of providing a new alternative. He variously described the cause of conflict as "Germanism" and "entangling alliances." In a speech in South Dakota (September 9,

1919), he declared: "Your choice is between the League of Nations and Germanism. I have told you what I mean by Germanism—taking care of yourselves, being armed and ready, having a chip on your shoulder, thinking of nothing but your own rights. . . ."[8] Speaking earlier to the U.S. Senate (January 22, 1917), he explained his remedy to avoid new war in different terms: "I am proposing that all nations henceforth avoid entangling alliances which would draw them into competition of power, catch them in a net of intrigue and selfish rivalry, and disturb their own affairs with influences intruded from without."[9] Instead Wilson wanted "a concert of power," a League of Nations. The point is that Wilson (and the American people generally) became aware of balance-of-power alliances and their effects really only in the final phase of a balance that on the whole had worked well for a long time. In this last or declining phase of recurrent crises, the balance mechanism indeed came to look like entanglements permeated by "selfish rivalry." Such a judgment did not do justice to the role of the balance of power taken as a whole; Wilson's views help to explain the rather remarkable persistent antipathy with which American leaders for the ensuing three decades regarded the device of balance-of-power alliances. (Even the North Atlantic Pact in its early years was described by Americans not under the frank and accurate label of a balance-of-power alliance but under the euphemism of "regional collective security.")

Woodrow Wilson, presiding over the end of a century of American historical innocence, called himself an idealist. In many ways he was, particularly in his attempt to replace power politics with a new kind of international system. But at least in one sense he was a realist: he knew that the tried and true remedy of simple American abstinence from any important involvements in European affairs would no longer assure American security. At least one American leader (and there were others) had concluded by 1918 that the era of security without real effort that America enjoyed for so long was now gone. But the analysis of the cause-and-effect relationships that had brought on World War I left much to be desired. Later experiences affected American thinking on international affairs and will concern us at length in the chapters ahead. There can be little question, though, that our experience between 1815 and 1914 was poor preparation for understanding the problems that lay ahead.

The Effects of the Domestic Environment

THE fact of *how* the American nation was formed, with cultural diversity interacting with unparalleled economic opportunity, had important

[8] For text see *Addresses of President Wilson*, Senate Document No. 120, 66th Congress, 1st Session, pp. 83–88.

[9] *Congressional Record*, Senate, January 22, 1917.

effects. The United States is the sole great power in the world whose population came from across the seas by immigration and occupied a large, rich, and sparsely settled continent.

Many other nations have been settled in large measure by overseas immigration. Latin America, Australia, New Zealand, Canada, South Africa, all come readily to mind. However, in few Latin American nations did the Europeans essentially displace or eliminate the natives. In most Latin American nations the opposite was true: intermarriage produced a new part-native, part-European culture, as in Brazil. At the opposite extreme, in South Africa, the Boers and their descendants drew a rigid color line; in later years they attempted a degree of physical separation the world today knows as *apartheid.* In Canada, in Australia, in New Zealand, the natives were relatively few in number and as in the United States were essentially displaced by the European immigrants; frequently they were placed on reservations or in areas isolated for their use. Neither in Australia, New Zealand, nor Canada were there simultaneously the rich abundance and enormous territorial area that the American people came to control. Although large, Australia is comparatively poor, contrasted with the United States. New Zealand is comparatively rich like the United States but is much smaller in area. Canada's large size is even further exaggerated by the conventional Mercator map, and she has important sources of wealth but has a tiny population compared to the United States. Unlike Australia and New Zealand, Canada is the only one of these three nations which presently has a large non-British population (although Australia is now changing somewhat).[10]

If one surveys all the larger nations of the world it is difficult to find an exact parallel to the American mix in these respects: a large nation with a large population primarily originating overseas, which has duplicated the American experience of blending many people from many cultures into one nation enjoying vast economic resources and a very high standard of living. If, then, the American experience represents a unique blend of these factors, we ought reasonably to expect that their product will be a distinctive national flavor in our approach to problems.

From the very beginning the American nation represented a cultural blending. New Sweden (Delaware) had been founded by the Swedish West India Company (1638). The people who settled it were not only Swedes but Finns. It was annexed (1655) by Peter Stuyvesant, Governor of Dutch New Netherland (New York). New Netherland in turn became New York (1664) when a British expedition took control. These earlier events were to have later repetitions as parts of New France became the Northwest Territories of the United States, as the French of New Orleans

[10] In March 1966, Australian law was changed to permit some nonwhite immigration. By September 1968 the government had accepted 376.

and the Spanish of Florida, New Mexico, Texas, and California passed under the American flag. Even in the earlier period, Pennsylvania was largely settled by the Germans and Welsh, just as the Scots and Irish took over the Carolinas. As the area of the original thirteen colonies passed into British hands, a system of government familiar to Englishmen became the predominant political form. The largest cultural group in the infant United States was English. However, since these colonies possessed large non-English groups, the American people collectively were never simply English people overseas. The Scots and Irish were as un-English in outlook as any Dutchman, Swede, or German. Colonial population grew "from about 85,000 in 1670, to 360,000 in 1713. By 1754 it had quadrupled again to about 1,500,000. This increase owed much to heavy migration of non-English people—Irish and Scots, Germans and French—favored by a liberal naturalization act of the British Parliament in 1740."[11]

Great waves of immigration continued to swell the numbers of the American people in the nineteenth century and into the twentieth these trends continued. To quote Morison again: "During the decade of the 1820's, only 129,000 'alien passengers' entered the United States from foreign countries; in the 1830's the number swelled to 540,000, of whom 44 per cent were Irish, 30 per cent German, and 15 per cent English; this figure was almost tripled for the 1840's, and rose to 2,814,554 for the 1850's. Roughly half of the immigrants from 1840 were Irish, with Germans a close second."[12] The census figures for the later decades of the nineteenth century for certain midwestern states show what this meant concretely as new settlers poured from Europe into that area. For example, the 1880 census figures for Minnesota show 72 per cent foreign born or with at least one foreign-born parent. Even California's figure was 60 per cent. The 1900 figures are 74.9 and 54.9 respectively.

It is not only that America from the beginning was culturally diverse, with important effects, as we shall soon see, on the character of American nationalism. What was also important was that the continental area into which these European millions poured was only lightly populated by Indians, who were relatively easily subdued or expelled. Not that life for the early pioneers on the Eastern seaboard was secure and unthreatened, but the threats were overcome. Symbolic of what was to come of this was the sale of Manhattan Island for $20 worth of beads and trinkets. An immensely rich land was there for the taking.

[11] Samuel Eliot Morison, *The Oxford History of the American People* (New York: Oxford University Press, 1965), p. 140.

[12] *Ibid.*, pp. 479–480. Compare against total populations of 9.6 million in 1820, 12.9 in 1830, 17 in 1840, 23.2 in 1850, and 31.5 in 1860. The first restrictive immigration act was the Johnson Act (1921), which set up quotas based on "national origins."

In the early colonies for a time economic constraints were in operation (e.g., the use of indentured servants on the great estates of the Hudson Valley); soon ended were systems of land tenure artificially limiting the acquisition of wealth by the many, despite their own willingness to work. "Go West, young man!" was advice being followed by droves of people long before Horace Greeley. This abundant and inexhaustible bounty of land stood in tremendous contrast with Europe's formal land tenure system, in which all was already owned; for those who reaped its bounty it was an entirely new psychological experience. Marx later dreamed of the destruction of property barriers, which he saw as the origin of classes, foreseeing the erection of a new society in which everyone could contribute according to his abilities and receive according to his needs. Something not far from the first part of that dream was a reality in the United States, even as Marx wrote. The hand of government had a light touch in this America, and taxes were few and far between. In Chapter 3 we shall look at how the effects of this experience profoundly influenced the American character, and how it imbued that character with an all-pervasive fundamental optimism. There we shall also see what other fundamental attitudes arose from the unusual historical experience we have already examined.

First, however, we must discuss the important effects that cultural diversity had on American nationalism and the American political process.

In the United States people of many cultures worked side by side on free and abundant land, in an environment characterized from the beginning by a virtually classless society, in a setting in which (slaves apart, and even that only for a time) man was not subordinated into a permanently inferior position by the accident of birth. In such a land only certain kinds of political institutions were ultimately practical. Only certain kinds of political arrangements could be compatible with the nature of the new American nationalism, to undergird and reinforce it.

Consider the logical consequences of the great mixture of cultures in a largely unfenced, unformed land, in which many of the problems to be resolved had no traditional or customary answer. Captain John Smith's experiences in the founding of Jamestown (1607), the first permanent English colony in the Americas, set the pattern. Confronted with an Indian problem, he played a role in a complicated drama in which Pocahontas, the chief's daughter, had a prominent part. Plagued by a scarcity of food and shelter in a physical environment that had yet to be mastered, and with an overabundance of "gentlemen" not accustomed to manual labor, Smith hit upon the well-remembered formula: "He who does not work, neither shall he eat"—a formula followed fairly faithfully ever since in the United States, even down to the present, when sons of well-to-do parents sometimes deliver newspapers for the "experience."

Two facts about this environment were fundamental: first, it involved strange new problems for which European ways contained no fully useful or transferable solutions; and, second, peoples from different European cultures had their own different preconceived solutions to problems. The effects of these two facts on the American character were lasting, as Chapter 3 will indicate. Not so obvious were the effects that produced the new system of government, which permitted the U.S. to prosper.

If we consider the immediate prelude and aftermath of the Philadelphia Convention that produced the American Constitution (1787), we gain a first important insight. The Federal Convention was called by the Congress of the Confederation "for the sole and express purpose of revising the Articles of Confederation" and exceeded its mandate, indeed set it aside, and instead produced a blueprint for a much different Federal Union. This document was filled with ingenious compromises. One of these permitted each former colony equality in the Senate, while retaining a separate population formula for the House (and even here slaves were counted on yet another compromise basis). The double break with European (especially English) tradition is apparent, for the dual chambers of the British Parliament had other origins and operated quite differently, then and later. Presidential elections constituted still another area for compromise. It was here that the complicated and indirect election via an Electoral College was born.

One could continue the illustrations, but the point is that the new American Constitution represented many adroit compromises for which European precedent and tradition offered little preparation. When this Constitution was offered for approval, a second significant development occurred: it was immediately amended (a stipulation that was made by a variety of the states when they agreed to ratification). The first ten amendments are known today as the Bill of Rights; they were and are collectively powerful brakes upon any tendency which the Federal government might develop toward overbearing tyranny. Thomas Paine's formula, "That government is best which governs least," found a ready reception in the hearts and minds of the people.

These latter developments are often interpreted (correctly) as signifying suspicion on the part of the states that they would lose their individual identities if no safeguards were added to the Constitution. It goes deeper than that. Unless one wants to ascribe the depths of this so prevalent feeling merely to a parochial local patriotism that insisted that "Virginia shall remain Virginia," one is forced to probe beyond and ask why this viewpoint commanded such substantial support.

Two observations can be made. First, the variation in circumstances and problems from one former colony to the next was not unknown or hidden from view. Popular opinion rightly held that given that diversity, much local and individual autonomy was absolutely necessary. This answer does not really explain why the Bill of Rights *per se* was added.

One could argue that *state* diversity was already amply protected by the compromises built into the original unamended Constitution. We come to the second observation. Whether altogether consciously or in part unconsciously the American people realized that in a land where unforeseen kinds of problems had been experienced and where novel solutions were frequently needed, the individual right to dissent would have great practical importance, especially in view of the mingling of many cultures already to be observed in the United States. If English cultural responses to problems would need substantial alteration when applied to American circumstances, it was even truer that the answers given to problems by a multitude of foreign cultures would be even more diverse. All would be in need of both integration with different views and modification to fit American circumstances. To accomplish this task with all possible viewpoints expressed, the habit of wide and free discussion had to be set upon the solid rock of Constitutional provision. Even today in New England the Town Financial Meeting is a perfect illustration of this principle in operation.

Consequently, while it is possible to examine the Bill of Rights from the standpoint of pride and moral approval, as a way-station toward democracy, it does not do the provisions full justice. They were (and remain) eminently practical political arrangements for a nation confronting unusual circumstances both in physical environment and cultural diversity. How else could the U.S. have succeeded so well as a political entity?

What happened in the United States is that a fixed and even deified *method* was evolved for a people of many backgrounds to use in resolving problems as they appeared, in virtually any way they saw fit. The *solutions* to problems have varied with the times, but the *method* has remained the same. The free debate and compromise method has been used throughout American history to supply an endless variety of answers and solutions—most of them peacefully and ultimately accepted, with the exception of the slavery issue and Prohibition. After the original constitutional compromise, the slavery issue led to a whole series of later compromises and ultimately brought on the Civil War, which led to a further series of compromises. In more recent times segregated schools that could be "separate but equal" became illegal on the grounds that separate is *not* equal. The struggle and revision and new compromises over these racial issues is well known. When one looks back upon this illustration, one can speak of an evolving conscience. In political terms one can speak even more meaningfully of an endless revision of what was previously agreed, toward some new compromise. Except for the resort to arms in 1861–1865, this method of problem-solving has remained constant even while the solutions have varied in endless succession. Illustrations from such other areas as taxation and medical insurance are not hard to find. If one wants to describe with some precision that ambiguous phrase, "the American way of life," one must recognize that it really has no fixed content, only a fixed method for problem-solving. This fact describes above all else the essential character of the American domestic political environment.

Today as before, the political process continues; and it is threatened today as before, by those who are tempted to withdraw from the original agreement. The process has not been frictionless and was never designed to be. What one can say about it is that it has survived "Know-Nothing" movements, hysterical "ban German from the schools" movements (World War I era), and the Joseph McCarthy era. Lately, we have vigorous dissent over the Viet-Nam War, which arouses much criticism (some of it rightly, for the burning of American flags by Americans *is* disturbing); this dissent ought to be seen in the same perspective. What would or should be far more disturbing would be the spectacle of a United States fighting such a war, with all its ambiguities as to methods, goals, and results, with no substantial opposition or debate. From a quite conservative point of view, one would have to ask whether such a debate-less America could survive the tough road ahead. One may argue that a homogenous American culture has now evolved that makes the former regard for American diversity no longer necessary (although the validity of that argument is questionable). One may argue that America is now facing problems for which traditional and approved solutions can simply be applied, and thus there is no real need for debates. The truth would seem otherwise. The real meaning of contemporary debates over United States foreign policy is that the American people are still coming to terms with these new problems. They can see that there is actually something of substance to be said in favor of two quite different policies: the total involvement, so characteristic of us since 1945, and a more limited involvement. It is because they see some merit in both alternatives that much debate is needed, now as before.

How the American nation was formed thus directly influenced the political system we have evolved. At one and the same time it has made us remarkably open minded about what policy we may choose to attempt and has—fortunately—equipped us with the means for its re-examination.

An Assessment

CHAPTER 1 considered two handicaps that the United States has in dealing with world affairs: first is the widespread American assumption that *we* are the conscience of the world and understand universal man's aspirations, that nations are proceeding toward common goals along a single spectrum of progress; and second is our tendency to ascribe our good fortune and substantial success essentially to our own efforts and wise decisions, a tendency that encourages us to believe that we have ready answers to other peoples' problems. In Chapter 2 we have shown that America's experience has been fundamentally unusual (and even, in its mix, unique) in three important areas of experience. First, the effects of our geographic isolation have been profound. The United States is the sole great power in the world without great power neighbors nearby. Second, the effects of historical experience have been enormous. The United States is the sole great power in the world whose major period of historical experience as a nation was in the rather peaceful century between 1815–1914. Third, the effects of the domestic environment have been pronounced. The United States is the sole great power in the world whose population came from across the seas by immigration and occupied a large, rich, and sparsely settled continent with such outstanding politico-economic success. The facts of *where* the United States came to exist, *when* it happened, and *how* the American nation was formed have had and continue to have extremely important consequences. These facts of where, when, and how are intimately related to her two handicaps in dealing with world affairs.

A people formed *e pluribus unum* ("from many, one") can be pardoned if they are tempted to assume that they think like all, since they in fact originated from all. Yet, by the very nature of the American experience, the many were blended together under economic, geographical, social, and historical circumstances that made them typical of none. This experience proved to be an important source of our moral, spiritual, and national strength, but it hardly qualified us to become the "conscience of mankind." As to the second handicap, the record shows an early prudent regard for our own limited strength. It shows wise foreign policy decisions to concern ourselves with understandable, important, and limited goals. What the record does not indicate is that we really understood the important effects of British policy, of the balance of power, of the uniqueness of the 1815–1914 historical age. We erred not in taking credit, but in taking too much.

We would do well to understand how really different we are, how really different has been our experience, and how really different is our outlook. Much that is central to our image is admired and accepted throughout much of the world. The admiration is for our success; it is not a demand for guidance or prescription. The American goals of abundance and peace are accepted; other nations cannot, and know they cannot, follow the American path to get there. That procedure is beyond their capabilities. Our resources, rich as we are, do not make it possible for us to do this for them.

We turn in Chapter 3 to an analysis of the American character. If the unusualness of the American experience affects our approach to foreign policy problems and has made us what we are, we must also understand what it *is* that we are: how we tackle problems, what our attitude toward problems is, and what weaknesses and strengths derive from these habits and outlooks. If our experience has been different, our attitudes and character will have unusual features too. In Chapter 3 we shall be asking how Americans tend to look at life and how and where we are different. If the inquiry is meaningful, we shall understand both ourselves and other nations better.

CHAPTER 3

The Impact of American Attitudes

N O NATION is immune to its experiences and environment; on the contrary, the national attitudes and traits, the national character as a whole, reflect the history of a people. To the extent that those experiences and the environment combine certain unusual features, the mix of attitudes, too, will have unusual aspects. What is striking in the American approach to problems is the strong emphasis on ability to make progress and resolve difficulties—an emphasis not at all unknown elsewhere, but certainly measurably stronger in the United States.

Speaking of a whole nation in terms of behavior traits involves large-scale generalizing with fairly obvious limitations. "Typical Americans" and "typical American attitudes" are myths at close quarters; these generalizations lose firmness as descriptions of any flesh-and-blood individual person or particular issue. Two hundred million people do not speak or respond or feel with one voice, action, or heart.[1] Such usage will likely involve over-simplification. One can become the victim of one's own phrasing, falsely assigning a corporate personality and describing mythical collective traits. But if there are *no* distinctive national traits, neither can there be a nationalism; if there is no *national* character, no real differences in outlook distinguish people from nation to nation. The frontiers dividing them would be only arbitrary administrative lines. We know from observation that this is not true. Differences are real, and do exist, even though one can only generalize about the national group within certain limits, and only so far.

In the absence of conclusive data, the characterizations herewith are necessarily somewhat crude and impressionistic, particularly where the effort is made to tie these "characteristics" to foreign policy performance. Nevertheless, understanding of these national differences is so important to understanding the foreign policies of nations—especially so in the case

---

[1] A point made explicit earlier in quotations of views on foreign policy, and a point explored further in Part Two when we consider public opinion and competing interest groups.

of the United States—that it is better to run the intellectual risks in making the attempt than to forego the prospect of an improved (even if imperfect) understanding of the *whys* of American foreign policy. By speaking of national character and national attitudes we are trying to describe only those qualities that would appear to be generally true about Americans as a whole, highlighting what seems particularly true of Americans in comparison with other peoples and other cultures.[2] In looking then at our approaches to foreign policy problems, we may be better able to see where they are typical of many or most peoples, and where they are different or even unique.

Whatever their "real" character, foreign policy problems are also in part that which is believed. Suppose it were true that peoples generally thought little of closing out a commitment that had proved untenable, but the American people believed the opposite to be true. Our behavior in that case would deviate from the usual and be significantly at variance with real conditions. How Americans approach problems (realistically or unrealistically) stems from our attitudes, which in turn derive from our experience (usual or unusual). In our characteristic responses we will reflect our national "character" (i.e., our group attitudes) formed by that experience.

What kind of attitudes, then, do we have as the result of the unusual experiences described in Chapter 2? In what ways, if any, are these attitudes changing as a result of contemporary experience? How well do these attitudes equip us for dealing with other peoples with different experiences?

Attitudes about Government and Politics

THE first important observation relates to our general approach to political action. Americans, formed by compact out of many diverse cultures, will inevitably place great stress on the contractual nature of government. Government will be seen as "holding the ring" procedurally, while program preferences are argued out and new departures taken. In a society with a short history such as ours, traditions will restrict far less, and the range of possible new programs will be very broad.

Of all the cultures that have shaped us, the English influence was naturally greatest. Yet the English Constitution was never reduced to a single formal document with a given number of articles, sections, and paragraphs. Consisting instead of a long chain of habits and usages interspersed with landmark statements of principle such as the Magna Charta, the English Constitution was evolved organically out of a long and changing experience. Indeed some of the provisions of the Magna Charta

---

[2] By contrast, in Chapter 6 we shall explore many of the differences among Americans.

make strange reading today; yet Englishmen know very well which parts still prevail. In the United States, by contrast, although "liberal construction" (interpretation) of the Constitution by the Supreme Court has stretched its provisions to cover contingencies that the Founding Fathers could hardly have clearly foreseen, the ultimate finding in law has to turn upon some phrase, some provision of that basic document or its reasonable or logical extension. However much some aspect of the Constitution is temporarily ignored in time of stress, the Constitution ultimately prevails. A recent illustration is the redressing by the courts of the rights of West Coast Japanese-Americans who were arbitrarily interned after Pearl Harbor.

The American Constitution not only explicitly reserves certain responsibilities to the states and reserves other rights to individual citizens; it also divides in principle the powers of government among the executive branch, the Congress, and the courts. The British executive is a part of Parliament, and Parliament has ultimate power over the courts. In theory the British Parliament can enact any legislation and make it constitutional (always within the bounds of the unwritten rules).

Certainly the contrast is real and observable between these two systems. The American system of government originally was and still is a very definite departure from "mother country" methods. Although the basic rights of Englishmen were taken over into American practice, they were also written down so that there could be no mistake; this procedure was not considered necessary in the English culture with its long and organic experience in working out these principles.

Many foreign nations have subsequently imitated the American example, producing constitutions modeled after ours. Relatively few have achieved anything remotely resembling our own faithfulness to our basic law. Either new versions have been produced to give legitimacy to new governments as they have taken power, or old versions have been retained and ignored. Latin American practice offers copious illustrations of both tendencies. Brazil in the last decade is a recent example of this kind of development.

Our innate habit of respect for written law, so much ingrained in us, has served us well. There is a built-in temptation to Americans to claim a moral superiority over governments less constitutionally scrupulous. One should probe instead beneath the surface to find why the American Constitution proved viable while many others did not. Certainly its very flexibility (especially by interpretation) has made an important difference. Underneath there has been a more vital element involved: its suitability for a people blended from many, in laying down workable ground rules for reaching successive new consensus. It is here that two related strands in the American political character are clearly revealed, for although the Constitutional ground rules for working out new solutions to new problems have been held sacred, the solutions are judged on their practical merits. As we said in Chapter 2, there is a fixed *method* for finding solutions, but the *content* of the solutions can vary greatly. What this means is that *American idealism* and *American pragmatism* find a happy marriage in our domestic instruments of government. The idealism speaks to a "government of laws, not of men." The pragmatism speaks to an open and evolving mind as to what ought to be done about civil rights.

The domestic practicality of our idealism encourages us habitually to seek foreign policy solutions with these same dual features and frustrates us when we are not successful. We feel that idealism and practical, useful results ought to go hand in hand in our foreign policy just as they have done so successfully at home. Consequently this habit and expectation are reflected in much of our foreign policy programs and in our attempts to find suitable ways of participating in international relations.

Looking from this perspective, one understands why the American people have been so prone to emphasize the United Nations. Inarticulate ofttimes as it may be, an instinctive feeling is common to most Americans that the UN will prove useful and workable because it, too, blends the essential elements of a fixed constitutional method for handling international affairs with an open-mindedness about solutions to international problems. This instinct leads us to elevate UN decisions and their potential efficacy above what is sometimes justified. If there has been a falling-off in this faith, it represents a disillusionment with the actual workings of the UN rather than a rejection in principle of the thought that it should ultimately work.

These American attitudes toward the UN contain subtle nuances of differences from the attitudes of many other members. They account for what might otherwise seem somewhat erratic U.S. voting behavior. The older European nations tend to approach the UN rather warily (especially now that there is so strong a non-European and even anti-European membership). They look not so much to improving the condition of the world as to keeping things from deteriorating. French policy in the UN exemplifies this very note of conservative caution; British policy reflects it only slightly less. On the other hand, the Afro-Asian nations approach the UN on a dual basis. Their scarce economic and diplomatic resources force them to concentrate their efforts where they can presumably have maximum effect. Also they see the UN as a lever from which to move a lethargic world; they demand enforcement action on Rhodesia, on South Africa. The Soviet Union and the Communist nations generally, while seeing in the UN an instrument for encouraging change toward socialism, react negatively to the notion that the UN should be given greater military, constitutional, or political powers; they fear these may ultimately be used contrary to Soviet interests. Latin America welcomes the UN partly as a means of escaping from the overwhelming shadow of the "Colossus of the North," while paying a prudent regard to American wishes in voting. The attitude of the United States (and its financial willingness to support UN activities) is most unusual and distinctive, for the United States "needs" the UN less than most and supports it more (and more altruistically) than any.

It is sometimes said that U.S. policy in the UN reflects a wish to be loved, to be popular. This is a surface observation of a phenomenon with much deeper roots. The U.S. *believes* in the possibility of effective compromises between diverse national cultures because her own way of life and her own national experience seem to show this approach to be feasible. What contributes to American frustrations over an adverse vote in the UN is a sense of uneasiness that America has not accurately reflected "the conscience of mankind." Our whole history reinforces our conviction that by our very nature and composition we do. What is lost in this translation of American effort from domestic to foreign problems is an understanding of the point made previously: precisely because the American people became one from many, they represent a new national product, a distillation not truly representative of any. In the American predisposition to envisage the UN as a superlegislative body, the seeds of some frustration and even error are implicit. The members of Congress represent districts within a single nation, and the enacted laws (if they survive the courts) will endure; in the UN, on the contrary, members represent nations who will not concur in or carry out the will of the majority where they consider any resolution contrary to their own interests. To make the assumption that the UN will be otherwise is dangerous; it is even more dangerous if the U.S. acts on that false assumption.

Needed as a corrective is not cynicism or contempt, but a certain amount of caution. The analogy many Americans draw between the UN and our own experience breaks down in the assumption that scrupulous adherence to this method (international organization) ought to provide effective changing solutions to international problems. America's happy marriage of domestic idealism and pragmatism cannot be satisfactorily replicated for international behavior through the UN device. This truth has forced the U.S. on occasion to follow a more pragmatic course of action outside the UN—such as forming NATO.

A second important observation about American attitudes on government and politics relates to the greatly increased support for large and ambitious governmental programs at home and abroad since the 1930's.

Early colonial experience with British rule led to the widely held conclusion that government regulation could be arbitrary and restrictive, that personal liberty and economic advantage could be severely circumscribed by laws and regulations—especially those enacted from across the seas. The taxing power ("no taxation without representation") was an obvious illustration; regulations prohibiting the construction of American shipping or its free involvement in world trade were equally important illustrations of harassment.

Contrasting strongly in colonial days with the power of government to harass was the ineffectualness of government to protect. Continual colonial complaints made their slow way to London on the lack of effective security arrangements made in America by the British government. The raising of native militia regiments and the less formalized defense arrangements that dotted the American frontier were testimonials to this lack, rather than an indication of colonial preferences to bear arms. So it was that when the American Constitution came into existence, the local right to bear arms was incorporated (leading today to the argument between the American Rifle Association and those who want to control the indiscriminate distribution of firearms). So it was also that the powers of the central government were limited to the end that functionally and geographically government would be located as near the actual problem as possible. So it was, finally, that the powers of both Federal *and* state governments were restricted by the reserved rights of individuals as citizens. In an age of poor communications and transportation, in an age when the need for complex national solutions to overall problems was severely limited, these arrangements fitted the circumstances quite well.

We all know what changed later in these circumstances. Great arterial highways in an "interstate" system demand federal control and supervision. Pollution of rivers on a grand scale endangers the drinking-water supplies of towns and cities far away from the original pollution. Great harbors at the foot of multimillion population cities cry out for multistate cooperation and federal regulation. There are also the obvious problems of national security in a far less secure contemporary world. All of these great changes in circumstances have produced equally great changes in attitudes about the proper scope of governmental activities. The regulatory function of government has vastly increased. Interdependence on the part of all of the American people in many if not most areas of life is now acknowledged and government's role has changed accordingly. Yet the fact of change should not obscure the constant: both earlier and now the scope permitted to government turned on the perception of problems to be solved. The content determination has been consistently pragmatic.

With these changes in domestic attitude have also come changes in outlook on foreign policy. Reared originally in a land far away from any constant and sustained military threat (especially in view of technological limitations and the interactions between British policy and the

continental balance of power), we found our "natural" security threatened
by the end of the nineteenth and early twentieth centuries by a whole
series of changes described earlier. We became convinced that positive
American actions were necessary—a conviction which led to the intense
involvement that typifies our foreign policy today.

Here again we can gain valuable insight into the American character,
if we first look at the domestic aspects of this development and then
at its foreign policy implications.

Many middle-of-the-road Americans have been much upset by the
growth of "big government." Rotary and Kiwanis clubs all over America
are still subjected to luncheon speeches on its dangers. And yet government becomes even bigger. Constant invoking of the theme that power
should be returned to the states has had little impact for two reasons.
One reason (more important in current political terms but less important
fundamentally) is that it usually turns out that "conservatives" want an
end to deficit spending and "give-away" programs other than those
which bring money and tangible material benefits into their *own* community. They want economy in each case to be made somewhere else.
Each such suggestion in a pluralistic society such as ours cancels the
others out. The second, more fundamental reason is that since the social
needs are so obvious and had been neglected past toleration on the
rural-dominated state level, the pressures on a federal legislature (which
continues to be redistricted as populations shift) have increased steadily.
From the New Deal, through the Fair Deal, the New Frontier, and the
Great Society, the line of progression is almost unbroken. Significantly,
the Eisenhower Administration came to power on a platform of economy
in federal expenditure and a return of functions to the states, but little
along those lines was actually achieved. Indeed, at least one important
new federal spending project of enormous dimensions was begun—the
Interstate Highway program.

This progression baffles the "conservative" who is still trying to find
out why it all failed, especially if his idea of Americanism is largely
coterminous with insistence on private property rights. The "liberal" is
not at all astonished at these developments (although uncritically disposed to view an even bigger Federal government with too much
equanimity). The actual clue to why these things have been done is implicit in the arguments previously made: the basic American approach
to government is that anything is all right that is not constitutionally
illegal and which a majority can agree on as an action program.

Interestingly enough, now that in the last years the U.S. Supreme Court
has forced an equitable redistricting in hopelessly lopsided state legis-
latures, the way so long closed has again been opened for the people to
demand from state representatives (and perhaps receive) the things
that by popular majority they want to have and to have done. In the

years ahead, a healthy rebalancing of the respective strengths and powers of the state and Federal governments may take place. There is no ingrained reason why states cannot better perform certain functions that the Federal government has assumed by default.

The relevance of these observations to foreign affairs lies in the fact that the American tendency in politics is pragmatic to the highest degree, that the conviction that "something should be done" is not long thwarted by any considerations but those of legality, common sense, and moral sensitivity. Of these last three qualifications only the first is fairly much what it sounds like, for pragmatism thinks it *is* common sense, and moral sensitivity can become blurred in complicated issues where moral arguments can be advanced both for and against doing what is contemplated. In foreign affairs Americans are highly motivated by the idea of "getting the job done," and are highly impatient to "move it forward." This trait is both a strength and a weakness, depending upon the particular case and the particular "principles" being followed.

Consider the zeal with which in the post-World War II era we collected allies—more than three and a half dozen. In a UN of over 120, made large by the accession of numerous rather artificially based nation-states, one third are allies of the United States (and frequently enemies of still other allies of the United States). Enthusiastic over building a "position of strength" against communism, we were not deterred by such internal contradictions in the coalitions we created. Convinced that the U.S. had erred in the interwar period by "sitting it out," we moved after 1945 quite close to taking a stand on any and every international dispute or problem.

Not only did we take a stand, but we usually took it quite soon. For example, for many years after 1945, it became the practice of the U.S. State Department to react to notes from the Soviets virtually as soon as they were received. A time schedule of response like German Chancellor Kiesinger's plan to answer a 1967 Soviet note a couple of months later would have appeared in John Foster Dulles' time as completely astonishing procedure. More recent practice shows a distinct gain in maturity. The over-early, off-the-hip response is now much less frequent, as the procedural handling of the Cuban Missile Crisis (1962) and the Middle Eastern Crisis (1967) illustrate. Yet the opposite tendency is not altogether dead. Whatever one thinks of the merits of the "fast-draw" U.S. action in the Dominican Republic coup (1965), most observers would probably agree that we ran a serious tactical risk, since the U.S. commitment was made public before Organization of American States (OAS) action put a retroactive blessing on it.[3]

[3] If the OAS had *not* endorsed the action, the U.S. would presumably have been guilty of violation of Articles 15 and 17 of the OAS Charter.

Very little analysis has been made of the impact of fast communications on U.S. foreign policy. Although no one would argue that hearing news late is best or early warning of developments wrong, the fact that the U.S. possesses a much more extensive and elaborate network of communications than almost any other people results in a constant temptation for government to react on early and incomplete knowledge. Newspapers and television facilities, with their constant programming needs, exert steady pressures in the same direction. In a nation such as America, where the pace of life is quick, and in which the appearance of efficiency is in part customarily maintained in the business, professional, and governmental fields by a steady, tight scheduling, there remains a daily possibility of doing something now and thinking about it later. In this dual respect the U.S. is again rather distinctive in its handling of foreign affairs. Abroad, not only are communications less efficient and fast, but there is more temperamental inclination to react more slowly. Those European diplomatic services with longest experience in handling international affairs are most prone to consider that problems left alone will go away—which they sometimes do.

A related facet of this same phenomenon, stemming from the same framework of experience, is the American tendency to think that all problems are ultimately soluble. This attitude is by no means restricted to application in the realm of politics and government, or foreign affairs. Its roots go deep into the general American experience with life.

Thus contemporary American attitudes about government and politics are distinguished by idealism in approach, pragmatism in content, expectations of relatively rapid progress in the solution of problems, and a general willingness to attempt to exert U.S. influence abroad.

Attitudes about Human Relationships

To THE extent that Americans prefer to think of themselves as "typical" (at least of what the peoples of the world would be like if they could), they will not tend to think their own experience peculiar or extraordinary except in the quantity and quality of American domestic success in attaining "universal" goals.

Yet the factors already mentioned have been prime and quite unusual influences on our outlook. These include the relatively classless society built from the interaction of multiple cultural influences, the "clean slate" aspects of an environmental framework where authority or acceptability derived hardly at all from custom, and the extreme natural wealth of the extensive American domain. If we add other factors not yet mentioned, these tendencies are further reinforced. Each has some relation to foreign policy and how we conduct it.

Consider the extreme mobility of the American people. Not only do

Americans indulge in extensive sea, land, and air travel (itself rather unusual experience) but they transplant domiciles at what must be an unprecedented rate. The frontier experience was from this point of view an exercise in mobility. Although some whole areas of the country were settled originally by influx directly from abroad, more usually immigrants settled for awhile in or near their arrival ports and gradually moved West. Southern Indiana settlers came in large part from the Cumberland area, just as western New York State was opened to settlement by transplanted New Englanders. Daniel Boone's progressive migrations were not unusual, and the great influx to California with and after the 49'ers came from much further East. In the original sense of the term the frontier did not disappear until 1912, when the last "territory" within the continental limits of the United States was admitted to the Union.

Migration to Hawaii and Alaska continues right now, and such areas within the continental limits as Arizona and especially Florida continue to grow significantly through migration. *Newsweek* (January 1957) reported that every week since 1951 an average of 2,600 new "settlers" had migrated to Florida to make a new home—a tendency accelerated in the last decade, with more expected. In July 1958, the U.S. Census Bureau released figures showing that in the twelve months ending in April 1957, about one out of five Americans (32 million) moved. Of these 32 million, about 20 million stayed in the same county, five million moved to different counties in the same state, and five million moved to different states. Of persons aged 20 to 24, more than 40 per cent moved. In ten years (1947–1957) 18.5 to 21 per cent of Americans moved each year.

It is a safe wager that almost any American college or university instructor who asks his class how many of them still live in the place in which they were born will see few hands raised. If you ask an American where he comes from, he is likely either to name off a string of places or else settle for the most recent, which will generally turn out not to have been his location for very long.

What are the implications of this extraordinary mobility on foreign-policy matters? Americans have necessarily had to adjust to this way of life, creating many devices that cushion the shock of transplantation—such as transfer credits among colleges, transfer certificates for church memberships, a customary invitation to the Rotarian and Kiwanian to take up membership in the club in the new locales. Each is likely to regard his voluntary move as a part of personal or professional progress, as something desirable and more normal than not. In the process the nation's once quite strong regional differences have been eroded, and greater national unity has been the by-product. The transplanted American rarely looks back on the change with regret, although perhaps with a vague nostalgia. In short, he is not aware that other peoples generally have different experiences and, when they have the same experiences, may regard them quite differently.

If, for example, Germans have been expelled from eastern areas presently held by Poland, and some 40 per cent of the people of the Bonn Federal Republic grew up elsewhere, and if these areas lost to "free Germany" pass out of German control for 20 or 30 years, the American is highly likely to assume that Germans will generally settle into the new localities with much the same willingness as he would. Continuing annual large rallies of the "expellees" (for which in the U.S. there is only such a shadowy and marginal equivalence as the college reunion) may be valued at less than their potential political meaning. An American may wonder about the continued existence for so many years of compact masses of Palestine refugees in the Gaza Strip (fostered deliberately in part, to be sure, by the policy of Arab nations), but he will more easily conclude that in time they will make the best of things. Unless he thinks in terms of racial analogies, he will find trouble in relating the evidence of minority groups existing intact in foreign countries for centuries— such as the Volga Germans transplanted and broken up finally by Stalin in World War II—with anything in his own experience.

A second factor, with interrelations with the first, is the American sense of historical time, already alluded to. Now, we must put it in perspective.

The American sense of history is very weakly developed. It is not just that our own national existence does not top the two-century mark; temperamentally we live in the present or future tense. Change has been our hallmark, and change is quickly accepted. We take pride in adjusting, in refusing to cling to the "outmoded" past, even in welcoming with recurrent but weakening optimism the "advances" dutifully and regularly incorporated in each new model year or each new television set, automobile, or gadget. We tend noticeably to believe that change *is* progress, and vice versa. (Even the "new Left," rejecting the standard American dream, believes that the future can be better.) So we look steadily forward as we move past the checkpoints of progress: the advent of television, the elimination of polio, the manned trip to the moon. It is a matter of "common sense" that we are better off now than we were then. (Part of the contemporary student unrest is a reaction against such beliefs, for we are now also better able to destroy our own civilization.)

What this outlook leaves us short of is an appreciation for the perennial aspects of the human predicament. Since change is progress and the present is better (and the future even better), we do not incline to look backward and we are consequently frequently short on an appreciation of the long roots of things.

In many ways the American attitude toward handling foreign affairs reflects the fact that we "just found out about it." Because of the long immunity (1815–1914) from serious disturbance from abroad, because we have been woefully short of much widespread knowledge about the background experience of so many foreign peoples (whose way of life we think we know via the osmosis of continuing cultural absorption), we were grossly underprepared for the new role in international affairs that we took on after 1945. We were (and remain) more optimistic about putting things to rights than a sober study of man's long history would justify. We are equally taken aback by the historically long-ingrained but newly revealed arrogance of contemporary China (which became even more accentuated through the humiliations China's weakness brought her from George Washington's time forward). We are predisposed to assume that communism (which is after all relatively recent) overcomes historic Chinese frictions with Russia going back through the centuries. Not keeping in mind that China counts her own history continuously now for some 4,000's of years, that she remembers the long period of being the cultivated center of a barbarian world as "normal" and the short, more recent period of weakness as "abnormal," we become confused at the emotional strain and stress with which China conducts her frustrated policy. Impressed by the widely known fact that both China and Russia are "communist," we do not take as seriously the less known fact that China remembers the loss of over 500,000 square miles of "her" territory to the Tsars.

Plunging into a vigorous policy in the Far East, into a Viet-Nam War for the "freedom" of a faraway people, we optimistically conclude that— as we quoted Secretary Rusk earlier—"we are coming towards the end of an era when men can believe it is profitable and, even, possible to change the *status quo* by applying external force. [Those who persist in so doing] represent ideas and methods from the past, not the future. Elsewhere in the world those committed to such concepts have faded or are fading from the scene. . . ." Perhaps. A sober regard of world history encourages the contrary belief. Is it assumed that a great change is now taking place because the future is always automatically better? Or was it to occur, as Senator Stennis asked dubiously in 1967, through the U.S. playing policeman to the world? Ironically, Rusk's prediction was followed by the third round of the Arab-Israeli War.

Behind the assumptions about change and the future lies ultimately a view of man himself. What is it that makes men "tick," and how does this affect things? Here we embark upon even more treacherous terrain for effective generalizations; but if we do not try to see more concretely the American image of man, we cannot ultimately grope with the general American expectation that all problems can be solved with time and effort, and that change is progress.

Traditional American appraisals of the nature of man cover a spectrum of viewpoints, with one predominating much more than the rest.[4] One minority view is that man is a sinner and remains so, saved, ultimately, if at all, by the grace of God. A second minority view is that man is a mixture of good and evil, led by the blinding light of revelation toward an effort to do good and be better, and saved ultimately, when he is, by good works and the grace of God. The majority view holds that man is the son of God, occasionally falls from His graces, but is on the whole good, and in the end, with few exceptions, saved. This view, if it *is* (as argued) the majority view, is also quite obviously an optimistic view.

Not that such a view is held still with the pristine simplicity of the beginning of the twentieth century. The last six decades have been filled with too much war, bloodshed, and destruction. The large shadow of potential worldwide thermonuclear destruction hovers uncertainly just off stage. Such shadows mar the picture but do not destroy it. If Americans were asked whether Africa would one day overcome its problems, they would probably mostly say yes. If Americans were asked whether mankind would ultimately use nuclear power to man's benefit, they would probably mostly say yes. If they were asked whether Secretary Rusk's view that change wrought by force was gradually being outmoded, they would, more than not, probably say yes—in the long run.

Such views, if they are indeed held, can be proved neither true nor untrue in any objective sense, any more than the predictions as to man's future made by communism or other secular faiths can be finally judged in the here and now. Only the fullness of time will reveal what is correct. These views have significance, then, not because they are or are not objective statements of reality, but because they strongly influence what we do in the here and now. *If* Americans generally believed that no combination of positive and constructive actions in world affairs could possibly be of lasting benefit in improving the condition of the world, they might still act, but hardly with the same vigor of purpose. It is because Americans have experienced progress themselves that they tend also to believe that progress is really possible. Because they have been able to find a suitable set of changing solutions to their own problems, their own history has not been so discouraging; and because they have experienced the dismal side of historical experience less than most, they remain optimistic about the outcome. These attitudes contribute the essentials to a distinctive American political style—in both domestic and foreign policy. Although such approaches to problems may or may not be based on false premises, they do arise out of a rather unusual his-

---

4 Although the reader will recognize that the following statements can be roughly equated with the formal creed of particular American churches, it is not the assumption of the author that statistics on the relative membership strengths of these churches would be of much use in assessing the degree of adherence each enjoys in a fundamental philosophical sense.

tory. We should not assume that such attitudes are usual abroad or that they are widely shared. If we understand this point we shall be less disappointed with the reactions of others. And if we further understand that our own experience is far from the world's norm, we shall also better adjust to the recurrent setbacks and disappointments we shall encounter. Hopefully such a state of mind might insulate us from the real danger implicit in overly ambitious goals—that finding frustration with attempting too much, we ultimately settle (as once before) with trying too little in world affairs.

An Assessment

THIS chapter has described what are considered to be the distinctive attitudes with which the American people approach problems, especially problems of politics and foreign policy. These attitudes are environmental in source; they were formed by our experience. As such the attitudes are not immutable. Changing experience can alter them in time, and will, but they arise out of an unusual history and they are not attitudes shared by much of the rest of the world. Specifically, the American attitudes are higher on optimism and shorter on patience. We expect to accomplish more than most and do it more quickly. This combination makes us more vulnerable in several respects. It encourages us to underestimate the tenacity of problems and to think in rather ambitious terms. It leads us to the brink of temptation to take on a larger role than we (or anyone else) may ultimately be able to fill. It exposes us to frustration when intractable problems remain unsolved, and it may end by shaking our faith that all problems can be solved with enough good will and effort.

In our own domestic experience problems *have* been solved; the rule of law has generally prevailed; the combination of a fixed method of procedure, but changing contents for solutions, has worked well. Part of the reason for this success is precisely because two ingredients were present: the absence of a single, ingrained, formal, and traditional structure shaping our "way of life," and the presence of a multiculture society. The latter made a way of finding suitable compromises absolutely essential; the former permitted those compromises to be unstructured by tradition-bound limits. Because the American scene was not set in its outlines by centuries of class relationships, because it had no traditional feudal past that laid its restraining hand upon change, the solutions that could be reached for problems were remarkably open to the arguments of logic and the shifting pressures of political forces. This distinctive political experience is not duplicated in, or is at least not widespread in, the world arena. There the roots of some contemporary problems literally go back for thousands of years. The great Jewish exodus in Roman times has a direct relationship to the present tensions between Arabs and Jews.

The antagonism and conflict between Teuton and Slav has a thousand years of active history behind it. The gradual and growing mutual impingement of Chinese and Russian has very long roots in the spread of these two cultures toward one another. These are not problems to which new solutions are applicable merely on the basis of logic, common sense, good will, or good intention. In a nutshell, the difference between the American experience and the general experience is that our own problems had so few intractable historical roots.

Consequently, we cannot expect ultimately to have as substantial success with our foreign policy if we approach international problems without taking this factor into account. It is not simply a matter of "improving" the UN or raising living standards abroad that will be of use (although these efforts *do* have uses).

After a long hiatus from meaningful world affairs between 1815 and World War I, and confronted with the problems of the world arena, in our 1945–1950 conceptualization of those problems we tended to think in the image of two "ways of life." We tended to divide the world into those in the "free world" who presumably shared our sentiments, and those in the "communist world" who apparently or obviously did not. Only by President Kennedy's time were we prepared philosophically to accept the existence of a third or neutral bloc. And only more recently have we accepted even in principle the infinite variety of policies that individual communist (and other) states follow in the name of "national communism," "polycentrism," or even "de Gaullism." We have been unprepared for the infinite variety of interests that nation-states actually have, and we have been slow to abandon a simple view of all the world divided into two or three points of view.

Because of our own short historical experience as a nation and our even shorter active participation in world affairs, we did not have the perspective to assess the very unusual features of that post-1945 world. Lacking that perspective, we were encouraged to overstress its bipolarity. What was not appreciated was the degree to which bipolarity itself was the temporary reflection of a postwar era, that it deviated from the norm of international relations experience, and that it could not ultimately be expected to persist.

The more complex world of today *is* the norm. It is a world in which no one nation or two—regardless of their capability for wreaking physical destruction—can hope to lead or guide with any sureness of acceptable results. It is a more normal and more frustrating world than the world of the bipolar Cold War.

The foreign policy of the United States aroused debates, sometimes intensive ones, in the period before 1945. In George Washington's time, following the outbreak of the French Revolution, the issue was acute as to whether to support France (to whom we had alliance ties) against

England. Fortunately, we did not. Just prior to the War of 1812 New England mercantile interests were so opposed to our policy of an embargo on our shipping that a serious schism arose. It would not be accurate to portray our early history as one of continual consensus over what should be done in foreign affairs. Yet these controversies were over simpler and more immediately understandable problems than in our own day. They were disputes over alternative policies to ensure the security of a new weak nation surrounded by territories under European great power control. The controversy was not over the *strategy* behind the alternative policies: extending the national frontiers and maneuvering European powers out of positions in the New World. It was obvious enough that the strategy was in our national interest. Once the policies chosen achieved their strategic goals, our ventures in foreign affairs until the end of the nineteenth century were of modest dimensions. Although we did not assign appropriate credit to the actions of other powers in contriving the beneficial state of affairs between 1815 and 1914 by which we profited, there was in this period no substantial outcry for a vigorous program of involvements abroad. In these decades public sentiment went in one direction, public policy in another. While Americans cheered the Polish revolt against the Tsars, or financially supported Hungary's Louis Kossuth (1848), or aided the Irish in their struggle against the English, our official policy was unsentimental and uninvolved. In a word, American idealistic sentiment found an outlet abroad, but American pragmatism held us officially aloof in our actual policy. Idealism and pragmatism, the happy combination that worked so well at home by its innate natural harmony in meeting our needs, were made compatible in our foreign policy by the simple device of compartmentalization.

What occurred in 1917 for a short period, and then again after 1945, was the resumption or initiation of a vigorous foreign policy in which our idealism played a primary role, but in which sufficient pragmatism was apparent to make those policies at least temporarily acceptable to the American people.

Wilson's League "solution" was not only idealistic but drastic, and was ultimately rejected. For this and other reasons, the League proved impractical as a mechanism to achieve the purported results. Wilson's belief that it would do the job illustrates his lack of acquaintance with the more pervasive forces at work in international affairs. One can call Wilson an "idealist" for thinking the League would work, but his greater claim to the label arises from his conviction that *something* new was needed. It was, after all, not unrealistic for the U.S. to seek as a strategic goal better ways of maintaining peace. We stood only to benefit from a durable peace. What was unrealistic about Wilson's proposals was not the idealism of his goal but the weaknesses of his remedy.

In any event the American people retreated into "isolationism," to emerge once more on the world scene in 1945 with a substantial role to play. In this early Cold War period, a remarkably effective program gained a comprehensive support from the American people. The Soviets needed to be contained, Europe needed to be rebuilt, and the Marshall Plan, the Truman Doctrine, and the North Atlantic Pact did indeed all share the dual features of large conception (idealism) and effective progress and reform (pragmatism).

What made the European program a success for U.S. foreign policy was that the American people substantially agreed on the need for a program; that those who were helped could also help themselves, once we primed the pumps; and that helping them contributed to a stronger, more secure world for the United States. At a time when bipolarity did exist we helped our friends generously—and thereby did ourselves good as well. Idealism and pragmatism were at this point as happily married in foreign affairs as they had been domestically.

The tale after 1950 becomes more blurred as we became involved in the Far East. Increasingly, the strategic rationale of what had been so successful in Europe (aiding the recovery of those who could become viable and whose viability contributed meaningfully to the security of the United States) was less coherently followed. When the Viet-Nam War brought on a great controversy and much public debate, it was not fundamentally our idealistic motives that were being questioned in America. We knew our motives were good. What was being questioned was the pragmatic effect of what we were doing. Some cried out about the "murder" of civilians through bombing, but all war is murder in a sense, and there had been no outcry against bombing of North Korea (because much more public unity existed on the unavoidability of American involvement there). Behind the moral or moralistic cries and countercries were serious strategic questions of far-reaching significance, such as whether the Viet-Nam War was a desirable (necessary) war for the United States to fight at all. The point is that the practicality or pragmatism of U.S. Far Eastern policies was by no means automatically agreed on by the American public.

The United States, in the 1960's, was groping to play a role in world affairs that would be both idealistic in conception and fortunate (pragmatically, from the standpoint of U.S. national interests) in results. But the happy marriage of idealism and pragmatism that has served us so well domestically and after 1945 in Europe, obviously failed when extended to Far Eastern problems. Given our attitudes, it is apparent that there and elsewhere we are temperamentally capable of taking on too much, of expecting too much, and of ignoring too much the underlying roots of the problem we are handling. (It *is* possible that the devastation to which Viet-Nam has been subjected weakens her historic ability to resist Chinese domination.) Given our attitudes we have the tendency both to expect more good results than are ultimately likely, and to ignore other possibilities in the situation in which our work could be done for us. (It is hard to conceive that the U.S. must take on the major responsibility for containing Chinese expansion when the Soviet Union by geography cannot escape the problem.) Given our attitudes we are likely to involve ourselves in situations without enough historical feeling for what kept things within bounds (in Asia or elsewhere) before we decided after 1945 to take on world problems in a large way.

In this chapter we have sought to make clear what distinctive attitudes toward foreign policy have been produced by the unusual experience of the American people, and what the strengths and weaknesses implicit in those attitudes have to do with the conduct and degree of success of U.S. foreign policy. Out of all that has been said, one clear warning arises: the U.S. temperamentally is likely to err on the side of attempting too much once it begins to go outside the framework of traditional or clearly understood national interest concerns. Later we shall ask how we should decide the strategic questions mentioned here: where and when to be involved—or where and when not to be. We turn now in Part Two to the evolution and coordination of the instruments of foreign policy-making, for they, like our attitudes in conducting policy, have important effects upon the results achieved.

PART TWO

Foreign Policy-Making: Politics, People, and Organization

CHAPTER 4

National Security Coordination and Foreign Affairs

S O FAR the background experience that has influenced the general attitudes of the American people toward foreign policy problems has been stressed, with little but passing attention to internal U.S. governmental organization for foreign affairs and the complex interplay of politics, people, and organization that shapes its functioning.

Here in Part Two we shall look at foreign policy-making from two perspectives already sketched out in the Introduction and Chapter 1. We shall ask how the governmental system for foreign policy purposes has been altered since the 1930's to reflect the changing scope and content of the much more ambitious involvement of the United States in contemporary world affairs. Second, we shall probe the interrelations of politics, people, and organization against the background of Part One to discover, if possible, why the tendency has existed to downplay or ignore consideration of the grand strategic alternative foreign policy choices confronting the United States. If we tend to ask the wrong strategic questions in the wrong order, why do we do so and to what extent, and how could corrections be made to improve our capability for strategic choice?

Unquestionably, the President of the United States is the central figure in foreign policy-making. But for all his power, prerogatives, and influence in this area, his options are much more drastically limited than might appear. Most important in setting parameters for his effective action or initiative are seven constraints: the provisions of the Constitution, the "dead hand" of the past, the public willingness to accept change, the responsiveness of the bureaucratic machinery, the reactions of Congress, the press he receives, and the external international relations environment he confronts. Each constraint interacts significantly with several of the others for any issue; each varies in importance from issue to issue; each plays some part in every issue. We shall give examples of each constraint here, with fuller analysis later.

To illustrate the first constraint, U.S. Constitutional provisions in President Wilson's term of office decisively influenced the wording of key provisions in the League of Nations Covenant. Article 16 specified the League sanctions actions to occur in the event of a breach of the Covenant, once a member was "deemed to have committed an act of war against all other members of the League" by its refusal to obey Covenant provisions. The original text had provided that such violations would produce *a state of war.* Substitution of one phrase for the other stemmed from Wilson's reluctant recognition that only Congress could declare a state of war for the United States. When the Second League Assembly, "interpreting" Article 16 in 1921, deliberately used precisely this point of difference between the two phrases to weaken the automatic character of sanctions, the potential effectiveness of the League for dealing with the crises of the 1930's was substantially undermined.[1]

The same Constitutional provisions played a role in the Viet-Nam War. Since no declaration of war was requested by the President, or made by the Congress, much controversy was to occur (as we shall see) over the meaning of the Gulf of Tonkin Resolution and related issues such as drafting men in "peacetime" and sending them into combat.

The "dead hand" of the past is a serious constraint. More than a year elapsed between President Johnson's announcement of limitations on bombing of North Viet-Nam (which led to the Paris negotiations beginning in 1968) and the first reduction of U.S. forces in Viet-Nam (announced in June 1969). It is simply very difficult to reverse course, as all Presidents have found. U.S. policy on the China question, which President Kennedy had shown interest in altering, was much the same when President Nixon took office.

Bureaucratic organization has a vital effect on what a President can and cannot accomplish. If the U.S. had been disposed in the 1930's to carry out a foreign policy such as characterized the 1960's, the gaps in instrumentalities of government alone would have ensured a grand failure. Our lacks were many. These were: lack of intelligence (no Central Intelligence Agency, National Security Agency, or Defense Intelligence Agency); lack of coordination of armed forces command (no Joint Chiefs, no single Defense Department, no unified and specified com-

---

[1] Paragraphs 3 and 4 of the League interpretative resolutions tell the story:

"3. The unilateral action of the defaulting State cannot create a state of war: it merely entitles the other Members of the League to resort to acts of war or to declare themselves in a state of war with the Covenant-breaking State; but it is in accordance with the spirit of the Covenant that the League of Nations should attempt, at least at the outset, to avoid war, and to restore peace by economic pressure.

4. It is the duty of each Member of the League to decide for itself whether a breach of the Covenant has been committed . . ."

mands); lack of a sizable and professional State Department, and lack of real machinery for national security affairs (no National Security Council). No active U.S. policy, regardless of its wisdom, could have succeeded with such handicaps. Yet the critical factor is not just the availability of appropriate bureaucratic organizations, but how well they actually serve to equip the President with the advice he needs to make effective decisions. President Kennedy's overhaul of the structure was very much influenced by what he considered its failure at the time of the Bay of Pigs episode (1961). His improvisation of an "Excomm" (Executive Committee) for the unwieldy National Security Council in 1962 was a reaction to this same point. Critics of the extensiveness of Federal expenditures for the military in 1969 were only gradually comprehending the weaknesses in bureaucratic linkage between contingency planning in the Defense Department and its sister activities in the State Department, compounded by the weaknesses in linkage to a total program-budgeting concept for the allocation of national resources to national security purposes.

Reactions by Congress to presidential initiatives are illustrated any week in the public press on some issue. Efforts by certain Senators, for example, in 1969 to avoid commencing an ABM deployment, have obvious foreign affairs connotations, particularly since President Nixon seemed essentially to be arguing that he wanted the program in motion as a bargaining point when he began strategic missile arms control talks with the Soviets.

Press and television reaction to presidential performance is of critical concern to any Chief Executive. President Franklin D. Roosevelt was a master of press relations, not the least of the reasons why he was elected to an unprecedented fourth term. His "fireside chats" are still remembered with appreciation by many professional politicians today. President Kennedy's gift for phrasing was magnified in its effects by television coverage, and his campaign TV debates with Richard Nixon played an important role in his close victory. Important here, too, is the fact that the President can project himself virtually at will into most American homes through TV coverage at times of his own choosing. President Johnson's effectiveness on TV in the first years after Kennedy's assassination was quite pronounced. Only later, after Viet-Nam disillusionment set in, did he seem to some to appear too often. His 1968 TV announcement that he would not seek re-election had a profound effect, and was undoubtedly instrumental in allowing peace negotiations to begin. President Nixon, in his first five months in office, received an excellent press. Even allowing for the "honeymoon" grace accorded a new President, his boxscore was impressive. This fact makes it all the more worth noting *The New York Times* reaction to his early June 1969 speeches, which the *Times* headlined as "[Nixon] flings down a challenge on foreign and defense policies." Max Frankel's review article said (with italics added):

> the next day, at the Air Force Academy, assessing the importance of military power and weapons, Mr. Nixon *appeared to see only two gradations of truth—* of those who were with him and those who were not.
>
> "You are under attack from those who question the need for a strong national defense, and indeed see a danger in the power of the defenders," the President told the cadets *provocatively*.[2]

Most Presidents, at one time or another, have been accused in the public media of exactly the same thing. Over a long period, whether justified or not, such criticisms can chip away political support.

Outside America's frontiers lies a world only partially shaped by American influences and desires. Its state of tension or relaxation, the role certain nations essay to play, its technological features, all decisively influence the foreign affairs program of any President. Coolidge, in the calm between two storms, could opt for a policy that no President after Hoover could justify, and which Wilson before him could not realistically have chosen. There is an interaction here between the extent of choice and the vigor of foreign policy involvement open to a President, and the world conditions such a policy must confront; and that interaction is highly complex. Wilson could not ignore the fact of World War I, whereas Coolidge had no such situation to react to. Yet nothing in the fact of World War I's existence in Wilson's time foreordained a particular policy reaction to it on Wilson's part. All that can be said is that Wilson had to deal with it and Coolidge did not. Eisenhower, from this point of view, confronted the fact of war in Viet-Nam, as did Kennedy, Johnson, and Nixon after him. No one of the four had a "Coolidge option," but it is still noticeable that Eisenhower refrained from making a U.S. combat commitment under fairly similar circumstances to those in which President Johnson chose to intervene: "our side" was about to lose.

In this chapter and the following ones we shall see these seven constraints in many formulations, affecting a great variety of events. In the remainder of this chapter we shall be concerned with the first of the two perspectives sketched out at its beginning: how the governmental system for foreign policy purposes has been altered since the 1930's to reflect the changing scope and content of the much more ambitious involvement of the U.S. in contemporary world affairs, and how it relates to the responsiveness of the bureaucratic machinery to the President's problem of coordinating national security problems. These changes in the system came about under the impetus of our greater involvements abroad; they made possible the still greater involvements that followed.

2 *The New York Times,* Section 4, (June 8, 1969), p. 1.

We must be careful with a point of this kind. We do not mean to imply that if one takes away the large armed forces and the aids to their deployment (such as foreign bases abroad and fast deployment logistics ships) there will be no more "globalism" in our foreign policy. There is, of course, some temptation toward greater involvements in such circumstances. Yet the larger truth is that elaborate weapons systems or a far-flung network of foreign bases are more the symptom and reflection of something else than they are themselves the cause. Having bases in the Philippines in the 1930's, or on Okinawa in the 1960's, leads or can lead easily to other foreign policy commitments in Asia. Having the ability to deploy troops at great distances permits such deployments. But the cart is largely before the horse if we make too much of this, and attention is too much directed away from the essential cause-and-effect interaction. Bases in Spain or Okinawa have been created because of a foreign policy of worldwide commitments. They are not the cause of those commitments in the first place or in any essential sense. Cut the commitments and the symbols of those commitments will begin to disappear. But cut the symbols and the commitments will still remain; only the efficiency of carrying out the commitments will be drastically affected. Truth's balance here would seem to lead to the conclusion (which the historical evidence supports) that the elaboration or reduction of the visible symbols of an ambitious foreign policy follows in the train of what is attempted, rather than vice versa.

The Revolution in the U.S. Foreign Policy System: Primitive Beginnings

SINCE the President is the central figure in foreign policy-making, the ultimate test of the bureaucratic organizations and linkages as they have evolved is how well they assist the President in making wise and informed judgments. While the changes in the Department of State, the creation of a single Department of Defense, the innovation in systematic intelligence gathering all may separately be weighed in terms of how well these organs can now discharge their particular missions, the overall question is how well each of these increasingly sophisticated parts of the total foreign affairs-national security process functions under the President as an entity. Effective coordination is the key organizational problem.

The rather elaborate and sophisticated machinery of today emerged from primitive beginnings, and more recently than one might suppose. As late as January 1925, President Calvin Coolidge could remark with much truth, "The business of America is business." The bulk of America's energies, the real thrust of its concerns, and the career choices of talented individuals all indicated a "business psychology." Not only did the contents of United States foreign policy largely bear this orientation out; so did its organization for foreign affairs. Until the Rogers Act (1924) there were no formal and specific requirements for entry into the U.S. Foreign Service at each level, nor did the service have any real organizational structure in a modern sense. Before 1924, even senior appointments were often made in a casual way which makes amazing reading today.[3] Individuals who accepted appointments under these conditions were not necessarily poor choices—frequently they were excellent choices—but a complete career service concept had not really been accepted. President Theodore Roosevelt's Executive Order (June 1906) had laid a foundation for change, by providing that appointments at the lower consulate grades were to be made only after examination. In 1909, by a similar order, President Taft extended the merit system to the appointment and promotion of diplomatic service personnel below the grades of minister and ambassador.[4] Totally inadequate salaries frustrated the intent of this order, and hardly any but the sons of the wealthy could afford making diplomacy a career. This delay in establishing a merit system for foreign affairs careers in government is less surprising if we recall that the same kind of reform for the U.S. Civil Service as a whole was only instituted with the Pendleton Act (1883). Until then the "spoils system" predominated. It does not seem too much to argue that "serious" government and a spoils system were virtually contradictions in terms.

The haphazard career nature of the civilian side of government between the 1880's and the 1920's had ample reflection on the military side. True, West Point had been established before the end of the eighteenth century (as a school for gunners and sappers), and the Naval Academy came into existence on the eve of the Mexican War. In both services a career pattern existed, but merit features were virtually nonexistent. As late as the 1880's promotion in the Navy went directly with length of service: officers frequently became admirals (if they lived long enough) shortly before compulsory retirement at 62. Only with the Naval Personnel Act (1899) was this system (designed to keep political influence out of promotion) altered. There is an obvious relevance to the Pendleton reform (1883), which made this change possible.

The small size of the armed forces (already noted earlier) also kept advancement slow, then and later. Dwight D. Eisenhower, in his *Crusade in Europe* (p. 2) points out that the total Army enlisted strength on July 1, 1939, was less than 130,000. His own career illustrates. He was commissioned as second lieutenant in 1915, served 16 years as a major, and became a temporary colonel in March 1941, some 26 years later.

---

[3] See for example the autobiography of Lloyd C. Griscom, *Diplomatically Speaking* (New York: Literary Guild, 1940).

[4] J. Rives Childs, *American Foreign Service* (New York: Holt, 1948), pp. 9–10.

In fiscal 1930 no more than $700 million was spent on the entire military establishment, out of a total government expenditure of just under $4 billion.

Whatever the effectiveness of West Point and Annapolis education may have been in those days, the opportunity to follow further regular professional military studies was limited or nonexistent. The Army did establish an Artillery School at Fort Monroe, Virginia, and new Infantry and Cavalry "Schools of Application" were set up by General Sherman in 1881; the Navy had no equivalent until much later. On the other hand, the Navy pioneered with the establishment of a Naval War College in 1884,[5] a move not imitated by the Army until 1901. (Interestingly enough, Lt. Tasker Bliss, U.S.A., a member of the first faculty of the Naval War College, ultimately became the founder and first commandant of the Army War College.) The significance of the war colleges is that they enabled mid-career officers to study the art and science of war in an organized fashion. If one adds that the Atlantic Squadron (which in effect *was* the U.S. Fleet) had never exercised as a squadron until Admiral Luce in the 1880's initiated it, one begins to understand further dimensions. Add to this the paucity of strategic and tactical doctrine, the then prevalent tendency of Congress to conceptualize naval action in terms of coast defense, and the obsolete Civil War vintage ships which made up most of the Navy (1884), and we begin to see how remote the total picture is from our ideas of military effectiveness as an important part of foreign policy.

Command relationships and Washington defense organization reflected equally primitive notions. Until Elihu Root forced a reorganization (1900) there was no Army General Staff. The Navy had eight completely autonomous "bureaus" until the office of "Chief of Naval Operations" was created (1915). Not until Admiral King in World War II became both Commander-in-Chief U.S. Fleet and Chief of Naval Operations did the Navy "for the first time [have] a single professional chief in fact as well as in name."[6] Even after that time, CNO's authority as such was more limited than his Army counterpart until as late as the mid-1960's. The post of Secretary of Defense did not exist until 1947. Before that time liaison between the U.S. armed forces components was by committee in Washington.

As to intelligence activities, before World War II the most important of these were conducted by MI-8 in the War Department and by the

[5] The Naval War College was the first of its kind in this country. The Berlin "Kriegakademie" founded by General von Scharnhorst (1810) was the prototype. The Royal Military Staff School in England came in 1873; the École Militaire Supérieur in France in 1878.

[6] Walter Millis, Harvey C. Mansfield, and Harold Stein, *Arms and the State* (New York: Twentieth Century Fund, 1958), p. 109.

Office of Naval Intelligence in the Navy Department. An early success was the breaking of the Japanese diplomatic code, making it possible during the Washington Naval Disarmament Conference in 1921 for the American delegation to be privy to Japanese plans. Such intelligence activity, begun in conjunction with World War I, was virtually unknown in the U.S. government before 1917.[7] It shortly became less known again, for Secretary of State Henry L. Stimson in 1929 was presented with intercepted diplomatic dispatches several days after assuming office and gave orders for all code-cracking operations in the State Department to cease. Since the State Department was financing the Army code-breaking activity, this too was suspended. Stimson later explained that "Gentlemen do not read each other's mail." (Years later he took a leading part as Secretary of War in pushing those same activities.) In the Office of Naval Intelligence (ONI) some work continued, but there, as in the Army, intelligence was regarded as a stepchild and as a very poor path to professional advancement. Not until the highly successful Office of Strategic Services (OSS) and ONI activities in World War II did the conviction grow that something like the present Central Intelligence Agency (and its sister organizations, the National Security Agency and the Defense Intelligence Agency) was badly needed.

The Revolution in the U.S. Foreign Policy System:
World War II and After

THE picture just given of the primitive machinery for making and co-ordinating foreign policy reflects the modest dimensions of U.S. policy until World War I, if not World War II. World War I brought certain changes toward a more efficient machinery, but few of them endured in a meaningful way. For example, a Council of National Defense was established in 1916. It had been suggested by the Naval War College and was discussed by Congress as early as 1911. Admiral Mahan, testifying before the House Naval Affairs Committee, asserted: "It seems to me that there is very little appreciation in this country of the relation between diplomacy and the Army and the Navy." As though to lend credence to Mahan's assertion the Secretary of War supported the bill but saw no reason to include the Secretary of State! Before one is too severe, consider Ernest R. May's comment:

In the archives of the McKinley, Roosevelt and Taft Administrations, I have yet to find a letter from a Secretary of State, asking for a military cost accounting before some diplomatic stroke. Although Taft's Secretary of State did

---

[7] One thinks of Nathan Hale and some use of spies in the Civil War. Thereafter one is hard pressed for other illustrations.

occasionally ask the fleet to back up his diplomacy, he never inquired ahead of time about the fleet's location and make-up.[8]

The Council of National Defense as established did provide for limited arrangements for high level civil-military collaboration on national policy. Continuing to exist on paper into the 1930's, it was far from the real thing. So was much of what came next. Its first formal working successor was the Standing Liaison Committee, established in April 1938.[9] Proposed by Secretary of State Hull because of concern over Axis activity in Latin America, it consisted of second-rank departmental officers: General Marshall as Chief of Staff of the Army, Admiral Stark as Chief of Naval Operations, and Under Secretary of State Sumner Welles. This new arrangement was better than the complete lack of formal coordination shown during the earlier Manchurian Crisis, but it had one great weakness. Each member reported to a separate superior officer (i.e., the Secretary of War, of the Navy, and of State), and these officers were themselves not formally in direct contact other than via Cabinet meetings (which under President F. D. Roosevelt as well as most other Presidents were no more than sounding boards for presidential ideas). In addition, although incidental, the relations between Welles (in whom Roosevelt had special confidence) and Hull (whose value to Roosevelt was more in the domestic political rather than in the diplomatic realm) were not too good.

Looking back on this record from today's vantage point and knowing what was coming, one may wonder at the slow progress. After all, World War I was but the curtain raiser for World War II, whereas World War II in turn ushered in decades of Cold War and strenuous U.S. involvements in world affairs. Nevertheless, as public opinion polls clearly show, the predominant American mood almost until the beginning of World War II was to dismiss World War I as an aberration. The battle over the Neutrality Acts exemplifies this. If war should come again, it was felt, *this* time we would not be so foolish as to become involved. We wanted peace, we wanted to be left alone. Catching the mood of the times, the Deputy Chief of Staff of the Army, Major General Stanley D. Embick, denied a request (May 1938) for the construction of B-17 bombers on two grounds: it would interfere and overlap the Navy's mission, and "Our national policy contemplates preparation for defense, not aggression" (and bombers were "aggressive"). The naiveté of this neat distinction also underscores the lack of political-strategic sophistication still prevailing in the military establishment. A parallel

[8] Ernest R. May, "The Development of Political-Military Consultation in the United States," *Political Science Quarterly*, 70, No. 2 (June 1955), 164.

[9] In my discussion of the evolution of machinery here and below I have relied heavily on the excellent treatment in Millis *et al., Arms and the State.*

ingenuousness permeated the political side of the house. Secretary of State Hull returned from the Moscow Conference in World War II announcing that balance-of-power alliances were now definitely to end and collective security reign instead—this at a time when alliance activity in the years ahead was to be a very brisk business: NATO, SEATO, CENTO, and so forth.

Early in 1941, the Standing Liaison Committee was displaced by informal weekly meetings on the level of the Secretaries: Stimson, Knox, and Hull. After the Arcadia Conference (June 1942), the Joint Chiefs of Staff began regular meetings on an *ad hoc* basis. Admiral Leahy, as President Roosevelt's personal Chief of Staff, presided without vote. "JCS came into being without any formal charter or executive order of any sort, not even a letter; indeed, when an executive order was later proposed to legitimize it and define its work, the President rejected the idea as unnecessary and cramping."[10]

Subsidiary coordination machinery began to be invented on many other levels to coordinate military and political policy. Some of this machinery did not work very well. One outstanding failure (with consequences to this day) stemmed from a relatively low-level War Department-State Department coordinating group charged among other things with decisions on the Allied occupation zones in Germany once Hitler was defeated. This group left the U.S. representative on the European Advisory Commission (which made the joint Allied recommendation on the zones to the heads-of-state conferences) without adequate instructions on access rights to be obtained from the Soviets for travel between the American Zone in Germany and the American Sector in Berlin (one hundred miles behind what would soon be called the Iron Curtain). Space precludes giving here the details,[11] but the Army seems to have held back from asking specific commitments from the Soviets primarily on the grounds that at a time when war was still continuing it could not be foreseen which access routes would be usable, and that the right to be in Berlin implied the right to get there. In the tedious and dangerous Berlin crises that periodically punctuated the postwar period, the U.S. as a consequence had to depend upon this logic rather than on any written grant of access by the Soviets to Berlin.

The full story of this period makes incredible reading today. Item: Secretary of State Hull was not even invited by President Roosevelt to attend the important great power Teheran Conference. Item: en route to the Teheran Conference, when President Roosevelt sketched out a

10 *Arms and the State,* p. 105.

11 Full details are given in Frederick H. Hartmann, *Germany Between East and West: The Reunification Problem* (Englewood Cliffs, New Jersey: Prentice-Hall, 1965), especially Chap. 3.

plan for occupation zones that would abut at Berlin (and thus do away with the access question) on a National Geographic map, he turned this map over to the military who, uninstructed, kept it subsequently in a Pentagon safe, where its existence was not officially known in the State Department. Part of the breakdown in overall coordination stemmed from reluctance on Hull's part to be fully involved; even so, the organizational apparatus improvised for World War II was still far from what a great power needed for effective and responsible participation in world affairs. Both the individual pieces of the apparatus and their smooth functioning in terms of one another left much to be desired.

The Hot War was so quickly succeeded by the Cold War that the new organizational procedures that had come into existence were not this time abandoned. Instead, they were formalized and improved upon.

A first major step came with the National Security Act (1947). A National Security Council was established, with the President as chairman. Other members included the Secretary of State, the Secretary of Defense (a job then of still quite limited powers), the three service secretaries (including one for the new separate Air Force), the chairman of the new National Security Resources Board (ultimately abolished), and others whom the President wished to add. The new Central Intelligence Agency —itself a great advance over the previously uncoordinated separate intelligence services—was placed directly under the National Security Council, and the Joint Chiefs were given a Joint Staff (which greatly improved their capability). General Marshall, now Secretary of State, initiated early in 1947 an important reform in the State Department by establishing the Policy Planning Staff under George Kennan.

Experience with the new arrangements brought further changes. In 1949 an amendment to the National Security Act set up the Joint Chiefs of Staff as a four-man board on a permanent and statutory basis. The statutory chairman was again without vote, but he was no longer to be a personal *ad hoc* representative of the President. By the same amendment a "Department of Defense" was created. (Until then the Secretary of Defense had presided with uneasy and incomplete authority over the three military departments without any apparatus directly responsible to him.) New subcabinet positions were authorized, including a Deputy Secretary of Defense and three Assistant Secretaries. The same amendments dropped the three armed services from permanent seats on the National Security Council (although the President remained free to invite them). Further changes, such as in 1953 and 1958, were to be made, but the general outlines remained fixed. With the Chairman of the Joint Chiefs in charge of the Joint Staff, and with the Commandant of the Marine Corps authorized to sit as an equal when matters concerning the Marines are on the agenda, the broad outlines of a full-fledged modern administrative machinery for both control of the armed forces and liaison between Defense and State on the highest level had been evolved.

How well it worked was another question. In sketching so far only the broad evolution of coordinating devices on the highest level, we have not yet considered two important questions: the effect of varying presidential attitudes toward this apparatus, and the related question of what degree of coordinating responsibility will be given to the State Department as compared with the White House staff. How the President, as the central figure in foreign policy-making (and Commander-in-Chief of the armed forces), chooses to handle national security problems makes a great deal of difference.

Coordinating Devices and Presidential Style

PRESIDENT Truman was the first Chief Executive to hold office under these new arrangements. His initial approach to the National Security Council (NSC) was cautious, for he felt it possible that the new institution might infringe upon his constitutional duties and authority. Until the Korean War (1950) he did not regularly attend Council meetings, preferring to deal more directly with the Departments through his Cabinet officers. The NSC produced papers and sought to establish guidelines for coordination, but it was kept at first in a strictly advisory role. Once the Korean War broke out, the pressures for coordination grew. Truman now ordered all major recommendations on national security policy to come to him through the Council. Even so, he stressed as before his own responsibility for making final decisions. Equally important, he used the NSC staff more as a personal staff than strictly as an NSC staff. When the Executive Secretary of the NSC in 1950 became the chairman of the Senior Staff—an interagency planning group, which under Eisenhower became the NSC Planning Board—a State Department official was replaced by an individual without departmental ties. Truman permitted a small unit within the NSC staff to see that reports on the status of national security programs were readily available, but he refused to delegate executive responsibility for the implementation of the programs.

Eisenhower came from a much different background of experience and was acquainted throughout his professional career with the needs for staff work and coordination; and he took a very different attitude toward the NSC. He was determined to produce an overall strategic plan and concerted action by the many agencies involved. Not only did the NSC now function more actively, but a Planning Board and an Operations Coordinating Board (OCB) were created as subsidiary units. The Planning Board coordinated Department recommendations and prepared policy papers for the NSC, while the OCB produced operational guidelines for carrying out NSC decisions, once made. For most of his tenure, Eisenhower used the NSC not for all operational and intelligence matters but for those requiring a "policy." NSC business came to him through a Special Assistant for National Security Affairs directly on the White House Staff, with the NSC staff reporting via the NSC Executive Secretary to this Special Assistant. By 1960, the Special Assistant not only chaired the Planning Board but the OCB as well (which until then was headed by the Under Secretary of State), and the previous distinction between policy formulation and operational coordination was lessened.

Eisenhower not only held frequent NSC meetings and required all long-range policies to emerge via this procedure, but he also held "special NSC meetings" of a less formal kind to decide current problems, something like Kennedy's later "Ex Comm" procedures.

Both advantages and disadvantages accrued to the Eisenhower system. Critics charged, then and later, that the NSC became a vast "paper mill," processing policies that turned out to have little relevance to the real problems which emerged. Eisenhower evidently believed that the system would surface the real issues for his decision, and that his decisions would be carried out efficiently by the system once they were made—a view that proved to be highly optimistic. Yet there was something to be said for what was admittedly a ponderous way to concert views and have agreed, coordinated policies. Observers of President Kennedy's later, more free-wheeling, style frequently missed this feature.

President Kennedy, coming to office, chose McGeorge Bundy as Special Assistant for National Security Affairs, opting for a "single, small, but strongly organized staff," which, he said, would "assist *me* in obtaining advice from, and coordinating operations of, the government agencies concerned with national security."[12] Under Eisenhower, the NSC had primarily functioned to secure advice and coordination from the various agencies and departments; now, the new emphasis was clear. Abolishing the OCB (February 1961), Kennedy announced his intention to increase the responsibility of the Secretary of State in this area. The State Department would become the principal coordinator, with the President taking a more direct interest personally in policy matters, even dealing himself with policy-making officials.

Shortly after Kennedy took office, the Bay of Pigs fiasco strengthened his distrust of the formal procedures of the NSC, and also led him to seek a more vigorous direct relationship with the State Department, which in turn produced disillusionment. The State Department, with its slow responses, was far from fulfilling the role Kennedy originally intended. His personal staff, centering on Bundy, came to dominate much of the interagency coordination. Where Kennedy had sought to revitalize the

[12] Press release, President-elect John F. Kennedy, January 1, 1961. (Italics added.)

State Department role (whose downgrading we have seen in the erosion of State Department senior officials from controlling positions in the NSC and Senior Staff), he actually ended up concentrating much more direction in the White House. As Sorensen remarks, "The President was discouraged with the State Department almost as soon as he took office."[13] At the same time, the Defense Department, under Robert S. McNamara, gradually achieved a degree of autonomy which would not have been possible under Eisenhower.

Kennedy was fond of creating special task forces for particular emergencies, the most famous of which was the "Ex Comm" device for the Cuban crisis in 1962. Similar *ad hoc* groups were created to deal with Laos and Berlin, and a Special Group for Counterinsurgency (CI) included both Bundy and Attorney General Robert Kennedy. The distinguishing features of these groups is that they operated largely apart from the regular NSC apparatus and they included a key White House staff member even when they were chaired by an Assistant Secretary from State or Defense. Kennedy used the regular meetings of the NSC primarily for long-range questions.

President Johnson's conception was again different. Bundy's successor, Walt W. Rostow, played much the same role as Bundy had, but Johnson used the White House staff generally less aggressively, preferring closer relations with the Secretaries of State and Defense. Johnson also attempted to delegate operational coordination to the Secretary of State. The NSC met frequently, but, as under Kennedy, its regular agenda was usually weighed toward long-term issues. Competent observers agree that, under Johnson, the most important high-level meeting was the "Tuesday lunch." Normally it concerned operational matters and included Secretaries Rusk and McNamara, the Special Assistant, and (later) the Presidential Press Secretary, the Director of Central Intelligence, the Chairman of the Joint Chiefs of Staff, and the President. The Tuesday lunch reflected Johnson's feeling that a smaller group than the NSC, chosen on the basis of their ability to contribute to decisions rather than primarily or exclusively because of their organizational affiliation, was preferable for the "real" work. Since no minutes were made, however, each participant interpreted decisions according to his own understanding. Their subordinates frequently were also left unsure of the nuances of what was intended.

This survey, centering on the high-level coordination aspect, reveals something of a back-and-forth swing, even more marked if we now consider President Nixon's conception. Before noting the new change, however, we must understand the implications of President Johnson's National Security Action Memo 341 (NSAM 341) of March 1966. Two

---

[13] Theodore Sorensen, *Kennedy* (New York: Harper and Row, 1965), p. 287.

questions are intertwined, as noted in the preceding section of this chapter and already partially discussed: what the NSC will be and do depends not only on presidential preferences but also on *where* the coordination of operations is basically attempted. Operations coordination, in turn, has two aspects: field coordination abroad by agencies located abroad, and coordination at the center of government for operations abroad. Field coordination itself has varied, as we shall see in Chapter 5. Washington coordination under Truman was still rudimentary. Under Eisenhower it was centered increasingly in the OCB. Under Kennedy it was located primarily in the White House staff, either directly or through *ad hoc* groups that always had important White House staff membership. President Johnson attempted to move more responsibility for coordination of overseas operations out of the White House. By NSAM 341 Johnson assigned to the Secretary of State "authority and responsibility to the full extent permitted by law for the overall direction, coordination and supervision of interdepartmental activities of the United States Government overseas." NSC or *ad hoc* bodies would continue to coordinate national security in the general planning-policy sense, but the Secretary of State would become the prime coordinator and implementer for overseas operations (other than directly military combat in nature). To accomplish this, NSAM 341 created a permanent interdepartmental committee, the Senior Interdepartmental Group (SIG), chaired by the Under Secretary of State and exercising, subject to appeal, the power of decision. Related subordinate Interdepartmental Regional Groups (IRGs) were to be chaired by the regional Assistant Secretaries of State.

The procedures of NSAM 341 were slow to gather momentum for a number of reasons. They had shown promise but had not proved themselves by the time President Nixon succeeded Johnson. Moreover, Mr. Nixon, as Vice-President under Eisenhower, unquestionably was impressed by both the advantages and disadvantages of the Eisenhower system. Seeking like Kennedy and Johnson to give the State Department a greater role, he was also alert to the problems implicit in doing this outside the NSC system. For if the SIG-IRG approach makes real sense it must become, in effect, the NSC operations arm in addition to coordinating lesser-level problems. Otherwise, the indirect character of the link between NSC and SIG-IRG will erode the meaning of NSC discussions that will be translated, if at all, primarily through SIG-IRG. NSC will become an abstract debating agency. Yet if there is to be a direct link between SIG-IRG and NSC, the White House staff must play an important role. Can this be achieved without eroding either the State Department's role or that of the NSC? To make the NSC effective it must have a coordinating arm which, unlike the old OCB, can have an executive chairman nearer the actual agencies that will execute.

Nixon's resolution of these problems is interesting and may well work. On February 6, 1969, he issued new guidelines designating the NSC as "the principal forum for consideration of national security policy issues requiring Presidential decision."[14] The IRGs (and the Political-Military Interdepartmental Group—a "functional" IRG) became "Interdepartmental Groups in the NSC system," chaired by the appropriate Assistant Secretary of the Department of State. Each group was to include representatives of the Assistant to the President for National Security Affairs, the Secretary of Defense, the Director of Central Intelligence, the Chairman of the Joint Chiefs, and other members determined by the chairman for each issue.

The former IRGs, now IGs, are to "discuss and decide" issues which can be settled at their level, "including issues arising out of the implementation of NSC decisions." They will also prepare policy papers for NSC consideration and "contingency papers on potential crisis areas" for NSC review. *Ad hoc* groups will be appointed if and as needed.

Papers from these sources or directly from departments are to be handled by an NSC Review Group, with membership from the same agencies, chaired by the Assistant to the President for National Security Affairs (Henry Kissinger). The Review Group is to screen issues for NSC attention, ensuring that "all realistic alternatives" are included and that the facts and costs are properly set forth, and either assign action to an IG or *ad hoc* group, or refer issues to the Under Secretaries Committee. Chaired by the Under Secretary of State, this committee (Deputy Secretary of Defense, Assistant to the President for National Security Affairs, Director of Central Intelligence, and Chairman of the Joint Chiefs) will handle issues referred to it by the Review Group and "operational matters pertaining to interdepartmental activities . . . overseas" not resolved by the IGs and not requiring higher action. Thus the SIG appears under a new name, but now as an integral part of the "NSC system."

The same order specified that the Secretary of State would continue "the overall direction, coordination and supervision of interdepartmental activities . . . overseas"—except for U.S. military field forces under a U.S. area military commander and activities of a single agency not affecting "significantly the overall U.S. overseas program in a country or region."

An Assessment

THE President's problem in formulating and conducting an effective foreign policy by no means begins and ends with the question of what

---

[14] For text see *Foreign Affairs Manual Circular No. 521*, U.S. Department of State, February 6, 1969.

bureaucratic organization he creates to link himself, his White House staff, the Departments of State and Defense, and the National Security Council. Yet, resolving this problem involves his most difficult single organizational choice. It will probably have the most to do with his success or lack of success in dealing with foreign affairs as they involve national security components. Since these components are the most important parts of foreign policy, the correctness of his organizational decisions in this area greatly expedite or inhibit the general thrust of his efforts.

We have seen that the present organization is essentially a post-World War II product. Regardless of the variations from Truman through Nixon, each was adjusting an organizational system that (compared to that before World War II) was highly modern and sophisticated. It was broadly appropriate and essential to U.S. policy in the new age, regardless of the administration-by-administration changes noted. It was also in great contrast to what had prevailed only three decades or so ago.

Although each successive reshuffling of the pieces of the organizational problem as described in this chapter has revealed new facets of that problem, it does seem likely that the Nixon system will improve on the earlier procedures. By simultaneously revitalizing the NSC and linking it to the advantages implicit in the SIG-IRG concept, it brings the State Department clearly into the operational coordination picture.

CHAPTER 5

The Department of State

THE President's relationship with the State Department today is a troubled one. He must rely heavily on it for the formulation and execution of foreign policy. Yet he has not always been pleased at State's responsiveness and efficiency, as indicated in Chapter 4. Even if he has confidence in his Secretary of State, a President may have little confidence in the Department. Franklin D. Roosevelt even ignored both his own Secretary of State and the State Department on important occasions. His real confidence was in the Under Secretary. Harry Truman had able Secretaries of State, but Dean Acheson also became a political liability for him. Dwight Eisenhower essentially had one Secretary for most of two terms, and trusted him a great deal, but John Foster Dulles was a dogmatic man with some tendency to go too far, and with little interest in administration. It was under Dulles that the McCarthy era witch hunt swept through the State Department. Kennedy and Johnson shared Dean Rusk, in whom both had personal confidence. But Sorensen states that Kennedy felt that the State Department "too often seemed to have a built-in inertia which deadened initiative and that its tendency toward excessive delay obscured determination. It spoke with too many voices and too little vigor. It was never clear to the President (and this continued to be true . . .) who was in charge, who was clearly delegated to do what, and why his own policy line seemed consistently to be altered or evaded. The top State Department team . . . reflected an abundance of talent ironically unmatched by production."[1] Lyndon Johnson is reputed also to have felt strongly that the Department of State was inefficient. His NSAM 341 was an attempt to upgrade its functioning. We shall see what comes under Nixon.

What are the sources of these State Department difficulties and how, if at all, can they be overcome? Some perspective is needed to answer such questions, particularly some acquaintance with postwar developments in the Department as it reacted to the great increase in foreign policy involvement by the United States. Six aspects will be considered: growth in total numbers, recruiting tendencies, career patterns (including

---

[1] Theodore Sorensen, *Kennedy, op. cit.,* p. 287.

rotation between posts at home and abroad), coordination of or integration with operational units in the foreign affairs area (such as the U.S. Information Agency), relations with the Defense Department, and the fairly unique problems in bureaucratic organization associated with the conduct of foreign affairs. These six aspects fall readily into two categories: personnel and organization. The first two sections of this chapter will take them up in that sequence.

Personnel Problems

PERSONNEL problems have included the very rapid expansion in numbers since World War II, the recruiting procedures and sources used, and the difficulties in establishing efficient career patterns (including rotation between home and overseas posts).

We have already pointed to the landmark legislation of 1924 that transformed the Foreign Service into a career program (and which integrated the then separate diplomatic and consular branches into a single service). Nonetheless, the Foreign Service, as the operating arm of the State Department, remained very small in size after 1924. The entire American Foreign Service (April 1, 1940) numbered only 851 Foreign Service Officers (FSOs). With the great expansion of the U.S. role in world affairs after World War II, the Department of State (and the Foreign Service), by contrast, underwent enormous growth. The Foreign Service Act (1946) completely overhauled existing legislation, thus providing many improvements to pave the way.

Table 5–1 gives total figures for the Department of State as of the end of 1938, 1948, and 1968.

TABLE 5–1

DEPARTMENT OF STATE PERSONNEL (AS OF DECEMBER 31)

	1938	1948	1968
FSO* (Foreign Service Officer)	766	1,360	3,379
FSR (Foreign Service Reserve)	—	110	1,448
FSS (Foreign Service Staff)	876	3,966	5,173
Civil Service	1,943	9,005†	4,028
Foreign Nationals	2,107	5,886	11,467
TOTALS:	5,692	20,327	25,495

* Includes noncareer Chiefs of Mission

† The 1948 figure for Civil Service employees was abnormally high because the Department was then absorbing certain wartime agencies and the employees were automatically transferred with the agency function. After a sort-out-period, many of these temporary employees were released. Source: State Department personnel records.

The complexity of the personnel problem, aside from absorbing this growth in numbers efficiently, included (and still includes) the parallel existence of two quite different personnel systems (with still other variations for reserve officers). While FSOs were personally vested with rank, Civil Service employees acquired rank according to position; while FSOs were promoted upwards or selected out, Civil Service employees had permanent tenure once they passed the initial probationary period. Reservists, for their part, could serve for only limited periods. When the question arose of changing many Civil Service positions to FSO positions (which we shall examine), this difference proved an important source of strain and stress. Although such a complicated personnel system can be made to operate, and does operate in some other government departments (notably Defense), it can operate best only if the logic inherent in one system is not mixed up with the other. The American Foreign Service Association Martin Report says:

> Part of our recent problems have arisen . . . with the attempt to administer both systems by a single personnel establishment whose administrative leaders have been sometimes largely Civil Service and sometimes largely Foreign Service. Drawing from their experience, these administrators have naturally tended at times to attempt application of perfectly valid Civil Service techniques to the Foreign Service with results that were not always happy. Sometimes the reverse has been true . . .[2]

By contrast, the Defense Department has traditionally maintained a careful and well-understood distinction between the two personnel systems, the "man in uniform" being handled quite differently from the civil servant. In the State Department the FSO often serves in the same kind of job as the civil servant and is not a "man in uniform"; therefore the distinction has proved much more difficult. The Martin Report concludes that the answer is not to abolish the distinction but to maintain it more carefully.

Foreign Service Officer recruitment procedures have also caused problems and have produced changes over the last two decades.

In 1946–1947 recruitment for the Foreign Service, although quite professional, suffered from two disadvantages. First, the entrance test was a true ordeal, occupying most of a week. Its formidable character discouraged many who might otherwise have tried. Second, the nature of the test (and the preferences of the examiners as shown by the results) put a premium on attendance at Ivy League and "prestige" institutions. Although this tendency produced a Foreign Service manned by well-

[2] See "Toward a Modern Diplomacy, A Report to the American Foreign Service Association," *Foreign Service Journal,* Vol. 45, No. 11, November 1968, Part Two, p. 16. The whole report is well worth reading.

qualified college graduates, it did not produce a Foreign Service representative of the American people.

The first disadvantage meant little until after World War II; the Foreign Service in any case was small, it did not matter that only small numbers took the test. Even fewer were appointed. When the U.S. after World War II took on a truly global policy, the Foreign Service had to expand drastically to match. Eventually this need was to produce a much simplified written ("objective type") test that could be taken in a day. Successful candidates would then (as before) receive oral and physical examinations. At the same time, the number of localities where the test was offered was expanded considerably. Now it no longer took a fair-sized investment of money to try one's hand at the Foreign Service examination. Other means of expansion were also used. Officials in a variety of wartime emergency organizations which were being disbanded were, if qualified, offered opportunities for "lateral entry."

The most important effect of the second disadvantage was to limit opportunity for all-United States recruitment. Certain institutions supplied the majority of successful Foreign Service candidates. Indeed the same generalization tended to be true after World War II of the Foreign Service Reserve, the U.S. Information Agency (USIA), and the Agency for International Development (AID), etc. James L. McCamy's study based on one-quarter of the names listed in the State Department's *Biographic Register, 1960* (which includes data on the personnel of eight key groups concerned with foreign affairs) shows that of the 3,101 people sampled (965 in the Foreign Service proper), officials with college degrees received them from 540 different institutions. But, taking graduate and undergraduate degrees together, 27 universities granted half of the total degrees, and of these 27 universities seven granted a fourth of all the degrees.[3] The first ten institutions, accounting for over 30 per cent of the total, in order were: Harvard, Columbia, California System, Yale, Georgetown, George Washington, Wisconsin, Chicago, Minnesota, and Princeton. For the Foreign Service, Foreign Service Reserve, USIA, and AID, for either undergraduate or graduate degrees (a total of eight categories), these first ten universities appear in three-quarters of the categories. By 1960, the Foreign Service had been making deliberate efforts for some years to recruit more widely and to broaden the educational base from which Foreign Service Officers were being drawn. McCamy's figures indicate that significant geographic concentration still persisted despite these efforts. One can argue that good undergraduate candidates from other areas of the nation were taking graduate degrees at these few institutions and then entering the Foreign Service.

[3] James L. McCamy, *Conduct of the New Diplomacy* (New York: Harper, 1964), pp. 210–211.

This, of course, was true. Before 1960 graduate fellowship opportunities were much more limited than Federal support after that time made them.

Even so, changes were going on toward greater dispersion of opportunity. McCamy's list includes all levels in the Foreign Service. If one looks at the data for the beginning levels, some change is apparent. Of Class 8 Foreign Service Officers certified for appointment between January 1, 1957 and July 1, 1961, some 226 out of 724 (31 per cent) attended one of the first ten institutions on McCamy's list. Later State Department figures show that of the 519 Class 7 and 8 appointments between July 1, 1965 and June 30, 1968 only 129 of 519 (24.9 per cent) attended those ten institutions as undergraduates. (Graduate figures were 114 of 402 or 28.3 per cent.) This trend would seem to be very desirable, if only because it spreads opportunity more widely.

Widening the basis of recruitment *may* in time help in part to create a somewhat more balanced Foreign Service from another point of view. Just as the military officer in the "McNamara era" was being accused of lack of sophistication in, and even contempt for, systems analysis and other modern management techniques, the FSO in the postwar period has frequently been accused of similar sorts of parochial behavior. It is said that the older FSO has often been indifferent to management and administrative problems, preferring to get on with "real professional questions"—i.e., substantive policy problems in foreign affairs. He has given less attention to in-house efficiency. Compounding this attitude (which apparently has existed) is the inability of the Secretary himself to find time for these problems. The Martin Report cites the fact that Secretary Rusk personally represented the United States at 125 conferences, 109 of them overseas. To the 376 days thus consumed (including travel time) one must add almost 100 days at the UN—a total time use for his incumbency of twenty per cent. There is great need for a full time, high-level administrator. Moreover, with the steady widening in the spectrum of activities affecting foreign affairs, the Foreign Service must come to include more specialists in scientific and other areas not traditionally thought of as germane. This consideration has interlocking features with the problem of career development. The Martin Report makes much of the "inertia" that a small and "closed" service (involving entry only at the bottom) will normally exhibit and in which many of today's senior FSOs received their grounding. It quotes Charles E. Bohlen's comment on the effects stemming from the early isolationism: "When I joined the Foreign Service in 1929, this traditional stance was still very much in mode. 'Observe, analyze, and report,' we were told, 'but, above all, don't get involved.'"

Career patterns (including rotation between posts at home and abroad) have represented a third serious problem area. Until the Foreign Service Act (1946), regular home leave for FSOs was not an essential condition of service, and it was not uncommon for Foreign Service personnel to remain abroad for many years without returning home at all. In some extreme cases individuals remained abroad for more than two decades! Service at posts at home was highly restricted since relatively few positions in the State Department were manned by FSOs.

In 1954, as a result of the Wriston Committee Report, drastic changes were approved. In concept the policy posts at home and abroad were merged as a pool of positions to which FSOs could be ordered. As a corollary, those in the Civil Service whose policy positions were progressively integrated into the new pool were offered "lateral entry" at an equivalent rank into the Foreign Service. This development had advantages and disadvantages both in principle and practice.

In principle the advantages were greater than the disadvantages, for the change helped to eliminate a situation where home officials with little personal foreign experience and inadequate bases for judgment handled the reports and recommendations of field officers. It made it far less possible for FSOs to lose contact with their own culture and provided fresh points of view at home. At the same time it disrupted the career patterns of home officers who had in many cases no aptitude or desire for field service, and who had entered the State Department with quite different expectations. Balancing this defect was the opportunity for others to serve abroad who wanted just such a chance. Overall, the "lateral entry" device was also excellent from the point of view of infusing new blood into a still rather "closed" service.

From the standpoint of practice, the advantages and disadvantages were something else. Unquestionably, "Wristonization" with its disruptive features made the State Department for perhaps a decade too preoccupied with itself. In practice, rotated officers, arrived home, frequently found the Washington scene less exciting and tended to think of their service abroad as their "real" career. This was especially true when they were assigned to functional or geographic areas at home quite far from their service abroad. As less experienced Washington bureaucrats, they frequently had trouble in learning Washington's complex style of transacting business, and were frequently less effective than those they displaced. Yet the reverse effects also could be noted, and many of those rotated to home posts both brought and received fresh points of view.

With the passage of time the situation has moved back somewhat toward the earlier center of gravity before 1954. Particularly in the functional areas of the State Department (as contrasted with the geographical), there is fresh recognition that continuity in positions by experts has advantages over rotation.

The Wriston reform did extend the logic implicit in the Rogers Act. Where that Act had formed a single service abroad out of the then separate Diplomatic Service and Consular Service, the Wriston change further amalgamated much of the home and foreign service so far as the State Department proper was concerned. It did not affect the "other foreign services" of the United States and the problems involved in their existence.

Organizational Problems

THE first organizational problem—coordinating or integrating other operational units dealing with foreign affairs—has never been entirely satisfactorily resolved from the standpoint of the State Department, although sometimes it has been better resolved and sometimes worsened.

Even leaving apart military and career intelligence personnel, the Department of State in modern times has never included under its direct administration all of the government personnel working abroad who are concerned with foreign affairs. Between 1927 and 1935, for example, the U.S. had in effect four or more foreign services operating abroad. In 1927, the Department of Commerce formed a separate foreign commerce service. In 1930, the Department of Agriculture established a smaller foreign agricultural service. In 1935, the Department of the Interior (Bureau of Mines) set up a similar but still smaller service involving mineral specialists. All of these changes were given congressional authorization. And we have not mentioned the foreign service of the Treasury Department! The confusion created by these rival services, each reporting to their own departments, led President F. D. Roosevelt (1939) to sponsor a reorganization act that merged the representatives from Commerce and Agriculture into the Foreign Service. In 1943, the Bureau of Mines representatives were similarly merged. But Treasury kept (and keeps) its separate identity.[4] Agriculture, too, in 1954 again created its own Foreign Agricultural Service.[5] As of June 30, 1964, only 7,200 of 30,000 U.S. federal civilian employees abroad worked for the State Department. Other departments and agencies represented abroad included: Justice; Interior; Health, Education and Welfare; Defense; Treasury; Agriculture; the Atomic Energy Commission; and the Federal Aviation Agency.[6]

Very complex problems arose at the end of World War II in especially acute form. The war had spawned the creation of numerous special organizations, most of which were disbanded after 1945. Some were merged into existing government departments; others became the nucleus for organs such as the present CIA. The propaganda activities eventually

[4] Childs, *op. cit.*, pp. 14–15.

[5] It maintains more than 60 foreign posts. See Burton M. Sapin, *The Making of United States Foreign Policy* (Washington, D.C.: The Brookings Institution, 1966), p. 262, for a detailed survey of this and other problems in organization.

[6] *Ibid.*, p. 252.

were consolidated primarily into the USIA; foreign aid became what is today (after six confusing changes in name) the Agency for International Development. Both USIA and AID are full-fledged participants in foreign affairs. Particularly, they engage in important operational aspects of foreign policy. How should USIA and AID be properly related to State? Should the Foreign Service once again be expanded and the personnel of these agencies, too, integrated?

In logic it is possible to argue the case either way. One can argue that USIA and AID are predominantly concerned with the execution of certain parts of policy, and only secondarily with policy formulation. Or one can argue that State not only formulates but executes policy abroad and that it is illogical to separate out certain functions. Whatever the logical case, certain practical and political elements affected the way in which the problem was handled.

During much of the period after 1945 it remained unclear how much sustained congressional support would be forthcoming for USIA and AID. Opponents of these programs formed a strong bloc in Congress. These opponents fell into two groups: those who, in the case of USIA, were suspicious of any government program of propaganda on principle, and those who favored the operation in principle but who were consistently critical of how it was carried out. Similarly for AID, another set of congressional critics sniped away at the inefficiency and ineffectualness of certain parts of the program. Indonesia under Sukarno for a time was a favorite whipping boy—until Sukarno himself put an end to U.S. aid with his famous statement (February 1965): "To hell with U.S. aid." Aid to nations such as the United Arab Republic did not deter Nasser from a fairly consistent anti-Western policy. As a consequence the foreign aid program each year became progressively smaller.

In the light of these developments the State Department, apart from its "closed" tradition, was not anxious to amalgamate these functions (and their personnel). Besides, there was an element in Congress that held that if USIA and AID, with all their defects, became entirely State Department activities they would be handled even more poorly, that State by its very traditions and general attitudes was too hidebound to carry out "action programs" of this kind.

The result was a compromise. In November 1961, AID became "an agency within the Department of State,"[7] with its Administrator reporting directly to the Secretary of State and the President for policy purposes but retaining direction of all AID personnel at home and overseas. USIA in 1953, on the other hand, was established as an "independent agency" within the executive branch. It "obtains policy and background information from the Department of State and other sources and prepares policy

[7] *United States Government Organization Manual, 1967–68,* p. 90.

guidance for operating elements of the Agency."[8] It maintains liaison with the White House, with State and Defense, and other agencies. In 1961, when the Peace Corps was established, it too became "an agency within the Department of State."[9]

Confronted with these problems the tendency in the last decade in governmental organization has been to seek the larger solutions through new coordinating devices (such as were examined in Chapter 4).

In Washington the SIG-IRG solution, continued now essentially within the new Nixon "NSC system," has sought to provide coordination under State Department leadership regardless of whether AID, USIA and other units are or are not directly under the line authority and administration of the Department of State. In the field, rather than try the older gambit of integrating the variety of attachés (previously mentioned) into the Foreign Service, the resort has been to the "Country Team" concept.

On May 29, 1961, President Kennedy sent all U.S. ambassadors a letter whose provisions have been reaffirmed by both President Johnson and President Nixon (in much the same or even broader terms although in a different form).[10] Its key paragraphs read:

> You are in charge of the entire United States Diplomatic Mission and I shall expect you to supervise all of its operations. The Mission includes not only the personnel of the Department of State and the Foreign Service, but also the representatives of all other United States agencies which have programs or activities in. . . . I shall give you full support and backing in carrying out your assignment.
>
> Needless to say, the representatives of other agencies are expected to communicate directly with their offices here in Washington, and in the event of a decision by you in which they do not concur, they may ask to have the decision reviewed by a higher authority in Washington.
>
> However, it is their responsibility to keep you fully informed of their views and activities and to abide by your decisions unless in some particular instance you and they are notified to the contrary.

President Nixon's formulation (1969) said succinctly and even more positively:

> Chiefs of Diplomatic Missions in foreign countries, as representatives of the President and acting on his behalf, continue to be in charge of all elements of the United States Diplomatic Mission and to exercise affirmative responsibility for the direction, coordination and supervision of all activities of the United States Government in their respective countries.

---

[8] *Ibid.*, p. 543. More recently (1968) its officer corps has been granted professional status and its recruitment is on the same professional basis as for FSOs.

[9] *Ibid.*, p. 94.

[10] Nixon's directive is in his announcement of the reorganized NSC system, the final paragraph.

Although what this means in practice varies considerably, there is no question but what in principle it permits an ambassador to have substantial, if not complete, control over American officials in his country, at least where the U.S. maintains no large armed force engaged in field operations. Since career promotion opportunities for such personnel abroad will continue, however, to be in the hands of the many home agencies represented, what we see is a rough check-and-balance system. The official abroad not employed by the State Department, who runs afoul of either his home agency or his ambassador, will probably be in trouble professionally. Assuming that it is not feasible or necessarily altogether desirable to incorporate all these officials into the Foreign Service, this way of attempting to square the circle appears to be a useful compromise.

State Department relations with the Defense Department and the intelligence agencies represent the second organizational problem. It is, of course, a two-way street. There must be an adequate consideration by State of Defense viewpoints, and vice versa.

In an earlier day and even through much of World War II, the arrangements for liaison either did not exist or did not work well. Suspicion and a wholly different outlook on problems separated military and State Department personnel, as examples already given illustrate. By mid-World War II, the experiments with political advisers, attached to the staffs of commanding generals, were in full swing, with quite varied results. Such State Department personnel had to learn a whole new technique of staffing to function well at all, while the generals and their staffs had residual suspicions about civilian outsiders in their councils.[11]

After 1945, serious efforts to improve this situation began to be made. But, as late as the Korean armistice negotiations, the U.S. general officers involved were by contemporary standards woefully unprepared to grapple with the political implications of what they were handling. As late as the Korean War, the number of senior Foreign Service Officers who could deal with the military aspects of national policy was woefully small. The number of each who had served in staff positions with the other was quite inadequate.

Important changes were made in two respects: a deliberate interchange of military and civilian officers was begun in staff positions in both the State and Defense Departments, and many senior officers from both sources were given more common in-service educational opportunities. Both developments helped, assisted even further in the 1960's by informal contacts, which came to exist on many levels and which reflected the close and friendly relationships of Secretaries Rusk and McNamara. In all, it represented quite a change from the attitude when Secretary of Defense Louis Johnson, in the late 1940's, backed by a

[11] The best of them undeniably had success. See the experiences of Robert Murphy in his *Diplomat Among Warriors* (Garden City, N.Y.: Doubleday, 1964).

presidential directive, required that all contacts between the two departments had to occur through his own office.

Within the Defense Department Foreign Service Officers were attached to the international affairs offices of each of the separate services, as well as to the Office of International Security Affairs (ISA) within the Secretary of Defense's staff. The combined civilian-military professional staff of ISA numbered 176 (104 civilians, 72 military) in September 1964.[12] ISA's head, the Assistant Secretary of Defense (International Security Affairs), functioned as the principal staff assistant for international security, coordinating with the Department of State on foreign policy problems involving the military. Within the State Department a Politico-Military Affairs staff under a Deputy Assistant Secretary for Politico-Military Affairs was established (May 1961), reporting to the Deputy Under Secretary. In September 1969 this office became the Bureau of Politico-Military Affairs. Its director, now ranking as equivalent to an Assistant Secretary, chaired the NSC Interdepartmental Political Military Group.[13] Military officers served here side by side with their civilian colleagues. Already as of 1963, about twenty State Department officers were on duty in or had completed tours in the Pentagon, and an equal number had come from there to the State Department.

The educational exchange program brought much larger numbers of officers from both sources together. Between 1946 and 1963 alone, more than 425 State Department officers attended the five U.S. war colleges and the Armed Forces Staff College and equivalent overseas defense colleges. (Most of these are ten-month courses.) Military officers in smaller numbers attended Foreign Service Institute courses, including the "senior seminar." Since the war college curricula all place heavy emphasis on the interrelationships of military and political policy, the development was a healthy one. In both State and Defense the U.S. increasingly was coming to possess an experienced corps of officers who understood policy coordination, who were trained in the dispassionate analysis of national policy, and who understood the interacting military, political, and economic effects of policy decisions. These psychological and educational changes were at least as important as the innovations in coordinating machinery (previously noted) in preparing the U.S. to pursue a more coordinated foreign policy.

The relation of the State Department to the intelligence agencies has fewer organizational problems, primarily because the "intelligence community" is so highly organized in itself, with a reasonably well-defined role for the State Department. The Central Intelligence Agency (CIA)

---

[12] Sapin, *op. cit.*, p. 158. Most of these civilians were, of course, Department of Defense employees.

[13] See *Foreign Affairs Manual Circular No. 536*, U.S. Department of State, September 18, 1969.

established in 1947, the Defense Intelligence Agency (DIA) established in 1961, and the separate service intelligence organizations are coordinated with the National Security Agency and the Department of State's Bureau of Intelligence and Research through the Director of Central Intelligence, who is chairman of the overall U.S. Intelligence Board (USIB) and the President's adviser on all intelligence matters, whether inside or outside the NSC system. USIB prepares National Intelligence Estimates (NIEs) which represent an agreed national analysis and interpretation available to all interested and concerned government agencies.

Within this system the Bureau of Intelligence and Research, apart from its "intelligence community" work, prepares reports and studies for internal Department use.

The third organizational problem turns on the fairly unique bureaucratic difficulties associated with the conduct of foreign affairs. The State Department, unlike almost every other government department, must maintain and operate a large number of major posts abroad, including both embassies and consulates, and also conduct its Washington business efficiently. Only the Defense Department, because of its need to deploy forces, and because of its gigantic size, approaches State in its bureaucratic complexity.

There is little use in surveying historically the many changes in organization that have occurred in almost two centuries in the Department of State. Whole volumes have been written on this theme. Also, there is nothing truer about organization in government than that the newest organization chart is always out of date. These cautions are introduced to warn the unwary that any description in print of government organization is likely to need amendment and is true only for the date specified (in this case, unless otherwise noted, 1967–1968).

There is, however, less drastic change in the organization of the State Department in recent years. (Perhaps the major recent change is the restoration of "political affairs" to a position of primacy, which it has not always enjoyed.)

Immediately below the Secretary of State in authority is the Under Secretary, and below him the Under Secretary for Political Affairs. Reporting "laterally" to the Secretary as "agencies" are AID and the Peace Corps (with the Arms Control and Disarmament Agency noted with dotted lines as "a separate agency which reports to the Secretary" and which functions "as the principal adviser to the President and the Secretary of State" on such matters).[14] Directly under the Secretary and his assistants are the rest of the "home office" in Washington and the missions to international organizations and abroad. Reporting through the Under Secretary for Political Affairs are the Deputy Under Secretary for Political Affairs and the Deputy Under Secretary for Administration

---

[14] *United States Government Organization Manual, 1967–68,* p. 532.

(under whom is the Director General of the Foreign Service, the Foreign Service Institute, Security and Consular Affairs, and Administrative Offices and Programs). A Legal Adviser, a Counselor, and the director of a Policy Planning group report to the Secretary of State and his assistants directly. The rest of the department is organized in twelve functional and geographical bureaus: Congressional Relations, International Scientific and Technological Affairs, Intelligence and Research, Economic Affairs, Public Affairs, Educational and Cultural Affairs, African Affairs, European Affairs, East Asian and Pacific Affairs, Inter-American Affairs, Near Eastern and South Asian Affairs, and International Organization Affairs. Each such bureau is headed either by one of the ten Assistant Secretaries of State or (as in the case of International Scientific and Technological Affairs or Intelligence and Research) by a Director with equivalent rank. (As noted, a new Bureau of Politico-Military Affairs was established in 1969.)

To illustrate the further subdivisions let us take African Affairs. Besides three "Deputy Assistant Secretaries" and other administrators and coordinators there are nine "Country Directors," each responsible for several adjacent countries. For example, Ghana, Liberia, Nigeria, and Sierra Leone are grouped together. Below this level are "desks" for individual nations, each headed by a responsible officer.

The Counselor and what after Kennan's time became the Policy Planning Council deserve a further word. Ranking as an Assistant Secretary, the Counselor serves as special adviser and consultant to the top officials and handles special problems. The Policy Planning Council, reorganized on July 3, 1969 as the Planning and Coordination Staff (PCS), continues as before to handle long-range policy planning on an advisory basis. But its director now also supervises the coordination staff formerly servicing the SIG (or Under Secretaries Committee as it became under Nixon). Both the Counselor and the director of the new unit jointly serve as Department of State representative on the NSC Review Group.

The organization just described is designed to cope with several kinds of problems. Life in State would be much simpler if the basic units of the department could be organized either functionally or geographically, instead of both at once—with a corresponding need for coordination. But either alternative would raise even more difficulties. A purely functional approach would defy the practical fact that each nation-state is separate, with problems and policies that may be slightly or extravagantly different —if for no other reason than that each has a separate set of governing officials with varying personalities. (This is even true of Africa where the divisions into nation-states are sometimes so tenuous and frontiers so arbitrary.) On the other hand, a purely geographical approach would be obviously inappropriate for dealing with international organizations and hardly adequate for fostering an appraisal of, say, economic affairs as they raise implications across national frontiers. So both are done; but an obvious problem of coordination results.

A second problem is that functional or geographic bureaus, charged as they are with the handling of daily business, will lose much perspective on the total impact of what is developing or at least become reactors to events rather than initiators of desirable changes. (Balancing this consideration is the fact that the geographical bureaus and desks can be manned by specialists who have been stationed in the country whose affairs they are now handling at home. But even here it is possible for the advantages accruing from continuity of such expertise to be partially blotted over by bias.) Here the role of the Planning and Coordination Staff can be crucial. Relieved of day-by-day responsibility for particular developments, the planning members of the PCS are in theory able to look at things as a whole, but even this healthy situation is counterbalanced somewhat by the natural tendency of those caught up in the daily affairs to think they are in a better position to judge. Also, PCS planning members, like everyone else in government, find themselves involved in paper work which erodes time for thought.

The utility of a Planning and Coordination Staff depends a great deal on how seriously the top officials of the Department take it and make its input meaningful. This devolves especially upon the Secretary himself and the Secretary is an extremely busy man. This is the third problem, for to be effective a Secretary must cultivate Congress, must maintain close liaison with the President, with Defense and other agencies, must frequently be himself a chief negotiator at conferences, and personally represent the U.S. abroad at gatherings of many kinds. He must somehow do all this while administering the affairs of a large department, coping with daily emergencies, and keeping some perspective on long-term effects. And he must somehow cram in many public speeches to audiences of influential Americans or else find himself without much popular support. Altogether, not an easy job!

The State Department in Operation

WE HAVE seen some of the major problems of the Department of State and what has been or can be done about them. Now we need more feel for how the State Department actually operates to coordinate worldwide activities, and a brief look at ambassadorial duties and the trend in ambassadorial appointments.

Communications, and their effective handling, are a vital part of operations. In 1967, the U.S. maintained diplomatic missions in 117 countries. Each such mission is in contact with State each day, and the flow of "telegrams" (really, communications of all sorts) stream back and forth incessantly. Of these many messages only a handful is referred to the

Secretary on any day or originated by him. Each incoming message must be routed to all who should be informed; each outgoing message has to be "cleared" widely before the "action officer" can release it. Normally, messages of less than serious import are acknowledged by or responded to by an Assistant Secretary as the responsible officer. (No official below that rank is empowered to "make" policy.)

A development since the Cuban crises (1961 and 1962) is worth comment. For a long time the Defense Department has maintained "situation rooms" or "war rooms" at hundreds of bases and in fleet units, varying in sophistication with the level of command. Those at the White House and in the Pentagon are best known. Equipped with elaborate communication and command facilities, they are manned around the clock, ready to respond to emergency. Curiously, the State Department had no real equivalent. There was always a "duty watch" after the great bulk of departmental personnel went home at the end of the working day, but it was not organized for fast reaction. Its principal duty in emergency was to alert key personnel to return to the office. The experience in 1961 led to a needed reform with the establishment of an Operations Center with power to take initial reacting steps. In June 1962, a 24-hour watch system was established. In every duty section a senior military officer who provides close liaison with the Pentagon is included. Since the Cuban Missile Crisis a connected innovation is the "task force" concept of handling crises from the Ops Center with a team working under the appropriate Assistant Secretary.

This facility is located high up in the State Department building and was integrated with an older feature of interest: facilities for conference discussions via radioteletype links that enable incoming and outgoing dispatches to be visually presented side by side. This device is available for conferences with key missions abroad and has advantages over ordinary telephone communications, useful as these are. For one thing, there can be a conference group at each end which includes all the appropriate officials. They can confer and discuss at any necessary length the questions or remarks put from the other end before responding. The fact that the messages are projected on screens allows each end to read, reflect, and reread. Finally, the entire sequence of messages is preserved in written form and is available for subsequent reference. In dealing with intricate questions the very directness of a phone conversation may be a disadvantage. (As most people are now aware, the "hot line" between Washington and Moscow is not a telephone but a teletype link. Either is technologically feasible, but with teletype error is less possible.)

The messages that go back and forth from State (as with Defense) are a prime source of information about government policy. Consequently every effort is made to transmit them in secure codes and ciphers and via means not subject to "wiretapping." In embassies located in nations with which the United States does not have friendly relations, there is need for elaborate security measures. In the Moscow Embassy, for instance, past experience demonstrates the versatility and ingenuity with which the Soviets eavesdrop. Some years ago it was discovered that a Soviet-presented Great Seal of the United States that was hanging in the American Embassy in Moscow had concealed transistors.

The mail has to be similarly safeguarded. A U.S. Diplomatic Courier Service operates on a global basis as part of the Foreign Service. Couriers, using mostly commercial transportation, deliver the mail in sealed "pouches" from one stop to another on a regularly scheduled basis. This represents quite a change from the days when John Quincy Adams (as American Minister to Russia in 1809–1814) dispatched most of his official mail via imperial Russian couriers. Actually, the U.S. did not develop its own courier system until World War I, when marines and soldiers performed as couriers. After the war this force was disbanded and the mail was normally carried by any American citizen who was considered reliable and was going in the appropriate direction. Such Americans were given letters appointing them temporarily as "bearers of dispatches" and could in return for their services expect preferential treatment at the frontier.

Quite consistent with the late modernization in coordination and casting aside of primitive instrumentalities of government, here too the change came about in relatively recent times. During the London Economic Conference (1934), President F. D. Roosevelt, astonished to learn that no official courier system existed, ordered one into existence.[15]

The competence of each ambassador to handle his part in this complex business is an important element in the overall success of State Department operations. The U.S. embassy abroad which he heads is connected to State as the Washington nerve-center and may vary considerably in size. From the staff of the Paris Embassy (with 97 Foreign Service Officers attached in September 1968, plus many others) to the staff of the embassy in Upper Volta (with 7 Foreign Service Officers, and few others) is a large numerical spread, reflecting the amount of business transacted. Whether large or small, each embassy is normally divided into major sections for administration, political affairs, economic affairs, and consular matters. Cultural affairs are handled by USIA. Missions may have a whole range of non-Foreign Service officials attached to them.[16] Besides the normal military attachés and representatives from USIA, AID, CIA or other agencies, there may be fair-sized military

[15] For a good treatment of these developments see Charles W. Thayer, *Diplomat* (New York: Harper & Row, 1959), especially pp. 386–392.

[16] In late 1968, nine embassies (including Paris) had as many as 1,000 U.S. citizens attached, about a fifth from the State Department proper, the remainder from 34 other agencies.

advisory groups sent to provide training in the use of U.S. equipment. Although these various officers may report to many different Washington departments and agencies, they are all, as indicated, under the administrative supervision of the American ambassador. But this supervision may be less than it sounds, for substantive tasks are assigned to these officials by their Washington offices and promotions remain in their hands.

It amounts to this: the ambassador must be informed of on-going activities at his post and must approve their continuance. Such non-State officials may not follow a separate foreign policy of their own making. Operating effectively in such an environment demands that the ambassador be not only a good representative abroad in the obvious sense of having negotiating ability. He must also be both a capable administrator of his own staff and be able to impart a unified sense of direction to that very diversely oriented staff.

In theory the ambassador and his staff do not make foreign policy. Washington (in one, presumably coordinated, voice) makes the policy; the embassy (with presumably an equally coordinated voice) carries it out. Thus the ambassador and his subordinates are not expected to deviate from their presumably coordinated instructions (even if they disagree personally with what they are told collectively to do). Yet, even assuming effective coordination, this division of responsibility is too pat. The embassy is fully engaged in relaying information, reports, and advice to Washington and is itself the prime source of the facts considered in Washington when policy is made; therefore it is both inescapable and desirable that the embassy views have an important (although indirect) impact on policy and its revision.

This short survey of the complicated duties of a U.S. ambassador today explains why two-thirds to three-quarters of all American embassies are directed by ambassadors who, rising through merit as career Foreign Service Officers, have reached the top. This represents a very recent change, true only since the end of World War II. In 1944, for example, Jefferson Caffery became the first professional career diplomat to head the Paris Embassy (although by this time many embassies of lesser size were headed by career officers). While rewarding wealthy campaign contributors with appointments as ambassadors still continued, after that time it became relatively rare. Noncareer officers sometimes were appointed (such as Senator Henry Cabot Lodge to South Viet-Nam in the 1960's and General Walter Bedell Smith to Moscow right after World War II), but these noncareer officers commanded an expertise in political matters and a corresponding respect of their staffs deriving from that fact. They were typically men with long governmental service and certainly not amateurs.

Two reasons account for the earlier, now largely discarded amateur political-appointee system. First, in the period when U.S. foreign policy was of quite modest dimensions (as in most of the nineteenth century), the embassies had in any case little substantive business to conduct. The second reason, already alluded to earlier, is that the entertainment costs connected with any sizable embassy so greatly exceeded the salaries given to ambassadors that only men of private means could afford to accept the honor of an appointment. Consider that the salaries for ambassadors and ministers set under the Act of 1856 were $17,500 and $10,000 respectively, which was enough at the time. These salaries were not increased until 1946![17]

One extreme illustration of the results of the political-appointee system came in the sometimes painful, sometimes hilarious hearings held by the Senate Foreign Relations Committee in 1957 on the question of confirming President Eisenhower's nominee, Mr. Maxwell H. Gluck, as Ambassador to Ceylon:

SEN. FULBRIGHT: How much did you contribute to the Republican Party in the 1956 election?
MR. GLUCK: Well, I wouldn't know offhand, but I made a contribution.
SEN. FULBRIGHT: Well, how much?
MR. GLUCK: Let's see; I would say, all in all, twenty or thirty thousand dollars.

SEN. FULBRIGHT: Why are you interested in Ceylon?
MR. GLUCK: I am not particularly interested only in Ceylon, but I am interested in a Government post where I can do some work and do some good at it.
SEN. FULBRIGHT: What makes you think you could do that in Ceylon?
MR. GLUCK: Unless I run into something I am not aware of I think I ought to do a fairly good job in the job I have been nominated for.
SEN. FULBRIGHT: What are the problems in Ceylon you think you can deal with?
MR. GLUCK: One of the problems are the people there, not necessarily a problem, but the relationship of the United States with the people in Ceylon. I believe I can—I think I can establish, unless we—again, unless I run into something that I have not run into before—a good relationship and good feeling toward the United States.

SEN. FULBRIGHT: Do you know who the Prime Minister in India is?
MR. GLUCK: Yes; but I can't pronounce his name.
SEN. FULBRIGHT: Do you know who the Prime Minister of Ceylon is?
MR. GLUCK: I have a list . . .
SEN. FULBRIGHT: Who is it?
MR. GLUCK: His name is a bit unfamiliar now. I cannot call it off, but I have obtained from Ambassador Crowe a list of all the important people there . . . I have a synopsis of all the people [and] sort of little biography or history of them, with what his opinion of them is; and so . . .
SEN. FULBRIGHT: That's all, Mr. Chairman. [18]

[17] Childs, *op. cit.*, p. 7.
[18] Extracts from Senate Foreign Relations Committee, *Hearings on the Nomination of Maxwell H. Gluck*, 85th Congress, 1st Session (July 2, 1957), pp. 1–4.

Mr. Gluck was nonetheless confirmed. His actual record in Ceylon was much better than one might have expected from this beginning.

An Assessment

PRESIDENTS like Franklin D. Roosevelt, who have by-passed their own State Department on important problems, have more frequently than not paid a price. The results can be expensive in terms of the national interests of the United States. Presidents like John F. Kennedy, who have taken much more than the customary share of direction of detailed foreign policy into the White House, have been forced to invest disproportionately large amounts of their time at a cost to something else—perhaps in Kennedy's case his legislative program that was stalled at the time of his death. Presidents like Lyndon B. Johnson, who have sought to place the State Department firmly at the center of foreign affairs coordination have been trying to achieve what is in principle the better solution— provided it can be closely tied into the "NSC system." In Johnson's tenure the tie between the SIG-IRG portion of the apparatus and the NSC remained only partially articulated. So we see the Nixon Administration's attempt to close the gap.

Even with the full development now of the "Country Team," and the revamped SIG-IRG apparatus presently incorporated into the NSC system, serious problems remain, which we have explored in this chapter. The major lines of solution to these problems, as attempted so far, are clear enough. Growth in numbers and changes toward wider recruitment for the Foreign Service, provisions for more adequate career rotation patterns from home to abroad, have introduced personnel reforms which are, in general, highly desirable. The resolution in principle of the old question of whether the State Department should physically incorporate all the foreign affairs operating agencies has been settled on what appears to be a workable basis both in Washington and abroad. The communication and understanding between the Defense and State Departments have become useful and effective.

All of these changes in no way guarantee a fully effective State Department. The duties of the Secretary of State, much like the duties of the President himself, remain almost too much for any one man. Whether proposals to create a second-rank post, with a title such as Foreign Minister, to share the duties of attendance at conferences and other protocol-type responsibilities, would work is a moot question. It can be anticipated that foreign officials would still try to have the man at the top personally attend to their business. More relief for the Secretary might be obtainable by a serious attempt to utilize a "Deputy Secretary" for congressional appearances, and an "Administrative Under Secretary" to handle the internal managerial functions, while the Secretary himself concentrated on overall policy and continued to attend international conferences.

In this chapter and Chapter 4 we have been looking at the changes in the executive side of the U.S. government and foreign affairs. In the next chapter we must see how Congress, in part as it reflects wider public views, fits into the total picture of interaction between politics, policy, and organization. It is here that we shall gain a more direct look at the second perspective with which Part Two is concerned: why has the tendency existed to downplay or ignore consideration of the grand strategic alternative foreign policy choices confronting the U.S.?

CHAPTER 6

People, Politics, and Foreign Policy

THE American political system contains important clues as to why the tendency has existed to downplay or ignore consideration of the grand strategic alternative foreign policy choices confronting the United States.

To begin with, that political system is designed to meet a great variety of needs, pressures, and demands—only some of which have a direct connection to foreign policy issues. Take as illustration any presidential news conference. At President Nixon's June 19, 1969 TV press conference, 24 questions were asked: seven were directly on Viet-Nam, three involved how American policy decisions related to foreign policy were being made, three concerned arms questions, one was on the Middle East, one on Latin America, three on inflation and taxes, two on the New York mayoral race, and the rest on scattered domestic issues. Even the apparently direct questions on foreign policy frequently involved domestic political considerations such as public concern over the U.S. casualty rate, Senator Ted Kennedy's opposition to an ABM system, and other Democratic proposals for cutting back Viet-Nam troop strength. Foreign policy issues as such are only a part of the total process, and normally they are a smaller part unless the U.S. is actually engaged in fighting abroad. Neither President, Congress, nor people give more than a proportion of their total political time and energy to foreign policy issues, and these issues are rarely pure (i.e., divorced from meaningful domestic considerations).

Second, if foreign policy issues are only a part of the total political process, it inevitably follows that only the most dramatic or most urgent issues receive substantial public attention, and even then it is rare for attention to be sustained. Public attention tends to be intermittent, focused primarily on issues that have reached the crisis (or, at least, decision) stage. There is typically little time or opportunity at that point to examine and explain the whole background of the issue. There is little public awareness of the total factual background, little public interest in a dispassionate and objective analysis of the assumptions made or rejected in reaching the decisions, little public time available to the President to put the whole question in a meaningful frame of reference that illuminates the *context* of the decision rather than its *content*.

Third, the American people as a whole tend to approach foreign policy issues with distinctive attitudes developed as a consequence of an unusual national experience; yet as individuals they vary widely in how much they agree or disagree on particular decisions or policies. That they agree on the general method of approaching political decisions (i.e., encouraging presentation of diverse views as a means of developing a consensus) in no way determines what the consensus will be. Since the *contents* of policies are determined pragmatically, it is possible for the American people to follow successively quite contrasting policies over the long term. Much depends on how they react to an issue from the perspective of their individual interests, biases, and preferences, and what majority opinion then turns out to be. But since there is much human inertia in the system, the most critical determinant, apart from "pressure groups," is the center of gravity of views of the most articulate and "independent" part of the public. Presidential elections are rarely decided by a public landslide vote; it only appears so because of lopsided Electoral College results. Because many of the opinions and preferences of great numbers of people remain fairly constant over long periods of time, the "independent" voter, as the "movable piece," acquires great significance in the American political system. When we talk about swings in public opinion it is this group we really have most in mind. They are the ones most responsible for, and responsive to, the presentation of the "other side of the question." If, rather suddenly in 1968–1969, the "military-industrial complex" or the campus ROTC is under fire (whereas previously one heard little concern expressed about either), it is not necessarily a sign of fundamental shift of opinion but it is a clear indication at least that the "independent" is having second thoughts about what he did not question before.

Taking the three factors (clues) together, it should be apparent that their total thrust is more against than for meaningful consideration of grand strategic policy alternatives. Fragmentation of political interest, the fleeting character of public interest in most questions, the inertia of the greater part of the public, are hardly fully counterbalanced by the sensitivity of the independent voter to public issues—especially since even then (as illustrated in the preceding paragraph), attention may come to focus more on symbol than cause, for the "military-industrial complex" and campus ROTC are hardly meaningful explanations of why U.S. foreign policy was encountering serious problems in the late 1960's.

Within this perspective, let us look further at the American political system and the interaction of people and politics with foreign policy.

Three Qualifications to a Model of
Political Group Interaction

IN examining the impact of political group interaction on foreign policy and U.S. foreign policy-makers, three major qualifications must be kept in mind to avoid undue simplification, for the relationship is more amorphous and complex than one might assume.

First, these interactions are "internal" to the American political process only in a strictly limited sense. Although they occur within the territory of the United States and affect the policy-makers of this country, they do not occur without relevance to events and forces outside the United States territory. A member of a congressional committee on foreign affairs does not respond something like a gauge to two opposite but simultaneous sets of pressures: one from the external foreign environment, the other from internal groups.

Too simple a model ignores the possibility that all or most of the pressures are being exerted in the same general direction. More important, a useful model must take into account the fact that the "internal" groups, in exerting pressures, are themselves reacting in some degree to their conceptualization of what constraints the external environment imposes. The degree to which a farmers' organization presses to keep the tariff high involves from the outset some appreciation of how much is realistically attainable in view of the overall foreign environment. Thus the policy-maker is not a middleman. He is not condemned to the unenviable role of explaining the facts of international life to American citizens and relaying to foreigners an appreciation of internal views of which they were unaware. In the very demands from abroad or from inside, the nature of the "opposition" has already *to some extent* been taken into account. Foreign policies which stand little or no chance of success because of external constraints are not likely to be seriously proposed or discussed to begin with. The process involves considerable feedback.

To use a foreign illustration: in 1967, when the Labour Government of the United Kingdom applied for membership in the European Common Market, it did so with assured domestic backing from Parliament and British pressure groups. British opinion had also attempted to "read the tea-leaves" on how de Gaulle and the other members of the Common Market would react to the British proposal and decided it might not be negative. Once de Gaulle and the others did react by shelving the British bid, a new assessment had to be made, and the process went through its next cycle.

Second, any category of policy-maker larger than a single individual is itself not monolithic but fragmented or susceptible to fragmentation on many issues. (Even the President, as a single individual, is subject to many conflicting internal desires.) Comparing "Congress" as a whole with the "executive" compares categories that, from a political system standpoint, only have real meaning under special and particular circumstances.

There are some issues on which the Congress as a whole is likely to line up against the President and the executive branch. If, for example, the Congress appropriates sums of money for three new nuclear-powered aircraft carriers, but the President (on the advice of the Secretary of Defense) impounds the money and refuses to spend it, the two branches are at loggerheads. Even here, the unity of view within the executive branch will probably only exist on the surface (since many within the Navy Department at least would probably like to have those carriers!). Perhaps a more black-and-white illustration occurs when a congressional committee is holding hearings and finds itself confronted with a government employee under instructions from the President not to reveal certain information. Quite often this situation comes about over information in personnel dossiers, or in relation to the "raw" (unevaluated) files of the F.B.I. Congress is likely to "demand" to be informed as a matter of public necessity, while the President is likely to insist on "executive privilege." Occasionally, a confrontation of the two branches turns on the relatively rare case in which a presidential nominee is not confirmed by the Congress (in this case, the Senate). Even here the Congress is rarely monolithic: *all* of it opposed; and it is more likely to delay than to refuse confirmation. In 1969 the two branches argued over the Senate's right to have access to "contingency plans" for aiding Thailand.

A Congressman not only has to take into account the nature of a foreign policy problem, the probable reaction abroad, and the desires of groups of his own constituents, but he will do so within a framework of views and biases of his own and a healthy regard (if he is to survive politically) for the views of his colleagues in the Congress, the impression he is making on the President, and the press he is receiving by virtue of his actions. If his constituents are fairly evenly divided on a certain issue, he may have a great deal of latitude. Even if his constituents are fairly unanimous he may for other reasons go against their wishes (knowing he will mollify them with later votes, or judging that the voters' memory will be short, or believing that they will not turn out a prominent representative from their state who brings them national recognition, among other benefits).

What does influence a member of Congress most? John F. Kennedy, writing his *Profiles in Courage* from the perspective of a U.S. Senator, listed three major pressures on a member of that body. First in his list was a desire to be liked, especially by friends and colleagues: "we are anxious to get along with our fellow legislators, our fellow members of the club, to abide by the clubhouse rules and patterns, not to pursue a unique and independent course which would embarrass or irritate the other members. We realize, moreover, that our influence in the club—and the extent to which we can accomplish our objectives and those of our constituents—are dependent in some measure on the esteem with which we are regarded by other Senators." Kennedy's second pressure was the desire to be re-elected, to continue in office. His third pressure, which he tied specifically to its most significant effect in discouraging political courage, was the "interest groups, the organized letter writers, the economic blocs and even the average voter." Kennedy quoted with relish Congressman John Steven McGroarty (California) who wrote one of his constituents in 1934:

One of the countless drawbacks of being in Congress is that I am compelled to receive impertinent letters from a jackass like you in which you say I promised to have the Sierra Madre mountains reforested and I have been in Congress two months and haven't done it. Will you please take two running jumps and go to hell.

Within the executive branch the responses to pressure groups and to public opinion are equally complicated although somewhat different in nature. The President (and by derivation his higher appointees) depend on public favor for their office, but the President only runs for election every four years. Permanent officials of government remain as Presidents come and go. Thus, they are largely personally insulated from outside group pressures. What does affect them are considerations of career advancement and the utility of any proposal for the interests of the United States (as they perceive them). They must also consider how a proposal affects the department for which they work.

Confrontations between two government departments may occur, or within the large Defense Department the Joint Chiefs of Staff may dig in to oppose the "civilian side of the house," led by the Secretary. Much more likely and usual, however, will be some difference in each group. *Within* the Joint Chiefs, different points of view will be expressed; and so too on the civilian side. There will be infinite variation from case to case in how monolithic the agreement really is on the lower levels.

Direct reaction to public opinion may be considerably less than one might suppose. James L. McCamy comments:

the officials who are primarily responsible for formulating foreign policy pay little or no attention to these particular factors of public opinion that might be relevant . . .[1]

This is, of course, less true at the most senior levels. McCamy goes on to quote W. Phillips Davison's study of the State Department:

---

[1] James L. McCamy, *The Administration of American Foreign Affairs* (New York: Alfred A. Knopf, Inc. 1950), p. 331.

In practice a policy-maker may be more influenced by reading his customary newspaper in the evening and thinking through the arguments advanced by columnists and commentators than by scanning his office mimeographed reports on public opinion.[2]

To sum up, the variety of views within government is very great, just as it is outside. Government officials do not live in an insulated atmosphere remote from the environment of the average citizen. Nor are they recruited from only special classes or backgrounds or live under peculiar conditions like the Turkish Janizaries. They come to their jobs and do their jobs with much the same array of backgrounds, interests, biases, and preferences as do the general run of professional groups in the United States. Being "in" government, whether elected or appointed, produces some elusive changes in outlook (a heightened awareness of the intractability of certain problems, a realization of the infinite bafflements that can arise in a bureaucracy), but these altered viewpoints are not fundamental. They affect views on the feasibility of change rather than specific preferences for or against specific changes.[3]

By the time we have taken all this into account, we are very far from a simple model of the American political process and U.S. foreign policy-making.

The third point about internal group influences on foreign policy is that such groups are rarely concerned with broad foreign affairs issues and, if they are, will probably be unlikely to deliver a meaningful vote at election time. Most organized groups have limited interests in foreign policy questions. Although farmers may be interested in tariffs, they are much more interested in domestic subsidies and the rising costs of living. Even if there are many "farm votes," and even if they can be organized effectively by their leaders, the tariff issue is only a limited one. An election will not likely turn on a tariff issue. Even where groups have very real foreign policy interests (as among ship owners and maritime workers), their attention is not specifically and exclusively foreign-trade oriented, and their views (as indeed in this case) may tend to be mutually self-defeating. Large groups who maintain general points of view on foreign policy questions, such as the American Legion or the

---

2 *Ibid.*

3 Sidney Verba *et al.*, in "Public Opinion and the War in Viet-Nam," *American Political Science Review*, 61:332–333, June 1967, show the division of congressional opinion as of October 1966 to be 48.5 per cent in favor of the basic course followed up to then; 26.4 per cent desiring a more decisive military action by the United States; 15.1 per cent for more emphasis on peace talks; and 10.0 per cent unascertained. A Stanford Survey of nine months later, asking somewhat different questions of the mass public, found 49 per cent in favor of the general policy followed; 23 per cent for major war if necessary; 19 per cent for withdrawal; and 9 per cent "don't know."

numerous *ad hoc* groups current in 1969 over Viet-Nam or the missile question, have such broad memberships who disagree on many other things that their total effect on foreign policy must be judged limited.

Group Pressures

THE impact of political group interaction on foreign policy and U.S. foreign policy-making is more amorphous and complex than one might at first assume, for the three reasons just given. What factors, then, are of prime importance in determining how the system actually reacts to pressures? Once we understand (1) that the dividing line between internal and foreign affairs is frequently nebulous and that there is continual interaction, (2) that the concept of categories of foreign policy-makers only holds true with important qualifications, and (3) that organized pressure groups rarely have effect on the most serious and important foreign policy issues, we are in a better position to assess what does happen. Looking now more closely at the effects or lack of effects of group pressures on American foreign policy, we can see five factors at work.

The first factor is that individual Americans have multiple interests. Since their allegiance to any one of the groups to which they belong is normally qualified by the existence of those other interests, the distribution of preferences often acts as a moderating force on pressures toward any great policy alterations. The pluralistic allegiances of the typical American voter frequently checkmate his ability to push vigorously for a given program, unless one of his interests is much greater than another. By virtue of his affiliations and interests, more often than not a voter belongs on both sides of a given question.

In pointing to the highly pluralistic nature of American society, cultural diversity is just the beginning. Religious, political party, professional, and economic groupings are of great importance. The voter is extremely rare (if he exists) who wholeheartedly stands behind the formal and official program of every organization of which he is a member. Some Protestant Democrats, for example, could not bring themselves to vote for Catholic John F. Kennedy for President. Some Catholic Republicans could not bring themselves to abandon their long-time political affiliation to vote for Kennedy even though they very much wanted to see the myth destroyed that a Catholic could not become President. Very few people (as indicated earlier) are consistently for or against government spending; they are for or against spending particular amounts for particular purposes.

Complicating the picture still more, Americans as citizens collectively favor spending for national defense. At the same time they usually favor reducing the national debt. In circumstances such as the Viet-Nam War, they will favor less spending on the "War on Poverty" program than would otherwise be permitted. The whole Civil Rights movement in 1967–1968 was undergoing convulsions, caught in a frustration between opposing or supporting the Viet-Nam war. Some Negro leaders went one way, some another. To some extent their frustration arose out of ideological and moralistic grounds (the war had racial overtones); to some extent it came from the economic facts of life (elimination of urban "ghettos" was not financially supportable during the war).

Even the issue of a voter's pocketbook, where dollars are directly involved, may not be at all decisive in resolving the balance of pressures that influence him (let alone the Congressman to be influenced). Sentiment, tradition, ideology—all are at least as significant in determining points of view as direct profit-and-loss calculations. As a profession, political scientists are disproportionately Democrats; they have a prejudice in favor of government. Knowing what government can do, they generally like to see it doing it. This professional bias or prejudice may be stronger than considerations of personal profit. As members of the higher education profession they are much more likely to favor a school bond issue even if it raises their taxes while not increasing their income. Naval officers (and the officers of the Army) are disproportionately Republicans. Perhaps this affiliation goes back to the days when the Republican Party stood for a large Navy, but certainly in the last decades it could be convincingly demonstrated that the Democratic Party has given far more generous support to the U.S. Navy. What we see is probably the sentimental attachment of the Navy officer corps to the more tradition-centered of the American political parties. Here, as before, sentiment, tradition, and ideology tend to put each of these groups somewhat (even if unequally) on both sides of a question—in these specific cases, the money issue versus sentimentality.

The second factor is that, in any group, the degree or intensity of involvement and commitment over an issue or attitude varies enormously. Effects on foreign policy vary accordingly.

Some pressure groups have very compact and specific purposes and a membership vigorously supporting those purposes. The American Zionist organizations (especially at a time when Israel is in peril) are fairly single-minded about aiding Israel. The members are not lukewarm about the objective, although when crisis in the Middle East is not at its peak, enthusiasm may waver. At the opposite extreme are the members of the very large American Bowling Congress; they exert little pressure at any time and, apart from nominal membership in their bowling organization, have little or nothing in common. It is hard to visualize their uniting on a program for broad political action. Compare the American Legion and the Americans for Democratic Action: the former is far larger than the latter but is generally ineffective in any normal political sense, because its focus is on overall patriotic loyalty rather than on any specific program. If the American Legion adopted any program other than "national readiness" and "national security," it would quickly come apart at the seams. Barring some very unusual set of circumstances, the likelihood of the American Legion, for all its elaborate organization, delivering an effective political vote to one party rather than another is nil. The ADA, on the other hand, although composed predominantly of Democrats, could quite conceivably (especially in view of the liberal dissatisfaction with the Viet-Nam War) have been induced to vote en masse in 1968 for a "suitable" Republican candidate.

What is true here of the voters is also true of Congress. A member of Congress who is Jewish normally needs no great pressing to favor Zionist programs. An anti-Semite in Congress, who feels vigorously opposed, will need no urging to implement his own bias. In between there are many members of Congress who will have no pronounced leanings one way or the other on this question. If they do not consider the Zionist program incompatible with other stands they favor, and if it is presented to them via voters from their own district, they may well vote for it even if personally indifferent.

The third factor is that, even where groups are cohesive enough to exert pressures, the degree of momentum of a problem has a distinct effect on whether pressures can have results. Where an issue is present in rather unchanging form over a long enough period of time, very distinct public attitudes may emerge. Excluding the lower groups of the public who typically in polls record that "they do not know" or "have no opinion," the informed public on an issue like seating the Chinese Communists in the UN is likely to be very clear over what resolution of the question they favor. By contrast, with a new or rapidly changing question, unless it is crystal clear in its implications or fits exactly within the confines of accepted principle, the public pressure will likely be ineffective since there is insufficient time for opinion to jell. For example, in the week before the June 1967 fighting in the Middle East, after Nasser closed the Gulf of Aqaba to Israeli shipping, the issue of whether they were international waters and should be forcibly cleared by the United States, alone if necessary, was overtaken by the rush of developments. In the Cuban Missile Crisis, by contrast, although events also moved very rapidly, it was apparent that public opinion was virtually unanimously behind President Kennedy's "quarantine" announcement. Developments came quickly in this case, but the issue fairly clearly involved the immediate and obvious national interests of the United States; no long gestation period was needed as lead-time before sentiment unified.

The fourth factor turns on the degree of understanding an issue permits. Most Americans favor disarmament with safeguards; yet most Americans would be at a total loss in assessing whether a particular plan offered suitable safeguards. Whether an antimissile system is needed, and what kind, is another complex question. Most Americans, while favoring an "adequate" defense, would be hard put to decide whether a specific system is adequate. On this kind of issue, unless the picture becomes clearer as time goes on, public sentiment as pressure is likely to be quite ineffective.

The fifth factor is what the public communication media choose to emphasize, and how much of a feeling of unanimity their treatment shows and/or creates. Where radio, press, and television all emphasize particular issues simultaneously, public interest in those questions is bound to grow. Where the point of view shown is highly homogenous, opinion may or may not veer in the same direction, but preoccupation with the question covered will certainly increase. In a presidential news conference, although the President, if he is adroit, can find ample opportunities for presenting his own point of view, he must be responsive to the questions asked or else risk appearing evasive. He may wish to place emphasis elsewhere than the questions direct, but he can only do so to a limited extent.

Many military men are convinced today that two important reasons why the Viet-Nam War fared so poorly in its public reception are (1) that it was the first American war to be televised at length and (2) the action covered was largely at the American end of the activities. Americans at home were given a graphic picture of the brutality and waste of war; at the same time they saw the effects of enemy fire on American lives: literally seeing Americans killed.

By inserting world affairs into everyone's living room, the mass media have not contributed much on the whole to an understanding of the complex cause and results of what is portrayed, but they have made Americans much more aware of what activities are going on. As a consequence they may encourage reluctance to become involved without clarifying how commitments can safely be reduced.

A realistic understanding of pressure groups and their effects must take each of these five factors into account.

The Consequences for Foreign Policy Change

WE can now reach some assessment of the interaction between public opinion on the one hand and government policy on the other, especially as the interaction affects changes in foreign policy.

Normally, the government is far freer to act on new issues than old ones existing for a long period of time. This contrast in flexibility exists because public opinion has formed on older issues, and they have acquired inertia in the international environment. To illustrate, if the policy on seating Communist China in the UN were to be revised, it would not only have to happen with due regard for internal American sentiment but also with an eye on the reactions of the many foreign nations who are aware of (and have themselves taken positions with some relation to) the policy followed by the United States.

The U.S. government, if it decides on a radical change of course, has a difficult political problem, especially if the older policy has been followed a long time without great or effective protest. Since its sources of information are elaborate, and since it must as a practical matter digest that information and react to it, government will likely become aware of the need for change before the general public has come to demand or expect it. In the late 1930's, as the war clouds gathered over Europe, there were many individual Americans with an interest in and a knowledge of world affairs who had grave doubts about the effectiveness of the Neutrality Acts to safeguard American interests and the national security. As a minority they counted little against the inertia of continuing the *status quo,* and the fairly general public indifference to its dangers. Under these circumstances the initiative had to come from government, specifically from a lead by President Franklin D. Roosevelt. Since Roosevelt himself had earlier favored the neutrality legislation, the political problem was doubly difficult: to induce change from what he had himself urged and which was generally still acceptable to the people. Events came to a crisis following the outbreak of World War II. Bound by the provisions of the 1937 Neutrality Act, President Roosevelt (September 5, 1939) had to proclaim an arms embargo against the initial belligerents on both sides. By September 10, arms supplies had been cut off not only to Germany but to Britain, France, Poland, Australia, New Zealand, India, South Africa, and Canada. Some $80,000,-000 worth of arms, already ordered by Britain and France and previously licensed for export, could no longer be sent. Roosevelt, calling a special session of Congress, appealed to it (September 21) for a repeal of the embargo provisions. Describing it as "most vitally dangerous to American neutrality, American security, and American peace," he told the Congress: "I regret that the Congress passed that act. I regret equally that I signed that act."

Congress, in complying with the President's request, replaced the embargo with the Neutrality Act of 1939—which allowed a "cash-and-carry" policy for arms and goods to belligerents but prohibited United States ships from entering war zones. In the next two years the United States steered a somewhat zig-zag course within these remaining constraints. In April 1941, the Red Sea was reclassified by the President from war zone status to permit Lend-Lease supplies to go to that area. By July 1941, the United States had assumed responsibility for the defense of Greenland and acquired bases in Iceland (700 miles from Scotland). United States shipping was being protected by the U.S.

Navy in areas that by any reasonable definition were war zones. At this point the neutrality acts were again amended and U.S. ships permitted to sail to belligerent ports through belligerent waters.

The foregoing gradual process was paralleled by a gradual evolution of opinion that made it possible. The ultimate complete change of policy reflected a complete change of opinion, with the government at each step asking for as much as it felt feasible. By the summer of 1941, public sentiment had shifted markedly from the quite negative response that greeted Roosevelt's "quarantine the aggressors" speech (October 5, 1937), in which the President proposed nothing more drastic than severing diplomatic relations with any country that continued aggression. In January 1937, the polls showed 70 per cent of the people with an opinion convinced that America's intervention in World War I had been a tragic mistake. The "Ludlow Amendment" sought to change the Constitution to forbid Congress to declare war (except in response to invasion) until the people had approved belligerency by popular referendum; this measure lost in the House (January 1938) by the narrow vote of 188 to 209—an eloquent testimony to attitudes on the very eve of World War II. By February 1939, some 48 per cent of the American people believed that U.S. entry into World War I had been an error (although 69 per cent were willing to take steps short of war to aid Britain and France); by October 1939 (just after World War II began), some 59 per cent believed our 1917 action mistaken. By this time, 21 per cent favored outright American intervention, while 46 per cent were willing to go to war if that was the only way to prevent a German victory. Thus, the repeal of the 1937 Neutrality Act and its replacement by continued but less crippling restrictions reflected a delicate balance between national policy requirements and the considerable public antagonism to any direct moves toward war. By January 1941, the percentage considering our entry into World War I mistaken was down to 40 per cent, and by December of the same year, it stood at 21 per cent; these facts shed light on the new policies and amendments to the neutrality legislation in that year.

Where the government embarks on a policy commitment consistent with public views, it has much more latitude. Whether it keeps that support depends upon whether the action continues to be considered correct.

The outbreak of the Korean War (June 1950) represented a reverse case of public opinion. Sentiment that year contrasted markedly with prewar isolationism. The pendulum swung far in the opposite direction, as we noted in Chapter 1. The polls asked whether U.S. action in Korea had been a mistake, and only 20 per cent said yes in August 1950 (at a time when U.S. troops were holding on desperately to the small beachhead around Pusan at the very tip of South Korea). Almost two out of three voters (65 per cent) said no (with 15 per cent undecided). By January 1951, following the brilliant amphibious landing at Inchon, the advance into North Korea, the entrance of Chinese "volunteers" into action, the disastrous defeat and withdrawal of U.S. forces, and the loss to the enemy of the South Korean capital, 49 per cent thought the war a mistake, while only 38 per cent persisted in their approval. Even after Seoul was liberated again, 50 per cent thought the war a mistake, while 39 per cent supported it. These were days when opinion everywhere was divided. (MacArthur's recall was announced by President Truman on April 11, 1951.)

The Viet-Nam War is a more recent illustration of an issue in which public opinion was severely divided. In 1966–1967 there were strong minority pressures to stop bombing North Viet-Nam; there were even greater pressures to use more military force to induce a decision. Virtually everyone wanted the war to end; many thought that involvement had been a mistake; few considered that the United States could simply abruptly pull out and leave an unsatisfactory situation to find its own resolution without an American presence.[4]

In noting the polls on American policy between 1937 and 1941, we have said nothing about the pressure groups that arose during that period. Two important groups emerged: one, the Committee to Defend America by Aiding the Allies; the other, the Save America First Movement. These groups represented a rough division of opinion, the first arguing for intervention, the second fighting an action against all measures that progressively threatened to end in U.S. involvement. These kinds of groups have emerged at other periods, on other foreign policy issues, although the clear-cut division into two large groups has seldom been duplicated since. Readers of *The New York Times* at any point during the Viet-Nam War could read whole page advertisements, replete with hundreds of signatures from prominent individuals. Pressure groups of this kind have obviously a more fluctuating base of membership than those groups that find their common core membership in an ethnic, economic, professional, or political view setting. The membership of this second kind of pressure group, concerned as it is with the "biggest" issues, will cut across the more narrowly interest-oriented groups. Such "big picture" groups might be thought of as having essentially little consequence on the foreign policy formulation environment, because the polls already indicate the rough division of opinion. It depends. Such organized groups (depending on how *well* organized they are and how

---

[4] In October 1967 the Harris Poll showed 37 per cent wanting to "get out as quickly as possible" while the same percentage said we must continue to "fight to get a negotiated peace." The Gallup Poll two years later found 57 per cent supporting Senator Charles E. Goodell's resolution to withdraw all U.S. troops by the end of 1970, with the fighting turned over to the Vietnamese.

cohesive they remain) are able to indulge in propaganda and organize demonstrations; they may as a consequence attain publicity, which in turn may give them further effect.

The limited effect of polls *per se* on political judgments arises partially out of the inherent weaknesses of polls themselves. We saw, for example, that at the same time that 59 per cent of Americans responding considered U.S. entry into World War I a mistake, some 46 per cent were also willing to go to war again if that was the only way to prevent a German victory. In 1967, one could ask whether Americans would be willing to continue to fight in Viet-Nam if that action was the only way to prevent a Communist victory. One could ask the same question for Thailand— or for Indonesia. The trouble with this kind of question is that it really bypasses significant issues—such as whether U.S. involvement *is* necessary in such conflicts in order to avoid Communist victories, or whether a substitute course of action could attain the same end without shedding American blood. The ability to conceptualize alternative strategic solutions to the problem, which such a question, to be answered effectively, would imply, rules it off the pollster's agenda. He asks—necessarily— rather simple questions requiring yes and no answers.

Yet as Abraham Lincoln once said, "There are few things wholly evil or wholly good. Almost everything, especially of Government policy, is an inseparable compound of the two, so that our best judgment of the preponderance between them is continually demanded." We would recognize readily the limited efficacy of asking the public: "Do you favor, if necessary, buying a new automobile if this is essential to avert a depression?" We would realize that as a guide to Detroit for setting production quotas, a response to this question would not be too helpful. Also, presumably the individual judgment on this question (like a question concerning intervening in World War II to "save" the allies) would fluctuate like the stock market. We have not said there is no value in this approach, but that its value is limited quite sharply.

The difficulty with polls is that they cannot yield meaningfully sharp divisions of opinion over complicated questions whose apparent meaning and implications continually change. What polls can and do indicate are general attitudes on large questions. As such, polls are useful and have an effect; primarily the effect is in revealing the gross parameters that policy-makers cannot exceed unless they use persuasion to bring about change, or unless events alter public sentiment in such a way as to expand flexibility.[5]

[5] In the Sidney Verba article, *op. cit.*, p. 333, they conclude: "The public opinion we have been discussing (i.e., the opinion on Viet-Nam) does not seem to possess much potential for controlling or limiting the alternatives of the administration. If anything, it mirrors the complexities of the debate in Washington and probably reflects a permissiveness in either direction (i.e., reduction or escalation)."

In conclusion, the American political system as it affects foreign policy, is extremely complex. Foreign policy issues are only a part of the total political process, and very few issues receive much sustained and widespread public attention. Consequently, the independent voter, because he stays more informed, and because he can tip the balance if major segments of the public are relatively inert or slow to change, has at all times great political importance. His views are the most relevant to the likelihood of change. However, like other Americans he is a person of many and ofttimes conflicting sympathies and interests; therefore the total effect in inducing real pressure for change may be mitigated. Inside and outside government the same fragmentation of interests can be seen. As the views of different interest groups compete, and as their views find expression in the mass media, the government finds itself far freer to act on new issues than on ones that have been around for a long time. But public inertia against change, accompanied by competing and mutually exclusive proposals for change, can seriously limit the government's freedom of action (even where the "government" has more of a single point of view than the general public has).

The ability to conceptualize and promote consideration of the grand strategic alternative foreign policy choices confronting the United States is, on the whole, relatively limited in the overall American political system. Many more factors conspire to prevent it than to encourage it. Only when a policy has clearly moved close to exhausting itself in futility does the re-examination begin. In Chapter 7 we shall consider the interaction of Congress and President, especially from this point of view, bearing also in mind that the American pragmatic approach to problems does permit new departures once a new consensus is reached.

CHAPTER 7

Congress, President, and Foreign Policy

THE Founding Fathers, concerned over the possibility of executive tyranny, took care to limit the powers of the President in all important areas of governmental activity. Although the Chief Executive was to be Commander-in-Chief of the Army (and other armed forces), it was left to the Congress to raise and equip that army—and the states were also guaranteed a militia. Presidents were to have necessarily large discretion in foreign affairs but only Congress could declare a war; and only with the Senate concurring could the President ratify a treaty or make an ambassadorial appointment. Without action by the House of Representatives to authorize expenditures and provide funds, no meaningful government activities were ultimately possible. Enumeration of these points makes the Constitutional conception clear: the President could propose innovations; the Congress would then agree or disagree and set the limits of what would be done. Or the Congress could propose and the President either accept or veto. Implied was the view that between them, and in their interaction, a suitable foreign policy for the American nation would emerge.

Congress Vs. President: An Overview

Now that we are approaching almost two hundred years of experience with these arrangements, we can see what different combinations of actions have proved possible under them. Apart from temporary fluctuations introduced by "weak" versus "strong" Presidencies (and other special but temporary circumstances such as the decade following the American Civil War), it is also possible to note certain long-run tendencies. James A. Robinson referred to foreign affairs particularly when he summed up in his *Congress and Foreign Policy-Making* (1962) by saying: "Congress's influence in foreign policy is primarily (and increasingly) one of legitimating and amending policies initiated by the

119

executive to deal with problems usually identified by the executive; and second, that one of the key reasons for this development lies in the changing character of the information or intelligence needs in modern policy-making."[1]

Several points need to be made to give perspective on the changing roles of Congress and President in the realm of foreign policy. First, it is generally agreed that the President's powers in this area are, by the very nature of government, greater than in other areas. As the Supreme Court expressed it (1936), the President has "a degree of discretion and freedom from statutory restriction which would not be admissible were domestic affairs alone involved."[2] It is not just that his information is greater (although this is so and has always been so, for he has access to the flow of dispatches from embassies abroad). It is also inherent in his position as head of state. He receives foreign emissaries, he represents the United States on visits abroad, he designates the officials sent abroad. As both head of state and national political leader he sets the tone and tenor of policy through speeches and addresses (and today, over television and through press conferences).

Second, it is not possible for Congress effectively to legislate the detail of foreign policy. However specific legislation becomes, it can do little more than enunciate principle and create organization. An Agency for International Development can be established and Congress can provide that its funds be used along certain lines (for example, that a certain percentage of the money be spent on a limited number of countries), but at some point it must leave the devising of concrete programs to the executive. This power over detail is ultimately very real power. Congress is a large collection of individuals preoccupied with legislation in many areas and does not have the time or energy to do more. Where, as we shall see later, the Congress has attached detailed restrictions on presidential execution of foreign affairs programs, Congress has most frequently felt forced to allow the President to override or ignore those restrictions if he finds, in the specific case, that they would be contrary to the national interests of the United States.

Third, the degree of presidential discretion is found to fluctuate with the degree of complexity and importance of foreign affairs to the United States. This quality has not been static. The initial decades were marked by high U.S. involvement in international relations; but for much of the nineteenth century and into the twentieth, the U.S. played a voluntarily limited role. In that period, which was a time when our apparatus for foreign affairs was quite naturally primitive and uncoordinated, the question of the relative power and roles of Congress and President in

[1] James A. Robinson, *Congress and Foreign Policy-Making* (Homewood, Ill.: Dorsey Press, 1962), p. *v*.

[2] *United States v. Curtiss-Wright Export Company*, 299 U.S. 304.

foreign affairs was debated in low key. There simply were not many foreign affairs to argue about. Conversely, after World War II and the establishment of global commitments and involvements, the argument— as could be expected—moved ultimately to the forefront of national discussion. Since the Senate has the greater constitutional grant of powers in foreign affairs, it is natural that by the mid-1960's the Senate and its Committee on Foreign Relations were at the focus of discussion.

The recurrent arguments and clashes between Senator Fulbright and President Johnson (1965–1968) over the Viet-Nam War were symptomatic of the congressional effort to play its constitutional role under the difficult conditions that prevail today. Congress not only is attempting to deal with presidential initiatives based qualitatively on more adequate information and intelligence and quantitatively on the extensiveness of our worldwide commitments; it is also attempting to deal with this problem within a context which derives from the interlocking features of the nature of modern armaments and the characteristics of contemporary, almost instantaneous warfare.

It is obvious that a great source of Senate discontent over the Viet-Nam War arose not just from the difficulty of achieving an American victory without either physically destroying Viet-Nam or bringing in other major powers such as Communist China. It arose also from the dilemma that the President had involved the U.S. in a large-scale conflict without a declaration of war and that a declaration of war might well bring on newer and greater problems than it solved. A declaration of war would inevitably have escalated the conflict in a number of directions. Viet-Nam was only the latest case, for the President after 1945 was using American armed forces consistently without any declaration of war (as in Korea, the Lebanon Landing, the Cuban Missile Crisis, and the Santo Domingo Affair), sometimes on a war basis and sometimes not, with the Congress both unable and unwilling to control effectively what should and should not be done once the events were fully in motion.

These observations are not meant to imply congressional weakness or presidential arbitrariness. It simply better served the national interests to keep the situation fluid. Indeed the situation of the 1960's was foreshadowed from earliest times by presidential decisions on at least 125 occasions to deploy U.S. armed forces into combat or danger of combat without asking Congress for a declaration of war. What was different in the 1960's was that sending the Marines into Cuba could have devastating, immediate, and virtually unlimited results compared to the 1920's and 1930's, and that the area to which we were now sending Marines was global in scope rather than restricted to the Caribbean area. The much more ambitious policy of the U.S. was coupled with its attendant dangers in a nuclear-armed, quick-reacting world and led to a severe case of Senate dissatisfaction for which no easy solution existed. In short, the Senate dilemma of the 1960's was no different *in principle* from earlier U.S. armed involvements in undeclared wars. But the dilemma was made more acute in a highly armed, fast-reacting world in which the U.S. was playing an extremely active part. These factors affected declared wars as well. Although the U.S. Congress might have chosen *not* to fight the War of 1812, or take part in World War I in 1917, even by 1941 Congress had been largely reduced to formalizing an actual state of affairs that could not be ignored.

Given these circumstances one might conclude that Congress had best leave these problems to the President. But, even if it wanted to, it could not—not alone for constitutional reasons but because any feeling of national unity would probably quickly evaporate. When the U.S. is engaged in a declared and acknowledged conflict, especially where it feels it has been the victim of attack, it is relatively easy to maintain national morale. In circumstances such as Viet-Nam, on the other hand, where public opinion is drastically split, a lack of congressional debate would soon reduce national morale to the vanishing point.

One cannot justifiably, in the light of these considerations, charge Congress with failure to discharge its duty if undeclared wars are sometimes fought by the U.S. Closer to the bone of truth would be to argue that the U.S. by the 1960's had been allowed to drift into questionable involvements without prior *effective* congressional debate. The essential difficulties implicit in a Viet-Nam War were fairly obvious before they were encountered in practice. (Most of those difficulties had been discussed as early as 1954 when the U.S. decided *not* to intervene at Dien Bien Phu.) They could largely have been anticipated—and certainly were by scholars. But in granting the President initial and rather unlimited discretion on the situation, Congress did not face up in its own debates to what could come of it. Consequently the public at large had little conception of what was implied by the actions taken.

In the Senate Foreign Relations Committee hearings on August 17, 1967, all of these issues stood starkly revealed.[3] Senator J. W. Fulbright admitted that Congress had made a serious mistake in using the broad language of the Gulf of Tonkin Resolution (August 7, 1964). The Resolution declared that "The United States is, therefore, prepared as the President determines to take all necessary action, including the use of armed forces, to assist any member or protocol state in the Southeast Asia collective defense treaty requesting assistance in defense of its freedom." The Senate (Fulbright said) intended this as a response to the North Viet-Nam PT boat attack on U.S. fleet units, but President Johnson had subsequently used it to send almost a half-million American troops to Viet-Nam.

Fulbright agreed with Under Secretary of State Nicholas deB. Katzen-

[3] Quotations are from excerpts in *The New York Times* (August 18, 1967), 14.

bach's argument that the President actually needed no congressional authority to answer the 1964 North Viet-Nam attack with force. Fulbright said: "I think in all fairness the circumstances were we were responding to an attack. As you have said, the President didn't need this authority to respond to an attack. And I agree with that. . . . But we did resolve, we did act and I have said many times I think wrongly, precipitously, without due consideration, to giving authority far beyond that particular attack. . . ."

The obvious question arises: Why did the Senate pass what was not needed? The answer is given in the same hearing and helps shed light on why the Senate committee was disgruntled.

Katzenbach: It seems to me that if your complaint is the drafting of the [Tonkin] Resolution of Congress it ill becomes. . . ."
Fulbright: That resolution was drafted by the Executive and sent up here. We didn't draft it, but we did . . . accept it.
Katzenbach: Mr. Chairman, it wasn't accepted without consideration.
Fulbright: Yes, it was largely without any consideration.[4]
Katzenbach: . . . the language of that resolution, Mr. Chairman, is a very broad language. . . . It was explained in the debate. You explained it, Mr. Chairman, as head of this committee.
Fulbright: But I misinterpreted it.
Katzenbach: You explained that bill and you made it clear as it could be what the Congress was committing itself to.
Fulbright: I not only didn't make it clear, obviously, it wasn't clear to me, because I did make statements that I thought this did not entail nor contemplate any change in the then existing policy, and of course there has been great change in it. It is the waging of war that really concerns us. . . .

The hearings moved to a still thornier point. Senator Gore, alluding to the commitment of combat troops in Viet-Nam, said that he regarded this "as one of the most tragic mistakes in American history. I did not intend to authorize it. Now, I think it is clear that Congress is in large part at fault in not being precise." He went on: "The President has now directed planes to bomb targets within seconds of the most populous nation on earth." Did Katzenbach think the President should "seek authorization of the Congress to undertake such provocation . . . ?" *Katzenbach:* "No." *Gore:* "Do you think the Tonkin Bay (*sic*) Resolution is sufficient?" Katzenbach responded that the authorization was "adequate" to deal with the situation as it existed. He went on: "In any event, when the Congress has authorized . . . the use of the armed forces . . . I do not believe that the Congress can then proceed . . . to tell the President what he shall bomb, what he shall not bomb, where

---

[4] The total time for committee and Senate floor consideration of the Gulf of Tonkin Resolution is estimated at only eight hours and 22 minutes.

he shall dispose his troops, where he shall not." Gore retorted that Katzenbach seemed to be saying that the resolution authorized a war with China. Katzenbach responded that the resolution "is quite precise in what is authorized. . . . Now in the course of that authorization, there can be risks. . . . Other people could be involved." Katzenbach was then asked whether the resolution authorized the bombing of Laos or China? Katzenbach took refuge from the line of questioning in verbiage about "a purely hypothetical question that it would be hard for me to see anybody could have contemplated and could have discussed under this situation." The senatorial response: "You say it would be difficult to interpret this resolution in the light of the hypothesis. It was equally difficult for the Congress. I doubt if any Congressman could foresee the bombing of targets within 10 miles of China. . . . It seems to me that the thrust of your testimony is that it is incumbent upon the Congress to consider in detail and precision the grant of authority involved in its action."

The hearings just detailed were technically over proposed Senate Resolution 151 which declared that "a national commitment by the United States to a foreign power necessarily and exclusively results from affirmative action taken by the Executive and Legislative branches of the United States Government through means of a treaty, convention or other legislative instrumentality specifically intended to give effect to such a commitment."[5] When asked the position of the Department of State on this resolution, Katzenbach had answered: "I could not support [it] because it seems to me that . . . it tries to do precisely what the Founding Fathers of this country declined to do in writing the Constitution," that it took a position "on matters that . . . have worked out well in terms of distribution of functions between the Executive branch and the Congress" and that it would erode the President's capacity for conducting foreign relations. (The Senate passed the resolution.)

That Katzenbach's position and the continuing escalation of the war did not satisfy important members of the Senate was obvious. Of the August 1967 American bombings within 10 miles of China, Senate Democratic leader Mike Mansfield said it was a "very dangerous extension of the war." Fulbright called it "dangerous and stupid," while Senator Charles H. Percy (R., Ill.) wondered aloud how the U.S. would react "if the Chinese bombed Mexico within 10 miles of the Rio Grande." Although Senator Ralph W. Yarborough (D., Tex.) had not previously been an administration critic, he said of hints and rumors about a possible invasion of North Viet-Nam: "This step is where I get off." Speaking specifically of Katzenbach's testimony, one of the committee members (unnamed) said: "This is the wildest testimony I ever heard. There is no limit to what he says the President could do. There is only one

5 *The New York Times*, Section 4 (August 20, 1967), 1.

thing to do—take it to the country."[6] Later, on a television program, Fulbright alluded to President Johnson's comment that the Senate had a "remedy" it could use (i.e., repeal the Gulf of Tonkin Resolution) and rejected that course as "a direct slap at a leader in time of war. It will not be done that way. The disillusionment, the dissent, that will be expressed in other less direct ways."[7] Fulbright cited the congressional uproar over the commitment potential in the administration's decision to dispatch three transport aircraft to the Congo (July 1967) and the subsequent administration curtailment of that action. In mid-September 1967, reflecting congressional revolt over the issue of separation of powers, the House voted 233 to 144 to repudiate an Executive Agreement to construct U.S. Navy minesweepers in Britain.

The debate just recorded illuminates two high points in a continuing controversy: the extent of proper congressional vs. executive power, and the role of Congress in debating and acceding to commitments. It is indeed a good question whether specific congressional powers (such as the declaration of war) can be as effectively exercised in the contemporary world as they were in past times. The key role of Congress in debating the general policy that should be pursued can hardly be over-emphasized. Real congressional power over foreign affairs lies in this realm,[8] and when it is not effectively exercised (as in this case), real problems are going to emerge as time goes on. Congress's role as a microcosm of informed public opinion is a very critical role, and it is one which has remained unchanged in principle since Washington's day. The greater sources of information and intelligence data available to the executive branch may induce Congress to yield to what purports to be more complete knowledge; but where and as Congress yields without a full and effective debate of the strategic policy alternatives, it fails in this crucial role. One must ask whether Congress is now so organized and conducted as to hold effective debates over critical national issues.

The Decline in the Congressional Role of Debate

THE storm in Congress which broke in 1967 had its origins in the Gulf of Tonkin Resolution of 1964 and is only a later manifestation of a general postwar decline in the effective exercise of debate in Congress as a means

6 *Ibid.*

7 *The New York Times* (August 21, 1967).

8 Robinson, *op. cit.*, p. 14:
. . . it is worth noting that quantitatively Congress initiates more foreign policy proposals than the executive. In the period 1949–58, 80 per cent of the Senate bills and resolutions originated with Senators and 20 per cent with the executive . . . yet none of these are the measures which command the greatest amount of time of the Committee [on Foreign Relations] or occupy the attention of the "attentive publics."

of illuminating the implications of foreign-policy decisions initiated by the executive. Beginning in the post-World War II period with congressional approval of the Truman Doctrine, it continued thereafter. One might argue that the Congress had backed Truman's actions for Greece and Turkey because it had specific aims in mind, which were successfully realized. As a consequence, Greece and Turkey were indeed effectively supported; communism lost its foothold in Greece, and Turkish determination to resist Soviet pressures was undergirded and reinforced—but the Truman Doctrine was not restricted to these specifics. It spoke of a struggle between "two ways of life." Truman had said (March 12, 1947): "The peoples of a number of countries of the world have recently had totalitarian regimes forced upon them against their will. . . ." The United States should "help free people to maintain their free institutions and their national integrity against aggressive movements that seek to impose upon them totalitarian regimes. This is no more than a frank recognition that totalitarian regimes imposed on free peoples by direct or indirect aggression, *undermine the foundations of international peace and hence the security of the United States.*" (Italics added.)

Did the Congress consider in 1947 how far this particular declaration (open-ended as it assuredly is) could ultimately take the United States? It would appear not. The primary congressional amendment to President Truman's plan of support was a proviso that under certain conditions the aid to Greece and Turkey would be terminated—particularly if the UN General Assembly or Security Council decided that the aid was no longer needed or desirable. Congress was not expressing concern over the aid program as such, by this amendment. It was seeking to deal with a main criticism advanced: that direct aid to Greece and Turkey "by-passed" the UN, which the United States had so recently pledged to support.

The congressional role in the debate over the Truman Doctrine was not a failure from our point of view because it failed to negate Truman's plans. Any realistic assessment of the national interests should have led to exactly the specific aid action authorized. The failure lay in the tacit acceptance of the more grandiose future strategic implications of the Truman Doctrine without an adequate exploration of the dangers of open-ended, wholesale commitments in the abstract. For by 1965 that road led straight to Viet-Nam.

The congressional failure was not unique; at the time, Congress was not alone in not comprehending the dangers of foreign-policy formulations of this kind. In American opinion-making circles generally there was insufficient appreciation of the distinction. George Kennan's famous article in *Foreign Affairs* on containment also was a highly open-ended advocacy of strategic policy that was accepted widely, without thorough debate. (Years later, when ex-Secretary of State Acheson fell out with

Kennan's proposals for disengagement, Acheson was to argue that Kennan had abandoned containment, whereas Kennan argued that containment led logically—if and as successful—to disengagement. Whatever the merits of their arguments, both obviously thought their initial agreement was much greater than proved true.)

The fact that Congress at the time of the Truman Doctrine was dominated by a Republican majority also played a part. As with the Marshall Plan, which was discussed and debated in Congress just after the Truman Doctrine, the acceptance of these measures by the influential Republican Senator Arthur H. Vandenberg played an important part in obtaining congressional approval. Republican acceptance of these Democratic proposals was hailed at the time as effective "bipartisanship" in the field of foreign affairs. No one can reasonably argue that the Republicans should have frivolously opposed measures that obviously contributed to the national interests of the United States. The Congress on both sides of the political spectrum was undoubtedly reflecting "informed opinion." Yet there was a failure. Bipartisanship came to be so extolled as to seem desirable in its own right. It became risky politically to argue the pros and cons of the whole policy. Bipartisanship tended to put fairly narrow parameters around the debate. It removed much of the element of an organized, skeptical examination of alternatives that a "loyal opposition" normally supplies. Indeed once the Cold War became more frigid (as it soon did with the Soviet blockade of Berlin in 1948), it became hardly possible politically to go back to the strategic policy implications of the Truman Doctrine and hold the debate that should really have been held then.

As it turned out the lost chance remained lost for a very long time. Event succeeded event, and the air of sustained crisis continued. Moreover, until 1950 and the outbreak of the Korean War, the dominant issues in foreign policy were Europe-centered. They were also issues on which the nation and the Congress substantially agreed with the President's policy. For example, Congress played no important overt role in the decision to institute an airlift to supply blockaded Berlin, but there is no real question that it would have given full support. It was not asked perhaps because this was so obviously true. When the lessons of the Berlin blockade were assessed, they led logically to establishing NATO to provide more organized measures for collective defense of Western Europe. The Vandenberg Resolution (1948) provided congressional approval of the concept that in turn led to NATO and was adopted by the House and then the Senate (64 to four). The debate in the Senate took place during one afternoon and aroused little interest or controversy.[9] In one sense the Resolution led to a revolutionary

[9] Robinson, *op. cit.*, p. 45. See also Stephen K. Bailey and Howard D. Samuel, *Congress at Work* (New York: Holt, 1952), pp. 383–87.

departure in the long-established policy of the U.S. to refrain from alliances, which in another sense was already implicit in the Truman Doctrine decision.

Throughout this discussion we have been speaking principally of the role of congressional debate in opening up issues. As indicated here and in Chapter 5 by material quoted from congressional hearings, much comes to light through these channels. If one adds the formidable amounts of liaison contact between the executive and the leaders of Congress, one does not paint a picture of lack of consultation or lack of congressional discussion or influence with the executive. The point is a narrower one, but important, and it rests on a value judgment: that as far as national morale is concerned, the most important effect Congress has on foreign policy issues is through its debates in hearings and in plenary sessions. The truth seems to be that Congress never debated in either forum the full strategic implications of where the Truman Doctrine could *eventually* lead in global terms, because the first Europe-oriented steps were in any event highly acceptable in principle and proved on the whole highly successful in practice. The first full realization of this "sin of omission" did not really begin to dawn upon the Senate until the Fulbright-Katzenbach hearings.

Besides a general public approval of the main lines of American foreign policy in the 1950's in Europe, and the blossoming of bipartisanship, a third factor inhibited effective congressional debate in these years. Coincident with the shift of American interest to Asian affairs after the Korean War began, the "McCarthy era" commenced. This strange phenomenon of a Senator who rode roughshod and so long unscathed over fundamental American principles of political decency has much to tell us of the unreal atmosphere of public life in the United States between 1950 and 1953. It is highly instructive that he rose to great power at exactly the time of the first real crisis in public opinion over postwar foreign policy. If the points made above are accepted, one important reason for the failure to debate fully the implications of the Truman Doctrine is that there was general acceptance of the actual policy toward Europe which the Doctrine implied. Once the controversy over involvement shifted strongly to Asia, and especially once American blood began to be shed there, the unanimity began to evaporate. Yet no effective debates in Congress over strategic alternatives marked this change. Why not?

What the Truman Doctrine intended to convey was that the U.S. had embarked on a policy of containing communism in the person of the Soviet Union. Since communism in the late 1940's appeared to be fairly synonymous with the Soviet Union (if one discounts Titoism), and since there was agreement on containing Russia, it did not at the time seem important to most people that communism be distinguished from Soviet actions. When the Korean War broke out, it was at once assumed that the Soviet Union was the directing force behind the Korean aggression. This "second front" had to be met, particularly because the overt nature of the aggression in effect openly challenged a crucial tenet of American policy. Initially there was fairly unanimous support of this commitment, but when the Chinese entered it and the war continued on without "victory," public dissension increased. General Mac-Arthur began to advocate forceful sea and air measures against Communist China. Such action, while "anti-Communist," would obviously have entailed adding a new major enemy to the one already being contained by popular consent.

Later we shall examine the political-psychological dimensions of the general public reaction of the American people to the Korean War and other postwar crises. Here we are concerned with the narrower point of the congressional role. Congress as a whole was not consulted (although particular leaders discussed the initial Korean War commitment with the President in the White House). Most members of Congress read about the early decisions (which, of course, had to be taken in a hurry) in the newspapers. Yet there is little doubt that Congress would have endorsed the action. In the sequel, as dissension arose, the reaction of Congress to the Viet-Nam War was foreshadowed. There was understandable reluctance to disapprove formally of what was being done. There was also a fluid situation for important parts of the time, so that it was difficult to debate the changing conditions. Once stalemate set in, the alternatives again seemed blurred except for the extreme courses of assaulting China proper or simply withdrawing outright. In response to the prolonged negotiation phase of the Korean War—a period of great frustration—the Congress, for a number of reasons, again did not debate the issues effectively.

Important among the reasons was that "communism," which already had played some role in the elections of 1948, became a primary issue in the elections of 1950, 1952, and 1954. The famous "Hiss case" and the arrest and execution of the Rosenbergs dominated this period, as did McCarthy's far-ranging witch-hunt. Cutting across all this was the disagreement over previous policy toward China. The question by now was being put, with serious political implications, as to whether the Democrats had "lost" China to communism by 1949–1950 as a result of foreign-policy error and/or subversion and treason in high places. With characteristic unrestraint McCarthy charged the Democratic Party with "twenty years of treason." Eisenhower's election in 1952 did not end this outcry. Eisenhower no doubt in part was elected precisely because of it. When President Eisenhower assumed office he did not move against McCarthy, even despite the fact that McCarthy had smeared the reputation of General George C. Marshall, for whom Eisenhower

and most of the American people had great respect. Only the Senate—
and then very late—ever took action against McCarthy's excesses.

In this period, the welter of charges and countercharges over China
and the drastic probes of the executive branch (which McCarthy's committee spearheaded with all their interacting and cumulative effects)
paralyzed important parts of even routine governmental functioning.
Although extreme statements were made more by Republicans than
Democrats, the fact was that the differences of opinion were many
shaded and virtually defied party labels. In this atmosphere, useful
debate was simply not possible and did not occur.

Later, after the Korean War, the meeting at the summit of Eisenhower
and Bulganin-Khrushchev (1955) restored some calm—at least outwardly—in international and national affairs. When the next great crises
simultaneously occurred in 1956 over the Hungarian revolt and the
Anglo-French-Israeli war with Egypt, the administration's decision not
to intervene against the Soviets in Europe and to "pull the plug" on
England and France produced surprisingly little debate—perhaps because congressional opinion generally was on the side of these decisions.
The Eisenhower Doctrine, proposing aid to any Middle East state that
requested it when threatened from without or within by communism,
again was not made an occasion for any sustained and effective congressional debate. This Doctrine's first and only use, in Lebanon (1958), was
generally approved. By 1959–1961, with the Berlin Crisis again heating
up, the response of Congress to this familiar issue ran a familiar course:
We would not yield to threats. Only in the wake of the abortive Bay
of Pigs episode, which marred President Kennedy's first months in
office, was there real debate in the Senate, a phenomenon to be repeated in the Santo Domingo episode under President Johnson. We
have already mentioned in detail the Gulf of Tonkin Resolution and its
aftermath.

What does this survey tell us? As might be expected, it shows a
Congress that mirrored the views of the American people as a whole,
but also a Congress that over most of these years offered little effective
consideration of strategic alternatives. Perhaps the most damaging part
of the record is the virtual lack of any thorough consideration of the
merits or lack of merits of the policy of refusing to recognize Communist
China or seat her in the UN. These policies were followed by both
Democratic and Republican administrations and therefore never were
debated along party lines. Because they contained politically explosive
issues, these policies were never debated effectively by Congress on
nonparty lines. Yet if Congress does not do this job, where is it to be
done and what role can Congress really hope to play in foreign affairs?
And if the legacy of accumulated issues is allowed to grow unchecked
for too long, at what point does the pattern become irreversible?

Perhaps in the end one must conclude that it is unreasonable to demand that Congress give clear debate to alternatives when these alternatives are also not being given sufficiently clear debate in other circles outside Congress. It is certainly true that responsible discussion of these issues by informed persons outside Congress (especially the intellectuals) exceeded what Congress did. But in fairness we must note that in much of the postwar period a great deal of intellectual energy on foreign affairs went into the discussion of models, abstractions, deterrence theory, and the like—for a net loss (whatever the other gains) to the thorough discussion of policy *per se*.[10]

The President's Role

M UCH in the foregoing chapters has directly or indirectly sketched out the President's role in making foreign policy. We have seen the general constraints he confronts, the coordination problems he must solve, the political system in which he must operate, and the role of Congress as it reacts to his initiatives or lack of initiatives. Since he is in control (if anyone is), his role is ultimately crucial. How does he try to fill it?

The answer—even if confined only to the post-Pearl Harbor presidents—varies considerably. Truman, as he approached the end of his tenure in office, and thought about how Eisenhower would probably handle things, said: "He'll sit here and he'll say, 'Do this! Do that!' And nothing will happen. Poor Ike—it won't be a bit like the Army."[11] Truman's remark stemmed from a lifelong experience with American politics, which had taught him the inexpediency of trying to run things primarily through executive fiat. Truman knew how little can be accomplished, even with all the enormous power of the presidency, without carrying along substantial agreement in the Congress—let alone within the executive branch, which theoretically is responsive to the every wish of the President. Truman was well aware of the enormous practical limitations imposed on the President's effectiveness merely by the difficulties implicit in communicating effectively with a large bureaucracy. By the time his decisions were being implemented by remote control in the second, third, and fourth bureaucratic layers beneath him, he knew that they often changed appreciably—even unwittingly. He knew that those charged with carrying out policies that they did not personally agree with and in the making of which they had not participated were uncertain instruments to rely on, if only because they had not really comprehended the "why" of what was being done.

[10] For example, the program of the annual meeting of the American Political Science Association in 1967—at the height of public arousal over Viet-Nam—had no session devoted to the question as such at all.

[11] Richard E. Neustadt, *Presidential Power* (New York: Wiley, 1960), p. 9.

Where Truman erred was in assuming that Eisenhower's military experience had poorly equipped him for understanding these particular principles, for any successful general has had to deal with exactly these same problems in a somewhat different setting. Most generals arrive at the point of saying "Do this!" after a long staff processing of alternatives and plans for implementing them. They rarely issue important orders after mere inward contemplation and to a staff which is caught completely by surprise, never having thought of such a course of action. More importantly, what was different in Truman's background and experience, as compared to Eisenhower's, was the kind of problems they were each used to solving, the different content of those problems, and the different interested constituencies which had to be considered.

Even if one compares Kennedy with Truman or Johnson, although all three had been Senators, their personality differences were quite pronounced, and their way of making decisions equally varied. Or compare F. D. Roosevelt with Johnson: although both were noted for political skill, their methods were greatly contrasting. F. D. Roosevelt chose to break loose new ideas from the bureaucratic glacier by establishing competing organizations, a method certainly at the opposite extreme from Eisenhower's proliferation of coordinating staffs and committees encouraged to arrive at agreed positions to be presented to the President. Kennedy chose to wipe out much of the Eisenhower coordinating superstructure and communicate directly to a great degree with action officers. Johnson, while communicating directly, too, established new coordinating devices such as the SIG.

What most usefully should be kept in mind about the Presidency as an institution (with resultant effects on foreign policy) is that each President comes into the White House confronted with three interlocking circumstances growing out of the constraints listed in Chapter 4. *First*, he is already committed by his predecessors to certain courses of action. From a commitment point of view he does not have a clear slate. He may personally believe that it was unwise to associate U.S. prestige so directly with Chiang Kai-shek, or with the defense of Quemoy and Matsu (directly adjacent to the Communist Chinese mainland), but he cannot easily turn away from such commitments or alter them. It is not just that he may arouse a storm of protest from a "China Lobby" or from right-wing groups. Sudden or drastic change is simply too dangerous and unsettling in too many quarters around the world. Almost invariably, because of these constraints, policy alterations are taken more in the form of small course alterations, like a sailboat tacking. The whole process is replete with "trial balloons"—normally speeches delivered somewhere under the top level leadership to "test the wind." As one illustration (and one which revealed that the course proposed was acceptable) we can cite former Under Secretary of State Dean

Acheson's first public proposal of what came to be known later as the "Marshall Plan." Acheson's speech came on May 8, 1947, although today most people associate the proposal with Secretary Marshall's speech (June 5, 1947).

Again, in 1963, when the Kennedy Administration concluded that the time had come to express a change of policy toward Communist China, it was the Assistant Secretary for Far Eastern Affairs, Roger Hilsman, who was chosen. Hilsman's speech, which accepted the reality of Communist China's continued existence, marked the first fresh approach on this problem since Dulles had spoken (1957) of the Communist regime as a "passing and not a perpetual phase"! (Dulles had concluded his speech: "We owe it to ourselves, our allies and the Chinese people to do all that we can to contribute to that passing.") Reaction to the fresh approach (1963), which did not signal friendly relations between the U.S. and China, but at least accepted the premise that Communist China would not wither away in the glare of American displeasure, indicated public acceptance of a change.[12] But the change was still a very small alteration. Quite in contrast in the reaction it aroused is President Roosevelt's "quarantine the aggressors" speech cited in an earlier chapter.

Second circumstance. The President is confronted with a bureaucracy, which in large part has permanent tenure. The responsiveness and dedication to duty of these permanent officials will have important effects upon how successfully he is able to carry out his programs. Presidential appointments begin at the Cabinet level and extend basically to the Assistant Secretary level. Below this level *legal* responsibility and authority to make policy ends. That is, the lowest policy-making official is normally an Assistant Secretary, although in practice this may turn out for a number of reasons to be rather far from the truth.

Complementary in its effects is the fact that Congress is not under the President's direct control. Congress may even be under the rule of the opposition party. The point here is that large parts of the institutional apparatus must be accepted by the President and somehow effectively utilized—for he has no power to change these facets.

Third circumstance. Quite in contrast to the second circumstance is the fact that each President has to provide and appoint his own White House staff and policy-making officials. Within the very limited time after election and before assuming office (a period today much shorter than before the Lame Duck Amendment did away with March inaugurals), he must select and appoint an enormous number of persons whose abilities in the end will determine his success. In recent times

[12] For details see Roger Hilsman, *To Move A Nation* (Garden City, New York: Doubleday, 1967), pp. 350–357.

some Presidents have organized veritable talent-scouting operations to fill this need. Kennedy in this way appointed as his leading Cabinet officials two individuals whom he had either not previously known or had known only casually: Robert S. McNamara and Dean Rusk. On the other hand, Kennedy managed to bring into the White House some able assistants (such as Theodore C. Sorensen) who had already worked with him closely for many years. No man before becoming President has among his close associates or personal staff anything like the numbers and range of talents that a President needs merely to fill the ranks of his Special Assistants, let alone all the other posts. President Nixon, for example, chose Henry A. Kissinger to handle White House national security affairs, although Kissinger was previously Nelson Rockefeller's adviser.

Even if it were the fact (which it will not be) that the President is personally well acquainted with each of the policy officials he appoints, and they with each other, it still remains true that each and every one of them would be assuming a new job, and virtually simultaneously. The whole "high command" will be new. Even if they have served previously in closely related jobs, the new job will still be different. They will all have to learn to work well with all the others even as they begin to cope as individuals with their new jobs. This is where the point of greatest strain in the system occurs. Some fall by the wayside and are replaced; others are shifted. But all must learn on the job and find ways to be effective with one another. A little reflection will indicate how difficult this all is, and how unusual. In most institutional settings the new head rises from the ranks; or, if he is brought from the outside into the new company, factory, church, or university, the greater part of the policy apparatus remains unchanged and only the very top is new. But Presidents—despite the example of the 1968 election—only occasionally serve terms as Vice-Presidents (and the duties of that position are not automatically helpful in learning the next rung up), and when the President moves in he brings with him not dozens, but hundreds of brand-new officials.

These three interlocking circumstances combine to limit what a President can normally hope to accomplish in the first part of his first term. All three circumstances have a negative effect on substantive change, however much different the spirit or image the new Presidency projects. In Roosevelt's first term the first months saw enormous activity sparked by the President. But that was at a time of national crisis when the normal rulebook is thrown away. Similarly, when Truman suddenly became President, we were at war; he had much more freedom of action than he otherwise would have. Eisenhower did not initially attempt to push vigorously for policies, especially as he began office with a much more passive concept of the Presidency than we think of as usual today.

Kennedy's initial months in office were marred by the Bay of Pigs—an affair which retarded his ability to push his own programs. Johnson came into office at a tragic moment and succeeded far above the norm in imparting early momentum to policy, but he could count upon an emotional desire in the Congress to pass Kennedy legislation, as an act of collective contrition. Nixon's experience in his first year was again nearer the norm as he painfully and slowly moved to disengage in Viet-Nam.

None of this should be construed to mean that the President does not possess and exercise very large powers in foreign affairs. We know that he does, and we know (and have seen) that Congress in the late 1960's was concerned over the opposite point. These considerations are introduced to give a more balanced picture. Although the Congress may feel that the President is more free than he should be, the President almost invariably feels that his scope for innovation is extremely limited.

The conflict implicit in these two points of view was limited under Truman because his activist policy and the commitments he made had general approval—at least vis-à-vis Europe and at least until the events which marked the second phase of the Korean War. Under President Eisenhower the conflict was not as marked as it later became, because Eisenhower generally restricted himself in foreign policy to avoiding new substantive (as opposed to *declaratory*) commitments.

Consider that although Dulles as Secretary of State "fathered" SEATO, Eisenhower as President carefully avoided committing ground troops and armed forces in Viet-Nam. Although Chiang Kai-shek was "unleashed" to attack the mainland, he was also given to understand that we would back no such move. Although Dulles spoke of "massive retaliation," the U.S. actually intervened with military forces abroad much less than in later administrations—the most significant of these occasions being the low-risk landing in Lebanon. Even Eisenhower's "doctrine" lay virtually in limbo since most Middle Eastern states had no desire whatsoever for inviting U.S. troops. Dulles spoke "liberation," but Eisenhower carefully refrained from intervening in the Hungarian uprising of 1956. The picture is clear.

Later under Kennedy and (especially) Johnson, new commitments *were* made, new actions authorized. And these, as we have seen, led ultimately to the controversy over the Viet-Nam War and the global commitments of U.S. foreign policy in the late 1960's.

An Assessment

DEAN Acheson liked to relay a story told by Chief Justice Taft. Taft had just had a talk with an eminent man about the "machinery" of government (to which we have now devoted several chapters). "And you know," said Taft with wonder in his voice, "he really does believe it *is* machinery."[13]

The reader of these pages will know that the "machinery of government" is *not* machinery but people organized within an institutional and political setting. Consequently the "machine" will operate quite differently under the influence of different persons. At the same time it is important not to go to the other extreme and conclude that the institutional framework is as changeable as the personalities of the people who man it. Instrumentalities such as the Policy Planning Council of the State Department and the National Security Council operate differently under an Eisenhower or a Kennedy. Their directors make a deliberate and conscious effort to do so. At the same time the instrumentality still continues to perform the same central *function,* even if in a different manner. Under one President the NSC may have policy more or less neatly tabulated in a series of agreed "solutions" to various "contingencies," and under another operate on a more free-wheeling basis. Yet it still remains the sounding board and major institutionalized device to render the President effective advice from all sources within the government that should be heard on national security questions. Whom the President chooses to invite to the meetings (beyond the statutory membership) will determine what he hears there. How the President supplements this advice from other sources, who the "inner group" of advisers will be, and how the President assures himself that he has heard all he needs to hear will vary greatly with the personality of each Chief Executive. Somehow he must learn to adapt these instruments successfully to his own way of doing business.

Our survey of the foreign policy process indicates that there has been vast improvement in the last decades in coordinating devices that permit intelligent national security decisions and in the professionalization of career personnel involved. Accordingly, the advice available to the President has improved in quantity and quality. These improvements do not guarantee the President balanced advice, but it makes it much more accessible. At the same time that the United States has involved itself in unprecedented global decisions, the stakes have risen and we have seen a growing uneasiness in Congress as to where a reasonable halfway house between overcommitment and undercommitment lies. There is a new (although perhaps too long delayed) congressional willingness to reassert Congress's traditional and essential role as forum for the debate over the wisdom of presidential and executive branch initiatives. In this role, when it is properly discharged, Congress leads national opinion to an informed understanding of alternatives. That Congress in the last decades did not always perform that role

[13] Related in Hilsman, *op. cit.,* p. 17.

effectively is true. But at the same time it is equally true that national opinion has only sluggishly reacted to a rapidly changed U.S. national security position. If Congress can be blamed for not leading the way better and more persistently, the blame can be charged to their account only part way. Any honest survey of the reactions of the American people to the successive crises in foreign policy that typified the post-1945 era must equally assert that the adjustment in popular understanding was frequently slow, imprecise, and partial. America's postwar preference for questionable and over-simple guiding rules to foreign policy was, as already noted in earlier chapters, certainly not confined to Congress, and the American political process does not tend to push consideration of strategic policy alternatives to the fore. Perhaps Congress should have understood the problems more quickly and led the discussion better, but it is hard to do this if the people themselves are not quite aware of the need for a more critical look at what is being done. Congress is, as we have taken pains to point out, a fairly accurate mirror of "informed" American opinion.

The most useful way to gain an appreciation of the American peoples' reaction to the foreign policy problem is to survey the major critical decisions and responses of the U.S. in these postwar years, attempting at each point to analyze the psychological effects on the American people *at the time*. It would be a distortion of important proportions if we were to look back on that past and judge it merely through our present perspectives.

We turn therefore in Part Three to foreign policy in operation, looking at the record of what occurred and its meaning to the American people. To provide a better insight into our reactions in the past two decades or more, we shall first look at the formative years in the American Republic's experience and the events leading to World War II. The greater part of Part Three will then analyze our reaction to successive "shocks" as we dealt with post-1945 affairs. In Part Four we shall attempt an analysis of the major problems this record reveals.

Foreign Policy in Operation

PART THREE

Foreign Policy in Operation

CHAPTER 8

The Formative Years

AMERICANS are abstractly aware that the present has long roots in the past. Yet in practice we often approach problems in foreign policy as though this were not so. We are impatient to "get on with it."

Indeed, the process of looking back at the record of American foreign policy needs to be highly selective. Nor will a bare chronicle of important events do. Even adding a policy analysis to observation of bare historical data is not enough, unless that analysis serves also to illuminate the emotional and psychological dimensions of the major events.

Ideally, in examining the record, we are engaged in a three-sided investigation: the events themselves, the strategic policy alternatives they represented, and the psychological perspectives within which those alternatives were judged. To the extent that we can accomplish this task we not only avoid discussing the period since 1945 as though it had no prologue. We are also able to see how we progressively made an adjustment in outlook to our changing circumstances.

Three Long-Range Trends

LOOKING back over the record of the first hundred and ten years of American foreign policy, we can see quite clearly three long-range trends or themes. First, there was the drive for continental supremacy, a drive which involved enlarging the American domain and reducing or liquidating European great power holdings in what is now the continental limits of the United States. Second, there was the closely related concern for hemispheric security symbolized by the Monroe Doctrine—a concern for limiting or liquidating European great power interests in the New World (especially north of the Brazilian "bulge"). Third, there was the studied avoidance of *substantive* commitments in either Europe or Asia (at least to the time of the Spanish-American War).

These three themes form clearly discernible patterns in our overall policy when looked at through the perspective of today. But we must keep in mind that what is clear today in hindsight was not always clear at the time. Even where the strategic objectives were understood and agreed, it was not always obvious at the time what tactical sequence of actions would best achieve them. Nor did the U.S. have more than a limited capability for controlling the course of events.

The basic clues to American success, despite the great gap between U.S. desires and U.S. power, and the overriding threat to U.S. interests which the combined strength of Spain, France, and Britain would have represented, were presented in Chapter 2. Distance and the balance of power both gave powerful assists to American hopes and ambitions. Despite the initial unfavorable facts that Britain (who held Canada and the West Indies), France (who held the Louisiana Territory and the West Indies), and Spain (who held Florida and Latin America) all controlled important territories bordering on the U.S., the American frontiers were successfully expanded and the European presence drastically reduced. In the process the United States actually fought limited wars with all three powers at one point or another: the undeclared war at sea with France between 1798 and 1800 (which, as a by-product, terminated the Franco-American alliance), the War of 1812 with Britain, and the simultaneous struggle with Spain over West Florida. Yet American judgment also played a significant part in the gains made. Accompanying these actions in the early period was a running debate in the U.S. over whose side to support—particularly whether to side with Britain or France. Practicality and sentiment often competed, but practicality won out. Despite widespread anti-British feeling, for example, Jefferson wrote to Robert R. Livingston, the American Minister at Paris: "The day that France takes New Orleans . . . we must marry ourselves to the British fleet and nation" —a necessity soon removed by the French sale of Louisiana.

What the record tells us above all in these initial decades is that we made no fatal mistakes, we profited by our opportunities, we were frequently at odds with ourselves as to the best course to pursue, and we paid inadequate attention to providing military power commensurate to our problems. That, on balance, we did well can be in part laid to the door of luck, in part to our willingness to experiment and change course, and in part to our seizing sometimes unexpected opportunities. Whatever the bitterness or divisions in public sentiment, no one was arguing that the European presence in the new world should be *increased*. This strategic objective of U.S. policy was not in dispute.

When Russia in 1821 extended its claims into the Oregon country, closing the Bering Strait to foreign commercial fishing, Secretary of State Adams informed her "that we should contest the right of Russia to *any* territorial establishment on this continent, and that we should assume distinctly the principle that the American continents are no longer subjects for *any* new European colonial establishments." In this pronouncement was not only the genesis of the Monroe Doctrine of 1823 but the authentic voice of perceived American interests speaking. As the capstone to three other events it spoke of a new American confidence, for it followed the Rush-Bagot Agreement (1817) (neutralizing the Great Lakes), the Convention (1818) between Britain and the U.S. (settling the disputed northwest boundary along the 49th parallel from the Lake of the Woods to the crest of the Rocky Mountains), and the Adams-Onis Treaty (1819) (by which Spain gave up all claims to West Florida, ceded East Florida, and set the western frontiers of the Louisiana Purchase from the Sabine River up through the Red and Arkansas Rivers to the 42nd parallel and then due west to the Pacific—thus ending Spanish claims to the Pacific Northwest). Beginning in 1822, the U.S. progressively extended recognition to the new Latin American states, who had successfully fought Spain for independence.

In 1823, with France's invasion of Spain to restore the Spanish king's powers, it was widely rumored that the next development would be a Franco-Spanish expeditionary force to Latin America.

British policy remained a vital consideration, then and later. The British, while not sympathetic to Latin revolt, wanted the colonies to remain free so that British commerce could exploit their markets. Consequently Britain opposed any restoration of Spanish rule, whether by Spain or France. When George Canning, British Foreign Secretary, proposed joint action with the U.S., Secretary of State Adams advised: "It would be more candid, as well as more dignified, to avow our principles explicitly to Russia and France, than to come in as a cock-boat in the wake of the British man-of-war." This argument prevailed; President Monroe proclaimed the Doctrine in his annual message in December 1823. Substantially embodying Adams' declaration to Russia, it added that the U.S. would not interfere with *existing* European colonies in the Western Hemisphere or become involved in Europe's affairs in Europe.

Thus by 1823, all three main themes of the formative years had made their appearance: continental supremacy, hemispheric security, and avoidance of substantive commitments in Europe and Asia. Great Britain, potentially America's most important foe, had actually, for her own reasons, acted in a way favorable to American vital interests, thus greatly improving relations.

Many issues involving British interests were to arise in the next decades: over Oregon and Texas[1] in the 1840's, over Britain's flirtation

---

[1] President Polk was speaking to the British attitude over the Texas issue when, in his annual message to Congress in December 1845, he said bluntly: "We can never consent that European powers shall interfere to prevent such a union because it might disturb the 'balance of power' which they may desire to maintain upon this continent." (Here we see another root of American distaste for the balance of power.)

with the Confederacy during the American Civil War. Despite repeated tensions and many critical issues, a third Anglo-American war was averted. Much of the credit for this accomplishment should be assigned to Britain's careful diplomacy, although where Britain's interests were truly at stake the U.S. was careful not to show itself uncompromising.

By the late 1860's, the U.S. had passed an important watershed in its capabilities. It was no longer vulnerable militarily within its own frontiers; and it had the national power that would enable it to play a larger world role—if it chose.

An Empire in the Pacific

THE signs of a new and large world role were soon forthcoming, although the dimensions of that new role (and its implications) only began to be clear at the turn of the century.

In the 1870's and 1880's the U.S. tentatively reached out into the Pacific and took a distinctly larger interest in Latin American affairs. By treaty with Hawaii in 1875, Hawaii promised not to cede territory to any third power, and in 1878 the Senate approved a treaty with Samoa giving the U.S. nonexclusive rights to a naval station at Pago Pago. Secretary of State Blaine tried but failed to bring an end to the War of the Pacific (Chile versus Bolivia and Peru) and other quarrels in Central America. In 1885, the U.S. even attended the Congo Conference in Berlin, although it did not ratify the general act. In 1887, the exclusive right to a naval base at Pearl Harbor was incorporated into a new agreement with Hawaii; and in 1889, the U.S. attended a new Berlin Conference which placed Samoa under the joint protectorate of the U.S., Great Britain, and Germany. In 1889–1890, with Blaine once again Secretary of State, the First International American Conference met in Washington. Although it did not establish the arbitration procedures Blaine sought, it did set up what became the Pan-American Union—the first permanent organ in the Inter-American system.

Symbolic of America's growing role was the Senate's confirmation of an Ambassador to Great Britain (1893). Ambassador Bayard thus became the first American emissary to hold that rank. Unquestionably, U.S. relations with Great Britain continued to be the persistent important issue in American foreign policy. Shortly after Bayard was sent, new troubles arose over the Venezuelan boundary dispute (the frontier with British Guiana). President Cleveland took a strong stand for arbitration and Secretary of State Olney sent his famous note. Olney set forth flatly the proposition: "Today the United States is practically sovereign on this continent, and its fiat is law upon the subjects to which it confines its interposition. Why? . . . It is because, in addition to all other grounds, its infinite resources combined with its isolated position render it master of the situation and practically invulnerable as against any or all other powers."

To some extent Olney spoke no more than the truth. If the American Civil War was a domestic disaster, with Americans killing Americans, from an international relations prestige viewpoint it was a triumph. No European power could doubt the enormous military force which the U.S. could place behind its goals if it chose. That the great military-technological revolution in warfare between 1855 and 1905, which saw modern industrial advances incorporated into weaponry, also permitted European military power to be projected at great distances counted relatively little in the face of a lack of coordinated European will to try. By the time of the Venezuelan dispute the attention of Europe's powers was focused elsewhere—either in gaining empire in Africa and Asia or watching each other suspiciously nearer at home. Olney judged correctly that British troubles in Africa and elsewhere would cause her to be cautious in the Americas. After President Cleveland (December 1895) laid the issue before Congress and proposed to create an international arbitral commission whether Britain agreed or not, using force if necessary to see the award implemented, tensions were high. Shortly afterward Kaiser Wilhelm publicly congratulated the Boers for their resistance to British pressures, and late in the same month the British Colonial Secretary said publicly that a new Anglo-American war "would be an absurdity as well as a crime . . ." Britain permitted the arbitration to proceed (and gained most of its claims as a result!).

By 1896 American attention was also being increasingly focused on the ruthless Spanish suppression of the Cuban insurrection. The publication in the *New York Journal* of a private (and stolen) letter by the Spanish Minister to the U.S., characterizing President McKinley as "weak and a bidder for the admiration of the crowd," further deteriorated relations. When the U.S.S. *Maine,* sent to Havana supposedly to protect American lives and property, was sunk by a submarine mine in February 1898, with a loss of 260 lives, popular sentiment erupted with the slogan, "Remember the *Maine!*" McKinley, at first against war, asked Congress on April 11 for U.S. "forcible intervention."

The Spanish-American War's major events are well known, including the destruction of the Spanish fleets in Manila and off Cuba, and the famous assault up San Juan hill by Col. Theodore Roosevelt's "Rough Riders." Less well known is the status of the military forces of the U.S. at its outbreak. The U.S. Navy's total personnel strength of about 26,000 officers and men was almost as large as the U.S. Army of 30,000. While the Navy's readiness was high (as its victories soon showed, for total casualties in *both* battles were one killed and nine wounded), the Army had been allowed to fall into neglect. America's ability to muster large forces quickly, already demonstrated in the Civil War, was again dramatically shown. Despite the shortness of the war some 274,000 were put into army uniforms before demobilization was completed. Of these 5,462 died from all causes including disease, but only 379 in battle.

Out of the Spanish-American War came America's empire and the true beginning of a global U.S. involvement. Not only were Puerto Rico and Guam acquired, but also the Philippines (for $20 million). Hawaii was annexed as a territory and Wake Island taken in 1900. Cuba was to be independent.

The U.S., and especially the American President, did not move to such decisions overnight. Part of McKinley's dilemma was that he did not want to see these areas pass into *other* hands once the weak Spanish rule ended. It was the Monroe Doctrine principle by extension, as it were. McKinley later told a group of fellow Methodists:

The truth is I didn't want the Philippines and when they came to us as a gift from the gods, I did not know what to do about them. . . . I sought counsel from all sides—Democrats as well as Republicans—but got little help. I thought first we would take only Manila; then Luzon; then other islands, perhaps, also. I walked the floor of the White House night after night until midnight; and I am not ashamed to tell you, gentlemen, that I went down on my knees and prayed Almighty God for light and guidance more than one night.

Then, finally, McKinley saw what had to be done.

And one night late it came to me this way—I don't know how it was, but it came: (1) that we could not give them back to Spain—that would be cowardly and dishonorable;[2] (2) that we could not turn them over to France or Germany—our commercial rivals in the Orient—that would be bad business and discreditable; (3) that we could not leave them to themselves—they were unfit for self-government—and they would soon have anarchy and misrule over there worse than Spain's was; and (4) that there was nothing left for us to do but to take them all, and to educate the Filipinos, and uplift and civilize and Christianize them, and by God's grace do the very best we could by them, as our fellow-men for whom Christ also died. And then I went to bed, and went to sleep and slept soundly.[3]

That the U.S. subsequently had to use armed forces of 70,000 to suppress Filipino resistance to the U.S. showed that there was more in the situation than McKinley allowed for. And yet his dilemma was very real. Seven decades later the American people were still trying to decide upon a feasible line of military demarcation for U.S. forces in the Pacific.

[2] That is, it would betray the Filipinos who had risen against Spain there.
[3] *Christian Advocate* (New York), January 22, 1903.

In any event, the die was cast. America's career as a Pacific power was under way.

Toward Increasing Global Awareness (1899–1917)

THE decision to take the Philippines is the true line of demarcation between a continentally-limited American foreign policy and one of worldwide dimensions. Until then our tentative excursions and involvements in Pacific affairs were capable of being liquidated without great debate. Leaving aside Hawaii, which controlled one of the direct approaches to the continental U.S., none involved the U.S. in any large role carrying with it the built-in likelihood of an even larger role. Samoa and Wake were footholds, easily to be given up if the decision had been made. But the Philippines were a different story, for the *first time involving the use of substantial American armed forces far from home.* Thus, this event represents the real turning point and keynotes a first dominant aspect of this period. While at home much of the domestic debate remained focused on such issues as whether the Constitution followed the flag (i.e., whether the Filipinos, for example, were to be treated as U.S. citizens or U.S. nationals), and whether the U.S. "mission" in the world necessitated assuming this "burden," the most important part of the change was exactly that U.S. troops were for the first time deployed in strength far from American shores.

In the aftermath of the Sino-Japanese War (1894–1895), with its fresh demonstration of Chinese imperial weakness, the great powers competed in demanding leaseholds and spheres of interest; China was unable to resist. Secretary Hay's "Open Door" note (1899) asked the powers to avoid discrimination on a commercial basis in these areas of China. Even though it did not at first lead to further commitments, it, too, was a definite sign that potential American interests in Asia were receiving expanded attention. Hay's public construal of the evasive and ambiguous replies as "final and definitive" great power acceptance of the Open Door principle (March 20, 1900) better described official American optimism than the actual facts.

Here, again, the dilemma was much the same as with the Philippines. Direct U.S. trade with China was small, but if the U.S. did not attempt some positive action, its interests might suffer by default. There is a close connection here to McKinley's reasoning on the Philippines, even though here there was no intention to take on positive commitments. (Much later in time, American popular mythology would reconstruct the Open Door policy into America's first warning that it would not passively permit China's dismemberment.)

Signs of enlarged American interest in the outside world continued to accumulate. The First Hague Peace Conference (1899) included the

U.S. among its 26 participants. In January 1900, the Senate ratified a new treaty over Samoa, which divided those islands with Germany (Britain receiving compensation elsewhere). Thus American Samoa came into existence, with a naval commandant over a strategic base there. In the spring came the Boxer revolt in China. When the Boxers, seeking to expel the "foreign devils," occupied Peking and laid siege to the foreign legations, an international military expedition was organized to relieve the siege. U.S. troops took part—another highly significant, if for the moment temporary, involvement. This was the first time a significant U.S. armed force had been used on the Chinese mainland, even though for a strictly limited purpose.

Even before the siege was raised in August, Secretary Hay sent a new circular letter to the powers which this time went beyond the Open Door formula (although without any promise or threat committing the U.S. to action). The U.S. policy, the note said, was "to seek a solution which may bring about permanent safety and peace to China, *preserve Chinese territorial and administrative entity*, protect all rights guaranteed to friendly powers by treaty and international law, and safeguard for the world the principle of equal and impartial trade with all parts of the Chinese empire." (Italics added.) This concept became central to U.S. Pacific policy thenceforth, even if at first confined to mere declarations which avoided permanent or substantive commitments.

Nearer at home the next year (1901), a new treaty with Great Britain, acceded to reluctantly by the British, permitted the U.S. exclusive rights to construct and control an isthmian canal, provided it would remain open to the ships of all nations on an equal basis. The British would have preferred equal rights to control, but they had to face the fact of their inability to insist in view of troubles with both Germany and Russia. By agreeing to substitute this (Second) Hay-Pauncefote Treaty for the earlier Clayton-Bulwer Treaty, the British confirmed the strategic decision foreshadowed in the Oregon, Alabama Claims, and Venezuelan controversies: to avoid contesting important U.S. interests in the Americas.

These first years of the twentieth century involved the U.S. much more closely in Caribbean affairs than ever before. The Platt Amendment (to an Army Appropriation Bill) expressed congressional desires (1901) on Cuba. While the U.S. had earlier rejected any claims over Cuban soil, it now insisted that Cuba also reject any right to make treaties with foreign powers (other than the U.S.) which might impair its independence. The U.S. sought and obtained a naval base and the right to intervene to preserve Cuban law and order. In 1903 came the Panama revolt against Columbia, with whom the U.S. had unsuccessfully tried to negotiate canal rights. With the tacit approval of the Roosevelt Administration, the Panamanians rose up in revolt and declared their independence. The day *before* the revolt, President Roosevelt ordered the U.S. Navy to the area to maintain "free and uninterrupted transit" across the isthmus. U.S. recognition was extended three days after the revolt began, and the U.S. now negotiated a canal treaty with the new state of Panama. By the treaty's terms, ratified by the Senate (1904), a financial settlement with Panama gave the U.S. full sovereign rights in a 10-mile wide canal zone. The U.S. also guaranteed Panama's independence.

When a threat of European intervention arose again over Venezuela after its dictator's refusal to pay debts, and a blockade was actually established at the end of 1902 by British, German, and Italian warships, Roosevelt played a more restrained role, guided by his earlier comment (in his annual message of 1901) that the Monroe Doctrine was not designed to "guarantee any State against punishment if it misconducts itself" as long as it did not result in "acquisition of territory by any non-American power." Ultimately the issue was arbitrated, with the U.S. endorsing this means of settlement.

Financial insolvency in the governments of the area continued to cause trouble. The Dominican Republic was next. Roosevelt this time went beyond his earlier position by announcing the "Roosevelt Corollary" to the Monroe Doctrine: where "chronic wrongdoing" led to situations requiring "intervention by some civilized nation" in the Western Hemisphere, the U.S. might be forced "however reluctantly . . . to the exercise of an international police power." The U.S., profiting by a change of regime in the Dominican Republic, "accepted" an invitation to administer their customs (and thus restore financial stability).

With the same energy Roosevelt plunged into both Asian and European affairs, mediating the Russo-Japanese War and also urging Britain and France to agree to a conference at Algeciras to handle the explosive Moroccan question (then in contest between France and Germany). Not only did the U.S. send delegates to the conference, but Roosevelt helped persuade Germany to accept the settlement and also obtained Senate ratification (December 1906) of the Act of Algeciras! True, the Senate added a disclaimer that its action involved any departure from U.S. customary aloofness from European affairs.

Following some tensions caused by the scale of Japanese immigration into California, a "Gentlemen's Agreement" resolved the issue by coupling Japanese self-restraints on the flow of people to U.S. immigration laws. Characteristically, to put an end to any thought that such U.S. concessions as were made were the result of American anxieties about growing Japanese military strength, Roosevelt sent the "Great White Fleet" (the U.S. Navy) on a world cruise (December 1907–February 1909). These visits of ships of the now second naval power of the world again spoke more loudly (and more discreetly) of U.S. power than words might have conveyed. President Theodore Roosevelt did not invent the United States' newly found power to exert force at a distance, but he did more than any President of the United States up to his time to dramatize the bed-rock fact that that power was now in existence. Never again would decisions on U.S. commitments be made more simple by the elementary fact that we could not in any event do anything about it.

A dominant second aspect of these years was the increasing importance to both Japan and the U.S. of their relations with each other. The expansive drive of Japan in Asia came simultaneously with the more active Asian policy of the United States. Starting with the Spanish-American War, the question was being raised in increasingly acute form whether their divergent interests could be accommodated. In July 1905, the secret Taft-Katsura Memorandum between the U.S. Secretary of War and the Japanese Foreign Minister provided that Japan would give up any ambitions regarding the Philippines. The U.S., in return, would not interfere with Japan's plans to exercise control in Korea as a fruit of her war with Russia. Japan followed this in December of the same year by proclaiming Korea a protectorate. At the end of 1908 further stabilization in Japanese-American affairs was reached in the Root-Takahira Agreement. Each accepted the "existing *status quo*" in the Pacific, agreed to maintain the Open Door principle in China, and promised to promote China's territorial integrity by peaceful means. Whether this also included Manchuria, where Japan had paramount influence in the south, was not clear. In 1909, a U.S. decision to encourage further American commercial involvement in China (via a financial consortium) ran into opposition by other powers. This decision prompted Russia and Japan to agree overtly on a division of Manchuria into respective spheres of interest (1911). U.S. prestige was weakened. President Wilson (1913) abandoned the consortium concept. When World War I broke out shortly thereafter, and U.S. attention became focused on Europe, Japan was to take full advantage of her opportunities.

The years immediately before the war also saw new distractions for the U.S. in the Caribbean area. Nicaragua borrowed money with provisos for U.S. supervision of collection of customs. When the agreement touched off a revolt in Nicaragua, the U.S. (August 1912) sent Marines —a force that was not to be fully withdrawn until 1933. In 1910–1911 came the Mexican Revolution, bringing with it a long squabble between the U.S. and its southern neighbor. Incidents occurred at both Tampico and Vera Cruz which involved U.S. forces and led to an American bombardment of Vera Cruz. When Argentina, Brazil, and Chile offered mediation, the U.S. accepted the offer to extricate itself from a very unsatisfactory situation. U.S. Marines shortly thereafter were sent to Haiti.

By the year 1914, however, the theater of primary concern was

Europe, where World War I broke out in the first days of August. President Wilson proclaimed U.S. neutrality, asking Americans to be "impartial in thought as well as in action." Confronted immediately with British naval efforts to close off neutral trade in "contraband" with Germany, the U.S. steadily retreated from its historic stand for neutral rights. By the spring of 1915 Britain had proclaimed all German ports closed to shipping. Again, while Wilson at first opposed permitting loans to belligerents, by the fall of 1915 he had reluctantly agreed. (By the spring of 1917, U.S. bond purchases stood at $2,300 million from the Allies versus $20 million from Germany.) U.S. trade with Germany and Austria-Hungary declined drastically in the first two years of war: from $169 million to slightly over $1 million; but U.S. trade with the Allies went from around $800 million to around $3,000 million. So much for impartiality in action.

The German government's decision to sink *enemy* merchant ships on sight in the war zone led to a sharp warning by the U.S. in February 1915. (Germany had not said that neutral shipping could not enter the zone, but that they would do so at their own risk because of the misuse of neutral flags by British ships.) On May 7, 1915, the German submarine sinking of the *Lusitania* (with a loss of 1,198 lives, including 128 Americans) decisively turned American public opinion against Germany. So much for impartiality in thought.

The U.S. sharp notes to Germany which followed included a specific warning that other such acts would be considered "deliberately unfriendly." By the end of 1915, relations had deteriorated, as German sabotage efforts were disclosed in German documents obtained by the U.S. Secret Service. Germany felt forced to retreat from unrestricted submarine warfare and for the rest of 1915 concentrated on freighters rather than liners. By early 1917, the tension was again at a peak as a consequence of the German government's announcement (January 31) of its decision to wage all-out submarine warfare. Wilson severed diplomatic relations with Germany on February 3. In March, the Zimmermann Note was intercepted by the British who gave it to the U.S. Published in the American press, it made known Germany's attempts to bring Mexico into the war if the U.S. entered the conflict, promising the Mexicans the recovery of the "lost territory in New Mexico, Texas, and Arizona." On April 2, 1917, President Wilson, in a message to a special session of Congress, asked for a declaration of war against Germany to make "The world . . . safe for democracy." Once the declaration was made the U.S. became a part of the "Allied and Associated Powers," with America the principal "associated power." So came to an end America's traditional role of noninvolvement in European affairs.

It is apparent, looking at the record, that the real decisions that were ultimately to thrust the U.S. into a continuing active global role go back to the turn of the century. By the end of the Civil War, the U.S. had achieved all its initial policy goals. It had unified a continent, had substantially removed foreign powers from its vicinity in any meaningful sense, and had come to dominate its own approaches. With the Spanish-American War the U.S. clearly went beyond these traditional concerns and acquired continuing interests far from home in the Pacific. Two decades later American troops for the first time shed their blood in Europe. From now on the question would arise in ever more acute form: if the U.S. was to play a greater role and take on some global commitments, by what standards would the reasonable extent of such commitments be judged? Or was there any rational stopping place? Once one began to be involved, could one choose effectively among involvements?

CHAPTER 9

America, the Great Power

Awise decision on national involvements implies three things: (1) a well-conceived set of objectives implemented through (2) a strategic policy that takes account of, and advantage of (3) the basic forces at work in international relations. It is worth scoring each of the three Presidents who led the U.S. into a larger world role, between 1898 and 1919, against this yardstick. McKinley's argument for making the U.S. a Far Pacific power was based neither on well-conceived objectives nor on a real strategic policy; it comes down to essentially negative considerations: we did not really want the Philippines; we simply could not turn them loose. Teddy Roosevelt, a vigorous intervener, characterized his philosophy in 1900: "I have always been fond of the West African proverb: 'Speak softly and carry a big stick, you will go far.'" Under his leadership the U.S. indeed went far, but to what end, for what purpose? Action for action's sake would be too simple a tag to attach; yet the larger purpose, at least outside Latin America, remained obscure. Wilson, in his Fourteen Points (January 8, 1918) came the closest to stating well-conceived objectives and a strategic mission, but he both misunderstood the basic forces at work in international relations and misjudged the reactions of his own people to their new experience with world war.

The Versailles Settlement

The United States in the 1920's was by and large disposed to consider American intervention in World War I as a mistake. Mistake or not, it came at a critical moment. The very month war was declared, Britain lost 881,000 gross tons of shipping sunk. (Even the average monthly losses over the next year, which were less than a quarter of this figure, exceeded Allied replacement capacity.) In April, too, the costly failure of French offensives was followed by serious mutinies among French troops. (More than one out of every two Frenchmen, aged 20 to 32 in 1914, lost their lives in combat in World War I.) In the next months,

British, Russian, and Italian losses were all severe. Russia shortly collapsed. Her signature on the Treaty of Brest-Litovsk (March 3, 1918), within a year of America's entry, released huge numbers of German troops from the eastern front. In short, the war was being lost when the U.S. joined in.

American troops in 1917 numbered a mere 200,000. Yet by May 1918, a half million American fighting men were already in France—over 300,000 arriving in July alone. Some 29 of the 42 divisions sent over saw combat—1,390,000 men. To supply these forces the U.S. Navy expanded to a half million strength. While U.S. combat units joined the British fleet effort, other ships successfully convoyed not only these troops to Europe but almost four and a half million tons of cargo (by Armistice Day) to keep them supplied. There is no reasonable doubt that the eleventh hour contributions of the U.S. turned looming Allied defeat into ultimately smashing victory. On November 11, 1918, Germany agreed to an armistice whose terms included evacuation of all occupied areas, and whose significance was that it amounted to a *de facto* recognition that she had lost the war.

For an extremely low cost in lives (48,909 battlefield dead and 112,432 from all causes, plus 230,074 wounded) and a total direct war expenditure of relatively modest dimensions (about $22 billion), the U.S. had turned the tide, restored the balance of power, and won a prime seat at the Peace Conference. But now troubles began to multiply.

On December 4, 1918, Wilson set off for Versailles for what was supposed to be a preliminary conference of the victors. He was accompanied by no member of the Senate and by only one Republican in his peace commission. These well-known tactical errors were to have equally well-known consequences when President Wilson later asked for Senate ratification of the Versailles Treaty. When Wilson sailed he also left behind him a Congress slated to pass under Republican control. Wilson's appeal to the voters for a Democratic majority had backfired disastrously. If Wilson's domestic political support was now weak, so too was the degree of enthusiasm with which the British and French governments in particular viewed his Fourteen Points as the basis for a peace settlement. They had attached important qualifications to Germany's request for an armistice linked to the Fourteen Points (which they themselves had not formally accepted).

The psychological conditions under which the conference met governed much of the results quite directly—and indirectly for two decades afterwards. After enormous and prolonged costs in blood and treasure, the British and French, losing virtually a generation in the process, had "won." Public clamor for harsh measures was loud. Although the U.S. contribution had been both desperately needed and promptly and successfully given, the U.S. seat at the table had even so been purchased absurdly cheaply—and at the last moment. (Americans reacted in somewhat the same way, and quite justifiably, to Russia's claims for a share in the occupation of Japan as a reward for a week or so of fighting in World War II.) Western Europe could hardly be blamed for viewing U.S. proposals for an "impartial" settlement with suspicion, especially in view of the open question as to whether American involvement in European affairs would be more than momentary. How "associated" would the U.S. continue to be with the Allies?

France demanded the creation of a Rhineland buffer state or an indefinite Allied occupation of the area. Britain and France both insisted on heavy but open-ended reparations from the Germans. Italy argued for frontier rectifications in the north, which would bring some 200,000 German-speaking people under her control. Japan was determined to retain the German Pacific islands that she had taken during the war, plus maintain and expand her increasing grip on Chinese territory, especially southern Manchuria and Shantung.

Wilson argued in vain against most of these demands. He got French agreement on a long-term (rather than indefinite) occupation of the Rhineland by a security treaty guaranteeing France against Germany— which the Senate viewed with no enthusiasm at all. He essentially had to yield on the Italian issues and on the reparations question. The most he was able to get from Japan was a promise that eventually Shantung would be returned to China. As to Wilson's principle of self-determination, it became the vehicle through which large areas of Germany were given to her neighbors. Only some of these transfers were clearly justified by that principle. Especially in the East, Poland got areas that were, when doubtful, resolved in her favor. All German colonies were given up to the victors as "mandates." By the Versailles Treaty, Germany was also forced to accept responsibility for causing the war—a clause not justifiable on the basis of fact.

Indeed, the whole conference by this point had shifted from its original function as a preliminary peace session of the victors. Wearied by their disputes, and confronted with a Germany that could not well resume hostilities, the Allies abruptly summoned the Germans to Versailles (May 7, 1919) and told them to sign. Given an extension of time for consultation at home, and grudgingly permitted to offer counterproposals (which were largely ignored), the Germans were forced to sign on June 28. This flagrant disregard for normal peacemaking techniques became known in Germany (quite accurately) as the Versailles *Diktat*. It was indeed a dictated peace, a fact that Hitler later very successfully exploited. Its only major saving grace from Wilson's viewpoint was the provision for a League of Nations that was empowered to consider peaceful revisions of the harsh settlement—provided all concerned agreed.

One can understand the depths of emotion and hatred that World War I produced, and which led to the Versailles settlement. What is less excusable is that statesmen yielded to the popular pressures and the temptation provided by a momentarily weak opponent. If one asks why World War II was to follow so shortly, one must look at this treaty for much of the answer.[1]

Wilson now returned to a Senate quite hostile to *unconditional* acceptance of the Versailles Treaty (and the Covenant of the League, which formed its Part One). Most of the debate was preempted by the League issue so that it would be difficult to say that the glaring defects of the treaty received the consideration they deserved. Not that the U.S. could have altered them unilaterally. As it was, a coalition formed, prepared to ratify the treaty with 14 reservations offered by Senator Lodge. These reservations were almost exclusively concerned with the Covenant. Wilson embarked on a public campaign for the League that took him to 29 cities for 37 speeches before he collapsed; he told his supporters that the Lodge resolution provided not "for ratification but . . . for nullification . . ." The resolution was defeated. So was unconditional acceptance (38 yeas to 53 nays). Later reconsideration (March 1920) did not alter the result, although the vote shifted to 49 yeas and 35 nays—still short of the required two-thirds vote. Wilson had tried to have his way entirely. In the end he lost entirely. The U.S. thereafter, by joint congressional resolution, declared the war ended. In the presidential election that followed, the Democrats endorsed the League, while the Republicans rejected it in favor of some other (unspecified) form of "international association" to prevent war. Warren G. Harding, elected as Republican President, in his inaugural address outlined a new strategic mission for the United States, more modest than any we had previously attempted: "We seek no part in directing the destinies of the world."

Far Eastern Affairs and the Washington Conference

PACIFIC affairs were the first real test of whether we meant what Harding said. Actually, the retreat into what is miscalled isolationism, which came in the 1920's, did not turn out to be a refusal to *deal* any more with events far from our shores. That form of aloofness had come to a final end with the Spanish-American War. The change in the 'twenties came in no longer pursuing (even in the gingerly hedged form of an "associated" power) any role of *collective responsibility* for, as Harding put it, the "destinies of the world." Our participation continued; but it

---

1 The author remembers, as a teenager before World War II, learning about the Treaty of Versailles in high school. The authors of the text left the impression that it could hardly have been improved upon and that it met the needs of the situation quite well!

became *unilateral* for the most part and highly spasmodic and unpredictable in frequency. Our participation in conferences, when and if it came, was largely designed in practice to limit our involvements and commitments, while our verbal formulations continued to suggest something larger. Looked at from the perspective of other powers, our policy became something of an unknown quantity: if we began an action we might or might not abandon it halfway through. Yet neither could they count on our doing nothing. We shall see ample illustrations of this as we go on.

In 1921, the immediate problem for the U.S. was to achieve some agreement over naval armaments and Pacific affairs—each issue closely related to the other. Carried forward by the momentum of a large naval construction program authorized during World War I, the U.S. was already involved in a costly naval race with the British (whose historic policy of maintaining a navy equal in strength to the next two largest navies combined was in jeopardy). Also, the British had a treaty of alliance with the Japanese dating back to 1902 in its original form, and the Japanese naval construction program was substantial. These aspects of the problem, although they got much public attention, were really superficial.

Far more important was the question of U.S. relations with Japan, whose ambitions in China the U.S. continued to resist, and with whom any war (if it came to that) would inevitably turn upon the ratio of naval forces. Long-range airpower did not exist; a war with Japan would be primarily a war at sea. The question was whether Japan would limit her ambitions in China and whether a ratio of naval forces could be agreed upon with Japan, which would by its very existence be a tacit guarantee that neither Japan nor the U.S. intended an early resort to arms to settle issues between them.

Not only was the American problem with Japan in the Pacific Ocean areas extremely complex, but our own sense of priorities was in doubt.

Although we wished to limit Japanese expansionism, we made no real decision as to our policy's potential implications if Japan persisted in her China ambitions. By the Lansing-Ishii Agreement (1918) the U.S. recognized that "territorial propinquity creates special relations between countries, and consequently, the Government of the United States recognizes that Japan has special interests in China, particularly in the part to which her possessions are contiguous." Japan, for her part, agreed to the Open Door principle and the territorial integrity and independence of China. What did the Lansing-Ishii Agreement mean? To Japan it meant that the U.S. was conceding political rights to Japan in China. The U.S. interpretation was that the concessions were economic. But in either interpretation, how were they to be squared with the Open Door and China's integrity? Did the U.S. intend to back its policy toward

Chinese integrity with more than words? Would the U.S. settle for some modest dismantling of Chinese unity? What of Manchuria where Russian interest had long been strong and Japanese interest was pronounced? At the Versailles Conference the best that Wilson had managed over Shantung was that Japan, who had occupied it, would eventually return it to China.

American policy over China could logically lead to one of four contingencies. First, assuming no moderation of Japanese ambitions, the U.S. could give up the Open Door policy. Or, second, it could actively resist Japan—via a strong naval presence in Asia which was a *sine qua non* for a strong military presence. If, third, on the other hand, Japan would renounce her ambitions or limit her expansion, the U.S. could continue a strong naval presence in the Far Pacific to ensure that Japan carried through. Or, fourth, the U.S. could accept Japanese promises at face value and renounce the capability for a sustained naval offensive role in Japanese waters. Contingency one envisaged retreat; it was consistent with an end of the naval armaments race through an agreement but on rather inglorious terms. Contingency two meant a continued arms race, for Japan could be expected to compete. Contingency three would have similar results. Only the fourth contingency would meet basic U.S. desires for both Chinese integrity and an end to the arms race, and then only so long as Japan honored her promises. To cut to the heart of the matter, any U.S. program to bolster China and cut back on armaments build-up had to turn on Japan's promising to change her course, with some implicit guarantees that she would keep her word. This last is what was attempted by the package of treaties concluded at the Washington Conference, most of them concerned with the political aspects of the problem.

Of the strictly naval agreements, the most important provided for a ratio of capital ship tonnage strength for the U.S., Great Britain, Japan, France and Italy of 5 : 5 : 3 : 1.67 : 1.67. Capital ships of these nations (other than aircraft carriers) of over 10,000 tons displacement or having guns over 8-inch caliber were to be brought into this ratio by an initial scrapping of older fleet units and ships in process of being built.[2] Between 1922 and 1931, replacement construction allowances were specified which would reflect ever greater approximation to the exact ratios agreed. After 1931, for as long as the treaty was continued, the U.S. and Britain would have 525,000 tons each; Japan, 315,000; France and Italy, 170,000 tons each. Aircraft carriers were also limited, but using different formulas: for the United States and Britain, 135,000 tons; for Japan, 81,000; and for France and Italy, 60,000.

These ratios reflect a distinct strategic concept for the Far Pacific, a

[2] Substantial scrapping followed from this treaty. Even initially the British scrapped 20 in-service ships, the Japanese 10, and the U.S., 15. Total 1922 scrappings, including ships being built, was 78 units.

concept made even clearer when the political agreements in the treaties are taken into account. Article XIX of the disarmament treaty stipulated that the existing "status quo . . . with regard to fortifications and naval bases, shall be maintained . . ." in the Pacific, with certain exceptions. United States possessions near the American West Coast (except for the Aleutians) were to be unregulated, as were the Hawaiian Islands. Canada's West Coast was unregulated. So were Australia and New Zealand. What this meant was that U.S. or British bases within an operating perimeter of Japanese waters (such as Guam, Singapore, Cavite in the Philippines) were to stay as they were. To balance this, Japan promised to keep the Kuriles, the Bonins, the Loochoos, Anami-Oshima, Formosa, and the Pescadores as they were. No new naval bases in the *status quo* areas could be built; old ones could be maintained but not improved.

The Nine-Power Treaty of 1922 and the Four-Power Treaty completed the picture of intent. The first pledged the signers to "respect the sovereignty, the independence, and the territorial and administrative integrity of China," and the other provided for full and frank communication between the United States, the British Empire, Japan, and France, "to arrive at an understanding" as to what should be done "jointly or separately" if a "controversy" over "any Pacific question" were to arise. It also terminated the Anglo-Japanese Alliance on the grounds that this ambiguous obligation made it no longer necessary.

Of the other treaties in the package, the most interesting to note is the treaty between Japan and China providing for the restoring of Kiachow and the Shantung peninsula to China.

The U.S. Senate ratified all of the treaties, the Four-Power Treaty by a close vote and with a stipulation that "there is no commitment to armed force, no alliance, no obligation to join in any defense." We wanted Pacific affairs settled—but at no cost.

To this day, the essential strategic meaning of what was attempted at the Washington Conference is not widely and correctly understood. It is said that the conference failed to control naval armaments meaningfully, since it did not impose tonnage limitations on submarines, cruisers and destroyers.[3] The naval race could simply shift over to these types— which it did, with Japan in the lead. Even so, in fleet doctrines cruisers and destroyers especially are generally conceived as screening forces for capital ships. Capital ships held the vital key to the measurement of effective power in the vast Pacific. It is claimed that only obsolete ship types were controlled. Yet battleships *and* aircraft carriers were hardly obsolete in 1922; they were still being built and used for many years thereafter!

The truth is that the important weapons by which the U.S. and Japan

[3] Further limitations were accepted at the London Naval Conference of 1930 after the U.S. (1929) authorized the construction of 15 cruisers of 10,000-ton displacement.

could carry war to each other *were* controlled by these agreements. The U.S. force was greater (5 as against 3 in ratio), but the U.S. had two coasts to protect. Even if the U.S. concentrated its entire capital ship fleet in the Pacific, if it meant to operate off Japan it would do so some 3,900 miles from Pearl Harbor (its most western meaningful base)— well beyond optimum range, in a day when mobile fleet support was in its infancy or nonexistent. That is, the American capital fleet's operating capability, even if it was numerically larger, would be distinctly smaller than Japanese units operating on a short radius from resupply bases. Conversely, any Japanese thrust into the Eastern Pacific would suffer similar crippling handicaps for any sustained operations involving these ratios. Finally, such an agreement was fairly dependable in so far as capital units could not very well be built in secrecy or quickly. If secrecy were attempted (as in later years for Japanese construction), it would be a clear and timely warning.

The agreements meant in effect that the Japanese would be dominant in their home waters, that the Philippines would be difficult for the U.S. to defend, and that the Japanese would have distinct temporary advantages if they tore up their promises on China. Looked at from the vantage point of arms control, the Washington agreements were notable successes. Looked at in terms of Asian developments, they represented a postponement or avoidance of the central issues developing between Japan and the U.S. over China. Since the U.S. had not really faced the issue of whether she would actually fight Japan if necessary to preserve China, and since Japan at least for a time suspended her push to dominate China, the U.S. settled for the chance to terminate the costly arms race—an opportunity that the Japanese welcomed, too. In fact, Japan had at this point no definitive plans to push ahead in China. This was to come, but a decade later, and even then the Manchurian adventure was not endorsed by the civilian component of the Japanese government.

Whether future developments proved the Washington agreements to be desirable or undesirable, they did postpone the issue at a time when the U.S. felt unable to reach a meaningful decision on how far to commit itself over China. Whether the U.S. was wise to be concerned with China's integrity in the first place is still another question. Although foreign to our ways of thinking about problems, it is worth pondering whether a less active U.S. policy might not have led to a Japanese-Soviet embroilment in lieu of Pearl Harbor.

There is one further sense in which the Washington agreements were important. Because the U.S. had no inclination to involve itself substantially in European affairs, and because the "Chinese question" was in moratorium for a decade, the U.S. could essentially retreat into isolationism in the sense of refraining from meaningful collective commitments. Which it did.

Retreat into Isolationism

THE next decade was to show how far the U.S. was from matching its verbal declarations of policy to meaningful actions.

The economic dislocation caused by World War I, the vindictive and short-sighted reparations policy against Germany (which by its impossible scope guaranteed instability for all), sowed the seeds of the Great Depression of the 1930's. Contributing to the massive financial transfers problem was the U.S. effort to be repaid for war loans, although its effects were essentially postponed through the 1920's. If anything, political dislocation was even greater. The entire territorial heart of Europe had been disrupted and altered. Austria-Hungary's dismantling produced a number of new states who (with the exception of Czechoslovakia) had numerous unsolved economic and political problems. These mostly weak states were arrayed between two great powers who had each suffered substantially from the war's outcome: Germany and Russia.

Germany's losses were the direct result of being on the losing side. Russia's losses were ironically the direct result of having fought on the winning side. That is, Russia's inefficiency under the Tsars led directly to huge losses and dislocation, which set the stage for revolution. In the ensuing Russian Civil War, with its foreign interventions and related international wars (as with Poland), the Soviets emerged with frontiers in Europe substantially less extensive than before 1914. Consequently, both Germany and Russia in principle sought change in the *status quo.* If they cooperated to divide what lay between them, and if this brought about Western intervention, a new world war was highly likely. Indeed, all of this was to happen, but not yet in the 1920's.

In 1924, the U.S. participated in an effort to bring the German reparations issue under control. Germany's default on her payments had brought a Franco-Belgian occupation of the Ruhr in early 1923, but the inflation of the mark had continued to undermine any prospects of settlement. It not only became worthless but the French franc also lost a quarter of its value. The Dawes Plan, named after one of the Americans on the reparations commission, sought to stabilize German currency and provide a phased-down method of payments. In the same way the U.S. sent delegates to many League conferences, especially those dealing with nonpolitical questions, but we did not join the League and we retained full freedom over commitments. Nor did we join the World Court.[4]

The 1920's were not free of Latin American involvements for the U.S.

[4] The Senate in 1926 approved membership with reservations, one of which was not acceptable to other members of the Court. In 1935 the Senate voted against membership (although 52 Senators voted for it—short of two-thirds).

However, U.S. Marines were withdrawn from the Dominican Republic in 1924, Mexican relations were substantially improved in the late 1920's, and U.S. troops were finally withdrawn from Nicaragua in 1933. As early as 1928, a State Department (Clark) Memorandum in effect withdrew the Roosevelt Corollary to the Monroe Doctrine by defining it as covering "the U.S. *v.* Europe, and not . . . the U.S. *v.* Latin America." President Herbert Hoover's good-will tour of 1928–1929 to eleven Latin American states produced a new cordiality.

In 1928 came the Briand-Kellogg Pact which "outlawed" war. We, along with most of the world, signed and ratified this agreement. It had no enforcement machinery, it outlawed only "aggressive" war, and its signing took place in a flurry of explanatory notes excepting special obligations. Britain excluded any curtailment of her commitments to defend her Empire; the U.S. excluded the Monroe Doctrine. In today's perspective it is hard to recapture the enthusiasm with which this fairly innocuous agreement was then hailed. In 1930, the London Naval Conference carried naval arms control further, establishing cruiser limitations for Britain, Japan, and the U.S. along lines of the 1922 formula. Submarines were controlled at parity at a maximum of 52,700 tons each, and the capital ship ratios were continued to the end of 1936.[5]

Just as these optimistic signs were being posted, the bottom was falling out. The Wall Street stock market crash (October 1929) set in motion a severe credit contraction, which (May 1931) brought down the great Austrian Credit-Anstalt. By September, Britain had been forced off the gold standard. A proposal of President Hoover for a one-year moratorium on debts and reparations was accepted. Actually, from then on no payments were made[6]—both reparations and debts were dead letters.

At this critical juncture the long dormant Far Eastern area came dramatically awake. In September 1931, an incident at Mukden in Manchuria resulted in large-scale and continuing Japanese military moves that by January 1932 had given Japanese armed forces full control over South Manchuria. In the fall of 1931, when the League Council took up the question, the U.S. was invited to sit with the Council. While the U.S. sent a low-level representative, he had strictly limited powers. Secretary of State Stimson, for the United States, sent identical notes (January 7, 1932) to China and Japan, asserting that we did not "intend to recognize any treaty or agreement . . . which may impair . . . the sovereignty, the independence, or the territorial and administrative integrity of the Republic of China . . . or the Open Door policy. . . ." A few days afterwards the British substantially undermined any effects from this "Stimson Doctrine" by indicating they were willing to accept Japanese reassurances. Late in January, after the killing of five Japanese monks, the

---

[5] Some 9 capital ships were scrapped: 5 British, 3 American, and 1 Japanese.

[6] As is fairly well known, Finland continued later to pay the U.S. back.

Japanese intervened with naval and military forces at Shanghai. Stimson again sought to coordinate with the British who chose to work with the League instead. Then, on March 11, the League Assembly took a position closely parallel to Stimson's, and Japan at the end of May withdrew from Shanghai (but not Manchuria).

On September 15, 1932, Japan formally recognized the new regime in Manchuria as a separate state, Manchukuo. Shortly afterward, in October, the League investigation commission that had gone to the scene made its report. In this Lytton Report it was pointed out that the situation in Manchuria was extremely complicated:

This is not a case in which one country has declared war on another country without previously exhausting the opportunities for conciliation provided in the Covenant of the League of Nations. Neither is it a simple case of the violation of the frontier of one country by the armed forces of a neighboring country, because in Manchuria there are many features without an exact parallel in other parts of the world.

For example, the Manchurian authorities (although legally subject to China) had in the past carried out direct negotiations with Japan. Also, Japan by treaty had certain rights: the right to control a railway and a railway zone running from the sea into the heart of Manchuria; the right to have 10,000 to 15,000 troops there for its protection; and the right to exercise "rights of jurisdiction" over all Japanese subjects in Manchuria and to maintain consular police "throughout the country."[7] In view of these oddities the League was unable to find that Japan had committed clear-cut violations in the wake of the alleged incident in the railway zone which began the whole matter, and which led to the occupation of all of Manchuria. The Japanese view was that she had intervened to restore order, and thereafter the population had established a new government which turned to Japan for support.

Recent generations of Americans who "know" that Japan actually committed aggression then, and initially got away with it, ought to ponder the confused situation that existed. China in those years was torn by civil strife and Japan did have certain rights in Manchuria. Although the incident itself was contrived, the League was hardly to be blamed for treading cautiously in the confusion and urging Japan and China to settle the issue through direct negotiations. One might see certain parallels in the Israeli occupation of Sinai (late 1967), following the Third Palestinian War. Were the Israelis guilty of aggression? (But there had never been a peace settlement.) Were the Israelis in permanent occupation? (One would have to wait to see.)

Nor is it enough to say that the U.S., unsupported by Great Britain,

[7] *Commission of Inquiry,* League of Nations, Political Publications, 1932, VII, 12, pp. 126–127.

felt constrained to avoid more forceful action alone. In 1931 President Hoover opposed popular clamor for a boycott on Japan, and late that year Secretary Stimson told our Ambassador to Great Britain that "We do not intend to get into war with Japan." When, shortly thereafter, Stimson enunciated his doctrine, he did not couple it with any form of ultimatum; and when the League accepted the Lytton Report, the U.S. did not take any effective separate action. The fact was that the U.S. wished to see China preserved without any inclination to really make a true commitment backed by more than words. One can argue that the Open Door "commitment" should not have been made at all, or that, if made, it should have been honored. Its fruits were not long postponed.

War Draws Near

PRESIDENT Franklin D. Roosevelt in his inaugural address (March 1933) reformulated a strategic mission for the United States. "In the field of world policy I would dedicate this nation to the policy of the good neighbor—the neighbor who resolutely respects himself and, because he does so, respects the rights of others." But what if others did not respect *our* rights and interests?

The outlines of a much more restrained policy toward unilateral moves in Latin America, already apparent in the Hoover Administration, were reaffirmed and broadened. Spelling this out at the Montevideo Conference, Secretary of State Hull voted with the Latin American states in a unanimous declaration that "No state has the right to intervene in the internal or external affairs of another." Two days later (December 28, 1933), President Roosevelt said: "The definite policy of the U.S. from now on is one opposed to armed intervention."

Although the U.S. agreed to participate in the London Economic Conference (1933), we were unwilling to stabilize currencies and the conference failed. Even our limited cooperative links to Europe were weakening. On the other side of the coin, diplomatic relations with the Soviet Union were finally established. Latin American policy in the next years held close to the new lines. The Platt Amendment on Cuba was abrogated, troops were withdrawn from Haiti, relations improved with Panama. President Roosevelt, personally opening the Buenos Aires Conference (1936), asserted that non-American powers who attempted aggression in the Americas "will find a Hemisphere wholly prepared to consult together for our mutual safety and our mutual good." In the Declaration of Lima (1938) the Inter-American states declared they would resist "all foreign intervention or activities that may threaten them." Indeed, a new spirit was evident, even though at the time Argentina prevented any implementation beyond "consultation." Economic aid had been extended to Brazil, and negotiations were begun with Mexico for support of the peso and settlement of other issues. Philippine independence was pledged for 1946.

In Asia, after the Mukden incident (which had also extended Japanese control by early 1933 from Manchuria into neighboring Jehol), a Sino-Japanese truce brought hostilities to a close. With Shanghai evacuated by Japan, the situation there, while unstable, was technically peaceful. Renewed and continued war did not begin until a new "incident" occurred (July 7, 1937). Japan gave notice of withdrawal from the League (February 24, 1933) and denounced the Washington Naval Treaty (December 29, 1934), but she refrained from serious and continued provocations during 1933–1937. When Japanese planes taking part in new hostilities against China bombed the U.S. river gunboat, *Panay* (December 12, 1937), the U.S. demanded and received an apology. Only at the end of 1938 did Japan lay down an open challenge, declaring in November that the Open Door was "inapplicable . . . today and tomorrow."

Europe in these same years was undoubtedly the main theater of American concern. Hitler's advent to power in Germany was one main element (and a contributing factor to the American realization that a continued lack of relations with Soviet Russia was unwise). Yet Germany's armed power was weak initially—the Rhineland was not reoccupied, for example, until March 1936. World attention was directed more persistently at Mussolini's assault on Ethiopia in late 1935, and at the Spanish Civil War which broke out in mid-1936.

Mussolini's attack on Ethiopia produced the first of the series of U.S. neutrality acts by which America attempted to escape war. The 1935 version authorized the President, after a recognition of any state of war, to prohibit arms shipments to all belligerents. U.S. citizens could not travel on belligerent vessels except at their own risk. Roosevelt reluctantly signed but indicated that he thought the law might "drag us into war instead of keeping us out." Nor did the arms embargo cover steel, oil, copper, and other materials highly essential to war-making. (U.S. oil exports to Italian Africa actually rose drastically.) In 1936, a new Neutrality Act extended the previous provisions to May 1, 1937, and forbade any loans or credits to belligerents. These provisions said nothing about *civil* war, so when civil war broke out in Spain, Neutrality Act amendments were added to prohibit arms exports to "opposing forces in Spain." (Rebel forces under Franco were well supplied by Germany and Italy.) In May 1937, still further legislation authorized the President to allow "cash-and-carry" sales of raw materials, while retaining restrictions on munitions and loans. Travel on belligerent vessels was made unlawful. When the new fighting between China and Japan came in mid-1937, President Roosevelt did not invoke the new Act, since it obviously would have been to Japan's advantage. Although Roosevelt increasingly felt that the U.S. was unwisely limiting its own discretion, he could produce no immediate improvement. His "quarantine-the-aggressors" speech (October 1937) indicated his own changed strategic thinking and aroused adverse comment, proving that U.S. opinion substantially agreed with the point of view of Congress.

War clouds continued to gather over Europe. In March 1938, Hitler annexed Austria. The Munich Conference followed later that year, and Czechoslovakia's defenses were dismantled. In March 1939, Germany took over control of all of Czechoslovakia, annexed Memel, and exerted pressure on Danzig. In May, Italy and Germany concluded a military alliance; and in August, a Russo-German neutrality pact (with secret provisions for dividing Poland) was signed in Moscow. World War II began on September 1, when Germany invaded Poland and the British and French honored their pledge to assist the Poles. What now for the United States?

World War II

THE strategic policy issue posed for the United States by World War II was not initially faced; only slowly did the real issues appear. When victory was finally won, it was to be on terms that permitted grave tensions to continue in the heart of Europe.

In one of the radio fireside chats (September 3, 1939) for which President Roosevelt was justly famous, he said: "This nation will remain a neutral nation, but I cannot ask that every American remain neutral in thought as well." (Wilson, it may be recalled, had at the same opening act of war asked for Americans to be "impartial in thought as well as in action.") Bound by the law, Roosevelt cut off arms to all the belligerents. On September 21, though, he asked a special session of Congress to repeal the arms embargo. Although Roosevelt's triple appeal on the grounds of safeguarding neutrality, security, and peace left many members of Congress unmoved, the provision was repealed by the Senate (63–30, late October), and by the House (243–181, early November). Arms and munitions could again be sent—but on a "cash-and-carry" basis. Such provisions, of course, favored Britain and France, provided they had cash and could keep ships from being sunk in large numbers by Nazi U-boats.

The war itself was going very badly for Britain and France. Indeed, "our side" had still not taken its ultimate shape, for the Russians in October assaulted Finland, and Britain and France were seriously contemplating an expeditionary force to help the Finns against the Soviets! On the western front, a "phony war" continued without much action while Hitler decided to forestall Anglo-French movements toward Scandinavia (as a part of their projected aiding of the Finns) by seizing these areas himself, beginning in April 1940. Thus Hitler helped save the British and French from a major blunder; the Allied expeditionary force, belatedly sent to Norway, withdrew after a spirited but futile resistance to the Nazi occupation.

On May 10, 1940, the German offensive in the West began. The Lowlands were quickly overrun, and by May 28 evacuation of a third of a million British and French troops cut off at Dunkirk was begun. Churchill had by now become Prime Minister and asked the U.S. for urgent replenishment for the weapons abandoned at Dunkirk. Supposedly "outdated" or "surplus" arms were immediately sent—more than $43 million worth in June alone. By June 14, German troops were in Paris; and on June 22, France signed an armistice with Germany, followed by one with Italy (who had joined the attack).

Roosevelt had already asked for (and got) a tremendous preparedness program authorization from Congress. In airplanes alone, production was to be at 50,000 planes a year. Between August and October the Luftwaffe tried to soften up Britain for invasion. While the air campaign cost Britain 915 RAF fighters, the Nazis lost double—1,733 planes. The U.S. called up the National Guard at the end of August, and in early September the U.S. transferred 50 overage destroyers to the British in exchange for base rights in British Caribbean area territories (and Newfoundland). Conscription was instituted in September.

Events in Asia, too, were not promising. In September, Secretary Hull warned the Japanese that aggression against French Indo-China might bring about an adverse U.S. reaction. Japan went ahead and got Vichy French agreement for a Japanese occupation. Roosevelt answered with an embargo, effective October 16, on all exports outside the Western Hemisphere (except to Britain) on scrap iron and steel.

By the spring of 1941 U.S. sentiment was shifting, and government policy followed bolder lines. The U.S. Navy had been ordered to extend its patrol operations to 26° West Longitude as a partial counter to the increasingly successful U-boat attacks, which had by this point sunk about 688,000 gross tons of allied shipping. (In the next eleven months losses even so reached 2,314,000 gross tons.) In March 1941, Lend-Lease was authorized by Congress; and in April the U.S. assumed responsibility for the defense of Greenland (through agreement with the Danes). In July the U.S. acquired bases in Iceland—only 700 miles from Scotland. After an attack on the U.S.S. *Greer* off Iceland on September 4, the U.S. Navy was ordered to shoot first in U.S.-defined defensive waters. U.S. neutrality laws were amended in November to permit arming merchant ships and allow U.S. shipping to carry cargoes to belligerent ports. In the fall after Hitler's invasion of Russia on June 22, 1941, the U.S. extended Lend-Lease to the Soviet Union. In the Atlantic the U.S. was already at war. In fact the first, tentative war aims of the U.S. had already been announced (August 1941). Following secret meetings between President Roosevelt and Prime Minister Churchill at sea off Newfoundland, the Atlantic Charter was made public. Highly idealistic, it renounced (for example) territorial gain. The Soviet Union and more than a dozen other nations also endorsed it in the next weeks.

But it was in the Pacific that the final event in this prelude took place. Following Japan's move into Indo-China (July 1941), the U.S. froze all Japanese credits within its area, thereby virtually ending all trade between the two nations. Final negotiations took place in Washington, beginning in late November. Each nation took a position tantamount to requiring the other to cease and desist in the essentials of its Pacific policy. How events reached a climax is well known: at Pearl Harbor (December 7, 1941).

How narrow sometimes is the margin by which nations decide their fate! In the late summer before Pearl Harbor, although administration efforts to aid the anti-Nazi effort were increasingly gaining support, the nation as a whole, while tolerating bolder official moves, remained divided over the merits of "intervention." Nothing more dramatically illustrates the point than the House vote (August 12) by which Selective Service was extended—203 to 202.

Pearl Harbor changed all of this, for the U.S. had now been overtly attacked, and the nation girded itself to deal with this "unsought war." In the beginning the news everywhere was bleak. The Japanese were threatening Australia, having quickly spread their control over the whole vast Western Pacific while the U.S. hung on at New Caledonia (and fought a delaying battle at Bataan in the Philippines). In North Africa Field Marshal Rommel's forces advanced upon the Suez Canal while other German forces plunged deep into Russia. An eventual link-up in the Middle East of the two Nazi forces seemed possible, just as, further in the future, a Nazi-Japanese link-up in India was feared.

Looked at in today's perspective, the dismal year of 1942 was also, by its end, the turning point of the war. November was the critical month. In the Solomon Islands that month Japanese reinforcements for Guadalcanal (where U.S. marines had landed in August) were destroyed at sea. From this point on the Japanese-controlled area contracted steadily. That same month came the Anglo-American landing in French North Africa (November 8) in Rommel's rear. Rommel now faced a two-front war, and (November 12) British forces under Montgomery pushed the Nazis out of Egypt. In the Soviet Union, where the assault on Stalingrad began in August, the high water mark of German penetration was reached (November 19). From then on, the Nazis were forced into a slow but continuing retreat.

In mid-1943, Sicily was invaded and Mussolini resigned; by September 3, an armistice with Italy had been signed. Within a week a new landing at Salerno began the stubborn U.S. advance up the Italian peninsula, with the Germans bitterly contesting. On June 4, 1944, Rome was taken, and on June 6 Normandy was invaded. Almost simultaneously U.S. forces in the Pacific moved to take the Marianas. On April 26, 1945, the beginning of the end was signaled in Europe, as American and Russian armies met at the Elbe River; on May 8, military victory in Europe was a fact. Meanwhile, in Asia, Iwo Jima was taken in March; and in April, Okinawa was invaded. Then, on August 6, the first atomic bomb was dropped on Hiroshima, with a second bomb following a few days later on Nagasaki. Between these events, the Soviets declared war on Japan; and on August 10, the Japanese sued for peace. On August 15, military victory in Asia was also a fact. The United States quickly began a vast demobilization.

Military victory had been won. Had the U.S. also won the peace effectively? Arguments on this point were to continue over the next decades. For example, it was argued that the U.S.-sponsored "unconditional surrender" formula had prolonged the war unduly by discouraging German opposition to Hitler. What is more plausible, however, is that Hitler's ruthless vengeance against the "bomb plotters" had that decisive effect. In any event, when Japan offered terms for her surrender (specifically that the Emperor be allowed to retain his throne), the U.S. did agree to the condition.

Much more disturbing was the series of questions raised relating to Germany's division and occupation—provisions that permitted the Soviet Union to put its troops deep into the middle of Europe (where they have remained ever since), with profound effects on the balance of power.

Basic decisions on these and other points had been taken at a series of wartime meetings, primarily of the heads of government of the United States, the Soviet Union, and Great Britain—the so-called "Big Three." (France was not associated with these meetings, at first because she was an occupied nation, later because of disagreements over who should speak for France.) At the Cairo Conference (December 1, 1943), Roosevelt and Churchill, meeting with Chiang Kai-shek, agreed to strip Japan of her conquests, return Formosa to China, and create a free and independent Korea (a principle later accepted by Russia). At Teheran, following the Cairo Conference, the Big Three agreed upon the timing of the Normandy invasion (and the coordinated Russian assault) and approved in principle the Curzon Line as Poland's eastern frontier.

More critical yet were the decisions taken in the next two conferences at Yalta and Potsdam. At Yalta in February 1945, the Big Three agreed to establish a "democratic" Poland, which was to receive substantial German territories as compensation for the areas claimed by Russia from Poland in the east. Occupation zones were to be created in Germany. On a hopeful note, it was agreed that a United Nations Organization would be established through a conference at San Francisco in April 1945. Reparations from Germany were set at $20 billion as a basis for discussion. It was at Yalta, too, that Russia agreed to enter the war against Japan within three months of Germany's defeat. She was to reacquire essentially her status in Asia before her defeat in the Russo-Japanese War.

The final wartime conference at Potsdam (July–August 1945) reached a decision to establish a Council of Foreign Ministers, which would include France (and China, when Asian questions were before the Council). This Council was to prepare the peace treaties and handle questions of common concern. It was decided that Germany would be completely disarmed. All vestiges of Nazism would be eliminated, and "for the time being, no central German Government" would be established, although Germany was to be treated by the occupying powers "as a single economic unit." Russia would receive reparations from her own zone plus some "industrial capital equipment" from the western zones. Pending a peace settlement where "final delimitation of the western frontier of Poland" would be agreed upon, Poland was permitted temporarily to administer German East Prussia, Silesia, and large parts of Brandenburg and Pomerania. These territories, under Polish control at Stalin's insistence, were to run westward to the Oder-Western Neisse rather than to the Oder-*Eastern* Neisse line, which Britain and the U.S. had preferred. A glance at the map will indicate that the territories thus put under Polish administration were substantially larger than the Western Powers had envisaged. To put the point in reverse, if "Germany" is to be regarded as the sum total of the British, French, American, and Soviet zones of occupation (i.e., present-day West Germany plus East Germany), she was substantially *smaller*.

The most controversial aspects of these agreements (and ones taken by subsidiary organs as a result of these decisions), apart from the area left to Germany proper, were the size and territory of the individual zones and the question of Western access to Berlin (which was to be jointly occupied). To honor these agreements, American forces in Germany had to be withdrawn in 1945 from the proposed Soviet zone as much as 125 miles. Just as important, no *written* agreement was made with the Soviets on Berlin access. These points caused much trouble in the next decades, leading to the most persistent charges that the U.S. had won the war but lost the peace. They were given a new airing each time that a new American-Soviet crisis arose over Berlin in the postwar years. Since these decisions, taken during the war, had their real ramifications later, we shall wait until these later events are analyzed to give further background on how this state of affairs occurred.

An Assessment

THE United States, having reluctantly joined the fighting in World War I late in the conflict, made a substantial, and even decisive contribution to the victory. Having no territorial ambitions in Europe or Asia, it strove to produce a stable and generous peace. What it helped create was nearer to its opposite, even though the U.S. was most frequently on the progressive side. If the League of Nations was too daring a step— and not only for the U.S. but for the European powers who quickly whittled down the most important obligations imposed by the Covenant—the essential idea of a permanent conference of all the nations was sound in principle. Just as truly, the Versailles settlement in its largest outlines sowed the seeds of disaster even for those who argued for it most. It dismantled Central Europe, punished Germany unduly, and alienated Russia. One can say that Austria-Hungary was an anachronism; one can say that the advent of communism in Russia meant that the Soviets could not be brought to support a stable peace. These observations do not reach to the heart of the postwar problem: the two alienated great powers, Germany and Russia, were separated by a string of weak states (and potential victims). From a balance of power standpoint, it did not make sense. Either Germany had to be reconciled to the situation through concessions, or the Soviets had to become associated in a meaningful way with the maintenance of a stable *status quo*. Neither was done although each was attempted in turn on a halting and ineffective basis.

To say that the U.S. sensed these grave weaknesses in the balance of power structure, and decided to turn away and preserve its strength, would be to distort what actually happened. We did not turn away out of disgust but out of distrust—distrust that our proper part in world affairs included a meaningful and continuing role in coordination with friendly nations. Our efforts in the early 'twenties were confined to improving our own security position in Asia by bringing the Japanese to agree to preserve China. We did not face what we would do if she would not. Once Japan changed course, the issue was posed. The Stimson Doctrine was an acknowledgment of our failure either to face the implications or to change the policy. Granted that the economic paralysis that engulfed the major industrial states in the 1930's made political coordination extremely difficult. It is still the fact that, as war approached, we did very little about it in either ocean. Only after the actual outbreak of World War II, did the American government begin to face the issues. Even then, both Congress and the people remained divided over the merits of the strategic alternatives—as the one vote extension of Selective Service dramatically illustrates.

Caught up finally in the war, the U.S. again demonstrated its superb abilities to mount a military effort to defeat its enemies. Although it was not yet fully evident, a basic decision had been made by the American people that isolationism could no longer represent a meaningful strategic foreign policy choice. We had decided to be in and of the great events of the world in a practical and meaningful way. But enthusiasm and dedication, though necessary, were not enough. There also had to be devised standards for formulating and implementing policy. What were these to be? Could we evolve a set of objectives implemented through a strategic policy that took into proper account the basic forces at work in international relations?

In the first postwar years there were to be numerous shocks to our preconceived notions of what that postwar world with our willing participation would be like. Wartime decisions were to rise and plague us in these years. Soon we found ourselves allied to the very nations whose defeat we had so ardently sought in World War II. As we groped for a new strategic concept we made assumptions about basic phenomena in world affairs which turned out to be wrong—most obviously, for example, in our belief that communism could overcome nationalism.

It is to those postwar years that we now turn. As we observe and analyze these events we shall be attempting not only to probe the meaning of the events in terms of their consequences on the international relations of the time. We shall also be attempting to understand the psychological reactions of the American people to the impact of these events. For the shocks to former ideas which these events produced, and the new attitudes which thus came to be adopted, have led us to our present frame of mind and our present attitude toward today's problems.

CHAPTER 10

The New Age:
Initial Disillusionments

W E TURN now to the new age of American foreign policy, the period since World War II. Since this period of "all-out participation," as it might reasonably be called, began a quarter of a century ago, it will help first to recall the point of view in 1945, and then observe our sometimes painful education in the real world of international relations as we reacted to successive events. In looking at these successive shocks to our preconceived ideas, we shall continue to emphasize as faithfully as possible how it seemed *then*, as well as how it seems now. For the true value of looking back at these years is to see which of our preconceived notions in 1945 did not prove viable and useful in practice, what adjustments in these notions were consequently made, and (finally) where our present notions are still distortions or counterproductive to what we say or think we want. Our yardstick of judgment, as before, will be how well we linked objectives, strategic policy, and the basic forces at work in international relations.

Preconceptions

RAYMOND ARON, the noted French specialist in international relations, makes a useful distinction between what he calls "permanent allies" and "occasional allies," remarking that permanent allies are "those states that, whatever the conflict of some of their interests, do not conceive, in the foreseeable future, that they can be in opposite camps."[1] During World War II, the U.S. made no such distinction in its general approach to those principal nations also fighting the Axis powers. Our relations with France were limited, because France had surrendered and only de Gaulle and the "Free French" fought on from Great Britain. Those relations were also troubled, and not merely because of the personality of de

[1] Raymond Aron, *Peace and War—A Theory of International Relations* (New York, Garden City: Doubleday, 1966), p. 28.

173

Gaulle; the United States was genuinely perturbed over the question of who could speak for France. At the same time, the U.S. never doubted that relations with France would be close and cordial following the war, as they actually were for most of the time after 1945. Our relations with Great Britain were especially close, partly because the British wanted them that way. Many decades earlier in the Treaty of Washington which led to the settlement of the Alabama Claims, the British had virtually announced their intentions to avoid serious frictions with the United States, other than in the most dire emergency conditions. They and we both expected to be—later as before—permanent allies.

The most striking case is our relations with the Soviet Union. If (as was the case) the U.S. looked forward to continued or increased close postwar cooperation for mutual ends with the Soviet Union, the Russians for their part never did. We may have thought them "permanent allies." They knew they were "occasional allies," brought to a temporary and limited cooperation against a mutual enemy and held together in a common bond to that extent only.

We were not unaware of what we considered their "suspicious" attitudes toward our actions. Stalin and his followers made no secret of their belief that we were ready to sell them out at the first useful chance. This became obvious in their insistent demands for a second front (before the North African campaign, and before the Normandy invasion). Barely concealed (if at all) was their assumption that Western delays were calculated for the precise purpose of allowing Germany to proceed unhindered in the massive Nazi attempt to destroy Soviet power. When the armistice was arranged with Italy, they were highly suspicious. They consistently delayed in responding to our requests for shuttle bombing facilities on Russian soil. When we made airplanes available to them across the Pacific under Lend-Lease, they insisted on flying them from Alaska rather than have us fly them to Vladivostok. At the very end of the fighting they obviously expected us to accept an armistice on the western front that would permit the Nazis to continue their war with Russia (as the Nazis themselves attempted to arrange).

We persisted in attempting to convince the Soviets of our good faith. So much so that President Roosevelt bent over backwards (and too far) in showing Stalin in the Big Three conferences that he did not necessarily agree with Churchill. Roosevelt attempted the role of "honest broker" where there was far more at stake than making the American position a compromise between the views of the British and the Russians.

Soviet suspicions, on the other hand, were not unnatural. Substantial grounds for Soviet distrust had been created by Western policies between 1917 and 1939. First, the Western allies had intervened with troops and supplies to aid the Tsarist forces against the Communists (1918). Second, the West had attempted in the interwar period to erect a *cordon sanitaire* of alliances with Poland and the Balkans which would insulate the "Bolshevik virus" from the West. Third, it was reasonable (although incorrect) for the Soviets to assume that the failure of the British and French to thwart Nazi moves against Czechoslovakia (1938), or to press Poland to accept precautionary deployments of Soviet troops in Poland (1939), reflected an intention to turn Hitler loose on Russia. Naturally the Soviets were disturbed by the Munich Conference to which they were not even invited! Czechoslovakia under German domination brought Nazi power virtually to the Soviet frontier.

Without question, the West had amends to make if the Soviets were to accept their good faith. The question was whether the Soviets could in any event be brought to believe in Western good faith, and what could *reasonably* be done to convince them. Sacrifices of important Western interests to attempt that conversion could not be justified. As it actually happened, the most important concessions made were made far less consciously than this implies. The most serious concessions (involving Germany) *were not really seen as serious concessions*—on which more later. Subsequently, we became highly upset with Soviet actions which were far less important to American national interests. The Cold War did not begin over the Soviet position in Germany, with its very serious implications; it began, curiously enough, over the more peripheral question of Soviet actions in the Balkans (and Poland).

If the United States acted during the war as though Russia were a permanent ally, it also acted as though Germany were a permanent enemy. True, the U.S. shrank back from the drastic proposals of the "Morgenthau plan" for the pastoralization of Germany, but we proceeded to dismantle German industry and divide Germany as though we could without question consider these moves as in our permanent interests.

Both attitudes reflected the two sides of the same coin. We did not believe in the type of logic associated with the concept of counterbalancing national interests so central to an effective approach to the balance of power. Indeed, the UN was supposed to substitute collective security effectively in its place. We had not lost our faith that conflicts of interests among nations would yield to good intentions and good will.

In our concentration on defeating German power, we forgot what Soviet suspicions proved they did not forget: that destroying German power would leave Soviet ambitions in Europe without its most natural counterbalance.

The Cold War Begins

WITHIN two years of the end of the war in Europe, the U.S., to its surprise, was to find itself involved in an intense and overt competition with the Soviets.

Differences of opinion on how to treat the Soviets had, of course, existed both inside and outside the government before the war was over, but the prevailing point of view was to "trust" them. President Truman, coming into power in the last stages of the war, after Roosevelt's death (April 12, 1945), soon developed substantial suspicions about Soviet behavior. Unwilling to trust his own doubts, he made decisions on Germany, before and at Potsdam, which were serious mistakes. They may be pardonable since he was largely boxed-in by Roosevelt's prior decisions and mistakes. Nonetheless it is certain that he paid insufficient attention to Churchill's repeated warnings until it was too late to repair the most serious errors. Truman did have a choice on whether to order U.S. troops to assault Berlin from the west; he did have a choice as to whether to delay ordering American troops to withdraw westward from substantial areas of the Soviet Zone until he had obtained guaranteed continued access to Berlin and the Soviets had modified their highhanded conduct over Poland. This is what Churchill pleaded for—unsuccessfully.

Churchill clearly realized that the agreements on Germany and on a "democratic" Poland were working out in such a way that the Soviets were dominating the whole area of the Balkans between their frontier and what is today called the Iron Curtain in Germany. He clearly realized that there was no way of preventing the Soviets, who were in occupation, from dominating the Balkans. His discussions with Stalin on this point were designed to obtain at least tacit Soviet recognition that Greece would remain outside the communist area and within the British sphere of interest. On Poland he did not hope to influence Stalin (already in occupation) to follow a path of creating a truly independent Polish government, unless the bargaining card of U.S. occupation of the Soviet Zone area remained intact. Once Truman ordered Eisenhower to proceed with the withdrawal, Churchill had no cards to play. Later, when the U.S. became very upset about Soviet domination of the Balkans (and Poland), the British government (now under Attlee's Labour leadership) played a more restrained role.

From the British point of view the possibilities for effective action largely evaporated by the time Truman ordered troops withdrawn (effective June 21, 1945). In the spring, Eisenhower had opposed the suggestion to take Berlin. On March 30, 1945, he gave his opinion to Washington that "Berlin itself is no longer a particularly important objective. Its usefulness to the German has been largely destroyed and even his government is preparing to move to another area."[2] On May 4, 1945, three days before German surrender, Churchill urged delay on withdrawal: "The Polish problem may be easier to settle when set in relation to the now numerous outstanding questions of the utmost gravity which

[2] Dwight D. Eisenhower, *Crusade in Europe* (New York: Doubleday, 1948), p. 401.

require urgent settlement with the Russians." He spoke of withdrawal in terms (unfortunately for the effects of his plea to Truman) that implied that the zonal agreements ought not to be honored at all. It "would mean the tide of Russian domination sweeping forward 120 miles on a front of 300 or 400 miles. This would be an event which, *if* it occurred, would be one of the most melancholy in history. . . ." (Italics added.) (Truman, considering American honor to be at stake in carrying out a pledge, was unsympathetic to the argument that the Russians had not honored their word.) Churchill ended: "It is just about time these formidable issues were examined. . . . We have several powerful bargaining counters on our side. . . . First, the Allies ought not to retreat from their present positions to the occupational line until we are satisfied about Poland, and also about the temporary character of the Russian occupation of Germany." When Truman ordered withdrawal (to be done simultaneously with movement of U.S. troops into Berlin), Churchill answered despondently: "Obviously we are obliged to conform to your decision." After this the Soviets knew they could do what they liked in Poland. They also could with less risk defy the Potsdam stipulation (made after this withdrawal) that Germany was to be treated as an economic unit. To go further, one understands why Potsdam was such a dismal occasion for the protection of important U.S. interests when one remembers that it was held *after* the U.S. had surrendered most of the bargaining cards.

The irritation with which the U.S. watched the events of the year and a half after Potsdam fed further on our general inability to do anything about it, as Poland, Romania, and, later, Hungary were converted into Soviet satellites. It had been agreed that all of these areas would have "democratic" governments. On March 12, 1947, when the Truman Doctrine was announced, President Truman explicitly referred to these events: "The peoples of a number of countries of the world have recently had totalitarian regimes forced upon them against their will. The Government of the United States has made frequent protests [over] Poland, Rumania, and Bulgaria." Truman announced American intentions "to help free people to maintain their free institutions and their national integrity against aggressive movements that seek to impose upon them totalitarian regimes."

Although the Truman Doctrine went on to speak explicitly of support for Greece (from which the British were retiring) and Turkey, and did not call for a rollback of the Iron Curtain from the Balkans, the doctrine was generally seen as a declaration that the U.S. would not accept the Balkans remaining permanently under Soviet control. In this sense it reminded one of the Stimson Doctrine. Certainly by John Foster Dulles' time the general proposition of "containment" had blossomed forth into the concept of "liberation."

It is one of the ironies of this period that an important part of the reason that the Truman Doctrine was early taken to be a declaration implying eventual rollback came from the publication in the July 1947 issue of *Foreign Affairs* of the famous article by "X." Mr. "X" was shortly identified as George F. Kennan (later to become Ambassador to Russia), who was then prominent in the councils of the State Department. In this article Kennan called for containment of Soviet expansion and his article was generally interpreted as urging counterpressure on the Soviets to produce a break-up of the Soviet empire. What Kennan actually said was "to promote tendencies which must eventually find their outlet in either the break-up or the gradual mellowing of Soviet power." The reason that it is ironical is that in later years, before polycentrism fully asserted itself in the Balkans, Kennan became an advocate of "disengagement," which, to some of those who wanted to maintain a "position of strength" against Russia, smacked of reversal. Kennan himself was arguing by this time that post-Stalin conditions could now lead to some détente.

In this first shock of the postwar era the American people were reacting to what they considered a gross betrayal of Soviet promises over Poland and the Balkans. Where, they asked, were the "free elections" clearly promised in the Yalta Protocol? (Part II, "Declaration on Liberated Europe," spoke of "the right of all peoples to choose the form of government under which they will live," and provided specific steps, including: "(c) to form interim governmental authorities broadly representative of all democratic elements in the population and pledged to the earliest possible establishment through free elections of Governments responsive to the will of the people.") Now it turned out that in the Soviet view free elections in the Western sense would permit "reactionary" elements to regain control, and thus would not be really "free." Moreover, the only "democratic elements in the population" who could be represented under the formula were those who favored socialism! Although the West condemned the rigged elections which began to take place, the Soviets went right ahead. Since Communist parties enjoyed too little support to gain respectable showings even in drastically supervised communist-style elections, the Soviets resorted to "popular front" parties—forced amalgamations of democratic and labor parties with the Communists in a single party list. (The "Socialist Unity Party" of East Germany is perhaps the most familiar example.) All of this did not occur everywhere at the same pace. In Hungary the opposition remained strong; in Romania the king was actually retained as a front for a time. Yet by the time of the Truman Doctrine the overall development was crystal clear.

If one asks whether the national interests of the United States suffered as a consequence of this conversion of sovereign states into satellites, the answer is clearly yes. One can ask whether the United States had any leverage to alter the situation, and the answer is clearly no. Even if we had been willing to consider committing troops, we had few available. In fact, the government had no such intention. Yet, we made much of an issue which we could not readily change and which we did not intend effectively to try to change. By taking this line we contributed to our own frustration and widened the gap between our declaratory policy and our actual policy—something that was to return to haunt us in 1956, as Russian troops ruthlessly suppressed the Hungarian uprising while the U.S. stood helplessly by.

What is most instructive about recalling our attitude in 1947 is that it allows us to ask why the American people and/or government considered it worthwhile even to take the time to persuade the Soviets to make what we considered a promise of Western-style elections? We could hardly have been ignorant of the fact that the Balkan governments had pursued bitterly anticommunist policies between the two world wars. We could hardly have expected that free elections would put in power governments friendly to the Soviets—or even more or less neutral toward them. Yet apparently we expected the Soviets, in sole occupation in the area, impartially to supervise elections in these areas on their direct Western approaches, elections that would create regimes which would then assume power and follow stringent anti-Soviet policies! Even the United States has been known to balk at that degree of impartiality, as our policies toward Latin America have occasionally demonstrated. Why did Americans expect this fantastic degree of self-forgetfulness on the part of the Soviet Union?

Further, did we really consider that it was possible for true democracy to be established through elections in the Balkans—a string of nations whose past history of authoritarianism was undeniable? Why would they now be democratic, particularly surrounded by the ruins and hunger which were for them the immediate dividends of a lost war (for most had favored or aided the Germans)?

Finally, why did the U.S. assume that the clear historical trend in this area no longer applied? After all, the Balkan states have always been dominated by one or more great power neighbors and have never enjoyed freedom except when those neighbors have been all too weak to grasp for influence and control. With Austria-Hungary no longer existing after World War I to contest Russia for the area, the struggle was between Germany and Russia—who ended up dividing it in 1939. With Germany defeated, how could it have been possible for a situation to be created and maintained where the Soviet Union would not as a minimum exercise "influence" there? To expect the Soviets to turn away from their opportunity and pursue some abstract and foreign standard of justice did not make good sense. At their most benevolent, the Soviets were unlikely to pursue a policy in the Balkans more altruistic than the historic attitude of the U.S. toward Cuba and the Caribbean.

Having accepted too readily conditions permitting an undue Soviet presence in the heart of Europe, and having become futilely aroused over the less important Balkan area, the U.S. with the Truman Doctrine initiated an effective response to the challenge implicit in the dangerously expanded Soviet empire bordering on a still weak West.

The Truman Doctrine (March 1947) as implemented specifically toward Greece and Turkey was to prove a resounding success; so was its companion measure, the Marshall Plan. Kicked off in a trial balloon by Under Secretary of State Dean Acheson in a speech (May 8, 1947), the plan itself was announced by Secretary of State George C. Marshall (June 5, 1947): "It would be neither fitting nor efficacious for this Government to undertake to draw up unilaterally a program designed to place Europe on its feet economically. That is the business of the Europeans. The initiative, I think, must come from Europe. The role of this country should consist of friendly aid in the drafting . . . and of later support of such a program . . . This program should be a joint one, agreed to by a number of, if not all, European nations."

Like the Truman Doctrine's application to Greece and Turkey, the Marshall Plan's application to Western Europe was to prove equally successful. It is noteworthy that Marshall did not reject the idea of the Soviets and the new satellites taking part; and indeed Poland and Czechoslovakia indicated interest, and Molotov came to a conference at Paris to represent the Soviet Union. He also soon departed, condemning the aid program as designed to impair "the economic independence and sovereignty" of the European states by permitting "certain strong powers" to "make use of some European countries against others in whatever way" proved "profitable" toward establishing "domination." Unimpressed by these risks, 16 European states (all of noncommunist Europe, except Spain but including Iceland and Turkey) prepared a plan. U.S. participation was approved by the Economic Cooperation Act (April 3, 1948). The U.S. Economic Cooperation Administration worked in close collaboration with the sixteen-nation Organization for European Economic Cooperation and now began its fruitful efforts. It remains an open question whether Congress would have given generous support to this program if the Soviet bloc had actually taken part. On the other hand, Soviet participation on anything like a truly cooperative basis would have meant that the Soviets had opted for a quite different policy from the one they subsequently pursued. Détente was not on the face of things precluded as a potential Soviet strategy at this time. Communist ideology includes ideas of "ebb and flow," of retreat and advance. But the chances open to Stalin for advance implied continued tension with the West and seemed more appealing to him. The division of Europe was not yet complete but began to deepen from this time on.

The Fall of Czechoslovakia and Blockade of Berlin

IF IT could reasonably be argued that the West properly had amends to make to the Soviets for Western conduct between 1917 and 1939, and that U.S. determination to make an issue over democracy in the Balkans (as distinct from preserving a free Greece and Turkey) was a questionable tactic, it was more importantly true that the West had made grave mistakes in permitting an undue Soviet presence in Central Europe. Germany was the key issue; she was shortly to be the scene of the first major postwar crisis. The raising of the curtain on this crisis was preceded by a prelude over Czechoslovakia.

Unhappy Czechoslovakia had suffered greatly as a result of the Munich "deal." Delivered up to the Nazis as a sacrifice for "peace" by her own ally (France) and Britain, Czechoslovakia had been dismembered by Hitler. Resistance in the war years was ruthlessly countered by methods of suppression which, in 1942, were to make a small village's name known around the world—Lidice. At the end of the war, U.S. General Patton's advance into Czechoslovakia was halted before Prague was reached, and the honor of liberating the Czech capital gratuitously handed to the Soviets. Hailed between the wars as a "showcase for democracy," the Czechs were deemed by the West as naturally oriented in an anti-Soviet direction, even though the initial postwar election gave the Communist party the largest vote (38 per cent). A Communist became prime minister; another Communist controlled the police. (This procommunist vote was probably itself due largely to Munich—with which the Soviets had no connection.) When the Marshall Plan was announced, Czechoslovakia—an industrial state needing pump-priming —expressed interest but gave way to Soviet pressure not to take part. This Soviet veto created a cabinet crisis in Prague; and on February 20, 1948, 11 anticommunist ministers unwisely resigned in protest. This move indeed brought the government down as intended, but not in the way expected. Communist police and action squads took over and by February 25 President Beneš felt forced to accept a totally Communist-controlled cabinet. Beneš himself was soon forced out, and Czechoslovakia became a full Soviet satellite. Now the Soviet Union had an armed presence to the north (in the Soviet Zone of Germany) and an armed presence to the south (in Austria) and dominated even more of Central Europe. Soviet control of the daggerlike salient of Czechoslovakia (thrusting westward toward the heart of Western Europe) constituted a distinct additional military threat to the West.

Within a month of Beneš' surrender, events in Germany had reached the first stage of crisis when Marshal Sokolovsky (after a violent tirade) walked out of the Allied Control Council in Berlin (March 20), thus bringing four-power government to an end. On the last day of March the Soviet Military Administration announced that Western military passenger trains would no longer be allowed to transit the Soviet Zone to Berlin, without Soviet inspection. Next day, the Soviets prohibited rail freight from leaving Berlin without their permission. By late June, other measures had been added so that by June 24 all rail traffic had been stopped. The "technical difficulties" that the Soviets had alleged as an excuse soon overcame the canals and highways as well. West Berlin was under full blockade.

Looking back on the developments that led to this crisis, it is clear that East and West had become engaged in a continuing series of reprisals against one another. For example, charging Soviet bad faith over German reparations, the West discontinued further shipments of industrial reparations from their zones. Following the fruitless 1947 London Foreign Ministers' Conference, Secretary of State Marshall pointed out that Great Britain and the United States were paying "some [$] 700 millions a year to provide the food and other items to prevent starvation and rather complete disintegration" in their zones. Under the circumstances, "reparations from current production—that is, exports of day-to-day German production with no return—could be made only if the countries at present supplying Germany—notably the United States —foot the bill. We put in and the Russians take out."

As events in Prague reached their climax, a Six-Power Conference on Germany met in London (February 23–June 2). In early March, it announced plans for "a federal form of government" in the Western zones. This action triggered the Soviet walkout two weeks later in Berlin. Similarly, it was the London Conference report of June 1 calling for a meeting of the minister-presidents of the West German states no later than June 15 that inspired the further Soviet blockade moves.

Was the West justified in its action, inasmuch as it represented a definite turning away from the letter and spirit of the Potsdam Agreement? Clearly, yes; the situation in Germany had to be remedied. If we ask whether the Soviets violated the reparations agreement, the answer is also clearly yes. They were not sending the food and raw materials promised as their part of the bargain. But if we ask whether Soviet violation of the reparations agreement was deliberate, the answer is not so clear. The agreement itself called for "equivalent" exchanges, which was very ambiguous. From our point of view, the Soviet interpretation of what they owed us was quite unreasonable. From their point of view, the Soviet homeland had been devastated by the Nazis, the Soviet need was urgent, and the agreed reparations were far beneath original Soviet demands. It seems most likely that the Soviets deliberately decided to take via one method what they had been denied via another. In view of the chaotic conditions in Germany within which industrial dismantling was taking place and the unusable condition of much of what the Soviets took or received, they no doubt felt shortchanged. Yet even if this were so, it does not penetrate to the heart of Soviet motivation. The fact is that Soviet determination to strip and weaken all of Germany regardless of resulting starvation and chaos reflected a ruthless policy which the West did not and could not really share. The basic intentions of East and West in Germany were never the same.

Contributing to the American sense of frustration was the total collapse of German paper money. The printing press plates for the currency had been given to the Soviets who turned out vast quantities, using them to loot Germany. On June 20, to end this drain, the West introduced a new Deutsche mark in all their area except Berlin. (Marshal Sokolovsky had been notified on June 18 that the new marks would not be used in Berlin.) The Soviets retaliated with a new currency of their own, announcing on June 22 that their currency would be used in *all* of Berlin. On June 24, left with no option, the West introduced the new West German mark into West Berlin. It was that same day that the Soviets halted all Western rail traffic with Berlin.

A careful comparison of all these dates shows that the Soviet contention, at the beginning of the crisis, that the Western currency reform had been the cause of their counteractions against Berlin, does not stand up. Later they themselves threw this pretext into the discard. What the Soviets were really reacting to was Western determination to restore economic stability in Germany and form a free and representative government in the Western zones. This Western plan threatened the whole range of Soviet intentions: either as a minimum to keep Germany weak and helpless, or as a maximum, to create opportunities for absorbing all of Germany into the Soviet orbit. And so the trial of strength began over Berlin.

The position of the West was not, on the face of it, very strong. By August 1948, unless passage by road or rail was to be forced, some 2.5 million people in West Berlin had either to depend upon supply by air or surrender. Food stocks for 36 days and coal stocks for 45 represented a very thin barrier to humiliating and costly defeat. And winter was coming.

If we are to understand the next events we must again look backward, specifically to the question of Berlin access (and the related question of the zonal lines themselves). These problems originated during the war but, of course, received little attention outside governmental circles then. After the war they became the subject of much controversy.

The zonal lines envisaged a "temporary" occupation of Germany.

They were accepted at the Yalta Conference (February 11, 1945), and provided for three zones (and once French participation in the occupation was worked out, four) plus joint occupation of Berlin. There was no significant argument at Yalta as to the zonal lines themselves. Even at Potsdam, later, the argument was only over whether Poland should be allowed to administer that part of the Soviet Zone reaching to the *Western* or *Eastern* Neisse. The U.S., in the early negotiations before either conference, at first held out for what ultimately became the British Zone, but where the Soviet Zone would reach to in the west was never in real controversy. That line was derived from a British draft laid before the European Advisory Commission (EAC) as early as January 1944, accepted by the Soviets in February, and formally agreed to by the United States on June 1, 1944—in other words, just before the Normandy invasion that same month. (The EAC then reached basic agreement on the occupation plan [September 1944] and took it, as we saw, to Yalta for final acceptance the following February.)

Why were the Soviets conceded a line so far west and a zone of occupation containing large areas actually to be "liberated" by the United States? First, as General Clay was to write later, "there was a lack of confidence in some quarters" as to whether the Normandy invasion would even succeed. Perhaps it would be the Soviets who would need to retreat to honor the agreement. Second, the actual disposition of forces in June 1944 suggested that the junction of Allied troops in Germany would occur approximately on the East-West zonal line. In late June, with the West still consolidating the Normandy beachhead, Soviet forces were basically within Russian territory but had a westward bulge in southern Poland and a piece of northern Romania. A month later the Soviet offensive had closed to 400 miles from Berlin (with the Western forces 600 miles away). In August, the Soviets were outside Warsaw, but the West was still fighting in France. In the Battle of the Bulge (Christmas 1944), the last great German counteroffensive in the West held the Anglo-American forces on the German frontier. Not until March 2, 1945 (*after* the Yalta Conference), did the West reach the Rhine, while by February 7 (*during* Yalta), the Soviets had reached the Oder near Frankfort. One Soviet spearhead was only about 50 miles from Berlin.

In March and April 1945, a great change in this situation occurred as Eisenhower's offensive turned into a break-through. While the West by April 22 swept to the line of Hamburg, Magdeburg, Leipzig, Chemnitz, Nuremberg, and Stuttgart (well into the Soviet Zone), Soviet forces made very modest general advances. Their great battle—street by street for Berlin—absorbed much of their power.

Hitler's actions explain these very substantial changes. Foolishly stripping the eastern front of reserves to hold the British and American forces on the western frontier, Hitler permitted a Soviet breakthrough. Frantic then to stop the Russians, Hitler reversed his tactics and held the Soviets while allowing the West to sweep forward. Hitler could not have done worse by his people.

If the zonal lines decision thus becomes more understandable, a closer look at the Berlin access question confirms the popular suspicion that a serious mistake was made. President Roosevelt himself was the prime cause in this failure—a failure due essentially to the lack of high-level coordination between the State Department and the armed services. Although under Roosevelt a careful coordination of the armed services began to occur via the Joint Chiefs of Staff device, no effective equivalent linkage was made to State. We saw in Chapter 4 that when Roosevelt sailed for the Teheran Conference (November 1943), he did not even invite the Secretary of State along. When, enroute, he sketched out on a map a plan for occupation zones for the Joint Chiefs, no State Department representative was present. This map gave the British a southern zone and divided the north between the U.S. and the Soviet Union on a line running *through* Berlin, but the map ended up in a Pentagon safe. When, later, the plan was put forward in the low-level State-armed services coordinating group, it became the basis for a position paper forwarded to Ambassador Winant on the EAC, but without supporting arguments—primarily because the State Department neither knew about the plan's original source nor thought it feasible to get agreement on it. Winant refused to urge the plan without supporting arguments and sent George Kennan (then on his staff) to Washington. There Kennan ultimately talked to Roosevelt who accepted (April 3, 1944) the British-Soviet draft (which said nothing about access to Berlin).[3] In May Winant himself came to Washington and raised the access question. The War Department position was apparently that a presence in Berlin implied a general right of access and that the U.S. should not request specific routes which might, because of war damage, prove to be unusable. Whether Winant was to press for a general access clause is unclear.[4] The agreement made in June made no mention of the point.

Even if general access rights had been mentioned, the U.S. would have then been forced later to negotiate on specific routes. As it was, General Clay was sent by Eisenhower to Berlin to do exactly that (June

[3] The Joint Chiefs also gave approval on April 28. Kennan's own account can be found in George F. Kennan, *Memoirs, 1925–1950* (Boston: Little, Brown, 1967), pp. 164–171.

[4] Lord Strang, British member of the EAC, wrote that it was expected that the zones would not be "sealed off from one another" and that the EAC assumed "any necessary arrangements for transit could be made on a military basis by the commanders-in-chief when the time came."

29, 1945). Clay reports this meeting, which led to purely verbal agreements, as follows:

We had explained our intent to move into Berlin utilizing three rail lines and two highways and such air space as we needed. [Marshal] Zhukov would not recognize that these routes were essential and pointed out that the demobilization of Soviet forces was taxing existing facilities. I countered that we were not demanding exclusive use of these routes but merely access over them without restrictions other than the normal traffic control and regulations which the Soviet administration would establish for its own use. General Weeks [Clay's British counterpart] supported my contention strongly. We both knew there was no provision covering access to Berlin in the agreement reached by the European Advisory Commission. We did not wish specific routes which might be interpreted as a denial of our right of access over all routes. . . .

Clay reports he accepted "as a temporary arrangement the allocation of a main highway and rail line and two air corridors. . . ." The question was to be reopened in the Allied Control Council—where the Soviets had a veto. He goes on: "While no record was kept at this meeting, I dictated my notes that evening and they include the following: *It was agreed that all traffic—air, road and rail . . . would be free from border search or control by custom or military authorities.*"

In his memoirs President Truman records that he asked Stalin (June 14) for free access to Berlin (in return for withdrawal from the Soviet Zone). He adds that "The Soviet[s] agreed to provide unrestricted use . . . of the standard-gauge railroad from Goslar to Berlin via Magdeburg [and] the use of the Hanau-Magdeburg-Berlin autobahn but [the Allies] were refused free use of the Berlin-Frankfurt autobahn. The Allies were to have an air lane some 20 miles wide from Berlin to Magdeburg and two lanes from Magdeburg to Frankfurt."

Truman is apparently citing General Clay's verbal agreement, for the U.S. was never subsequently able to produce any agreement in writing (other than a low-level air lanes agreement that broadened Allied rights to the three lanes so familiar later).

Returning now to the blockade, General Clay decided even before the full stoppage to test the Soviet closure of the railroads. The train sent was shunted by the Soviets onto a siding until withdrawn a few days later. What next? The choice was to force passage of the autobahns or try by air (where our access rights were clearest). But Berlin had only two Western zone airfields and very poor winter weather conditions; could Berlin be supplied by air? It would need a daily airlift, even on an iron-rations basis, averaging 4500 tons!

As all the world soon learned, it could be and was done. Starting with very little, by December the daily average airlift exceeded 4500 tons; by February 1949, even with winter in full course, the average reached 5500.

By spring, it was 8000—equal to what had come in by rail and water before the blockade. With a new airport placed in operation, the totals continued to climb—13,000 tons on the record day.

The Soviets—having lost their first attempt to force the West out of Berlin—settled for a reciprocal lifting of the blockade and of Western countermeasures against the Soviet Zone, effective at midnight on May 11–12, 1949. Some 1,402,644 metric tons of food, coal, and supplies had by then reached Berlin in 277,728 flights. The airlift had lasted 11 months; at its height planes were coming in or leaving every 30 seconds.

The Soviet gambit had been a loss in more ways than one. It had caused the Americans and British to gain a close working relationship with the German people, putting an end to much of the residual wartime hostility. It had caused the French to cease obstructing Anglo-American moves to establish a West German government. It also caused 12 nations to negotiate and sign (April 4, 1949) the North Atlantic Pact. Duly ratified, it came into effect on August 24, 1949, a few weeks before Konrad Adenauer became first Chancellor of the new West German Republic. The Soviets had anticipated that U.S. withdrawal from Europe would surely occur soon after war's end, but they now found themselves confronted by an unmistakable American decision—already foreshadowed by the Truman Doctrine and Marshall Plan—to stay and hold the line in Europe.

The Fall of China and the Korean War

ON THE day in August 1949 that the Atlantic Pact came into effect, registering the revolutionary decision by the United States to play a strong role in Europe, American public opinion on all of these events had reached rough consensus. Although some still argued that Soviet moves were essentially defensive in motivation, and some warned against too enthusiastic a policy of new commitments, the Soviet challenge had aroused American ire. The outcome had added to American pride in their ability to respond. For 15 years or more after these events, NATO became predominantly a symbol of successful U.S. foreign policy. By that same day in August the bottom was rotting out of a principal plank in U.S. Asian policy: a unified China under the Nationalists. Nanking, the Nationalist Chinese capital, had already fallen (April 24) to the Communists. On October 15, the new capital at Canton would also fall. By December 8, 1949, the Nationalist capital would be on the island of Formosa.

The U.S. had tried to avoid this civil war between the Communists and Nationalists. President Truman sent General George C. Marshall on a special mission, which in early 1946 seemed to have attained success in arranging a government in which both groups would take part.

Amalgamation of troops into one Chinese army had also been agreed in principle. Each part of these agreements foundered on the mutual distrust of both Chinese parties. Whether they would have proved a viable solution is to be doubted. So between 1946 and 1949 the issue was fought out—ending with a Communist triumph on the mainland.

Stalin's attitude was distinctly negative toward this expansion of the Communist realms. He had strongly advised the Chinese Communists to make peace with Chiang Kai-shek, arguing that the conditions were not at all ripe for successful Communist revolution. From an orthodox ideological standpoint he could argue that what urban workers China possessed were essentially in areas under Nationalist control; they were too few and unorganized to be the focal strength of revolt. Whether this was the real basis of Stalin's negative attitude can be doubted. Certainly Stalin had never demonstrated any enthusiasm at any time for extending communism unless he was absolutely sure he could control it. Since the Chinese Communists had pursued a quite independent course during Stalin's whole tenure, he had little expectation that these maverick "agrarian socialists"—who had an odd brand of communism based upon rural peasants rather than urban workers—would follow his lead if they attained power. Stalin, too, had already obtained Nationalist agreement to what he desired from China—especially the use of Port Arthur as a Soviet naval base and (in the words of the Yalta protocol) a restoration of "the former rights of Russia violated by the treacherous attack of Japan in 1904. . . ."

Although neither the U.S. nor Russia thus sought Chinese Communist victory at this point, the Chinese Communists nonetheless won. To the American public, exposed in the newspapers to maps that portrayed a now grossly extended "Communist world," the prospects seemed frightening. The idea that communism was a single movement that was directed by one man from Moscow had a great hold on popular imagination. Now, while it could hardly be argued that the extension of communism in China was to the advantage of the United States, neither was it true then or later that the whole movement was responsive to one director. Things were not what they seemed, but the American public at the time was unprepared to assess the development as anything but one more shrewd aggressive act on Stalin's part—a move to open another theater of activity in a weakly defended or vulnerable area, now that his expansion in Europe had been stopped cold. After all the successful effort to save Greece, to hold Berlin, to restore Western European economic health, and to arrange for a viable defense through alliance— now the bottom had fallen out in China. The American people asked who had been responsible for the "loss" of China?

Writing in 1952, Sir Dennis W. Brogan summed up the prevalent American attitude:

The Communist triumph in China is discussed as if it were simply the result of American action or inaction, the results of the mistakes, and worse than mistakes, of General Marshall, Secretary Acheson, President Roosevelt, and the Institute of Pacific Relations; and as if the Communists or the Russians would not have "captured" China had American policy been represented and controlled by [American conservative or right-wing Republicans]. . . . Is this not to display the belief in American omnipotence in very striking form? [5]

Secretary of State Acheson himself—in an unusually frank assessment —said (January 1950): "Nobody, I think, says that the Nationalist Government fell because it was confronted by overwhelming military force which it could not resist. Certainly no one in his right mind suggests that. Now, what I ask you to do is to stop looking for a moment under the bed and under the chair and under the rug to find out these reasons, but rather to look at the broad picture and see whether something doesn't suggest itself." What had happened, said Acheson, was "that the almost inexhaustible patience of the Chinese people in their misery ended. They did not bother to overthrow this government. There was really nothing to overthrow. They simply ignored it throughout the country."[6]

Quite obviously the United States government, disillusioned by its long and unsuccessful effort to end the Chinese civil war and avert a Nationalist collapse, was now preparing to wash its hands of the whole matter. A "White Paper" on China was issued to set the record straight, and briefing notes were distributed for the use of U.S. embassies, which would be used to explain—once Formosa fell to the Communists—that Formosa's strategic and military value to the U.S. was limited. But the disassociation was not to be, for two reasons: domestic political reaction and the outbreak of the Korean War (June 1950).

Domestic political reaction to China's "fall" was gathering momentum even before North Korea assaulted South Korea toward the end of June. There was popular uneasiness but it had no direct focus. The Korean War provided that focus. It forced the United States' hand. After all, we had liberated South Korea. We had brought its government into existence. We had inspired the founding of the UN and pledged our prestige and support to it, if it should be confronted with any outright aggression. Now that promissary note was called. Improvised military help was rushed from nearby U.S. forces in Japan, and the issue was joined. At the same time, President Truman gave orders to the Seventh Fleet to prevent military action in the Formosa Straits during the course of Korean hostilities. (Otherwise a Chinese Communist offensive against

[5] Sir Dennis W. Brogan, "The Illusion of American Omnipotence," *Harper's*, 205:21–28 (December 1952).

[6] Dean Acheson, "Crisis in Asia—An Examination of United States Policy," *Department of State Bulletin*, 22:112ff. (January 23, 1950).

Formosa—which had been expected—might bring insistent pressures to fight the Chinese Communists on the mainland, and broaden the U.S. involvement greatly.)

The Korean War went at first poorly. Only a small perimeter around Pusan was still held, when (September 15, 1950) the situation was completely reversed by the daring U.S. amphibious assault at Inchon in the Seoul area near the 38th parallel. Now UN armies advanced in hot pursuit of the enemy up to the Yalu River frontier. In November, the Chinese responded with "volunteer" units that forced General Mac-Arthur's troops into retreat; and the General himself admitted to the Security Council: "We face an entirely new war." With the front finally again stabilized near the 38th parallel and a stalemate shaping up, the Communists agreed to truce conversations which began on July 10, 1951, and continued (with interruptions) for two years. On July 27, 1953, an armistice finally went into effect.

During all of these events (except in the initial weeks and immediately after the Inchon landing) public criticism and unrest increased, reaching a climax during the presidential campaign and election of 1952, which ended twenty years of Democratic Party tenure in the White House. (Senator McCarthy [February 1954] called that same period "twenty years of treason.") Acheson himself became a major political target. As Senator Hugh Butler of Nebraska put it once, "I look at that fellow, I watch his smart-aleck manner and his British clothes and that . . . everlasting New Dealism in everything he says and does, and I want to shout, 'Get out! Get out! You stand for everything that has been wrong with the United States for years!' "[7]

It is extremely difficult to reconstruct the oddity of those times. In the hotly emotional political setting of 1952 a man as courageous as John F. Kennedy hedged. (Even Eisenhower, after election, hesitated to take on McCarthy at first.) The Republican platform of 1952, with its charges of the "betrayal" of Chiang and the "loss" of the Korean War, appealed to the basic suspicions of the voters. Even the successful containment policy in Europe was characterized as "negative." What accounted for this "McCarthy era"—as it came to be called—was partly a cumulation of postwar resentments and partly a lively disaffection with the course of the Korean War itself.

The war had not gone well by the standards of the supposed scenario of a UN "police action." Collective security sanctions such as these were supposed to be overwhelming in their impact, quick in their military results, and clear in their moral consequences. All the UN members

---

[7] Quoted in Samuel Eliot Morison, *The Oxford History of the American People* (New York: Oxford University Press, 1965), pp. 1075–1076. Morison adds: "Nobody who did not live through that period will ever believe what a sound and fury" was involved.

would move as one (in view of the flagrant aggression) and would together crush the criminal nation—that was the concept. But the reality was that the Communist nations of course opposed the whole UN action, the "neutralist" nations exerted pressures generally to confine the fighting and restore peace by some degree of compromise, and only a few nations actually contributed armed forces. While two-thirds of the then 60 UN members offered some aid (medical supplies, food, money, transit facilities, even soap), only 16 actually provided armed forces.[8] By early 1951, the Unified Command had 250,000 U.S. troops and 26,000 troops from 13 other states, plus the South Koreans under its control. The nations who sent forces were largely allies of the United States at that time, or became so shortly thereafter. Beyond this grouping were only the Union of South Africa and Ethiopia (who for prestige reasons felt it necessary to respond since in the days of the League they themselves had pleaded for support against the Italians).

The American people pointed to the disproportionate U.S. burden, to the fact that help came almost solely from U.S. allies, and especially to the lack of conformity to the ideal "police action" scenario. In the end, even the aggressor's "punishment" was largely restricted to what he had lost in military operations. The North Korean government (at the end as in the beginning) was still in power; its territories were left largely intact by the armistice settlement, which essentially was a return to the *status quo ante bellum.*

A serious mistake by the Truman Administration added to the Democratic defeat of 1952. Confronted with the fact that large numbers of Chinese prisoners did not want to return to China, the U.S. decided on a novel approach of requiring only prisoners-of-war who so desired to be repatriated. Whether taken on humanitarian grounds or in an effort to gain a propaganda advantage, this departure from custom rebounded on the U.S. This issue by itself added 16 months to the negotiations for an armistice, during which, of course, U.S. casualties continued to mount. This new departure contained obvious disadvantages. For example, how could the U.S. ensure that its own men were given a free opportunity to return? In the specific context of these negotiations for an armistice designed to register a stalemate rather than a military victory, how were the Chinese to be induced to accept the humiliation that the U.S. formula contained? Not until the Chinese ultimately figured a way around the consequences, did they accept. (Essentially what they did was to stretch out prisoner-of-war interviews to where public awareness of how many Chinese would not return was dulled.)

Large numbers of Americans went to vote in 1952 convinced that the Democrats had not stood up sufficiently to Stalin in Europe, had "lost"

---

[8] A Chinese Nationalist troop offer was declined in the hope of keeping the Chinese question separate.

China, and were unable either to "win" or end the Korean War. In retrospect it is apparent that the advent of a Republican administration (under the circumstances) was very necessary to restore some measure of confidence of the American people in their own government. It was not true that China had been "betrayed" or "lost" because of American actions. Nor could one reasonably criticize the response of the government to the threat to Greece and to Berlin. At the same time, it was true that many important mistakes had been made in handling American foreign affairs, especially during the last years of World War II when the postwar policies of the Soviet Union were seriously misjudged.

An Assessment

GEORGE F. KENNAN in his *Memoirs* describes his lack of belief in 1941 that the Soviets could be made somehow into a real "political associate" of the United States in the postwar era. He characterized Soviet actions as reflecting "sheer self-interest" in a quite immediate sense. After quoting a note in which these points are made, he says that it

embodied the essence of the disagreement that was to hold me in opposition to our governmental policy for some five years to come; hold me in opposition until the movement of the pendulum of official thinking from left to right would bring it close to my own outlook in the years 1946 to 1948, only to carry it away once more in the other direction, with the oversimplified and highly militarized view of the Russian problem that came to prevail after 1949.[9]

The United States, failing to make the distinction between "permanent allies" and "occasional allies"—which it should have done—failed during World War II and immediately afterward to pursue a realistic policy toward the Soviet Union. Whatever excuses can be made for the Soviets, these are the facts: the Soviets proved willing to safeguard Hitler's rear in 1939–1940; they came into the war against Germany against their own obvious wishes; they accepted a nonaggression pact with Japan that freed the Japanese to assault the U.S.; they refused to open a "second front" against Japan until they defeated Germany; and they betrayed their completely ruthless policy toward Poland during the Warsaw uprising (when Red Army units were just outside the city and could have helped). These and other manifestations of Soviet policy were hardly such as to justify the assumptions that the American government—as Kennan notes—was making in this period.

Once the U.S. awoke to the true nature of Soviet policy in Europe, with the horse already stolen in Poland and half of Germany, we tried

---

[9] Kennan, George F., *Memoirs, 1925–1950* (Boston: Little, Brown, 1967), p. 134.

to lock the barn door in the Balkans where we had no hopes at all of making any impression other than on the sea flank (Greece and Turkey). Responding then to the challenge over Berlin, we made the Soviets back down where it really counted, and we proceeded with imaginative measures such as the Marshall Plan and the North Atlantic Pact. These moves represented well-conceived objectives, well executed, involving a clear strategic conception. Because they drew support and strength from Western Europe's desire to remain free, they capitalized on the basic force of nationalism in those states. By so doing they brought back a precarious stability to the European balance of power. Thus these moves served fundamental American interests in Europe at quite acceptable costs.

In Asia, led astray by a completely erroneous concept of Stalin's true attitude toward Chinese communism, anxious over the greatly expanded "Communist bloc," which we thought had been brought into existence in Asia at Stalin's command, we turned away following the outbreak of the Korean War from the decision to disengage from Chinese affairs. Feeling our word at stake, and our prestige deeply committed (which was true enough), we then engaged in a deeply frustrating "police action." Called off by an armistice registering a stalemate that was much preferable to full-scale war with China, the Korean War seemed in virtually its whole course an affront to American moral and political preconceptions. Much more significant, however, was that it placed the U.S. squarely athwart Chinese interests, and widened the containment concept to Asia without at the same time rallying significant Asian support. This last point was the most obvious strategic weakness in the policy.

By its emotional political backlash at home, the Korean War helped overturn a Democratic tenure of two decades. The change had the merit of bringing into power those who were most dissatisfied with what had been done, so that a new start could be made. In Chapter 11 we shall see where these new policies led, as they unfolded in the normal American way to the accompaniment of new formulas and doctrines.

CHAPTER 11

The New Age:
Liberation vs. Containment

I**T IS** quite clear that a new President of the United States, however much he is the central figure in foreign policy-making, and however much he may be committed publicly to change, rarely has much initial opportunity to alter or reverse foreign policy fundamentally. Rather, he can deflect it to one side or the other of its fixed course. As he continues in office he may by one deflection after the other ultimately change policy fundamentally. He may even in the end reverse it, as Harry Truman did Franklin D. Roosevelt's too optimistic appraisal of future Soviet behavior and its consequences for our own policy. This situation creates a dilemma for a new administration desiring change.

There are many reasons that a new President in a real sense inherits, and inevitably at first continues, the foreign policy of his predecessor, as Truman initially did. Especially is this natural when a Vice-President suddenly succeeds to power. Administrative problems assert themselves. A new President, besides learning the job by doing, is preoccupied with making appointments to his "official family," establishing a code of bureaucratic procedure reflecting his own personality. Only later can he proceed to substance. Even if he wished to change things both radically and immediately, certain inhibitions and obstacles exist. The vast bureaucracy of foreign affairs needs time to adjust, or even to comprehend the adjustment contemplated. Furthermore, sudden great changes are dangerous. Their usefulness is directly correlated to the interlocking reactions they produce from a whole host of foreign nations; the greater and more abrupt the change, the harder it is to know what is likely to come of it.

Even apart from these considerations, the political process in the United States encourages "center consensus" and discourages radical course changes. Each major political party, although portraying as vividly as possible its great differences with the other and conveying the image of "the great alternative," actually achieves political victory

194

by capturing the independent voter in the middle. Victory is not likely if the extreme implications of the "alternative" are too clearly spelled out. A successful strategy for achieving political victory involves solving problems akin to those confronting automobile manufacturers as they decide on new models and the promotion campaign to sell them: the new car must be different but it cannot be revolutionary. If the car is too radical, people will not buy it. In the same way, promises of a *radically* different foreign policy strategy may backfire. What the political platform and campaign speeches are really meant to convey is the ultimate direction of the new departures to be made, rather than an expectation of immediate and very radical change. This is not said in so many words, but it is fairly well understood by those who have any real experience with the process, including the "informed" voter. Thus the American political process discourages really clear-cut strategic foreign policy choices under any normal circumstances. Yet psychologically, at the outset of a new administration that has come to power by turning out the other party, some symbolic acts are needed to indicate that all of the campaign oratory has not been simply shelved. It is against this background that the foreign policy moves of the Eisenhower Administration, representing the first major shift in political power between the Democrats and Republicans in twenty years, must be understood. What the Republicans were saying to the voters is that the United States was going to quit yielding ground; if anything it was the Communists' turn.

Korea, Indo-China, and SEATO

IT WAS inevitable that U.S. Asian policy would receive first attention, since there the fighting still continued. While still a candidate, President Eisenhower had promised that one of his first acts would be to move the Korean War off dead-center. Even before assuming office and within a month of being elected, he made a dramatic visit to Korea. By this time, the armistice negotiations were well along. That they were successfully concluded at the end of July of Eisenhower's first year as President may be partly attributable to the new pressures Eisenhower sought to bring to bear (February 2, 1953), when he told Congress that the Seventh Fleet would "no longer be employed to shield Communist China," and cancelled Truman's neutralization of the Formosa Straits of June 27, 1950.

Whether the Chinese Communists thought that Chiang by himself could successfully invade the mainland would be extremely doubtful. At the same time, a distinct rise in the tension level resulted, and the Chinese Communists no doubt did obtain the impression that American frustration with the unending war might soon lead to further U.S. escalation. Stalin died in March 1953. In May, Secretary Dulles made it clear to Nehru in New Delhi that the war was going to end soon one way or the other; and very quickly after that conversation, Peking (probably influenced by both events) announced acceptance in the Korean talks of a new formula for the prisoner-of-war issue. The formula involved placing in neutral custody those prisoners who did not want to return—for a limited period, while they were interviewed. The Chinese Communists had conceived the idea of agreeing to this and then later claiming that the period was not to be one month by calendar but 30 (widely separated) days of interview; they were therefore able to salvage their prestige. The armistice was signed on July 27, 1953.

The fact not known publicly at the time was that Eisenhower and Dulles had extracted a pledge from Chiang Kai-shek to refrain from any offensive move without prior American consent. The public image conveyed by the new administration in dealing with the China problem was one of severely limited patience. Whether this stance was or was not designed to appeal primarily to a frustrated American electorate, it certainly alarmed America's European allies. Communist China's agreement to the Geneva formulas for ending the Indo-Chinese War (which we shall discuss in a moment) may have stemmed in part from the feeling that the U.S. temper was now to a point where rational considerations might no longer prevail.

Having publicly "unleashed Chiang Kai-shek," (as the newspapers put it—although the administration did not use this phrase) and having achieved a Korean armistice, the next question was what to do about Korea and Formosa in terms of treaty commitments. The Korean issue was handled first, with a draft treaty between the U.S. and South Korea initialed on August 8, 1953. It provided that the two nations would consult together whenever in the opinion of either the independence or security of either was threatened by "external armed attack." They would each move "to meet the common danger in accordance with its constitutional processes." U.S. troops were given the right to be stationed in the Republic of Korea. Signed on October 1, 1953, the treaty was accepted by the Senate (81 to 6) on January 26, 1954. The Senate stipulated that the U.S. obligation was confined to the then existing territory of South Korea.

With Formosa, similar arrangements were made. If there were "an armed attack in the West Pacific area," each would move "to meet the common danger in accordance with its constitutional processes." Formosa and the nearby Pescadores were specifically covered, but there was no definite mention of the offshore islands immediately adjacent to the coast of Asia that were still in Nationalist hands. U.S. forces could be stationed "in and about" Formosa and the Pescadores. In an exchange of letters it was also agreed that Chiang would not attack the mainland without U.S. consent. Senate approval (64 to 6) on February 9, 1955, included three reservations. By these the obligation was limited to "external armed attack," and military operations by either party from Nationalist territories could only occur after joint agreement.

Connected to this significant expansion of U.S. treaty obligations to areas to which, shortly before, the American government had been unwilling to be committed, was the Southeast Asia Collective Defense Treaty (SEATO).

SEATO's establishment was tied up with the results of the Geneva Far Eastern Conference (April–July 1954). Because the Korean War technically ended with an armistice (which would theoretically be later terminated by some peace settlement), and the long-fought Indo-China War had dragged on to a point where both sides sought negotiations (even if for different reasons), it was decided at the Berlin Foreign Ministers Conference of early 1954 to treat both questions at Geneva that spring. All concerned parties were invited to this conference, whether they had diplomatic relations with each other or not (as in the case of Communist China and the U.S.).

At the conference Korea became virtually a dead issue. Having fought each other to a military stalemate and negotiated an agreement, there was no reason for the parties to alter that verdict so soon by a further conference. Attention remained focused on Indo-China where French fortunes of war were moving steadily to a disastrous climax at Dien Bien Phu, which fell in mid-conference (May 7, 1954). For almost 10 years the French had struggled in Indo-China, delaying concessions to nationalist sentiment until they were too few and too late, never able in the chaos of the existing political party framework of the Fourth Republic (with its disastrously balanced line-up on the issue of either give up or really fight on the necessary scale) to bring the war to an end. With the war about to be lost, the new French Premier, Mendès-France, took office (June 19, 1954) on a pledge to end the war within 30 days or resign.

By June, Dien Bien Phu had fallen; the French had evacuated the southern part of the rich Red River Delta, held only Hanoi-Haiphong in the north, and had only partial control in what would become known later as South Viet-Nam. France had few cards to play. In this perspective the decisions of the Geneva Conference on Viet-Nam were remarkably favorable to the West. Viet-Nam was the largest Indo-Chinese state and was to be divided in two on the 17th parallel. In the ensuing 10 months, the French and such Vietnamese non-Communists as wished were to be withdrawn south, while Communist forces would withdraw north. Prisoners of war (PW's) would be freed and exchanged by August 20, 1954. An international commission (India, Poland, and Canada), together with Vietnamese commissions, would supervise the execution of these arrangements. Laos would be neutralized and would have elections in 1955; Cambodia also would be neutralized. In Viet-Nam elections were to take place before July 20, 1956. Since the French had substantially lost most of Viet-Nam by the time of the conference, the Communist agreement to the 17th parallel reflected pronounced moderation. Of course there was the promise of elections, which they felt sure they would win by one means or the other. These all-Vietnamese elections, however, were not held, as it turned out—a development linked to the difficulties in ending the Viet-Nam War in 1969. Probably Communist moderation stemmed also from the very real fear that the U.S. would engage in hostilities in Viet-Nam if the Communists pressed for a greater victory.

Military intervention by the U.S. had actually been discussed seriously in Washington in early April, as the siege of Dien Bien Phu tightened. Dulles had been told on March 20 that only an immediate air strike could avert disaster. Conferring with congressional leaders (April 3) he sought support for the use of U.S. air and naval power in Indo-China. Admiral Arthur W. Radford, chairman of the Joint Chiefs, supported Dulles, but the other Chiefs did not. When it also turned out that Great Britain's attitude was unknown, the congressional leaders, including Lyndon Johnson, strongly advised no action unless support from important allies was forthcoming. Prime Minister Anthony Eden gave Dulles no encouragement. There was agreement about the possibility of creating SEATO, but great disagreement about timing. The British insisted on waiting until after the Geneva Conference.

With American right-wing opinion strongly opposed to the Geneva settlement—Senator Knowland called it "one of the greatest victories for communism in a decade"—the U.S. reaction to the settlement was ambivalent. It straddled a line between refusing to endorse the agreement made (and thus communism's gains) but warning that the agreement must be kept in that no further Communist advances would be tolerated.

To implement some appearance or substance of a countermove and to counter the public disillusionment with further Communist gains even while Republicans were in office, Dulles pushed strongly now for SEATO. Meeting at Manila (September 1954) and reaching agreement on SEATO were the United States, Great Britain, France, Australia, New Zealand, Pakistan, the Philippines, and Thailand. They agreed that "an armed attack in the treaty area against any of the Parties or against any State or territory which the Parties by unanimous agreement may hereafter designate, would endanger its own peace and safety." They would act to meet the common danger each "in accordance with its constitutional processes." The treaty would remain in force indefinitely, subject to a year's notice of termination. Further, by protocol the SEATO nations agreed at Manila to extend the application of the treaty provisions to Cambodia, Laos, and South Viet-Nam by defining their territory as within the agreed treaty area to which SEATO would apply. It is in this way that the U.S. was obligated—more strictly, obligated itself —to defend South Viet-Nam. The rather tenuous legal argument in the 1960's that the U.S. was "bound" to defend South Viet-Nam thus came into existence. The U.S. Senate, acting during the first crisis over the offshore islands threatened by Communist China, agreed to SEATO's ratification (82 to 1) on February 1, 1955.

By early 1955, slightly more than halfway through his first term, President Eisenhower had thus substantially increased U.S. formal commitments in Asia. That his new treaties received such overwhelming support in the Senate indicates that the approval of the new policies was not confined to the Republican side of Congress. Once the United States had fought to save South Korea we could not gracefully wash our hands of its future, if we had wished it. We were obligated also by earlier bilateral pacts with the Philippines, Australia, and New Zealand. Almost simultaneously with SEATO Congress accepted the alliance with Formosa. Although this move was far from the 1949 concept of holding aloof from the final stages of the Chinese civil war while the Communists took Formosa, the actual decision to stand by Formosa was almost implicit in the events of the Korean War, in which Chinese forces had intervened against American troops. Whichever way one wants to assess these events—even if one argues that the U.S. advance into North Korea produced a conflict with Chinese forces that might have been avoided by a more prudent policy—once they occurred, the fact remains that it was no longer feasible in 1953 simply to resume the 1949 policy. Even if Truman and Acheson had continued in office, the same moves would probably have been made. Especially in this connection must we remember the crescendo of popular emotion that began to build up in the United States in 1949 after we "lost" China. Perhaps the 1949 policy would have been shelved even without a Korean War. After it, no other outcome was likely.

Thus, Eisenhower substantially revolutionized our previous policy in Asia by accepting these additional commitments, although some such course of action was probably almost unavoidable given the American political temper of the times. Whether that public attitude made these commitments wise was a separate issue.

Whether SEATO in particular was wise is a complicated question. Its membership included two European great powers, Britain and France, who were at the beginning stage of a fairly complete withdrawal from Asian involvements. It also included Pakistan (who was shortly to join CENTO) and the Philippines, Australia, and New Zealand, to whom we were already committed. Looked at in these terms, apart from its psychological impact (positive or negative) and apart from any gains made by improved coordinating devices (doubtful), SEATO really comes down essentially to the U.S. allying itself with Southeast Asia in the person of Thailand. She was the only new recruit, so to speak. As to the protocol protection of Indo-China, only the U.S. and the other already existing small power allies of the U.S in Asia ever took this very seriously. Despite the overwhelming approval of the American public for this pact, whose very name of SEATO deliberately paralleled the magic of NATO's name and implied similar success in Asia, the fact was that SEATO's membership was an admission of the lack of interest or even opposition by the major Asian nations to the U.S. proposals and policies. SEATO was (and is) unlike NATO exactly in that feature which made NATO, for all its later troubles, so useful and successful as a rallying point. SEATO lacked local great power membership—a warning itself that the strategy it embodied was probably deficient in capitalizing on the basic forces at work in Asia. By all of these acts of the first Eisenhower Administration, the *status quo* in Asia was intentionally frozen. By all of these acts the seeds were sown, for better or for worse, for the later Viet-Nam War. By all of these acts, for which the Chinese must also assume responsibility, the "Chinese problem" went unresolved. Although the strategic objective (containing communism) was clear, the strategic concept did not distinguish which communisms were a threat under which circumstances. Worse, the concept, because ambiguous, could lead to actions contrary to the basic forces of Asian nationalism, while ensuring only nominal Asian support on its behalf.

The fact that further serious problems were implicit in these new developments in Asia was not obvious to the American public. Since Communist expansive activities in Asia went into low gear for a time following the ending of the Korean War and the conclusion of these new alliances, the peace in Asia was deemed the result of the policies. Stability in Asia was, however, a passing phase, even if not realized at the time.

The German Problem After Stalin's Death

EVENTS in Europe (1953–1955) again centered on Germany and the Soviet position in Eastern Europe. How influential Stalin's death (March 5, 1953) was in inducing the Chinese Communists to agree shortly thereafter to the Korean armistice is a matter of speculation. By contrast, the fact that Soviet policy in Europe was immediately affected is quite clear.

On January 27, 1953, in one of those ringing pronouncements that seemed to come so naturally to John Foster Dulles—a man whose colorful phraseology contrasted so strongly with his reserved public character—he pledged over radio-TV to the "captive" people behind the

Iron Curtain that "you can count on us." In February, the administration encouraged a congressional resolution condemning "the forcible absorption of free peoples into an aggressive despotism." Stalin's death caused the resolution to be shelved; but on April 16, President Eisenhower underlined America's desire to see the "full independence of the East European nations" restored. Then on June 18–24, came the riots and resistance in East Germany, which culminated in a spontaneous insurrection in Berlin (and other cities) that was forcibly suppressed with the aid of Soviet armored units. On July 1, Eisenhower made clear to the press that the U.S. was planning no physical intervention in Europe.

The new Soviet government was nominally headed by Georgi Malenkov, in association with Molotov, Bulganin, Kaganovich, and Lavrenti Beria (the head of the secret police). On July 10, Beria was arrested on treason charges; he was executed that December. On August 8, Malenkov announced that the Soviets endorsed the principle of "a peaceful coexistence of two systems." On August 20, the Soviets further announced that they had tested an H-bomb "within the last few days." (The first U.S. hydrogen-bomb test had come in November 1952.)

To sum up U.S. policy toward Soviet interests at this time, although the U.S. had announced what the press interpreted as a policy of "liberation," we nevertheless carefully stayed out of involvement when actual unrest behind the Iron Curtain turned into active revolt. In view of the Soviet advances in the nuclear field, this was no more than prudent. Yet the U.S. continued in the next years to speak of liberation while equally determined not to intervene if it occurred—a policy which would arouse some soul-searching in late 1956 in view of events in Hungary.

The real focus of diplomatic attention in this period between Stalin's death and the summit conference of mid-1955 was Germany and the West's plans to rearm the Federal Republic. As early as May 26, 1952, the Bonn Agreement, looking forward to the restoration of West German sovereignty, had been signed. The following day, at Paris, the European Defense Community Treaty was approved by France, Italy, the Benelux nations, and West Germany. It was to be the vehicle for West German rearmament. In this field the Western move was basically defensive, for the Soviets had led the way: their East German "police units" (in reality, armed forces) were in excess of 50,000 as early as 1948, while the West waited until September 1950 (because of French opposition) to agree in principle to follow the same road. Throughout 1953 and more than halfway into 1954, the French vacillated, distracted by Indo-China but also shrinking from actually approving the rearming of their ancient enemy. That the French had themselves proposed the multinational EDC armed-forces concept in no way made them eager to see the final decision made. Premier Mendès-France, who had so energetically moved to resolve the Indo-Chinese issue, with equal determination forced the French National Assembly to face this issue too. When they did, they rejected EDC! While this shock was still being felt, Anthony Eden of Great Britain sprang into action and presented a substitute set of formulas designed to bring West Germany into NATO, while restricting the quantity and quality of German weapons. The new agreements were signed at Paris on October 23, 1954.

Soviet diplomatic attention during this period focused on preventing, first the EDC, and then the Eden-sponsored revamping of NATO, from being ratified. They tried simultaneously to stir French fears of Germany and convince the West Germans that a move in this direction would ensure Germany's continued partition. Soviet action immediately following the Bonn-EDC agreements (May 1952) had been highly dramatic. Between dusk of the night EDC was signed and dawn of the following day, the Communists closed off hundreds of secondary roads along which local traffic had been permitted between the two Germanies. A real Iron Curtain thus came into full existence. In mid-1953, unrest exploded in East Germany. After a sufficient delay to restore their control, the Soviets agreed to the Berlin Conference of foreign ministers (January–February 1954). All this conference produced on the German question was further deadlock. The West viewed with suspicion Soviet proposals for a provisional All-German government (formed by the two existing governments on a complete parity basis), which would then formulate a "democratic" election law and hold "democratic" elections. Molotov had made the meaning of "democratic" quite clear at the conference by saying that "complete freedom of activity for all democratic organizations . . . does not mean that we should not take any measures against the rebirth of activity on the part of Fascist and militaristic organizations. It is also necessary to exclude the possibility of any attempts at pressure by large monopolies. . . ." On the other hand, the simple insistence by the West on a really free election to form an All-German government that would be free to decide whether to join NATO (or Warsaw!) was completely unacceptable to the Soviets. Everyone concerned knew how that would turn out: the Soviets would have to withdraw, while the military frontier of the West would move forward to the Polish border. The failure of this conference led to the new Western agreements of October 1954 (already noted) and to new efforts of the Soviets to block their success.

On December 30, 1954, the French ratified the new arrangements. This time the West German Bundestag had waited for French action before ratifying the agreements, so Soviet efforts in January–February 1955 focused on West Germany. On January 15, 1955, Moscow in a public statement again offered "free elections," this time suggesting that the All-German election law "be drafted with due regard" for the electoral laws of the two German states, to "guarantee free expression of will for *all* electors [and] freedom for all democratic parties and organizations to conduct their electioneering campaigns all over Germany. . . ." (Italics added.) The Soviets added bait:

With the object of facilitating agreement on the holding of such elections, the Soviet government considers it possible, with the consent of the governments of the German Democratic Republic and the German Federal Republic, to agree to the establishment of appropriate international supervision of the All-German elections.

The West Germans indeed were now confronted with an apparent choice, as this Soviet "Statement on the German Question" said:

One course would lead to the reunification of Germany. . . . It would preclude the possibility of either part of Germany becoming a party to military alliances directed against other states, and would best be insured by the inclusion of Germany in a system of collective European security.

The other course, to which the Paris Agreements would commit her, would perpetuate the division of Germany, resurrect militarism in Western Germany, and make the latter a party to the planning of war.

The real possibilities implicit in these proposals are not known, primarily because Konrad Adenauer discounted them as merely devices to weaken West Germany's will to move to greater links with the West in a common NATO grouping. Fearful that prolonged discussions might divide German opinion and induce a "wait-and-see" attitude, Adenauer determined to ignore the Soviet statement, even though it seemed to be far less limited on the scope of "free" elections and even though it contained a promise of "appropriate" international supervision—a safeguard consistently demanded by the West.

The Soviets made one final try—in an event that today still remains obscure but extremely interesting in its possible implications. On February 6, 1955 (two days before Malenkov fell from power in the Soviet Union), an "interparliamentary conference on the German question" ended at Warsaw. Composed of 150 delegates "including representatives from the Soviet Union" (who would certainly not vote without instructions) it voted unanimously to offer negotiations

. . . on free, controlled elections in Germany, such as were proposed by Sir Anthony Eden, British Foreign Secretary, a year ago at the Berlin Conference of the Big Four. The resolution also suggested that the territorial integrity of a neutralized Germany should be guaranteed by the European states and the United States. The Warsaw resolution, voted by the Soviet delegates, went far beyond any offers made publicly by Vyacheslav M. Molotov on the reunification of Germany.[1]

---

[1] See *The New York Times* (February 11, 1955). *The Times* reports the ADN or East German News Agency dispatch on pp. 1 and 4.

Two days later (and three days before *The New York Times* story), Malenkov was out of power, never to return. The very day that Malenkov was removed, Molotov delivered a 16,000-word foreign-policy address to the Supreme Soviet, in Moscow. Said Molotov: German elections could be held "even this year" if the Paris Agreements were not ratified; otherwise reunification would be "impossible, for a long period." This was virtually the only remark he made on the German problem in 16,000 words!

Only one interpretation of this curious sequence of events would seem to explain all facets of it, for if this Warsaw gambit was simply a further and last propaganda move to avert ratification, why did Molotov not reap its propaganda advantages in his speech? Why make the move and then in effect ignore it? To believe that the Soviet delegates in Warsaw were carried away and went beyond their instructions strains credulity; any such resolution would almost certainly have been *proposed* by the Soviet delegates. We know that Malenkov, nominally still in power as premier in early 1955, had little real control within the Soviet Communist Party organs at that time. Khrushchev had already maneuvered himself behind the scenes into a powerful position. It is also apparent that a 16,000-word foreign policy address cannot be improvised and that Molotov was probably basically finished with his speech by the time the Warsaw resolution was proposed. In view of all of this, what is most likely is as follows: the Warsaw resolution represented a quite different German policy advocated by Malenkov; Malenkov managed to have it adopted at Warsaw; Molotov either opposed or did not know about the move; and Malenkov's action was the final straw in bringing about his removal.

Indirect evidence on this point came some years later from Khrushchev himself (March 1963). Making excuses for Stalin (who he said had been a very sick man), Khrushchev contrasted Stalin with Beria who had been "frantically reaching out for power, for leadership within the Party" in order to pursue non-Marxist goals:

Already in the first few days following Stalin's death Beria began to take steps to disorganize the work of the Party and to undermine the Soviet Union's friendly relations with fraternal countries of the socialist camp. For instance, he and Malenkov came out with the provocative proposal to liquidate the German Democratic Republic as a socialist state, to recommend to the Socialist Unity Party of Germany to abandon the slogan of the struggle to build socialism. The Central Committee promptly rejected these traitorous proposals with indignation and administered a crushing rebuff to the provocateurs.

The measures taken by the Central Committee safeguarded the Party and the country against the foul intentions of Beria, that inveterate agent of the imperialists.

While any efforts by Beria, arrested in July 1953, necessarily then stopped, Malenkov still remained free to maneuver after that date. One could argue that if Malenkov (March–July 1953) favored a change in Germany which would "liquidate the German Democratic Republic as a socialist state," he probably continued to have the same views later. If one *were* going to liquidate the GDR all it would take would be free and supervised elections such as Eden's formula prescribed in detail.

Malenkov evidently made a gamble and got a cold rebuff both from his own comrades and from the West. He was out of power as premier before the news about Warsaw was even widely known in the West. This also suggests that if Adenauer had shown more interest in the January "Statement," meaningful negotiations *might* have followed. Yet even if they had, Malenkov might well have been unable to prevail.

This is a formidable list of "ifs." In any event, by May 5, 1955, with the Paris Agreements now ratified by all the Western signatories, West Germany started on a course of unity with the West in NATO. For their part the Soviets had little to say about the whole question for some months after Molotov's long speech. In May 1955, they symbolized Europe's increased division by creating the Warsaw Pact, but almost simultaneously they accepted a treaty giving Austria neutral status (and providing for the evacuation of the troops of both sides). It was as though the Soviets were saying to the Germans: "This is the choice you threw away."

With the German issue now resolved for better or for worse, with the Soviet and U.S. stockpiles of nuclear weapons growing, with the change of leaders which had occurred in both super powers, and with the world momentarily free from major war anywhere for the first time in two decades, the stage was set for a new look at the situation. This new look came at a summit conference at Geneva, in July 1955.

The Summit Conference—Interlude Between Storms

SINCE the Geneva Summit Conference was a meeting of heads of government, Bulganin technically represented the Soviet Union (although accompanied by Khrushchev), Eisenhower represented the United States, Eden spoke for Britain, and Faure represented France.

In his keynote remarks President Eisenhower said: "We meet here for a simple purpose. We have come to find a basis for accommodation. . . ." The substantive issues Eisenhower listed were first, "the problem of unifying Germany and forming an All-German Government based on free elections"; second, disarmament; and third, Western distrust of the international Communist movement's intentions. Faure argued that bringing West Germany into NATO had provided a controlled framework for German rearmament, thus making any future

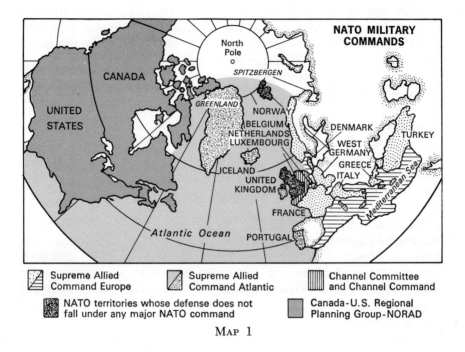

Supreme Allied Command Europe

Supreme Allied Command Atlantic

Channel Committee and Channel Command

NATO territories whose defense does not fall under any major NATO command

Canada-U.S. Regional Planning Group-NORAD

MAP 1

German aggression against the Soviet Union far less likely. Eden thought the "chief problem" was German unity: "Until the unity of Germany is restored there can be neither confidence nor security on this continent." Eden wanted "a security pact of which those round this table and a United Germany might be members" and declared himself "ready to examine the possibility of a demilitarized area between East and West." (Both suggestions were significant moves in the direction of earlier Soviet viewpoints.)

Bulganin was restrained, reviewing first the Soviet views on peace, disarmament, the Austrian treaty, and collective security: "The Soviet Government is of the opinion that our eventual objective should be to have no foreign troops remaining on the territories of European states." Germany should be unified "as a peace-loving and democratic state," but "the remilitarization of West Germany and its integration into military groupings of the Western Powers now represent the main obstacles to its unification." (Bulganin's speech was relatively general, and his remarks on Germany were substantially confined to those quoted.)

The third plenary session (July 19) saw Eisenhower attempting to reassure Russia on the "purely defensive" nature of NATO, even saying that "if any one of these nations [in NATO] attempts to act aggressively against any other, it is immediately moved against by all the remaining nations of NATO." Germany's forces would not be "complete or whole within themselves," and would be kept so "intertwined with the forces of the other Western nations" that it would be "impossible for them to conduct any effective military operation of any kind by themselves." At the fourth plenary session, Bulganin proposed a 50-year general European treaty on collective security providing for membership by both German states, "pending the formation of a united, peace-loving democratic German State." This treaty envisaged (after a transitional period) that both NATO and the Warsaw Pact would be phased out. It was not stipulated that by this time Germany would have to be reunited. Soviet policy was clearly shifting to a "two-German states" center of gravity.

On July 21, at the fifth plenary, disarmament proposals were made by both East and West. Premier Bulganin's plan involved reductions to fixed force levels, a prohibition of nuclear tests, and a pledge that each would "not . . . be the first to use atomic and hydrogen weapons." Eisenhower presented an "open skies" inspection proposal that would allow each side to overfly the other. Neither side showed enthusiasm for the approach to the problem taken by the other. The conference closed with a final directive to the foreign ministers (who were to meet shortly at Geneva, too) and final statements by all the heads of government. Bulganin noted the "relaxation of tension" he thought had been accomplished, terming "European security" as "the most important question" discussed. On his list disarmament came second, Germany third: "It was clear that . . . mechanical merger [i.e., simple reliance on free, Western-style elections] of the two parts of Germany" was "unrealistic." Representatives of both German states would need to be brought into any discussion on reunification.

What had the summit accomplished? Very little, substantively; quite a bit in diminishing the feeling of general tension. Indeed, close observation of these exchanges shows that the Soviets had put the important question of Germany essentially "on ice." The foreign ministers meeting that followed in no way thawed that ice.

The Crises of 1956: Poland and Hungary

As THE year 1956 began, the outlook for U.S. foreign policy seemed relatively promising. Treaty arrangements in the Far East were complete; NATO had gained West German adherence; a summit and a foreign ministers conference had renewed and continued the dialogue between East and West on Germany (first resumed at the Berlin Conference in 1954, after the long hiatus following the Paris meeting of June 1949, which ended the Berlin blockade). Whether such decisions as setting up SEATO or bringing West Germany into NATO were wise in the long run was a question little considered. The general American assessment was that tangible progress was being made.

What began as a quiet year for American foreign policy ended quite otherwise. Two very different events led to two quite diverse but fate-connected results: Khrushchev's "secret speech" and Nasser's seizure of the Suez Canal Company.

Khrushchev was party secretary and already held the effective power in the Soviet Union after Malenkov's demotion, even though Bulganin was premier. In February 1956, the 20th Congress of the Communist Party of the Soviet Union convened to hear a truly remarkable speech by Khrushchev. Indicting "the cult of the individual" which had been carried to an extreme under Stalin, he revealed that Lenin, "fearing for the future fate of the Party and of the Soviet Union," had "made a completely correct characterization of Stalin, pointing out that it was necessary to consider the question of transferring Stalin from the position of the Secretary General because of the fact that Stalin was excessively rude, that he did not have a proper attitude toward his comrades, that he was capricious and abused his power." So much had been known to the 13th Party Congress, which had decided to retain Stalin in his post. Khrushchev quoted a "new" Lenin letter of March 1923 to Stalin—one more forthright yet—in which Lenin point-blank demanded to know whether "you are agreeable to retracting your words and apologizing or whether you prefer the severance of relations between us." In the Soviet fashion the transcript of the speech at this point shows: "Commotion in the hall."[2]

As Khrushchev indicated, part of this information had been widely known 35 years earlier, but during Stalin's long rule all mention had been deleted from party histories of Lenin's opposition to him. As an illustration of Stalinist terror, Khrushchev went on to reveal what happened to the 17th Party Congress members in later years, pointing out that 80 per cent of the voting participants in that Congress joined the party either before the revolution or during the Civil War. They had been reliable Communists. And what was their fate? "It was determined that of the 139 . . . 98 persons, i.e., 70 per cent were arrested and shot (mostly in 1937–38)." (The transcript here shows: "Indignation in the hall.")

Khrushchev's revelations shook the hall. The details he gave about Kirov's murder (shortly before the terrorist period began) all but explicitly linked Stalin to it. He implied that Stalin had arranged the murder of a rival and then used it as an opportunity to kill others "suspected" of involvement. He revealed how demoralized Stalin was in the aftermath of the Nazi attack, failing even to attend a Central Committee plenum called for October 1941. Khrushchev's sensational speech was political dynamite, as he well knew. It was not given to the press;

[2] Lenin was seriously ill by the end of 1921. On May 26, 1922, he had a first stroke with a second one in December, which left him partially paralyzed. He died on January 21, 1924. This explains why Stalin managed to hold on at this point despite Lenin's disfavor.

and it was only in late 1961 that the Soviets dared to give wide publicity to this viewpoint within the Soviet Union.

A combination of pressures had caused the new Soviet leaders to make this daring move. Convinced from firsthand experience under Stalin that one-man power was intolerable, they sought to rally party opinion behind the principle of collegial rule, as in Lenin's day. Aware of the longing of the Soviet people for improvements in the standard of living and a repudiation of secret police terrorism, they determined to embark upon this delicate political maneuver. Because they, too, were in power in this period, they ran the risk of being tarred with the same brush. They had to convey an image of repudiating a distortion of a system in which they themselves were involved, and to do so without causing their own downfall. The management, too, of the satellites had to be put on a more healthy basis. Tito's successful opposition to Stalin had shown the dangers of a purely negative Soviet policy. People in Eastern Europe were as restive as the Soviet people, and the collegial principle had to be instituted there, too—both in de-Stalinizing the satellite regimes proper and in putting country-to-country relations on a more truly cooperative basis. Otherwise the whole pressure-cooker of the Soviet Communist world might erupt.

But bleeding steam from an overheated pressure-cooker is also a tricky operation. In retrospect, it is remarkable that the Soviet leaders achieved the basic transition they sought without more trouble abroad. At home they made the change, not without strains and stresses, but at least without bloodshed. Khrushchev (July 3, 1957) removed Malenkov and Molotov from the positions of power they still held; he dismissed Marshal Zhukov (October 26, 1957), and (March 27, 1958) he replaced Bulganin as premier. None of those dismissed was shot; and neither did Khrushchev attempt to become a new Stalin. All was accomplished on a basis of decisions by the party organs, and all were accepted without grave disruption.

Abroad in the satellites the process encountered more problems than at home, for the sensitivities of foreign nationalisms also entered the picture. Toward the end of 1956, the problem came to a head almost simultaneously in Poland and in Hungary. On October 21, 1956, a climax was reached in Warsaw as Wladyslaw Gomulka (himself previously confined to jail by the Polish Stalinist faction) took power at the helm of a "nationalist" Communist government. As the sense of emergency increased in Soviet-Polish affairs, the Soviet leaders flew to Warsaw. There they reached agreement with the Gomulka government: the head of the Polish armed forces (a Pole who had been a Soviet Marshal) was replaced, and it was agreed that Soviet armed forces movements within Polish frontiers would come only after previous notification to the Polish government. This arrangement was to prove enduring.

Events in Warsaw were echoed two days later in Budapest. Pressures built up against Stalinist Ernö Gerö and in favor of moderate Imre Nagy. Gerö invoked martial law and asked for Soviet help. But within a week, Nagy had become premier and János Kádár had succeeded Gerö as party secretary. Russia promised (October 30) in effect the same type of arrangements with Hungary she had agreed to with Poland. What seemed to be a settlement of the issue now rapidly evaporated, as Nagy's followers pressed for even greater concessions. By November 1, Red Army units were flowing into Hungary. Nagy proclaimed Hungary a neutral country and asked UN aid. By November 4, Nagy had lost, and Soviet tanks had crushed resistance in Budapest. Nagy himself took temporary refuge in the Yugoslav embassy, while Kádár headed the new Hungarian government. The tragic Hungarian revolt was over.

It was clear enough that the Soviet action of suppression, although ruthless, was taken reluctantly in the fear that the Soviet protective barrier in Eastern Europe might otherwise be lost. What encouraged the Soviet leaders to take the path of using force was the simultaneity of events in the Middle East, for on October 29, 1956, Israeli forces entered the Sinai Peninsula, and two days later French and British air operations began against the United Arab Republic. On October 30, the Security Council was deadlocked by Anglo-French vetoes; and on November 4, the Soviets cast a veto, too. Thus, in these crucial days of Soviet armed intervention in Hungary, world attention was fragmented, with most of it on the Middle East.

The Crises of 1956: The Middle East

THESE developments in the Middle East had a long history. The Palestine War had ended (1949) with armistice agreements that had never been translated into firm treaties of peace. From that time, tension, friction, and persistent small-scale violence had continued to characterize Israeli-Arab relations.

Arab resentment of Israel's "alien presence" on Middle Eastern soil was too deep-rooted to accommodate itself readily to a pragmatic recognition of the *status quo*. By derivation, the United States—considered in the Arab world as Israel's "sponsor"—became the focus of Arab frustration. To the surprise of Americans long accustomed to drawing a distinct line between Anglo-French colonial imperialism in the Middle East and American "benevolent involvement" to contain Soviet influence, the most orally violent sectors of the Arab world lumped all three states together, from at least 1949 onward. In their eyes England was castigated for her remaining holds on Jordan, Suez, and the Arabian Peninsula; France was opposed for her attempts to suppress Algerian nationalism; the U.S. was opposed as the main supplier of arms and backing to Britain and France, and as the protector and banker of Israel. Arab propaganda insistently painted Israel as a "disguised" form of a new Western imperialism. Thus, to the surprise of many Americans, the U.S. in Arab eyes (quite apart from any oil-connected neo-imperialism) became an "imperialist" power.

However, the events of 1956 had their immediate prelude in 1955. By that time (October 19, 1954), Great Britain had agreed to evacuate the British military base at Suez, which was the symbol of her domination of Egypt. Both Dulles and Eden had hopes of creating new defensive arrangements in the area, based upon voluntary cooperation by Gamal Abdel Nasser, the new Egyptian head of state. But when the Baghdad Pact (February 24, 1955) between Turkey and Iraq was next enlarged to include Britain, Pakistan, and Iran, Nasser reacted with rage. Nasser saw in its affiliation of Iraq with Western and non-Arab forces a blow at his plans for uniting the Arab world under his own leadership. The Soviet Union was angered at this new link in the chain of containment and came to an agreement with Nasser on a mammoth arms-cotton exchange. Announced on September 27, 1955, it sent shock waves around the world. To the West it represented a Soviet leapfrog action over the "Northern Tier" defenses, to a position of influence in the heart of the Middle East. As massive supplies of Czech arms poured into Egypt, it also upset the delicate military balance of strength between Israel and her Arab neighbors.

Nasser now began an exceedingly dangerous game, attempting deliberately to play off East against West. Counting upon the likelihood that the U.S. would prefer (for domestic, political reasons, among other things) to compete for influence in Egypt rather than simply write it off as lost, he began negotiations with both sides for financial underwriting of his pet project, the Aswan Dam. This dam was important to Nasser for two reasons: (1) it would add arable land and electricity sources large enough to double Egypt's national product; (2) it was also the very symbol to him of progress, of industrialization, of a greater Egypt. Eden and Dulles agreed to an initial grant of $70 million, plus $130 million later. The World Bank, for its part, would give equal backing. Together these $400 million would provide the essential foreign exchange needed for a project whose total cost approached $1,300 million.

In January 1956, Nasser rejected the Anglo-American terms that involved World Bank stipulations regarding sound Egyptian finances. Seeing a threat to Egyptian independence, he hinted at better terms from Moscow. With the West already uneasy over the state of Egyptian foreign exchange resources, so mortgaged to payments for Soviet arms, Nasser allowed rumors to spread in June of a Soviet offer of a low-interest 20-year loan of $1,120 million. Confident the West would raise the ante, Nasser was thoroughly enraged when Dulles informed the

Egyptian ambassador (July 19) that it was "not feasible under present circumstances" for the United States to support the Aswan proposal. Nasser in outraged pride reacted (July 26) by expropriating the assets of the Universal Suez Maritime Canal Company. With its annual $25 million profit he would finance the dam himself.

In 1955, almost one out of every three ships using the Suez Canal was British. Out of 108 million tons that went through as cargo, 68 million consisted of oil. On this supply of oil Britain and Western Europe depended. Egypt, for her part, was obligated by treaty to keep the canal open. The charter of the Canal Company would in any event expire in 1968, and it was obvious that Egypt would not renew it. Assuming compensation to shareholders, the Egyptian action on *nationalization* was presumably not illegal. Yet, Nasser's public record of unreliability toward the West, his antipathy for the British, his supplying of arms to the Algerian rebels, his consistent denial of canal transit to Israeli shipping, all made a clear picture to Eden of a man with "his thumb at our windpipe." Seeing in Nasser's actions parallels to Hitler's bold moves, Eden cabled Eisenhower (July 27) that the West "must be ready, in the last resort, to use force."

The United States wanted to avoid force, and for several reasons. Unhappy already with her "colonialist" image in the Arab world, she did not want to associate herself with what would be viewed in the Middle East in precisely that way. Furthermore, a presidential election was in the offing—a circumstance normally inducing administration caution. The canal itself was not an extremely important interest of the United States; avoiding war was, and so was avoiding a break with two of America's most powerful allies. Eisenhower sent Dulles to London, where Dulles agreed with Eden that ways must be found to make Nasser "disgorge" the canal, but reserving any resort to force by any party until diplomacy had proved ineffective.

Three attempts at a diplomatic settlement were tried between mid-August and mid-October. Each failed on the point of Egypt's accepting a form of international administration of the canal's operation. Anglo-French and United States views now grew far apart, with the former determined to use force if necessary and Dulles (September 13) publicly declaring—even before all diplomatic plans failed—that "the United States did not intend itself to try to shoot its way through the Canal." Keeping the U.S. intentionally uninformed, Eden and Premier Guy Mollet of France pressed ahead with their military plans, the French in the meantime increasing arms support to Israel. On October 29, Israel began hostilities in Sinai. Great Britain and France issued an ultimatum to both Israel and Egypt to cease fighting and withdraw troops 10 miles from the canal. Anglo-French air operations commenced as a prelude to landings. Before the canal zone could be seized, Egypt had blocked it with sunken ships. Thus, exactly when the Hungarian crisis was at full pitch, so too had the Middle East crisis reached the same stage. On October 31, Eisenhower said over TV: "There can be no law if we work to invoke one code of international conduct for those we oppose and another for our friends."

In the next days, while Dulles was operated on for cancer, a solution was found in the UN to end the fighting. On November 5, the UN Assembly created a UN Emergency Force of small and middle power contingents, designed to occupy the Israeli-Egyptian border with the consent of both parties (and allow the British and French to save some face by turning over their "responsibilities" for the canal to the UN). On the same day, Bulganin warned of Soviet readiness "to crush the aggressors and restore peace . . . through the use of force." Moscow suggested a Russo-American force, and then spoke of "volunteers" on a unilateral basis. Israel agreed to cease-fire, and the crisis ended as Britain gave up too. November 6, election day, was the peak of the tension. Eisenhower was re-elected.

The American actions in the whole Middle East crisis (and in the accompanying Hungarian crisis) left a good deal to be desired. Although generally approved at the time (and even afterward) by the American public, the U.S. rupture with its major allies in late 1956, accompanied as it was by public American moralizing, was eventually to play a key role in loosening NATO's bonds. De Gaulle (although not yet in power) watched the whole proceeding and drew his own conclusions. Nasser was saved at the last hour from the fruits of his own folly and felt encouraged to still further boldness.

On July 14, 1958, whether by order of Nasser or simply a coincidence that played into his hands, the pro-Western King and Premier of Iraq were assassinated, and it appeared that the new government of Iraq might move their country solidly into Nasser's camp. The pro-Western government of Lebanon was already threatened by Nasser supporters; Syria was already in Nasser's pocket; and the Jordanian king would likely be removed too. These factors, added together, meant that the specter of a new Arab empire dominated by Nasser, controlling much of the oil, the pipelines, and the canal, confronted the West. King Hussein of Jordan frantically begged help, as did President Chamoun of Lebanon. The U.S. responded (July 15) with landings in Lebanon (which eventually reached 14,300 men—with larger forces moved within striking distance for use if needed). Britain airlifted 3,000 troops to Jordan. By late 1958, these forces had been withdrawn. Nasser's hopes for dramatic gains had been frustrated.

In retrospect, it is hard to avoid thinking of the Lebanon landings as a belated American attempt to restore some stability to an area that its own actions had helped to unsettle. Viewed in perspective, the American actions of 1956 made those of 1958 necessary, because by undermining Anglo-French influence in the area, the U.S. had willy-nilly assumed a prime politico-military burden in still another area of the world.

An Assessment

PROPER evaluation of the foreign policy of the first Eisenhower Administration (and the Lebanon incident) is extremely difficult. On the surface level, the Dulles-Eisenhower policies can be characterized as follows: (1) avoiding military involvement and restoring peace in the Far East; (2) consummating Asian alliance arrangements that would guarantee continued stability; (3) successfully negotiating with the Soviets at the summit to register agreement on a lessening of tension; (4) being impartial in the Middle East, even when our own allies were involved; and (5) eventually, in Lebanon, showing our determination to keep the power balance in the area stable. On the surface it was a good record; and so it was assessed by the American people who returned the Republican administration to power for a second term.

At a deeper level and especially in perspective, each of these developments can be seen in a quite different light. The decision to "unleash" Chiang Kai-shek was essentially meaningless, both because Chiang lacked the ability to recover the mainland in any case, and because the U.S. never intended to help him try. Then there was the decision not to intervene in Viet-Nam. Should we consider it wise that the U.S. refrained from such a "can-of-worms" war? Or should we consider this decision a mistake—i.e., if we were going to fight there later, why wait until the French no longer shared the burden? In any event, Dulles wanted to intervene. As to the SEATO and other military alliances with minor powers, was this a victory or a public confession of the weak support for U.S. policies in Asia? No Asian great power (or large power, other than Pakistan) wanted in. What of the summit meeting of 1955, which was publicly hailed for its reduction of tensions? In retrospect one can see clearly that the Soviets were announcing there a "hard" two-Germanies policy that would soon lead to a new and greater crisis over Berlin. What of our impartial approach to friend or foe in the Suez crisis? Did it not sow the seeds for a later French independent nuclear force and reinvigorate De Gaulle's determination to go his own way? What about Dulles' handling of it from beginning to end? Was not the Lebanon landing in 1958—although desirable to show U.S. determination not to allow Nasser to dominate the whole Middle East—required to correct the 1956 impression that the U.S. shrank from the use of force? Eisenhower's comment that the Lebanon landing demonstrated "in a truly practical way that the United States was capable of supporting its friends" must have seemed ironical in London and Paris.

And while all these events were occurring, the status of the personnel of the State Department itself was being drastically overhauled. Between February and August 1953, the personnel strength dropped from 42,154 to 20,231. Some 16,000 of the reduction was by transfer to other agencies, but 5,000 involved terminations.[3] Among others who left the Department at Dulles' decision were John Carter Vincent, John Paton Davies, and George F. Kennan. How many of these changes can be reasonably construed as strengthening the handling of foreign affairs? It is hard to avoid the conclusion that during many of the decisions taken in these years the administration had less opportunity to hear a responsible representation of alternative policies.

[3] Louis L. Gerson, *The American Secretaries of State and Their Diplomacy, John Foster Dulles* (Vol. 17), (New York: Cooper Square Publishers, 1967), p. 111.

CHAPTER 12

The New Age:
Soviet Challenge

I<small>N THE</small> four years between 1958 and 1962, the Soviet Union pursued a political offensive for control over the heart of Europe, which led them to a dangerous flank maneuver in Cuba and almost thrust the world into nuclear war.

A half year after Western unity was shattered at Suez, and after having both successfully ridden out the Hungarian revolt and gained new stature for the Soviet Union in the Arab world, Khrushchev moved to consolidate his leadership at home. As indicated previously, on July 3, 1957, Malenkov and Molotov were removed from any effective influence on Soviet policy; on October 26, 1957, the army's leverage within the government was drastically reduced by the dismissal of Marshal Zhukov. Bulganin continued as premier until March 27, 1958, but Khrushchev was quite evidently prime leader. Even though Khrushchev did not want to become (and *did not* become) a new Stalin, his views on policy largely became the views of the Soviet Union. Significantly, Zhukov's removal came 22 days after the Soviet achievement in putting the first *Sputnik* into orbit in outer space, thus placing the Soviet Union dramatically in the front-runner position in space technology. (Not until December 18, 1958, did the U.S. more or less equal this record.) Khrushchev felt in control.

Khrushchev was a leader with flair and imagination, one who in press conferences issued salty statements liberally sprinkled with both homely Russian proverbs and ideological propaganda, one who did not shrink from bold actions. His "secret speech" of 1956 already noted, his "revisionist" doctrines of the same year not yet mentioned, his bold threats during the Suez crisis, and many other events to come in the next years all illustrate these facets of his character. And Khrushchev, although he was to revise the traditional ideology quite substantially, apparently did so because he took his ideology very seriously. Here was a Communist in power who clearly believed that the future belonged to communism.

As he once boasted, "we will bury you"—meaning that in "peaceful competition," the West was bound to lose. Quite a change from a cynical, tired Stalin, sincere enough as a Communist, but always so preoccupied with events as they affected his personal power that his ideology eventually became tool rather than guide. Khrushchev really believed in the communist utopian visions, and he thought that he exercised power at a time when enormous gains were possible. On the one hand, the West was in disarray; on the other *Sputnik* told all the world in no unmistakable terms that the Soviets were first in space progress, a symbol of more things to come! Khrushchev prepared to reap his harvest.

Squeeze Play on Berlin

SINCE the American position in West Berlin was exposed, it became the point of attack; and because, if Berlin went, so might Germany, American policy had little room for maneuver. These elements soon shaped up into a first-class crisis.

After *Sputnik* the Soviets pressed hard for a new summit meeting to dispose of "urgent international questions," such as American deployment of nuclear weapons in Europe. Foreign Minister Gromyko used this phrase at the end of February 1958 and also pointedly added: "Of course, the question of unification . . . into one state, wholly relating to the competence of these two German states, cannot be the subject of consideration" at any such summit. Even a discussion of the German reunification question was no longer acceptable! In March, Bulganin wrote to Eisenhower that it would be "inadmissible interference in the internal affairs of sovereign states . . ." On November 10, 1958, Khrushchev followed up these skirmishes by unleashing the first Soviet assault in the Second Berlin Crisis.

Khrushchev indicted the West for turning "the German question into an abiding source of international tension" by its "atomic arming of the Bundeswehr." (Technically, this was false; the nuclear warheads furnished to West German forces remained under U.S. control.)

We want to warn the leaders of the Federal Republic of Germany: The road followed by Western Germany today is a road dangerous to peace in Europe and fatal to Western Germany herself. . . . It is high time to realize that the times when the imperialists could act from 'positions of strength' with impunity have gone never to return.[1]

If West Germany wanted reunification it would have to establish contacts with the German Democratic Republic and seek rapprochement.

---

[1] *Documents on Germany, 1944–1961.* Senate Committee on Foreign Relations, 87th Congress, 1st Session, 1961, p. 339.

A peace treaty for Germany, "an entirely different matter" (because in it the Soviets would directly hobble Germany), was a question to "be settled primarily by the Four Powers. . . ."

The West, said Khrushchev, spoke continually about great power agreements for achieving German reunification, but if one looked at the provisions of the Potsdam Agreement, which was the major document, what did one see? The Soviets had "scrupulously observed" the provisions to eliminate German militarism and fascism, whereas the West had done the opposite, creating an army "headed by Nazi generals," which was being trained "in the spirit of revenge."

What was left of the Potsdam accord?

The so-called Four-Power status of Berlin, that is, a position in which the three Western powers . . . have the possibility of lording it in Western Berlin, turning that part of the city, which is the capital of the German Democratic Republic, into some kind of state within a state and, profiting by this, conducting subversive activities . . . On top of this, they have the right of unrestricted communication between Berlin and Western Germany through the air space, by the railways, highways, and waterways of the German Democratic Republic, a state which they do not even want to recognize.[2]

Was not the time to "denounce" this part of Potsdam at hand? "The time has obviously arrived . . . to renounce the remnants of the occupation regime in Berlin . . . The Soviet Union, for its part, would hand over" to East Germany its functions, and the West could deal with it. The Soviet Union would regard an attack on East Germany "as an attack on the Soviet Union . . ."

The seriousness of the Soviets' new assault on the West's exposed salient behind the Iron Curtain was not at first understood in Washington. Dulles (November 26), at a news conference, pointed to the Soviet habit of probing "weak spots . . . to find out whether they are up against firmness and strength and unity. If they find that, then I think the probing will cease." Asked why expected detailed Soviet demands had not yet arrived, Dulles speculated that Khrushchev "had spoken initially without the benefit of legal advice which is, of course, a very bad thing to do [laughter], that he had based his case upon alleged breaches of the Potsdam Agreement." Dulles went on to point out that Western "rights . . . in Berlin and the responsibilities and obligations of the Soviet Union do not in any way derive" from the Potsdam Agreement. In fact the subject was "not even mentioned" there. For the Soviet Union to claim that a violation of Potsdam would relieve it of "obligations which it assumed explicitly some four years later [at the time of the lifting of the blockade] seems to be a non sequitur, to put it mildly . . ."

2 *Ibid.,* pp. 341–342.

However Dulles misread Soviet intentions, his guess at the reasons for the Soviet delay was quite shrewd. Khrushchev indeed had gotten his barrage started without laying in the right ammunition. When the Soviet note of November 27, which "officially" began the crisis, arrived, the argument had shifted. Now it was alleged that the Western powers had "grossly violated" the Four-Power agreements on Germany, "including the Potsdam Agreement, which is the most concentrated expression" of those obligations. Those "who have grossly violated these agreements have lost the right to maintain their occupation regime in Berlin or any other part of Germany." The Soviet government would "no longer consider itself bound" and regarded as "null and void" the agreements on occupation, and would "at an appropriate time" transfer to the German Democratic Republic "the functions temporarily performed by the Soviet authorities" under these agreements. While "the most correct and natural way" to solve the Berlin problem was to give West Berlin to East Germany, to avoid "any painful break in the established way of life of the West Berlin population," it would be better to convert West Berlin "into an independent political unit—a free city, without any state, including both existing German states, interfering in its life. Specifically . . . the territory [could] be demilitarized . . ." To avoid "haste and unnecessary friction," and to provide "maximum possible consideration for the interests of the parties concerned," the Soviets proposed "to make no changes in the present procedure for military traffic . . . for half a year." If no "adequate agreement" was reached in this time "the planned measures" would go into effect, with the German Democratic Republic exercising full sovereignty. Soviet officials would "terminate all contacts" normally existing with Western officials on occupation questions. Any violation of this new situation would "immediately cause appropriate retaliation." Said the note in closing, the Soviets "are sincerely striving for the restoration of good relations" with the United States.

Except for Khrushchev's initial mistake on the Potsdam Agreement, these moves by the Soviets were well thought out. They were difficult for the West to counter, partly because the objective was ostensibly limited (a free city of West Berlin). Only if that objective were rejected would the direct challenge arise—after Soviet responsibilities had been turned over to German Communist authorities and the West had to choose what to do about it.

The West's response at the NATO conference of December was to make clear a determination "not to yield to threats." Shortly after this the U.S. State Department sent Khrushchev a detailed legal analysis of the Berlin position, the essential point of which was that Allied rights in Germany and in Berlin were derived "from the total defeat of the Third Reich. . . . The Soviet Union did not bestow upon the Western powers rights of access to Berlin. It accepted its zone of occupation subject to those rights of access." If this were not true the U.S. could as readily require the Soviets to evacuate those portions of the Soviet Zone captured by American forces. Since the rights to Berlin were not the Soviets' to bestow, neither could they "repeal those rights by denunciation of agreements or by purported transfer of control over them to third parties." On December 31, this analysis was followed by a note that rejected the Soviet contentions. The U.S. was willing to enter discussions over Berlin within "the wider framework of negotiation for a solution of the German problem as well as that of European security," but only if it was clear that the Soviet Union was not intending by its position either "menace or ultimatum."

When the Soviets answered on January 10, 1959, it was with a considerably milder tone. The same month, Mikoyan was sent to the United States to dissipate some of the tension. Dulles (January 13) was able to say that the Soviets had not intended the earlier note "as an ultimatum with a fixed time limit." But the American and Soviet positions on a suitable agenda were still far apart. In March, following Autobahn harassments, Eisenhower felt it necessary to make a strong speech in which he said: "Soviet rulers should remember that free men have, before this, died for so-called scraps of paper which represented duty and honor and freedom . . . . We will not retreat one inch from our duty. We shall continue to exercise our right of peaceful passage to and from West Berlin." In the same month, a new U.S. note proposed a May conference, with each side discussing anything it considered relevant; and on this basis the meeting was finally held.

The Geneva Foreign Ministers Meeting (May–August 1959) was one of the longest meetings ever held by that body. It was also to be the last such meeting for many years. Distinguishing it in format was the presence of two "German adviser" groups, one from each German state, who were given positions at small tables on the circumference of the large table at which the delegations of the major powers sat. From time to time each German delegation leader was allowed to address the conference. The presence of these two groups was a sop to the Soviet contention that only the Germans were now competent to discuss reunification (i.e., an "internal question"), whereas the major powers' function was to formulate and accept a suitable peace treaty draft (i.e., an "external question"). In practice all kinds of facets of the entire set of questions were discussed by the major delegations.

Certainly this conference differed from earlier conferences on Germany by its markedly increased display of Western procedural flexibility. Instead of merely proposing as before that supervised free elections be held as a first step throughout Germany and that the new All-German government could then bring the whole new unit into NATO if it chose (as it would), the West took pains to show willingness to cushion the resulting shock to Soviet interests. There could be stages and delays, there could be special arrangements to demilitarize the Soviet Zone, and so on. The electoral law itself would be prepared by a "Mixed German Commission" formed in proportion to the population of the two German states; there would be a time lag before elections were held.

The Soviets showed only slight interest in these proposals. At the ninth session for example, Gromyko said that the conference should discuss "in detail a peace treaty with Germany," which would prevent the rise of any "militarist state," and that any time spent discussing German reunification or elections "would simply be so much time wasted." Later in the conference, he offered guarantees that the free city of West Berlin would have "lasting and unshakable status . . . as an independent political unit." Quite clearly, almost as though it were a custom (which indeed in fact it was) in conferences on Germany, each side predominantly spoke past the other.

In mid-conference Gromyko proposed an All-German committee "on a basis of parity" that would "examine questions connected with" a peace treaty. Its work would have to be done in a year's time, during which the Soviets would not interfere with Western rights. American charges that this was a new ultimatum produced a reluctant Soviet explanation that they were trying to find some compromise formula between their wish for immediate change and the West's apparent wish for no change at any foreseeable time. Gromyko now changed the time limit to 18 months. When the West continued to press for an answer as to what then would be intended if at the end of the period the sides were still deadlocked, the most Gromyko would say was that the Soviet proposals did not attempt to address that question.

After a recess the conference resumed, but the impasse continued to its end. With tension high, Khrushchev made a personal visit to Eisenhower at the end of September 1959. Out of their conversations emerged the "Camp David formula." Eisenhower's version (September 28) was that further negotiations would be held, and "that these negotiations should not be prolonged indefinitely but there could be no fixed limit on them." Questioned next day in Moscow, Khrushchev answered that Eisenhower's version was correct: "We agreed indeed that talks on the Berlin question should be resumed, that no time limit whatsoever is to be established for them, but that they should not be dragged out for an indefinite time."

After a full year of tension, the Soviets had backtracked very substantially. However, the backtracking was from a position much too extreme to produce profitable agreement unless the West lost its nerve —which had not happened. It was announced that Eisenhower would repay Khrushchev's visit by going to the Soviet Union in the spring of

1960 and that Khrushchev's demands for a summit meeting would at last be met. It would be held in Paris in May.

The U-2 Incident and the Berlin Wall

THE tension thus reduced was soon drastically increased by an incident irrelevant to the German issue.

Even before the tension sky-rocketed, the truce continued to be very uneasy. When Khrushchev again threatened (in a letter to Adenauer) to sign a separate peace treaty if necessary with the German Democratic Republic, Under Secretary of State Dillon called it "skating on very thin ice." This drew the retort from Khrushchev that Dillon's speech "reeks of the Cold War spirit." Khrushchev said further that if a separate peace treaty became the only solution, the West "naturally will forfeit the right of access to West Berlin by land, water, and air." These remarks were made only a week before the scheduled summit. All they lacked to be a complete ultimatum once more was a specific time limit.

Then on May Day, all hopes for a useful summit meeting went abruptly into the discard. The Soviets shot down over Soviet soil a U-2 (spy) plane, piloted by Gary Powers, at first concealing the fact that they had captured the pilot alive. Once the U.S. then released a routine cover story that one of our weather planes had strayed off course with the pilot complaining of oxygen difficulty, the Soviets dramatically revealed that Powers had been shot down 1,200 miles inside Russia, complete with "spy kit." The U.S. government was in an extraordinarily embarrassing position. Eisenhower decided in a virtually unprecedented step to admit the U.S. violation of Soviet air space, terming it necessary, and saying that we would continue such flights as needed. (Later he said we would cease making them.) Khrushchev in these circumstances came to the summit demanding that Eisenhower apologize and punish those responsible. Since it was Eisenhower himself who ultimately was responsible, the summit broke up before it really began. Khrushchev flounced off, stopping in East Berlin to condemn the "aggressive act of American brasshats." To the West's relief he gave his opinion "that the best thing to do was to postpone the conference . . . until the dust has settled, so to say." He mentioned six to eight months. And he issued no new threats over Berlin.

Khrushchev's tactics in the U-2 case, luring the U.S. into releasing a cover story he could dramatically destroy, can either be construed as a scheme to initiate the conference with the U.S. badly embarrassed and off-balance or as a device to torpedo the conference itself. An embarrassed U.S. might be more conciliatory, but Khrushchev must have known this was unlikely. Consequently, it is more probable that he wished to avoid a summit that would again say no to Soviet demands and put Khrushchev's prestige in jeopardy unless he went the whole way and carried out his threats. Waiting six to eight months (which meant until a new U.S. President had been elected) would both buy time and give him a new opponent who might be more easily out-maneuvered than Eisenhower (whose handling of the Berlin crisis can hardly be faulted). What Khrushchev could hardly have anticipated was the additional windfall that the new U.S. President would begin his term under the cloud of the Bay of Pigs fiasco.

Inaugurated (January 1961) after winning a very close presidential contest, President John F. Kennedy (April 12) said that U.S. forces would not under any circumstances intervene against Castro's Cuba. Within a week anti-Castro forces were attempting to invade Cuba, with clumsy U.S. CIA backing. Castro defeated the force easily, taking some 1,200 prisoners. Kennedy took personal responsibility in April for the abortive invasion, as details kept leaking out of U.S. involvement, but he did not fully admit the extent of that involvement. In early June, he then met Khrushchev in Vienna to discuss the Berlin crisis. A secretly jubilant Khrushchev put full pressure on what he must have considered the inept young President, making it clear that the Soviets intended to shut the U.S. out of Berlin one way or the other.

Reporting to the American people on TV (June 6), Kennedy made no effort to disguise the severity of the crisis: "I will tell you now that it was a very somber two days." There had been "no discourtesy, no loss of tempers, no threats or ultimatums by either side." But the situation was undoubtedly serious. Kennedy said that he had made it clear on Berlin that "we are determined to maintain those rights at any risk. . . ."

Khrushchev's assessment of his opponent was implicit in Khrushchev's TV speech (June 15): "We ask everyone to understand us correctly: the conclusion of a peace treaty with Germany cannot be postponed any longer. A peaceful settlement in Europe must be attained this year." On June 21, he made the threat explicit: "At the end of this year, we . . . will sign a peace treaty with the German Democratic Republic." So much for the Camp David formula. Within a further week he said that if "certain Western Powers," believing they had the right "to resort to force," did so, they would be exercising the rights of highwaymen. "A highwayman can be beaten off only with a stick."

The U.S. (July 17) sent a formal note to the Soviet Union warning them that an attempt at a *fait accompli* "would have unforeseeable consequences." On July 25, Kennedy said on TV: "We cannot and will not permit the Communists to drive us out of Berlin, either gradually or by force. . . ." He announced increased defense measures, including the call-up of reserves, saying: "The solemn vow each of us gave to West Berlin in time of peace will not be broken in time of danger."

Khrushchev (August 11, 1961) called the West's declaration "that they will allegedly fight" for the freedom of Germans in West Berlin "a fairy tale. . . . We shall not be the first to press the buttons at our rocket installations . . . but if the imperialists force a war upon us we shall meet it bravely and deal a devastating blow to the aggressor."

Even as Khrushchev spoke, the lifeblood of East Germany was draining out through West Berlin as unprecedented numbers of German Democratic Republic citizens fled west. July's figures had been about double the norm; August's set new records. For the 10 years beginning in 1949, some 2,188,435 people had been registered in Germany as having escaped from East Germany, plus another million, who were registered with the West German police but had not passed through official refugee centers. That means that from 1949 to early 1961, the annual refugee flow averaged 230,000 per year—with most passing through from East Germany to East Berlin and then from West Berlin to West Germany. When one keeps in mind the hard core statistic that half of the total flow were people under 25 years of age (and 74 per cent were under 45), one understands the pressures building up in the Communist world to apply a tourniquet. Khrushchev's threats to force the West out of Berlin (if they had succeeded) would have allowed him to shut off the refugee flow; but they had now drastically backfired, and those who could fled. In the first 12 days of August more than 22,000 crossed over; on August 12th, some 2,400 came. (In annual average terms the August flow translates into two-thirds of a million.) On August 13th, at two o'clock in the morning, police and troop units of the German Democratic Republic began to seal off the West Berlin border. In the next days the Berlin Wall began to rise as three Red Army divisions continued to be deployed around West Berlin.

In late August, Khrushchev made two other moves. In a Radio Moscow broadcast of an interview with Drew Pearson, the usual threat was included that a peace treaty between the Soviets and the German Democratic Republic would end Western rights and that the Soviets had "firmly decided not to postpone any further" the signing of such a treaty —but no specific time limit was given. The second move was a Khrushchev announcement of hydrogen superbomb tests in the 50- and 100-megaton range "to discourage the aggressor from criminal playing with fire . . ." In October as tension continued, Khrushchev told the 22nd Soviet Communist Party Congress that he was no longer insisting upon the signing of a German peace treaty in 1961.

In the light of the foregoing, there can be little question that Khrushchev's initial offensive on Berlin had failed, that he knew it, and that he agreed to the Berlin Wall by way of a salvage operation. That the salvage operation was made the more essential by the boomerang effect of Khrushchev's own threats was ironical. But the stark fact is that a nation of 17 million people (such as East Germany) could not long survive a refugee flow of these proportions. The bitterness of the pill to be swallowed (by settling for the moment for far less than he had tried for) was partially compensated for by two other factors: (1) Khrushchev in building the Wall had changed the status of both Berlins, in that his wall itself defied the legally binding Four-Power status of Berlin, with freedom of passage east and west. (He was later to restrict the previously free movement of West Berliners into East Berlin, but he continued to permit Western officials entrance.) (2) Many commentators in the West interpreted the Wall as some sort of a Communist victory; and in the September 1961 election, Adenauer lost his absolute majority in the Bundestag, as a direct result of shaken West German confidence in his policies. These developments were welcome to Khrushchev, but when all is said and done it is hard to portray the Berlin Wall convincingly as a Soviet victory. It was—it is—a confession of failure.

American responses to these moves were sufficient, although criticized by the West Germans in their shock. There was a visit by then Vice-President Johnson "to show the flag" in West Berlin; the Berlin garrison was reinforced and a deliberate troop movement and rotation policy over the Autobahn was instituted to demonstrate American determination. In October 1961, after U.S. personnel who refused to show identity cards to East German guards had been stopped, U.S. military police escorted an American private car with Army plates 400 yards into East Berlin. Ten U.S. tanks and two armored personnel carriers were deployed as a sign of determination. By the next day, with Soviet tanks moved up, U.S. and Soviet tanks faced each other at 200-yard range. When, in the end, both sides withdrew, the East Germans strengthened the Wall to such extent that even tanks might not be able to breach it. Yet the American move had forced the Soviets to do precisely what they wished not to do—by deploying Soviet tanks they had in effect been forced to ignore their own argument that they no longer played any responsible role in Berlin.

Almost three years after the Wall went up, the Soviets on June 12, 1964, finally did sign a separate treaty with East Germany, but its terms did not purport to terminate Western rights.

The Cuban Missile Crisis

KHRUSHCHEV's determination to see significant gains for the Soviet Union and communism while he held power was not undermined by this setback. He simply looked elsewhere for further opportunities, but always with the central aim of improving the Soviet position in Germany. Although he spoke genially to capitalists of his philosophical conviction that by peaceful competition "your grandchildren, too, will be socialists," he certainly had in mind that what he himself did would make all the practical difference in bringing this about. The third act in the Khrushchev program was to have Cuba for the locale of its scenario. At least that is where the curtain would rise. If all went well it would fall in Berlin on a "free city," or perhaps even something better. For in 1962 Khrushchev was still far from willing to accept the meaningless separate peace treaty, which he was to accept in 1964.

As one might expect, the failure of the "Bay of Pigs" venture led to much public soul-searching in Washington and in the nation's press. All were agreed that it was a fiasco, some because it had been tried at all, others because it failed. A vocal minority in Congress was outraged at communism's continued foothold in the Western Hemisphere and pressed for vigorous action against Castro's Cuba, up to and including the use of force. Fidel Castro announced himself publicly after the "Bay of Pigs" as a convinced Marxist-Leninist and in the summer of 1962 sent his brother Raúl, the Foreign Minister, and Ché Guevara, the Finance Minister, to Moscow to arrange for supplies of Soviet arms and Soviet technicians to service and instruct. On September 11, TASS announced that "defensive" arms were being sent, adding explicitly that Soviet nuclear weapons were so powerful in range that there was no need to send these to bases outside the Soviet Union. But in point of fact, 42 medium- and intermediate-range ballistic missiles were then already in or soon to be on their way to Cuba.

Roger Hilsman (who in the Kennedy Administration first headed the State Department intelligence and then, later, became Assistant Secretary of State for the Far East) ascribes the Soviet motive in large order to *their* understanding of *our* understanding that they were not really ahead of the U.S. in intercontinental missiles.[3] This complicated proposition has to be understood against the background of the argument during the Kennedy–Nixon presidential campaign, at a time when U-2 flights over the Soviet Union had been suspended, as to whether or not there was a "missile gap." *Sputnik's* military meaning was that the Soviets were well ahead of the U.S. in thrust. Whether that meant they were equal or ahead or behind in numbers of missiles or in actual delivery capability was hotly argued. But by the summer and fall of 1961, says Hilsman, the American intelligence community had decided that the Soviets did not really have effective ICBM's, that in their attempt to move forward too fast in thrust, they had achieved "a behemoth . . . too bulky to serve as a practical weapon." Hilsman says further that it was decided to tell the Soviets that we knew this; which was done in a speech by the Deputy Secretary of Defense (November 1961) and by briefings of other nations. Hilsman claims that the Soviets suddenly

[3] See Roger Hilsman, *To Move A Nation* (Garden City, New York: Doubleday, 1967), Ch. 13, especially pp. 161–165.

realized that the "softness" of their system (other than in a first-strike situation) was now known to the U.S., and that Castro's request for arms opened an opportunity to make good the defects in Soviet defenses by establishing shorter-range missiles on the American flank in Cuba. How the massive shipment of bulky equipment and technicians—Hilsman describes it as equal to a hundred shiploads and comprising several thousand vehicles including fueling trucks, radar vans and equipment, together with over 20,000 men—was to be kept secret and the Cuban missiles "hardened" is not explained. One might even ask: Would the Soviets really have been substantially better off with "soft" missiles in both Russia and Cuba? Was it really ever likely that the Cuban missiles would or could be "hardened," and would that have really deterred the U.S. from a first-strike at the still "soft" Soviet Union?

Whatever these issues had to do with the Soviet decision, it is at least clear that the Soviet maneuver (if they could bring it off) would be of major psychological importance. It would "outflank" American defenses (which were primarily oriented toward a missile attack from the Soviet Union), bring significant new U.S. targets under a very clear threat, and induce U.S. caution if and when a new Soviet squeeze on Berlin was mounted. South America would be within target range, and therefore it might induce at least dissensions there. Khrushchev apparently involved himself in Cuba with at least one eye on rewards in Germany. If one accepts Hilsman's argument, one must accept the proposition that even with (or especially because of) a "soft" ICBM system in the Soviet Union Khrushchev was gambling on checkmating Western resistance, through the Cuban gambit. It is clear by any standards that Khrushchev was taking major risks in the hope of major gains. The difference in interpretations possible over Soviet motives runs in a narrow range between seeing it as a "defensive" move with "offensive" gains likely and seeing it as an "offensive" move, designed to yield "offensive" gains.

In early October 1962, no "hard intelligence" had yet revealed the Soviet move. Kennedy's response to domestic pressures to do something about Castro was to refrain from any new military moves but, as he said, "to watch what happens in Cuba with the closest attention." This meant especially U-2 flights over Cuba. On October 14, one such flight brought back pictures of a medium-range missile base in western Cuba, in the San Cristobal area. Later verifications gave a more complete picture of five other MRBM (1,100-mile) and three IRBM (2,200-mile) sites. The stage was now set for the most dramatic super power confrontation in the postwar period.

An interview between President Kennedy and Gromyko, Soviet Foreign Minister, had been arranged before these developments were known, for October 18. At this meeting Gromyko repeated Khrushchev's statement that the Berlin question would not be reactivated until after the American elections on November 6. But after that—and Gromyko said it twice—the Soviets would be "compelled" to sign a separate peace treaty with East Germany, which would end Western rights in Berlin. Gromyko also said that such Soviet missiles as were in Cuban hands were purely defensive. Reflecting on this interview and the continuing photographic intelligence that showed the rate at which the Cuban missiles were becoming operational, Kennedy concluded that the apparent gesture of political friendliness in avoiding tension until after the election had more to do with when the missiles would be in "go" condition.

On October 22, over TV, Kennedy publicly unmasked the Soviet maneuvers. He wasted no words:

> Good evening, my fellow citizens. This Government, as promised, has maintained the closest surveillance of the Soviet military build-up on the island of Cuba. Within the past week unmistakable evidence has established the fact that a series of offensive missiles is now in preparation. . . . The purpose of these bases can be none other than to provide a nuclear strike capacity against the Western Hemisphere.

This "sudden, clandestine decision to station strategic weapons for the first time outside of Soviet soil is a deliberately provocative and unjustified change in the *status quo* which cannot be accepted by this country, if our courage and our commitments are ever to be trusted again by either friend or foe." America's initial response would be a naval "quarantine" [blockade] against the further shipment of "offensive weapons." Kennedy gave clear warning: "It shall be the policy of this nation to regard any nuclear missile launched from Cuba against any nation in the Western Hemisphere as an attack by the Soviet Union on the United States, requiring a full retaliatory response upon the Soviet Union."

Next afternoon, the Council of the Organization of American States backed the American stand by recommending that the member states "take all measures . . . including the use of armed force," to cut off the flow of offensive weapons into Cuba and prevent those already there from becoming "an active threat." That evening (October 23, 7 P.M.), Kennedy proclaimed the quarantine: ". . . the forces under my command are ordered, beginning at 2:00 P.M., Greenwich time October 24, 1962, to interdict . . . the delivery of offensive weapons and associated matériel to Cuba." Force would be used "only to the extent necessary." To this proclamation "I have . . . set my hand and caused the seal of the United States of America to be affixed." There could be no doubt the U.S. was committed—and with unanimous hemispheric backing.

Wednesday the quarantine went into effect and the world held its breath. Eighteen Soviet dry cargo ships were known to be on courses toward the quarantine line. Reports of six Soviet submarines arriving for escort duty came in. Then the Soviet cargo ships nearest Cuba appeared to slow down.

Thursday, October 25, was another dramatic day of suspense. In the UN U.S. Ambassador Adlai Stevenson—with U-2 photos in hand—cross-examined Soviet Ambassador Zorin in the Security Council. "Do you . . . deny that the USSR has placed and is placing medium- and intermediate-range missiles and sites in Cuba? Yes or no? Don't wait for the translation. Yes or no." Zorin's answer snapped back: "I am not in an American courtroom, sir." Stevenson replied, "You are in the court of world public opinion right now!" Zorin temporized, "In due course, sir, you will have your reply." To which Stevenson rejoined, "I am prepared to wait for my answer until Hell freezes over, if that's your decision. I am also prepared to present the evidence in this room."

Secretary-General U Thant had already proposed that the Soviets voluntarily stop arms shipments and that the Americans voluntarily suspend the quarantine for two to three weeks. Kennedy in his reply pointed to the other half of the equation, "the removal of such weapons" already there that were being rushed to readiness.

On Friday, October 26, came news that 16 of the 18 Soviet dry cargo ships, including all five with large hatches, had turned around. Khrushchev's answer to U Thant that day confirmed the Soviet decision: he had "ordered . . . Soviet vessels bound for Cuba but not yet within the area of the American warships' piratical activities to stay out of the interception area" temporarily. But U-2 flights showed that work on the missile sites for the missiles already in Cuba was still being pressed. The U.S. had half a loaf, but that was not enough.

Direct exchanges of letters (radiograms) had started between Kennedy and Khrushchev. Two Khrushchev letters came, one on Friday (October 26) at 9 P.M., the other the next day. The Friday night letter (which remained secret) seemed to indicate that since Soviet missiles had been put into Cuba to frustrate any American invasion plans, they might be withdrawn if the U.S. gave a pledge to refrain from invasion. This letter had the genuine Khrushchev flavor, polemical and long. Saturday's letter was more carefully drafted and followed a harder line, demanding the withdrawal of Jupiter missiles from Turkey as the *quid pro quo*. (How ironical for Kennedy, who earlier had ordered the State Department to negotiate with Turkey the withdrawal of the Jupiters, but Turkish objections had frustrated action. To agree publicly to this move now would appear as giving way under pressure and might encourage other Soviet demands and delays.)

Kennedy decided on the bold but simple course of ignoring the Saturday letter and agreeing with Khrushchev's Friday "proposal."

As I read your letter [of October 26], the key elements of your proposals—which seem generally acceptable as I understand them—are as follows:

1. You would agree to remove these weapons systems from Cuba under appropriate United Nations observation and supervision; and undertake, with suitable safeguards, to halt the further introduction of such weapons systems into Cuba.

2. We, on our part, would agree [assuming such effective UN agreements] (a) to remove promptly the quarantine measures now in effect and (b) to give assurances against an invasion of Cuba.

Robert Kennedy personally handed this note to the Soviet Ambassador, adding verbally that unless the President "received immediate notice that the missiles would be withdrawn,"[4] other U.S. measures would have to be taken to see that it happened. Time was indeed running short, for the U.S. was determined to intervene with force to prevent the missiles in Cuba from becoming operational.

On Sunday morning, the Soviet answer came, first on Moscow radio and then with the delivery of a note: "In order to eliminate as rapidly as possible the conflict . . . the Soviet Government . . . has given a new order to dismantle the arms which you describe as offensive and to crate them and return them to the Soviet Union." The Soviets were "prepared to reach agreement to enable representatives to verify the dismantling. . . ."

The Soviet attempt to persuade Castro to allow verification by a UN team failed. Mikoyan was sent by Khrushchev as his agent, and he argued with Castro for most of a month before giving up. Convinced of Soviet good faith on this point, the U.S. carried out its own inspection by air. Eventually, the complications involved in the withdrawal of Soviet bombers and some 23,000 Soviet troops were ironed out. The world could breathe again.

So failed with finality Khrushchev's bid to exploit the Western disarray and the great space leap forward of *Sputnik*. As we saw, in the sequel the separate peace issue was essentially dropped, and the West remained as before in West Berlin.

The Congo Crisis

Overlapping in time with the Second Berlin Crisis and the Cuban Missile Crisis was the Congo Crisis. It represented still a third arena in which Khrushchev's challenge to the United States was to be largely blunted. The Congo question was handled essentially in the UN; therefore the clash of American and Soviet views and interests was neither as direct nor as vividly dramatic as in the tensions over Germany and Cuba.

[4] Theodore C. Sorenson, *Kennedy* (New York: Harper & Row, 1965), p. 715.

Yet in the end, the Soviet challenge quite as obviously led to their frustration and defeat. And the Congo crisis was never dull for any of those concerned.

Having ruled the Congo in paternalistic fashion for a half century, the Belgian government decided rather abruptly (following riots in 1959) to give the Congo independence (June 30, 1960). On that day, coming to power in a largely illiterate "nation" of 14 million people (and a handful of college graduates), Joseph Kasavubu was installed as President, and Patrice Lumumba as Premier. Sharing in fact in power was also Moise Tshombe, Premier of the province of Katanga—an area whose income from its mineral wealth was vital to any central Congolese government. Kasavubu was a moderate, Lumumba a leftist-leaning fiery nationalist, and Tshombe, a conservative. Barely was independence proclaimed, when the Congolese army of 25,000 men demanded two things: the ousting of its Belgian officers, and pay raises. Other factions of the population were disappointed that the end of colonial rule had not brought immediate improvements in their material condition and joined the mutiny. Belgians fled by the thousands as law and order broke down. On July 11, Tshombe announced that Katanga was seceding and requested Belgian military assistance to put down the revolt in the province. Belgian troops were also sent to restore order elsewhere and the Congolese government now asked the UN to send a force modeled on the UNEF (troops from neutral nations). On July 13, 1960, the UN African (or Congo) Force was created. This ONUC (initially drawn from Ethiopia, Ghana, Guinea, Ireland, Liberia, Morocco, Sweden, and Tunisia) had an early strength of 11,155 men, who were rushed to the Congo.

From the outset, the super powers agreed on the need for an ONUC, but they disagreed on the reasons for sending it. The Security Council vote (8 to 0) included both the U.S. and the Soviet Union on the affirmative side (with Britain, France, and Nationalist China abstaining). But Khrushchev saw its mission as preventing the Belgians from re-establishing colonial rule, whereas the U.S. saw it as a move to restore order (and insulate the area from the Cold War while preventing conditions under which communism might make gains). The Soviets charged the U.S. with collusion with Belgian "armed aggression," a charge that the U.S. rejected as "outrageous and untrue." In any event, with the African states firmly for UN action, neither super power wished to stand in the way.

Khrushchev announced that the Congolese leaders had sent him a telegram that their lives were in danger and that they might need Soviet intervention because of what Khrushchev called "Western . . . aggression." The Soviets at the UN demanded Belgian withdrawal within three days. The U.S. answer was that we would "prevent the

intrusion of any military forces not requested by the United Nations."[5]
The Security Council's position was to urge the withdrawal of Belgian
troops without delay and oppose any unilateral interventions.

Although the Belgian forces issue was important at first, the center
of interest soon shifted as a confused Congolese struggle for power took
the center of the stage. To prevent overt civil war the UN authority on
the spot closed all Congolese airports and shut down the radio station
in the capital at Leopoldville—a move which prevented Soviet aircraft
and trucks, which were being sent to the Lumumba faction, from arriving. Lumumba himself was taken into custody by the new army
strongman, Joseph Mobutu (September 14).

In the General Assembly (for the Security Council was deadlocked by
Soviet veto) the USSR charged that "the United Nations Command
and the Secretary-General personally have unmasked themselves as
supporters of the colonialists." But the UN by large majority upheld
the Secretary-General. There was also a vote on the crucial question
of which of the two Congolese "governments" should be accepted—the
Lumumba faction or the Kasavubu faction. With Lumumba not able to
plead his case, Kasavubu appeared before the Assembly. The Assembly
(November 1960) voted 53 to 24 (with 19 abstentions) in favor of the
U.S.-supported Kasavubu group.

On February 13, 1961, Lumumba's death "while escaping" was announced. The Soviet prospects for an effective intervention were now
largely blighted, although the Congo problem still preoccupied the UN,
which in this venture in restoring internal order found itself in novel and
difficult circumstances. Increasingly the center of gravity of the Congo
question became whether Katanga would be allowed to secede, and
whether the UN force mandate included preventing such action. The
Security Council (February 21), by a vote of 9 to 0 (with the Soviets
abstaining), authorized "the use of force, if necessary, in the last resort,"
to end the civil war.[6] But neither a victory for the now moderate central
government nor for the conservative Tshombe was of much direct
help to Soviet interests.

The Congo "crisis" as it directly affected the super powers was now
largely over. What then occurred through most of two further years was
an uneasy truce, interspersed by clashes between UN units and Katang-
anese mercenary-led forces (December 1961 and again in December
1962–January 1963). The Congolese government was led by Premier
Cyrille Adoula (after mid-1961) and pressed the UN to end the seces-
sion; and the first heavy fighting which followed (December 1961) convinced Tshombe of the need to show willingness to negotiate. The
failure of these negotiations led to the second round of fighting, in which

[5] *The New York Times* (July 24, 1960).
[6] UN Doc. S/4741, p. 147.

UN forces took over Katanga. When the UN ultimately terminated ONUC (June 30, 1964), it did not actually leave behind it a peaceful Congo, for fighting soon flared up again in the eastern Congo. In July of that year, President Kasavubu asked Tshombe to become Premier and suppress the rebellion. This Tshombe did with Congolese troops and white mercenaries. Then in October 1965, Kasavubu deposed Tshombe; and he in his turn was ousted in November by General Mobutu!

During these years when the ONUC was in the Congo its strength and composition varied. Indian troops eventually composed almost a third of the total. Generally speaking, the African troop percentage of the total continued to decline throughout the entire period.

An Assessment

BETWEEN the end of 1958 and the end of 1962, Khrushchev involved the Soviet Union in three important contests of power, in each of which he lost: (1) the attempt to squeeze the U.S. out of Berlin; (2) the attempt to turn Cuba into an offensive base for Soviet arms; and (3) the attempt to gain a position of influence in Central Africa. All these contests had in common a hope to change the *status quo* in favor of the Soviet Union; the failure of all three attempts in no way marked a Soviet retreat from its wartime-postwar gains. The dangerous extension of Soviet influence and power into the heart of Central Europe, which played so important a part in the tensions of the Cold War, still continued. Yet the blunting of Khrushchev's offensives, the meeting of the Soviet challenges, publicly revealed more than the inability of the Soviets to make further dramatic gains. It also showed, especially through the Cuban Missile Crisis outcome, that the U.S. would wage war if it must to protect itself, and that the Soviets were not anxious to push things so far. After the end of 1962, the world no longer believed that the Soviets were likely to risk war except in defense of their own obvious and immediate interests. Khrushchev's repeated failures were to undermine his own political position at home; by mid-1963 his ideological revisionism (which we have only noted in passing so far) had produced public indictment from Peking which viewed a Soviet "adventurism," followed by a "cowardly withdrawal," with nothing but contempt. Expressed another way, the Soviet failures, as they encouraged Sino-Soviet friction, helped to destroy the unity of the Communist world. Similarly, Russia's backdown on Cuba convinced Western Europe that a Soviet westward attack was increasingly unlikely, and that conviction in turn helped to destroy the unity of the NATO world. Thus in their defeat, the Soviet challenges led directly to the fragmenting world of polycentrism on both sides of the Iron Curtain—as we shall see in Chapter 13.

American policy throughout these crises (with the exception of the U-2 incident) can hardly be faulted. The U.S. showed a clear grasp of objectives and implemented a strategy that rallied its allies and gained world support. Not since 1947 had the U.S. performed so well in protecting its essential interests while avoiding the catastrophe of war.

CHAPTER 13

The New Age:
Polycentrism and Fragmentation

FTER 1945, it became popular to speak of a "bipolar world," dominated by the might of two super powers, a condition assumed to be more or less permanent. This was a distorted image except for its undoubted roots in the reality that two powers—the United States and the Soviet Union—were capable of using force at levels far above the traditional great power norms. (Even this became fully true only after the Soviet Union also possessed a significant nuclear arsenal.)

Certainly the tension from the interacting *foreign policies* of the United States and the Soviet Union dominated the postwar scene in the first decade. Other relatively powerful nations had interests to advance or protect, but most of them were much preoccupied with recovery from World War II. Even Great Britain had to keep an eye always on insistent domestic issues bound up with a shaky economy and could only play the shadow of her prewar role. France's role was small, largely negative, and much of the energies she could spare for interests abroad went into ultimately fruitless military actions in Indo-China and Algeria. Germany was emerging only gradually from the traumatic experiences under Hitler and of being divided into occupation zones, and was entirely focused on the immediate problem of reconstruction. Humbled in battle and shorn of empire, Japan again turned inward. China was torn by civil war and had no energies for a larger role. After her independence, India was fully engaged in anxieties over Pakistan and the arduous chores of making independence succeed. The whole "third world" of Africa and the former colonial areas were concentrating upon the painful processes that go with the birth of nations. Eastern Europe lay under the heavy hand of Stalin while Western Europe struggled toward renewed viability via the Marshall Plan and the devices we have previously examined. That left the center stage relatively free for the super powers. Certainly then the super powers dominated the scene, and

235

certainly their clashes were the biggest news, but partly their importance in the total picture of international relations was the product of a lack of competition. The fact that the United States and the Soviet Union held the center stage in world politics was magnified by the lack of contest by other nation-actors. Granted all this, unless the super powers chose to attempt to enforce their wills through violence, their ability to have their way was much less than appearances indicated. Not only was resort to force (which could involve the risk of confrontation and escalation with the other super power) a limited option. Even in the purely political arena and even if the other super power stood clear, should one of the other nations chose defiance, the ability of the super power to have its way would be distinctly limited. Tito's early defiance of Stalin was a case in point; so was France's persistent footdragging on the issue of West German rearmament.

In Eisenhower's initial years as President it was still popular in the United States to conceptualize and verbalize about foreign policy as though the world were divided into a "democratic bloc" and a "communist bloc." Not until about the end of the second Eisenhower term and the beginnings of the Kennedy period was there talk of the "third world." As a description of the complexity of foreign affairs problems, three worlds were better than two, but three was still far too modest a number. The proof of this lay in the events of 1956 and their delayed consequences. We have already noted the fundamental schism that arose in the NATO bloc over the Middle East in that year. We have also noted the first overt stirrings of "national communism" in the Balkans (outside Yugoslavia), which culminated in the Soviet suppression of the Hungarian revolt. What we must next do is to see how the polycentric tendencies clearly in existence by 1956 led in the following years to a loosening of the ties of alliance (or bonds of domination) on both sides of the Iron Curtain. Delayed by the Soviet challenge between 1958 and 1962 (examined in Chapter 12), the fruits of 1956 did not really ripen until 1963. So in this chapter we shall need first to look back at 1956 for the beginnings, and then forward to 1963–1969 for the consequences in "de Gaullism" and the Sino-Soviet dispute, and the interlocks in turn with American foreign policy.

Khrushchev's Revisionism

In Communist countries "doctrinal" discussions play roughly the role that foreign policy debates fulfill in a democratic nation. Thus the "theoretical" propositions advanced have important practical meaning.

Schisms and heresies among Communists are actually as old a story as the Communist movement itself—which is another way of saying that policy disputes are not new. Lenin, in his writings, was continually taking issue with others. In the period after communism took power in Russia, Trotsky finally had to go into exile for his stubborn insistence that a policy of "socialism in one country" would not and could not work. Stalin executed his rivals on many grounds, including deviationism. Even after the prewar period of Stalinist terror, differences of opinion among Soviet leaders obviously continued. Stalin wrote (1952) his last important work, *Economic Problems of Socialism in the USSR*, to argue for the validity of his own interpretations on "The Question of the Inevitability of Wars Among Capitalist Countries" and against rival views. In this last of his writings on political questions (for to Communists, politics *is* economics), he says:

> Some comrades affirm that, in consequence of the development of international conditions after the Second World War, wars among capitalist countries have ceased to be inevitable. They consider that the contradictions [sources of tensions] between the camp of socialism and the camp of capitalism are greater than the contradictions among capitalist countries, that the U.S.A. has made other capitalist countries sufficiently subservient to itself to prevent them from going to war with one another. . . .
>
> These comrades are mistaken. They see the external appearances which glitter on the surface but they fail to see those profound forces which, though at present operating imperceptibly, will nevertheless determine the course of events.

Stalin argued that the great nations of Western Europe, and Japan, were outwardly "on a dole," but this was a temporary condition caused by their weakness. Since there were no "guarantees" that such nations as Germany and Japan would not "again rise to their feet . . . wrest themselves from American bondage and . . . live their own independent lives," it also "follows from this that the inevitability of wars among the capitalist countries remains." Stalin went on: "It is said that Lenin's thesis that imperialism inevitably gives birth to wars should be considered obsolete since powerful peoples' forces have now grown up which are taking a stand in defense of peace, against a new world war. This is not correct."

What Stalin is explicitly rejecting is the proposition that rivalries among the non-Communist great powers would be suppressed in favor of maintaining a solid "democratic bloc" opposed to a "Communist bloc." Stalin was determined to coerce the nations under his own control and maintain their unity if he could, but he thought that "anticommunism" would not prove a sufficiently strong program to cause the West to remain unified. He expected imperialist antagonisms among these powers to destroy their apparent unity and lead to the danger of a new world war breaking out between two or more of them, a new world war into which the Soviet Union would be drawn—

attacked again, as in 1941. Stalin was highly skeptical of the concept of a bipolar world!

What was Lenin's thesis on war among nation-states? It was essentially that capitalist states, outrunning their own domestic markets through exploitation of their own workers (i.e., not paying wages sufficient to sustain consumption of their own output), had to seek additional markets and sources of cheap raw materials abroad. This phenomenon had led to colonial imperialism. And since the available colonies would eventually all be taken, new markets and materials could only be obtained by one capitalist nation through waging war to take by force what belonged to someone else. Thus capitalism and international war were synonymous. It is this thesis which Stalin explicitly reaffirmed: that there can be no permanent world peace so long as capitalism survives.[1]

The problem that even in Stalin's last years was leading "some comrades" toward revisionism was that the logic of Lenin's views led to the supposition of inevitable new war into which the Soviet Union and other "socialist" nations would clearly be drawn. Because such wars would probably involve reciprocal nuclear exchanges, they believed that in the end communism would triumph—but most or many of the victorious would be just as dead as the defeated. One of the clearest statements of this dilemma appeared in the September 1960 issue of *Kommunist* (the Russian theoretical monthly):

> The working class cannot conceive of the creation of a Communist civilization on the ruins of world centers of culture, on desolated land contaminated with thermonuclear fallout, which would be an inevitable consequence of such a war. For some peoples the question of socialism would in general cease to exist: they would physically vanish from the planet. It is thus clear that a *present-day nuclear war in itself can in no way be a factor that would accelerate revolution and bring the victory of socialism closer.* On the contrary, it would hurl mankind, the world revolutionary workers' movement, and the cause of the building of socialism and communism back by many decades.[2]

How escape the dilemma of an "inevitable victory" by communism involving the death and destruction which would go with it? Or, put another way, if communism could be expected with so much confidence to win in the end, it could only be because capitalists were too inflexible to accommodate themselves to the demands of the workers, and too in-

---

[1] Traditional Communist theory, it will be seen, includes no notion of international wars begun by "socialist" states as aggressors. Socialist states fight only in self-defense. The equivalent theory on "wars of national liberation" is more complicated because it holds that such wars are "civil," begun by oppressed peoples seeking freedom from colonial status. Such "aggressive" action by people unfree is deemed entirely legitimate.

[2] As cited in Zbigniew Brzezinski, "A Book the Russians Would Like to Forget," *The Reporter* (December 22, 1960). (Italics in work cited.)

flexible to yield control at home and abroad without bloodshed. The very guarantee of a bright future for communism was also the guarantee that the future would be of marginal appeal. In a nuclear age, how was one to convince Communists, if the capitalists failed to surrender in the face of the slogan-threat of "Better Red than dead," that it is still worthwhile to have communism "inevitably" triumph, even with whole-sale death for all as prize? Since Communists rejected the consolations of religion, they could not even console themselves with thoughts of a personal hereafter!

At the same 20th Congress of the Soviet Communist Party at which he made his sensational "secret speech" on Stalin's crimes, Khrushchev took a characteristically direct approach to the problem. He announced that "there is no fatal inevitability of war" between Russia and the West because "the Socialist [Communist] camp is invincible." He pointed to the weakening of Western influence in Asia, to increasing rivalries among capitalist states, and to economic problems in the U.S. This argument was not entirely inconsistent with Stalin's (who had predicted renewed capitalist rivalries), but by 1960 the new Khrushchev thesis had acquired further subtle aspects. At the Moscow Communist Conference of that year, responding to angry Chinese charges about the "insanity of decaying imperialism" and its warlike tendencies, Khrushchev said the Chinese were ignoring the fact that "the American bourgeoisie is divided against itself," with one group clearly seeing that nuclear war would be folly.[3] In these years Khrushchev also frequently pointed to the great numbers of workers in capitalist countries who were an additional force for peace. Khrushchev was gradually evolving a new thesis about war: the socialist bloc would be able to retain its unity because of the absence of class conflicts and would be too strong for the capitalists to attack, even if they could overcome rivalries and present a common front.

In Khrushchev's thesis—and this is the heart of his revisionism—capitalists do not automatically become warmongers simply because they are capitalists. There are different points of view held by capitalists and a spectrum of policy preferences expressed by them. In short, capitalist society, says Khrushchev, is (to use a Western term) *pluralistic.* Policy is decided by capitalists only after argument and compromise, and a decision against making war is entirely open to them. Capitalists are not foredoomed to act like capitalists simply because they *are* capitalists!

Yet see what a Pandora's box Khrushchev has now opened. For if capitalists are not foredoomed to an inevitable sequence of actions, if capitalists can consider alternatives and make rational choices, why then is communism still fated to be the way of the future? Marx and Lenin

[3] See Isaac Deutscher, "The New Communist Manifesto," *The Reporter,* (January 5, 1961).

spoke so confidently of communism's future because it was supposedly "scientifically" predictable. The whole history of mankind was seen as a repetition of class struggle waged in a dialectical sequence leading eventually to the final battle in which the proletariat would succeed. The whole process rested on two connected expectations: that exploiters would continue to play their exploiting role, and the dispossessed would rise up to challenge their rule. Traditional Marxist thought allowed for occasional capitalists who were personally charitable people, but individual variations were considered ultimately meaningless, because the *system* made exploitation inevitable. A good heart in a capitalist was essentially irrelevant. Yet here we do not see Khrushchev saying: "Of course, there are a few good capitalists who see the folly of war. But what can they do about the system?" Khrushchev instead is saying that the "good" capitalists will have an effective restraining influence and that the future is not foreordained. When he also says, "But your grandchildren will be socialist," he is arguing that his system will be the logical choice of the masses of the world, for they will see that it can do more for them. Communism, as it were, is now to win on its own merits through bold tactics in honest competition, rather than merely to await the prize awarded to it purely because of inevitable capitalist mistakes.

The Sino-Soviet Dispute

SO FAR we have ignored the Chinese reactions to Khrushchev's revisionism and the reasons for them. The Chinese were disturbed both by Khrushchev's "secret speech" attack on the Stalinist "cult of the individual," and by his claims that rational considerations could influence a still powerful imperialist bloc to refrain from war-fomenting activities. The attack on Stalin was not disturbing to the Chinese leaders because of any reverence for Stalin's memory. In his lifetime Stalin had done great damage to the Chinese Communist movement, bypassing them to deal with the Nationalists, and advising them on the very eve of successful seizure of power not to try it! But Stalin as a myth stood in Western minds as the symbol of the Communist monolith, a myth that was useful to a still weak China with substantial ambitions for change. Also, degrading Stalin might—and did quite soon, in both Poland and Hungary —lead to challenges by Communist states that could be dangerous. The unity of the whole movement could be broken, leaving China exposed. (Actually the events in Poland and in Hungary brought out some Chinese ambivalence. Within limits they were willing to encourage more independence, as in Poland. In the Hungarian case where things moved further, they argued for forcible suppression.)

Khrushchev's revisionism was not disturbing to the Chinese because of the anti-Stalinist bipolarity of the concept (camp of socialism versus camp of capitalism), but because it had overtones of the thought that one "can do business" with capitalism. Mao strongly believed that capitalism was in a highly exposed position. The liquidation of colonialism had deprived the capitalist bloc of valuable assets, which they were attempting still to manipulate (less directly than before) via the devices of "neocolonialism"—credits, loans, and ownership of resources, for example. These assets must be entirely destroyed and "national liberation movements" be supported that would remove Western puppets from power. In short, Mao argued, if the West were in a mood to pause at the brink of reckless actions by the thought of the consequences, then it was precisely in order to strike while the iron was hot and induce their downfall in the fringe areas where "salami tactics" (a slice at a time) could be used to greatest advantage. The challenge of "all or nothing" could be avoided and great gains made. But if Khrushchev were to use capitalist "reasonableness" as a pretext for calling off all-out struggle, then the *status quo* would remain. At the Moscow Conference (1957), fresh from his own unpleasant experiences in his "Hundred Flowers" gambit of encouraging criticism at home, Mao strongly condemned Soviet "revisionism" in all aspects.

How influenced Khrushchev was by Mao's criticisms is not really known. Possibly the activism of Khrushchev's policies between 1958 and 1962 had something to do with Mao's needling; but if so, from Mao's viewpoint the activism was probably misdirected. Actually, Khrushchev's assumptions about capitalist reasonableness did not indicate logically or necessarily any passiveness in policy, because Khrushchev could as easily assume that capitalist reasonableness would mean greater Western restraint in reactions. Khrushchev's offensive on Berlin and the flank maneuver over Cuba stood in any event in strange contrast in Chinese eyes to the Soviet failure to give the Chinese Communists real support (1958) during the Formosa-Quemoy-Matsu crisis. The failure of the Chinese "Great Leap Forward" through "backyard industrialization" still further soured Mao and Sino-Soviet relations. After his visit to the United States, when Khrushchev came to Peking and praised American achievements, the Chinese took it as though he were rubbing salt in their wounds. The Soviets had by this time (1959) backed off their 1957 agreement with Peking on providing China a sample bomb, although they had extended valuable technical aid for the Chinese' own nuclear effort. At the Moscow Conference (1960) the Chinese made a clear (if still indirect) attack on Soviet policies. Chinese charges of "Yugoslav revisionism" were countered by Soviet charges of "Albanian dogmatism." The final declaration of the conference papered-over their differences; but in 1961, Russia withdrew aid from Albania, and the Chinese promptly took her place. In March 1961, a Soviet-Yugoslav five-year trade agreement was signed, considered by the Chinese to be a direct affront. In this period, with Soviet technicians (and even blueprints) withdrawn from China, trade between them fell off 67 per cent (1960 to 1963).

At the 22nd Congress of the Soviet Communist Party (October 1961), Chou En-lai came at the head of the Chinese delegation. He claimed that the Chinese had been loyal to the 1957 and 1960 policy declarations. As to the attack that Khrushchev had made at the conference on the "Albanians" (i.e., the Chinese), Chou turned to the Albanian delegation and said: "This unity of ours has stood the test of time. No force can destroy it. . . . To lay bare a dispute between fraternal parties or fraternal countries openly in the face of the enemy cannot be regarded as a serious Marxist-Leninist attitude." To make the point doubly obvious, before leaving for Peking in mid-conference, Chou went to the Lenin-Stalin mausoleum in Red Square and put wreaths at the feet of both. Stalin's wreath had the inscription: "The great Marxist-Leninist." Khrushchev in his final conference speech was stung into his first direct reference to the Chinese, saying that no one was in a better position to reduce fraternal friction than the Chinese. Three days later, Stalin's body was removed from the Red Square tomb and reburied in a simpler grave in front of the Kremlin wall.

In mid-August, Prime Minister Nehru of India let it be known that he had agreement from the Soviets to manufacture Soviet military aircraft in India. The Chinese answered with their "frontier rectification" operation (October 1962)—an operation that virtually coincided with the Cuban Missile Crisis. This last event brought Sino-Soviet differences even more into the open. On November 18, 1962, *Pravda* said: "Neither bourgeois propagandists nor other falsifiers can conceal the main fact that Soviet policy saved world peace and preserved the Cuban revolutionary movement." The same day's *Peking People's Daily* said: "It is pure nonsense to say that 'peace has been saved' by withdrawing Soviet missiles."

From this point on, more and more lively charges began to be exchanged, but still with some restraint. Efforts were made to arrange bilateral talks, and these were scheduled for July 1963. Meanwhile, the Chinese prepared and illegally began to distribute in the Soviet Union an open letter to the C.P.S.U., dated June 14. The Chinese delegation arrived on July 5. The Chinese now resorted to scattering copies of their June 14 letter from the Trans-Siberian Express! Abruptly (July 14), *Pravda* published the letter, together with a rebuttal. The Chinese had written: "If the general line of the international Communist movement is one-sidedly reduced to 'peaceful coexistence,' 'peaceful competitions,' and 'peaceful transition,' this is to violate the revolutionary principles of the 1957 Declaration and the 1960 Statement, to discard the historical mission of proletarian world revolution and to depart from the revolutionary teachings of Marxism-Leninism." The Soviets began their answer by saying that in January they had argued "that open polemics" be discarded "so that disputed issues could be discussed calmly and in a businesslike manner." Said the Soviets, the Chinese had begun "retreating from the general course of the world Communist movement" as early as April 1960. The decline in Sino-Soviet trade and industrial plant deliveries ("dropped forty times") was "on the initiative of the Chinese leaders."

As to principles, the Soviets restated their conviction that "there is no fatal inevitability of war" between states. "This conclusion is not the fruit of good intentions but the result of a realistic, strictly scientific analysis of the balance of class forces in the world arena; it is based on the gigantic might of world socialism." The Chinese were saying that "an end cannot be put to wars as long as imperialism exists; peaceful coexistence is an illusion. . . ." But "the Chinese comrades obviously underestimate all of the danger of a thermonuclear war. 'The atomic bomb is a paper tiger,' it 'is not terrible at all,' they contend. The main thing, they say, is to put an end to imperialism as quickly as possible, but how and with what losses this will be achieved seems to be a secondary question. . . . We would like to ask the Chinese comrades, who offer to build a wonderful future on the ruins of the old world destroyed by a thermonuclear war, if they have consulted the working class of the countries where imperialism dominates on this matter?" The Chinese view may "engender the well-justified suspicion that this is no longer a class approach . . . but involves some entirely different aims."

As to Chinese charges that the Cuban missile deployment was an "adventurist" mistake and that the Soviets had then "capitulated" under American pressure, the Soviets responded that they had had "trustworthy information" of an impending "armed aggression by United States imperialism" and that the missiles had been sent as deterrence. Once they had an American "commitment not to invade Cuba," and thus frustrated "the plans of the extreme adventurist circles of American imperialism that were ready to go the whole hog," the missiles could safely be withdrawn. The Soviets (said the Soviets) were not soft on the class struggle; peaceful coexistence did not imply that the class struggle would cease in capitalist states or that the "oppressed people" would cease opposing the "colonialists."

On July 20, the Chinese delegation departed for Peking. The final negotiations over the Nuclear Test Ban Treaty, which commenced in Moscow the day after the *Pravda* exchanges just quoted, resulted in initialing of the Test Ban agreement (July 25), and signature (August 5). This agreement with the West was so obviously contrary to Chinese interests that it led to a new Chinese statement (August 15), in which the Chinese said that the Soviets a year before had asked them to forego nuclear weapons and that the Chinese had answered that what the

Soviets did was "a matter for the Soviet Government," but that the Soviets could not "infringe China's sovereign rights." The Chinese added: "We solemnly stated we would not tolerate the conclusion [of nuclear limitation treaties] in disregard of China's opposition."[4] On August 21, the Soviets answered that the Chinese wanted "by means of fabrications and low tricks to use this major event in international life . . . to impose upon other countries their adventurist platform on fundamental issues of war and peace. . . ."

Not to be outdone, as September began, the Chinese angrily denounced the Soviet statement: "Apparently the Soviet leaders have already become so degenerate that they now depend on telling lies for a living." The Test Ban Treaty was obviously designed to "manacle all the socialist countries other than the Soviet Union" while it would have "no restraining effect whatsoever on U.S. imperialism. It does not hinder the U.S. from using nuclear weapons in time of war or manufacturing stockpiles." The Chinese went on: "Even if we Chinese people are unable to produce an atom bomb for a hundred years we will neither crawl to the baton of the Soviet leaders nor kneel before the nuclear blackmail of the imperialists." Nuclear weapons could not halt national liberation movements. As to the Cuban crisis, Khrushchev in a "rash action" had embarked upon a "reckless course and irresponsibly played with the lives of millions upon millions of people." The Chinese had been "totally opposed to sending the rockets in." Unlike Khrushchev, the Chinese believed that the correct combination of strategy and tactics was a strategic offensive that would "dare to seize victory" but a tactical prudence "with regard to each specific struggle . . ." Only in this way could one avoid Khrushchev's "errors of adventurism in tactics and capitulationism in strategy."

Summed up, the Chinese were arguing that Khrushchev by his emphasis on "passive" peaceful coexistence was renouncing in advance the best opportunities for victory, while taking gambles where he could not carry through without unacceptable penalties, and that the reverse of this procedure was necessary.

These Chinese charges needled the Soviets into releasing (September 21) a further substantial statement that was a full-fledged defense of the Soviet position.[5] In it the Soviets denounced the Chinese for abandoning "comradely discussion between Communists" in favor of an attempt "to discredit the C.P.S.U. and the Soviet Union at any cost . . ." The "unseemly stand" of the Chinese on the Test Ban Treaty was "not supported by the peoples." Imperialism would be far less dangerous if

---

[4] For an excellent account see Desmond Donnelly, *The Struggle for the World— The Cold War* (New York: St. Martin's Press, 1965), pp. 457–481.

[5] It was bound in pamphlet form and distributed widely. See *Statement of the Soviet Government, September 21, 1963.* (New York: Crosscurrents Press, 1963).

disarmament could be achieved. Of course it was true that "as long as imperialism exists it will retain its aggressive nature, its contradictions. It is fraught with war. Proceeding from this fact the Chinese leaders contend that war is inevitable. Communists cannot take such a fatalist position." The Chinese boast that they would create their own atomic weapons even if it took a hundred years showed "that the schemes of the Peking 'giants' are quite transparent." Were "Chinese atomic bombs also needed for the defense of the socialist camp? Of course not." Mao Tse-tung (September 1958) said that China "need not organize the production of such weapons, especially since it is very expensive." What had changed since? "Has the nuclear rocket power of the USSR become weaker since that time?"

The Soviets heaped scorn on the Chinese "Great Leap Forward," as "a road of dangerous experiment, a road disregarding economic laws and the experience of other socialist states." As to Chinese charges that Chinese nuclear weapons were needed because the USSR was prepared to accept a "two Chinas" policy, this was "utter nonsense." In 1958, Mao had expressed his gratitude for firm Soviet support in the Taiwan Straits crisis; now the Chinese were arguing that the Soviets hung back until danger was past. "From our point of view, the very idea of having to acquire their own nuclear weapons" indicated that the Chinese had "developed special aims and interests that cannot be supported by the military force of the socialist camp."

The Chinese "allege that Soviet documents have taken out of context and misinterpreted quotations from statements by Mao Tse-tung that not all, but half, of mankind will perish in a future war" and about "the 'wonderful prospects' which allegedly will open before mankind after a thermonuclear war . . . Monstrous talk indeed. What 'wonderful future' can one speak of in view of the prospect of the annihilation of half of mankind!" The Chinese were not simply speculating about the future, they wished "to justify a definite policy." This was clear from another Chinese argument to the effect that "the question is what policy, after all, should be followed in the face of the nuclear blackmail and nuclear threat of American imperialism—to offer resistance or to surrender?" But this was not the issue at all; the question was whether to strive for peace or "compete with the imperialists in building up international tension?" To set the record straight on who was misquoting whom, consider, said the Soviets, what Mao Tse-tung actually said before witnesses at the Moscow Meeting (1957)—the "genuine text" rather than the "corrected" version later offered by the Chinese: "This pronouncement shows most nakedly the erroneous views of the Chinese leadership. 'Can one guess,' he said, 'how great the number of human casualties would be in a future war? Possibly it would be a third of the 2,700 million of the world population, i.e., only 900 million people. I consider even this a low figure if atomic bombs were really dropped. Of course, this is most terrible. But even half would be not so bad. Why? Because it is not we that wanted that but they. It is they who are imposing war on us. If war breaks out, atomic and hydrogen weapons will be used. For myself I think that in the entire world there would be such suffering that half of humanity, and perhaps even more than half, would perish. I had an argument about this with Nehru. In this respect he is more pessimistic than I am. I told him that if half of humanity were destroyed, the other half would still remain, but that imperialism would be entirely destroyed and there would be only socialism in all the world, and that in half a century or in a whole century the population would again increase by even more than half.' "

The Soviets summed up their major charge against the Chinese: "They regard the war variant in the development of events as inevitable and even more desirable than the peace variant." All kinds of evidence pointed in this direction. There was the Chinese-Indian border conflict, beginning in 1959, in which the Soviets had urged moderation but where the conflict had been allowed by the Chinese to develop with "the most negative consequences for the cause of peace." Soviet policy toward India was quite in contrast. Nearer at home, "starting in 1960, Chinese servicemen and civilians have been systematically violating the Soviet border. In the single year of 1962, more than 5,000 violations of the Soviet border from the Chinese side were registered. This cannot but make us wary, especially in view of the fact that Chinese propaganda is making definite hints about allegedly unjust demarcation, in the past, of some sections of the Soviet-Chinese border."

As to revolutionary activity, the "Chinese theorists, who repeat the sad anti-Soviet slander about a 'ban' on revolution, cannot, of course, be ignorant of the fact that revolution does not occur on orders from Moscow, or from Peking, and that once it is ripe, no 'ban' can stop it. And if they seriously believe in the possibility of starting a revolution by the incantation of a left revolutionary phrase, they are very far from Marxism-Leninism."

Communism, Post-Schism

THE year 1963 represented the high point of elaborate and frequent exchanges of charge and counter-charge in the "socialist camp." But it by no means represented the climax of the dispute that continued undiminished years later. Even the fall of Khrushchev (October 14, 1964) —whose defeats in foreign policy were complemented by failures in dealing with domestic problems—did not bring any great change. And there were good reasons.

For one thing, Khrushchev's "revisionism" and his quarrel with the

MAP 2

Chinese calls for a more "revolutionary" policy were points of view shared by Khrushchev's colleagues. Although Kosygin and Brezhnev were not as directly implicated from a prestige point of view and therefore could and did attempt to soften the public exchanges, they could not accept Mao's viewpoint any more than Khrushchev could. The real reasons for the differences were not primarily ideological, which is the second thing. They stemmed instead from differences in foreign policy problems and differences over how to resolve these problems.

The Soviets, especially after the shock of the Cuban missile debacle, could not help but regard the world situation from a more conservative viewpoint than the Chinese. Even before 1962, the Soviets were moving away from Stalinism and Stalinist policies, and they had challenged Chinese views, and for some very good reasons. Some relaxation of political and economic controls in the Soviet Union were absolutely essential to raising the standard of living of the Soviet people. Authoritarian controls over the East European "satellites" had to be transformed into a more workable partnership. With a continued Soviet armed presence in these areas increasingly unpalatable to virtually everyone but the weak East German regime, a more natural set of political and economic links between these nations was a very necessary reform. In these European nations the Soviets were not dealing with colonial areas rife with "national liberation" movements. The problem was one of consolidating "socialist gains." However offensive from the viewpoint of the West, from the Soviet point of view the drive to alter the status of West Berlin was probably undertaken as much for defensive as for offensive reasons, for its existence as an outpost of the West undermined the German Democratic Republic's future and thus also indirectly absorbed Eastern European energies in a very complex problem. Once the Wall went up, part of the problem was solved because the population of East Germany quit eroding. The temptation to go further proved irresistible in 1962, for if West Berlin could be neutralized, a really stable Iron Curtain line division of Europe would be more obtainable. But this gamble failed, and the Soviets were forced to weigh all that they could lose by trying to gain more.

In the Middle East area and Africa an urban proletariat hardly existed; and once freedom from colonial rule was largely established, the Soviet Union had a basic choice to make—and made it by 1955–1956. It could seek to undermine such governments as Nasser's (but with little prospects for truly "socialist" replacements—because the Egyptian workers movement was minuscule); or it could utilize the anti-Western orientation of such self-labeled socialist (or even bourgeoise) rulers to advance its own obvious national interests, by weakening Western strength in these areas. Generally this second alternative was the Soviet choice, as we saw. In the same way, in India and Indonesia, the existing leaders could be strengthened or the opposite could be attempted—with the likely outcome of "fascist" military governments brought to power there as the result. In short, "revolutionary" opportunities were in scant supply. A Congo leader here, a Castro there, but little else. In the long run the situation would be different.

But to the Chinese the whole prospect appeared quite otherwise. Confronted with American support of an alternative government in Formosa, confronted with American naval power off the coast, confronted with actual American armed forces in Korea (and later Viet-Nam), the Chinese felt under direct pressure from a nuclear-armed power. Frustration over the need for urgent industrialization and the competing heavy demands for a large military establishment which delayed economic progress, as well as frustration over the need to at long last rectify frontiers imposed on the Chinese in two centuries of weakness, combined to produce an activist and revisionist policy. Southeast Asia, in particular, seemed to offer great hopes for "national liberation" movements that would weaken the West. Confronted with so much to do, with so many competing demands, and impatient with the constraints implicit in the situation (China could not afford to have all its neighbors simultaneously hostile), the Chinese launched out on a policy which eroded much support in Asia and built frustration even higher. The Indian border was altered—but at great cost. The Indonesian subversion backfired. And the party hierarchy at home protested the continued delay in substantial economic progress at home. Mao and those who supported him saw a very different world around them than the Soviet leaders did.

In the years after 1963, the Soviets continued their basic policies and the Chinese followed theirs. The differences between them remained great. In January 1966, for example, the official *Peking People's Daily* charged that "the Soviet Union is preparing the ground to strike a new deal with U.S. imperialism just as the Lyndon Johnson administration is quickening its pace towards a wider war of aggression against Viet-Nam." Similar acid comments continued in 1967–1968. Actual armed clashes on the frontiers followed on a serious scale in March and August 1969, while Chinese Deputy Chairman Lin Piao in April told the 9th Party Congress: "U.S. imperialism and Soviet revisionism are always trying to 'isolate' China . . ." Even as Sino-Soviet border talks began in late 1969, one Chinese broadcast quoted Mao: "Make trouble, fail, make trouble again, fail again . . . until their doom."

In Europe the moderate policy of the Soviets, and their quarrel with the Chinese, produced a noticeable show of independence in the former satellites. Romania was the leader in this trend, partly because Romania was very discontented with the economic role allotted to her by the all-bloc Council for Mutual Economic Assistance (COMECON). Cast primarily in the role of agricultural supplier, Romania wanted to industrialize. In July 1963, COMECON bowed before Romania's adamant rejection of the current proposals. As the Soviets and Chinese increasingly sought to find friends and supporters for their positions among (especially) the Communist parties in power, the Balkan nations took advantage of the altered circumstances to follow more closely their own conceptions of their own national interests. After the formation of the "Grand Coalition" (CDU and SPD) in West Germany under Chancellor Kurt Kiesinger (December 1, 1966), Romania was the first to respond to the West German bid for full diplomatic relations in 1967.

West Germany's diplomatic offensive was made possible by the party coalition that for the first time put the elements who advocated a less rigid policy toward the East in the majority, and it caused a veritable schism in East Europe (1967). Clear lines developed at that time, with Hungary, Romania and Yugoslavia disposed toward better relations with the West; and with Poland and Czechoslovakia (who had frontier problems to settle with Germany) rallying to the "support" of the German Democratic Republic. In early 1968, full diplomatic relations were resumed between West Germany and Yugoslavia, while the Czechs began to give serious consideration to better relations. Meanwhile the Soviets took the diplomatic position toward West Germany that she could not countenance closer relations between Bonn and East Europe unless concessions were offered by Bonn in terms of its political role in West Berlin. The mild terms of this reaction by the Soviets was quite in contrast to Khrushchev's pressures and threats between 1958 and 1962. Although the Soviets continued in early 1968 to reassure East Germany of support (and continued likewise to maintain substantial troop strength there), they tried to avoid a public break with the "liberal" East European states (including, by then, Czechoslovakia) over the issue of the relaxation of tensions with West Germany. There could be no doubt by mid-1968 that "polycentrism" (and a consequent degree of independence in the pursuit each of their own version of "national communism") was becoming a reality in Eastern Europe. The exact limits that the Soviets were willing to permit became clearer (August 1968) with the sudden Soviet occupation of Czechoslovakia. But even then, the Soviets were forced by popular Czech resistance to compromise on their demands and temporarily restore to power Czech party leader Dubcek, who had led the way to Czechoslovakia's new liberalism! It was highly unlikely that the clock could really be stopped for more than a time—even by armed occupation. When, in the fall of 1969, Dubcek was downgraded from power, the Czech mood was sullen; in December, Dubcek was named Czech ambassador to Turkey.

Within 20 days of the Soviet invasion of Czechoslovakia, Radio Peking was devoting much air time to denunciation of the move, comparing it, in a variety of East European languages to U.S. actions in Viet-Nam.

In the fall of 1969, following Willy Brandt's formation of a new government in West Germany, with the Social Democrats in coalition with the Free Democrats, a whole new series of conversations began between the Federal Republic and the Soviet "bloc" states.

De Gaulle and the Change in NATO

CHARLES de Gaulle was the resistance leader in World War II of the "Free French," temporary President in the immediate postwar years, and Chief Executive of the Fifth French Republic from 1958 to 1969. He never stirred the affections of the American people. Indeed, in the 1960's, he enjoyed a worse public image in the United States than the Soviet leaders, for at least "they" were on "their" side and de Gaulle (although supposed to be on "ours") stubbornly set his own course. By 1967, because of de Gaulle, much of NATO's structure in France was being liquidated, and NATO headquarters itself was relocated in Belgium. While France, in de Gaulle's words, remained "the ally of her allies" (i.e., she was still a member of the North Atlantic Pact), she was no longer taking real part in the coordinated defense command and training arrangements that were the really distinctive feature of NATO. France in 1968 was the West's "Romania," and de Gaulle the moving force in NATO's schism.

Was all of this simply explained by de Gaulle's personal sense of "grandeur," or was there more to it? To answer this question requires an effort to free oneself from a purely American perspective, because looked at in terms of French responsiveness to U.S. views in the 1960's France—and particularly de Gaulle—was "guilty" on all counts.

Part of the explanation is simply that nations with old and close ties (which describes the U.S. and France) tend to have family quarrels, because so much is expected of them. Furthermore, U.S. postwar policies were generous in conception and implementation and restored France to strength—thus arousing American expectations of French gratitude. Americans assumed that gratitude would be demonstrated by French adherence to U.S. lead. It is also true that Anglo-American relations with de Gaulle during World War II irritated a proud and sensitive man who was also jealous for his nation's damaged prestige. But there is more to it. "Gaullism" in its deeper roots grew out of three factors not yet mentioned: France's historical experience in the twentieth century, the U.S. handling of the 1956 Suez crisis, and France's concern in the 1950's–1960's over the apparent desire of the U.S. to follow foreign policies considered at least in significant part to be contrary to French national interests.

The historical experience of France in the twentieth century has not been at all pleasant. Twice invaded and overrun by the Germans, bled by the casualties of numerous wars, cursed with a system of government characterized by weakness and impermanence, the French suffered many disasters and few successes. Even the period of apparent dominance in European affairs in the 1920's was only transitory, leading to worse troubles. The instability of the French political system provided a built-in tendency toward weak decisions. Munich was the capstone in foreign-policy weakness, but at home there were added the German occupation and the schisms represented by the Pétain Vichy regime. After World War II, although the French were still economically weak, they poured out yet further blood and treasure in an endless war in Viet-Nam and in strife in Algeria. Never was the decision taken by the postwar Fourth French Republic to either "win" or withdraw. Only with Mendès-France (1954) was the decision taken on withdrawing from Viet-Nam, and only after de Gaulle took power could the decision be taken on Algeria.

While France (1956) was still battling in Algeria against rebels armed with Nasser's help, she intervened against Nasser after his nationalization of the Suez Canal Company—only to be met by American opposition to the use of force. Whatever one thinks of the wisdom or morality of France's action against Nasser, the fact remains that the U.S. cut the ground out from France's feet. De Gaulle, who was not yet in power, watched France's humiliation as her major ally deserted her.

After de Gaulle's coming to power (1958), the overall divergence between French and American foreign policy grew ever greater, but not everywhere and not all at once. On the critical question of responding to Khrushchev's boldness there was no essential difference. France was less willing to negotiate than the U.S., holding that the solution was for Khrushchev to drop his threats, but France still supported opposition. In 1962, during the Cuban Missile Crisis, France carefully avoided any actions adverse to American interests. In 1963, the signing of the Test Ban Treaty produced a divergence, for France in refusing to sign continued her testing and continued developing her own nuclear *force de frappe.* Much friction developed over NATO (already noted), over de Gaulle's veto of the British entry into the Common Market, and over de Gaulle's insistence on keeping the supranational features of the Common Market restricted by French veto rights. These last policies flew in the face of the American enthusiasm for Western European unity. All of these moves were accompanied by acid comments by de Gaulle on the "special relationship" between Great Britain and the U.S. For example, speaking (1963) of the Anglo-American Nassau Agreement, he said pointedly: "Of course, I am only speaking of this proposal and agreement because they have been published and because their content is known." The idea of an integrated NATO nuclear force, discussed again at Nassau, left de Gaulle particularly cold.

The whole nuclear Multilateral Force (MLF) concept was a brainchild of American officials seeking to respond to de Gaulle's criticism of defense arrangements that left France in the position of being confronted with decisions made essentially by the U.S. He wanted a "hand on the nuclear trigger," as the phrase had it: consultation and agreement before any decisive actions. The U.S. proposed that instead of attempts at effective consultation there should be a nuclear force that would be multi-national (i.e., have integrated units composed of the forces of different NATO nations) and be in charge of NATO nuclear weapons.

De Gaulle's idea of effective consultation implied that important actions could occur only with common consent, but the U.S. was unwilling to relinquish its ultimate right to decide its own course and refused. Yet an MLF force would obviously be quite meaningless in reaching to the heart of French objections in any real sense. De Gaulle was confronted with the fact that however international the window-dressing the U.S. nuclear arsenal would not be used unless the U.S. government ordered American officers to do so. Worse in de Gaulle's view, once that order was given France would be involved whether she wished to be or not.

De Gaulle's own solution to the problem was certainly somewhat more sophisticated than the mechanical mirage represented by MLF, but what de Gaulle wanted was not really attainable that way either. If one nation feels that its life and death are in the hands of other nations allied to it, then naturally it wants as large a say as anyone else in the decision. But could the French have as large a say in a decision to use American weapons as the U.S. itself? Hardly. What the two nations were up against was the dilemma fundamentally implicit in the fact of sovereignty itself. If a nation could not really decide on ultimate questions, was it truly sovereign? A federal union of the U.S. and France could conceivably resolve this question; but not consultations, and certainly not the naïve MLF.

France was not so much in doubt that Americans would "die for Paris." What de Gaulle was asking was whether Americans would die *"because of* Paris," i.e., because of some French-initiated action. If France could do only what the U.S. endorsed, she had no real freedom or meaningful sovereignty. One could argue that the U.S. would endorse anything for which Frenchmen themselves would risk massive death and destruction—but what about 1956 and Suez? De Gaulle felt the solution lay in two connected moves: one, to remove NATO troops from French soil (if they were not under French command) and, two, build his own independent nuclear force. The first move would have the drawback of weakening NATO, but had the advantage that France's cooperation in any decision was not automatically foreordained by the very fact that forces on her soil were committed whether she liked it or not. Moreover, American and German forces in Germany would still shield France from Soviet advances. The second move (which American military commentators greeted with some derision) was not intended to lead to a capability equal to the super powers. De Gaulle reasoned that a French ability to kill 30 to 40 million Russians would not be ignored by the Soviet Union simply because not even half of the Soviet people would thereby be slaughtered. When we remember the Sino-Soviet dispute on this point, it is probable that de Gaulle's reasoning was correct, provided the French *force de frappe* has sufficient "invulnerability."

Connected to the French moves was another consideration, this time in the field of military strategy *per se.* France felt that the McNamara theory of "graduated deterrence" was a form of invitation to the Soviets to hazard military adventures. Because a Soviet action (under the McNamara theory) would not automatically bring on a full nuclear response, the Soviets might be tempted toward "graduated adventurism." De Gaulle wanted no risk of Soviet advance being finally brought to a halt only by a massive nuclear effort after the Soviets were in or near French territory. By effectively denying NATO its rear area (once NATO troops were off French soil), de Gaulle in effect forced NATO back much nearer to the strategy of massive and immediate nuclear retaliation. This military fact of life received surprisingly little attention and no real public official commentary until October 1968.[6] Yet a NATO

[6] At that time, General Lyman L. Lemnitzer, NATO Commander of Allied Forces in Europe, commented that denial of French spaces would force commitment of reserves, including nuclear weapons, "at an earlier point in the conflict." *The New York Times* (October 16, 1968).

whose logistical tail is in Belgium and whose front-line deployment is in narrow-width West Germany has no real space to sacrifice during some more or less leisurely graduated escalation. By his moves de Gaulle restored NATO in reality to the military doctrine that they had publicly discarded!

In a broader field of concern, de Gaulle saw in America's involvement in Viet-Nam an unintended insult implicit in American optimism that the U.S. could win where the French had lost. But beyond that, U.S. involvement meant a weakening of her ability to respond to European problems simultaneously with a tendency toward increased armed conflict in Asia, which de Gaulle felt was dangerous. By 1968, these views were rather widely shared in Europe.

De Gaulle's idea of a "Europe of the nations" and his assertions that Europe ran from the "Atlantic to the Urals" caused much confusion in the U.S. The first phrase seemed to many Americans a somewhat mystical reversion to "outmoded" nationalism, another evidence of de Gaulle's refusal to be modern and proceed with meaningful Western European integration where he had an opportunity. Yet de Gaulle's rejection of a small and tightly integrated Europe had certain merits. The small Europe solution certainly had little to offer as a means toward German reunification. It tended to ignore the promising growth of polycentrism in Eastern Europe. Indeed the very strength behind polycentrism was that of nationalism—in this case "national communism." Did not its growth indicate that national *differences* still remained very meaningful? Was full political integration in Western Europe at all necessary for the enjoyment of a significant rise in West European standards of living?

De Gaulle's emphasis in the second phrase, since it arbitrarily divided Russia at the Urals, seemed even less comprehensible to Americans. But what de Gaulle was trying to convey was not that all of Russia lies in Europe, but that Eastern Europe and Western Russia *are* parts of Europe, and that Europe is, after all, a continent and its problems need handling on a continental basis. Where the thrust of U.S. policy was for making "our part" of Europe a solid entity in competition with communism's part, the thrust of de Gaulle's policy was to attempt to emphasize the common interests of all European nations to resolve problems (such as Germany's division) that confront all and threaten all if merely left to drift.

This last point probably explains more than any other the relatively close relationship between France and West Germany in the 1960's. Although de Gaulle's willingness to settle for the Oder-Western Neisse line as a united Germany's eastern frontier caused Germany some concern, a part of that concern was purely tactical. The Germans do not wish (even before negotiations begin) to accept the union of the Federal Republic and the German Democratic Republic within their existing *de facto* frontiers as the *de jure* frontiers for the whole. And, of course, there are also significant elements in Germany who want improvements in a united Germany's frontier at some expense to Poland. Even so, when this is taken into account, one is struck by the closeness of Franco-German relations. In spite of French NATO policy, French troops remain in West Germany. The Germans feel, too, that America's involvement in Viet-Nam and Asia means that progress on resolving German and European problems is thereby hindered. In the West German policy of opening up diplomatic relations with Eastern Europe there is much more than an echo of de Gaulle's phrase, "Europe from the Atlantic to the Urals." Who, more than the Germans, must realize that progress in Europe depends upon all-European solutions?

In 1969, after de Gaulle's retirement, French nuclear policy remained essentially unaltered.

An Assessment

THE wonder is not that the reality or appearance of bipolarity remained in existence for so short a period. The wonder is that it endured so long. For the world to be truly divided between great rival blocs, especially two of them, assumes a high tension level and a wholesale willingness to suppress counterbalancing national interests. This is antagonistic to the natural tendencies of nations to strive toward their goals with a high degree of national independence, unless they feel a strong sense of overt threat.

What kept the tension level very high for a very long period in Europe was the division of Germany. It still is the greatest single factor in keeping tension levels high. What has changed is that (1) West Germany is seeking to establish new relations with Eastern Europe; (2) Eastern Europe is now free from Stalin's bondage and attempts to reciprocate; and (3) the essential spirit of de Gaulle's foreign policy (despite his blunders) was in accord with these developments. Simultaneously the American deepening involvement in Asia has encouraged Europe to take a fresh look at its problems. For it is not unjust to the U.S. record of creative approach in the immediate postwar years to Europe's problems to say that by the 1960's the U.S. had little constructive to contribute to those problems. Primary responsibility for Europe lies with Europe, and nothing can alter that fact. As the 1970's began, both Western Europe and Eastern Europe showed growing signs of impatience with the arbitrary division of the continent.

As to the schism in the Communist camp, although of benefit to the U.S., the U.S. could hardly claim the credit. Indeed American foreign policy throughout the postwar period has in its central thrust tended to unify the Communist nations rather than the reverse. This is one of the severest criticisms that can justifiably be made against it. In Asia the U.S. involvement in Viet-Nam, as often before, threatened to mitigate the Sino-Soviet discord.

So, in this survey of postwar events and the U.S. reaction to the crises that marked them, we come to the present. In many cases, as we have gone along, we have pointed to factors that should enter into the assessment of U.S. policy. In Part Four, which follows, we shall confront the question squarely: What does this record of American reactions to these events tell us about the strengths and weaknesses of our approach and the validity of our political strategy?

PART FOUR

The Problems of Foreign Policy

CHAPTER 14

Alternative Strategies for U.S. Policy

BALANCE sheet for U.S. foreign policy in the new age of increasing involvements after World War II must give full marks to much that was constructive in conception and capable in execution. Conversely, the important mistakes could be traced predominantly to our limited and unusual experience as a nation. Views as to what the world is like, what kinds of solutions will cure its ills, what our constructive contribution can be (and its limitations), and through what methods, strategies, and tactics that contribution can best be made, naturally are profoundly influenced by experience—an experience that U.S. policy-makers of both major parties share. Where the limitations of our experience had greatest negative consequences was in our failing to ask the right strategic questions in the right order. That, plus our impatience, inclined us almost automatically to ask first what we should do, rather than what we want done and who might do it. If U.S. errors after 1945 were in the direction of assuming unilaterally too much of the burden, these errors stem from a failure to understand the conditions under which other nations would and could be forced to act in our essential interests. Before attempting, in the next four chapters, to analyze our major military, socioeconomic, and political policy dilemmas, it will be useful here to look systematically at the assumptions behind our approach to world problems.

The Strategic Questions Debated

IN Chapter 1 we made the point that the three most important strategic decisions involve where to deploy politico-military power to hold the line, whom the line should be held against, and how the line should be held. Deciding these three aspects of strategy wisely is indeed the proof that one has a well-conceived set of objectives implemented through a strategic policy that takes account of and advantage of the basic forces at work in international relations.

When, as in *The New York Times* (February 26, 1967), a round-up of largely critical views by prominent individuals before the Senate Foreign

259

Relations Committee and elsewhere is presented, it is these questions
they are asking. The article title is "Are We Overextended?—Six Views,"
but its content thrust is less on whether we have the power to pursue
"globalist" commitments (although no nation *is* unlimited in its power)
and more on whether these many commitments are desirable or necessary. They are asking what we *should* be attempting in Europe, Asia,
and elsewhere. (Compare with Rusk's comments which follow, noting
how central the adequacy of his guiding formulas—defend freedom,
stop communism, deter aggression—is to this debate.)

In the *Times* article Senate Majority Leader Mike Mansfield's views on
Europe are reported. Speaking before Soviet occupation of Czechoslovakia dashed hopes for détente, Senator Mansfield called for "a selective
but substantial reduction of our troop commitments to NATO" which
"could become central to furthering" bridge-building efforts. Former
ambassador George F. Kennan noted, "We stand today at something of
a parting of the ways with respect to our approach to the Communist
world. If we . . . carry our differences against individual Communist
powers as though we were still dealing . . . with the grim monolith of
Communist power that confronted us in the days of Stalin, we may be
neglecting and discarding the only chance that I can see to spare ourselves . . . the immeasurable catastrophes of a world war among nuclear
powers." Professor Henry Steele Commager recorded his "feeling that
we do not have the resources, material, intellectual or moral, to be at
once an American power, a European power, and an Asian power. . . .
It is not our duty to keep peace throughout the globe, to put down aggression wherever it starts up, to stop the advance of communism or
other isms which we may not approve of. It is primarily the responsibility
of the United Nations to keep the peace . . . if that organization is not
strong enough to do the job we should perhaps bend our major energies
to giving her the necessary authority and the tools."

Retired General James E. Gavin saw the "United States' troop commitment to Europe [as] far in excess of today's needs." Although NATO
was necessary, Gavin stressed the need to encourage a stronger, more
independent Western Europe. Senator J. W. Fulbright, Chairman of the
Senate Foreign Relations Committee, noted the "quite fundamental
changes . . . in the world during the past twenty years [but] we continue to apply the vocabulary created two decades ago to the shape of
current events. . . . We know only that aggression is usually an action
that Communist countries take and that the United States abjures.
Equally, we therefore appear to know instinctively that fighting in
Lebanon or the Dominican Republic, for instance, somehow does not
involve aggression."

Former Ambassador to Japan Edwin O. Reischauer said: "The threat
of unitary world communism sweeping Asia has largely faded, and the

menace of Chinese domination—if ever it was a real menace in the military sense—is growing weaker. . . . We should seek to minimize our military involvement and military commitments in Asia, because our vital interests are not likely to be threatened in most of Asia, because our type of military strength is not very effective in meeting subversion and guerrilla warfare . . . and because our military presence is likely to stir up anti-American reactions."

A debate is not complete without the opposing views. No one has more ably enunciated the basis for the present policy than former Secretary of State Dean Rusk. One of the clearest defenses he made deserves quotation at length. Dated January 4, 1967, in form it is a response to a letter from student leaders on the U.S. policy in Viet-Nam, but in fact it contains a complete intellectual justification for how U.S. strategic problems have been conceptualized in the 1950's and 1960's by successive administrations.

There is no shadow of doubt in my mind that our vital interests are deeply involved in Viet-Nam and in Southeast Asia.

We are involved because the nation's word has been given that we would be involved. On February 1, 1955, by a vote of 82 to 1 the United States Senate passed the Southeast Asia Collective Defense Treaty. That Treaty stated that aggression by means of armed attack in the treaty area would endanger our own peace and safety and, in that event, "we would act to meet the common danger." There is no question that an expanding armed attack by North Viet-Nam on South Viet-Nam has been under way in recent years; and six nations, with vital interests in the peace and security of the region, have joined South Viet-Nam in defense against that armed attack.

Behind the words and the commitment of the Treaty lies the lesson learned in the tragic half century since the First World War.

After that war our country withdrew from effective world responsibility. When aggressors challenged the peace in Manchuria, Ethiopia, and then Central Europe during the 1930's, the world community did not act to prevent their success. The result was a Second World War—which could have been prevented. . . .

This was also the experience President Truman had in mind when—at a period when the United Nations was incapable of protecting Greece and Turkey from aggression—he said: "We shall not realize our objectives unless we are willing to help free peoples to maintain their free institutions and their national integrity against aggressive movements that seek to impose upon them totalitarian regimes."

These are the memories which have inspired the four postwar American Presidents as they dealt with aggressive pressures and thrusts from Berlin to Korea, from the Caribbean to Viet-Nam.

In short, we are involved in Viet-Nam because we know from painful experience that the minimum condition for order on our planet is that aggression must not be permitted to succeed. For when it does succeed, the consequence is not peace, it is the further expansion of aggression. . . .

Look back and imagine the kind of world we now would have if we had adopted a different course. What kind of Europe would now exist if there had been no commitment to Greece and Turkey? No Marshall Plan? No NATO? No defense of Berlin? Would Europe and the world be better off or worse? Would the possibilities of détente be on the present horizon?

Then turn the globe and look at Asia. If we had made no commitments and offered no assistance, what kind of Asia would there now be? Would there be a confident and vital South Korea? A prosperous and peaceful Japan? Would there be the new spirit of regional cooperation and forward movement now developing throughout Asia? . . .

. . . We regret all the loss of life and property that this conflict entails. We regret that a single person, North or South, civilian or soldier, American or Vietnamese, must die.

And the sooner this conflict can be settled, the happier we and the Vietnamese people will be.

The differences in opinion are obvious; the question is who is right? Do the formulas which worked well in Europe work equally well in Asia? Has the European situation changed so that even there adjustments in U.S. policy have become necessary? What fundamental considerations must be taken into account to answer such questions?

Looking at the record of commitment and involvement which marks the new age of U.S. foreign policy and such debates over its wisdom, one is struck by the centrality of four functional problem areas. Today, in each of these four problem areas there are substantial differences of opinion over the most useful and realistic way to conceptualize what is involved. *First* is communism. We have been torn between seeing it as a unified, militant, subversive, revolutionary bloc bent on undermining and destroying "free world" democracy, and thinking of it alternatively as a competing ideology taking different forms in different states loosely united by their common outlook. *Second* is foreign aid and the uncommitted. We have been torn between seeing foreign aid as an instrument to retard the spread of communism and seeing it as a moral obligation of the wealthy nations to the poorer peoples of the world. We have similarly hovered between the view that "he who is not with me, is against me," and the view that "he who is not against me, is with me"— meaning that we have not been sure whether we could or should convert the uncommitted, enroll them in one of our many alliance blocs. *Third* is the United Nations, conflict resolution, and the whole area of "peace-keeping." We have moved back and forth from considering the UN as the main focus of U.S. policy efforts to the other extreme. We have not always been certain whether UN peace-keeping activities could and should be strengthened, and our attitude has varied especially as the organization itself has changed. *Fourth* is military security. We have altered our doctrines from "massive retaliation" to "graduated response";

we have tried to outrun the Soviet armaments program on the one hand and urged them to settle for an equal destructive capability on the other (and to refrain from antimissile systems). We have sought to unravel the complex interrelations among armaments, arms control, weapons systems (both defensive and offensive), and strategy.

All four functional problem areas have been approached in quite different ways at various times in this postwar quarter century. Partly this was inevitable simply because we live in a world of constant change. Partly we have been uncertain of the correct approach because there have been substantial differences among the American people as to which approach corresponded most closely to American needs and which approach was most useful and realistic in the world as we saw it. In other words, an important part of the argument has turned on the *perception* of the problem and its world environmental setting. It is here where Rusk's views most importantly clashed with those of his critics.

Arguments over U.S. objectives necessarily include disagreements over perceptions (i.e., an objective appears more or less realistic depending on what one thinks reality is). Arguments over alternate strategies to attain these objectives will again inevitably reflect differences over perceptions. Even arguments over tactical implementation of strategy in some part reflect differences in perception.

It is of limited utility to examine U.S. objectives apart from perceptions, or strategies apart from objectives, or tactics apart from strategy. If we could agree on what the world is like and on what makes it "tick," we could presumably agree on what objectives the U.S. could hope to obtain, which strategy would be most appropriate, and which tactics were necessary. The problem of analysis of U.S. foreign policy therefore includes all four parts, and the sequence of consideration is important: perceptions, objectives, strategy, and tactics.

Perceptions

WHAT is the world like with which foreign policy must cope? What makes it "tick"?[1] It is a world presently divided into more than 130 sovereign units, varying from the city-state modesty of the Vatican to the geographic and demographic hugeness of China. Although varying tremendously in national power, each sovereign unit is the same in two respects: (1) its government makes decisions for itself (taking into account whatever factors it wishes in reaching its decisions), and (2) each unit must face the possibility of becoming involved in war. The international "system," then, has a very large number of actors who have

[1] It is not necessary for the reader to agree with the analysis here; it is necessary for him to decide whether he does agree or not. For the assumptions made here lead in the next sections to conclusions whose validity rests on these assumptions.

greatly varying characteristics (location, size, and so forth) but who will also have certain similar behavioral traits (the need to make security-conserving or security-enhancing decisions). The historical experience of a nation will affect very importantly how that nation perceives its security problem and what kinds of actions (or lack of actions) that nation may decide on. Two factors limit the strategic choices to a fairly narrow range of alternatives.

First, the amount and kind of national power which gives backing to foreign policy decisions already is a significant practical limitation on freedom of selection. Being sovereign, any nation, however small, could choose to attack alone a much more powerful neighbor. Such behavior in fact does not occur. Location tends to focus security decision-making: those who are near enough as neighbors, or those whose great power mobility allows them to deploy forces in the area, are of most concern. No nation is worried over conflict with more than a relatively few other nations.

Second, a nation's choices among structural or organizational patterns as "solutions" to its security problem are very limited in number, although each has more than one form. Only three basic options are available: to "go it alone," making no alliances (the pattern of *unilateralism*); to make alliances by joining other nations who have similar security concerns, either on a "regional" basis or otherwise (the pattern of the *balance of power*); or to rely for protection on the collective security features of a world organization such as the United Nations (the pattern of *collective security*).

An important fact is that the range of organizational alternatives is narrow; equally important is the fact that the range of consequences that flow from the choice of such alternatives is broad. Looking at the balance of power pattern, for example, since alliance networks can and do take various forms, they can and do produce varying results. The choice of a unilateralist pattern may have effects on other nations (or on the system as a whole), which may vary tremendously (as when Switzerland remains neutral compared with U.S. "isolationism"). Therefore, although the range of basic *options* is very limited, the results are far less so. Various kinds of total power systems will emerge, depending on the options chosen and the form in which they are implemented. Alliance systems, for example, may and do vary widely in their form—and effects.

Any option chosen by any nation will reflect its own conception of its security problem in view of the total power system and especially that part that affects it most directly. The system is anything but static, since individual choices of options will be continually reviewed in the light of the total system at any one time. Thus it is misleading to think of any "actor" as a "set piece" except in a transitory sense. This means that, at a given time, the policy being pursued by Indonesia and the security choices she has made cannot be regarded as absolute and unchanging but, rather, relative and flexible. Cambodian policy likewise can be expected to reflect changing Cambodian conclusions as to how well its interests are served by a given course of action. If each nation makes its choices out of a calculus of interests which frequently needs review, and alternative choices are available, what behavior, if any, is typical of nations confronted by severe threats?

We come at this point to a critical question, reaching to the very heart of the American foreign-policy problem. Do nations that have realistic reasons to be concerned about their security capitulate and make their peace with the nearer power or powers, who are the apparent source of their concern, unless they are guaranteed by great powers located quite far away? Or, in the absence of such guarantees, do they pool their strength and strive to maintain national integrity as best they can? Will the answer to this question be the same for Cambodia as for Japan and India, or for France and West Germany? How valid is the "domino theory"; and, if valid at all, under what circumstances?

This is not an easy set of questions to answer concerning any individual nation. Cambodia, for instance, has fears clustering on Thailand, Viet-Nam, China, and the United States and might therefore act in a number of ways. How much specific concern she feels about the actions of any one of these other states and what policy courses they are following will influence her decision. All we can be sure of is that Cambodia will know she has no hope of matching Chinese or American power, although she might hope to compete on more equal terms with either Thailand or the Viet-Nams (but again, probably not with both areas acting in concert—if this were to occur). Larger powers are less dependent on guile and agility. India is hardly likely to allow herself to become a Chinese puppet, whatever the Asian policy of the U.S. One can say that India is too weak to resist, but one would have to reserve judgment on this point. How easy would it be to occupy and hold India even if India could not prevent the occupation? And what are still other powers such as the Soviet Union doing while China is taking over India? In Europe, de Gaulle's independent policy toward NATO was not an indication of French conviction that security is unobtainable.

Looking at 1938 we see Czechoslovakia giving up without a fight; but in 1939, Poland fought against hopeless odds.

Answering the question on response to security threats (capitulation vs. opposition) for any individual nation necessitates careful and complex analysis, of its friends and foes as well as of its location and political stability and power. We can more confidently and simply answer the question for the international system as a whole. Unless one wants to argue that the advent of nuclear weapons now makes possible what never proved possible before, one must conclude from the historical evidence that the system as a whole rejects one-power control. No one nation has ever come near taking over the whole world. Those who have by their actions shown a desire for gross territorial expansion have invariably been repulsed by a union of those threatened. Nuclear weapons may make possible world destruction; they do not necessarily make possible world conquest. At this point we reach the realm of balance-of-power theory.

As with any ancient concept, the mere passing of many years allows simplistic notions, heresies, and false generalizations to cluster around it like the barnacles on a ship's bottom. The resulting travesty of good sense exposes the concept to easy ridicule. Yet if the concept endures, it is likely to have some real meaning. Without going into an extensive discussion of the many questionable things said in the name of balance-of-power theory, we can rest the case on its essence—which is that nations tend ultimately to combine against the most radical disturber of the territorial *status quo*. It is easy to point to cases where they did not when they should have. (Consider the failure in the 1930's of Great Britain, France, and Russia—let alone the United States—to combine against Nazi Germany.) Yet in the end they tend to do so, even be forced into it by the recklessness of their opponent. (Hitler attacked Russia of his own will and took the initiative in declaring war on the U.S.)

What causes the ultimate tendency to combine against the most radical disturber of the peace is that those who combine do so because they are confronted by a common and inescapable threat. The nearer and more immediate the threat, the greater the tendency. In neither world war did the U.S. feel threatened before Britain, France, and Russia did, because we were geographically more remote from its source. Hitler's real threat to U.S. interests depended on his ability to defeat first the powers who stood as a barrier to German expansion. Today, although the existence of ICBM's theoretically allows the destructive power of the Soviet Union to be launched against the U.S. even without a Soviet attack on her European great power neighbors, the basic workings of the balance of power tell us this action is highly unlikely. The Soviets would have no reason for such action unless they wished to conquer Europe. An attack on the U.S. alone, even if it were considered feasible by the Soviets, would be tantamount to a declaration of intent to take over Europe.

One can argue that Western Europe might seek peace at any price to avoid nuclear devastation. But if Europe's will to defend itself was that weak, the Soviets would surely choose to take advantage of that weakness and impose their hegemony directly on Europe, foregoing the presumably mutual nuclear devastation a war with the U.S. would entail. If convinced that Europe would not fight in her own defense, the U.S. would have to decide whether to fight at that point on its own.

Assuming this nightmare problem arose, would not the enormous growth in Soviet power automatically force other large, non-European power centers to weigh making common cause with the U.S.?

Speculations of this kind—assuming a supine attitude by proud European states toward their own national integrity—are far from reality. The fact of the matter is that the U.S., geographically remote from both Europe and Asia (except in ICBM terms), has a fortunate security position conferred by nature. Nations can (as the Soviets can) directly attack the U.S., but they have no reason to do so apart from interdicting U.S. interference in actions nearer their own frontiers. They cannot otherwise erode the security flanks of the U.S. without expanding nearer at home into the territories of near neighbors. If the Soviet Union or China were to do this, they would threaten all the rest of the nations in their immediate area, and threaten them far more immediately than they threatened the United States. In short, geography guarantees the U.S. allies; and nuclear weapons do not alter that fact.

If it is not logical to assume that a Soviet threat to Europe would be resisted by Europe or that a Chinese threat to Asia would be resisted by Asia, why is it logical to assume that if the U.S. were confronted by one or both of these dire possibilities she would nonetheless fight and die? What would make all the rest cowards while we remained heroes?

These observations about balance of power behavior tell us a great deal about the pros and cons of alternative strategies available to us. Let us consider U.S. objectives in this perspective. Here we must discuss what alert readers will have already noted by its heretofore conspicuous absence: the role of ideology.

Foreign Policy Objectives

WHAT should be the U.S. goals? Is it enough for the U.S. to survive in an insecure world, or must we make each part of it share our own beliefs? How far-reaching should be our objectives? How many sets of beliefs do we think there are in the world: two, three, as many as there are nations, or even more? What is the relation of our tendency to give a small-number answer to this question with our tendency to conceptualize our prime strategy in the simple and restricted terms of containing a Communist bloc?

Early in this book we sketched the particular and unusual nature of American historical experience and its results in American national characteristics as well as in the specific qualities of American nationalism. Pains were taken to stress the sources of American optimism, pragmatism, and idealism. We pointed out that American idealism in the form of a view of the proper functioning of government among men (consent of the majority, American freedoms, and so forth) had an obverse side in the Yankee practicality of these formulas for settling many novel questions in a very novel setting, among men from many national backgrounds. Because of this, ideas as systems have bulked large in American history. One finds one root here of the tendency toward slogans and formulas that adorn (or distort) our foreign policy. We take ideas seriously because our very system of government is abstract in orientation. A "government of laws, not of men" is a tribute to ideas about government, and by holding to this abstract *procedure or method* we have been able to arrive at specific successive *contents* or policies acceptable to the majority. Thus our habit is to proceed from the general to the particular.

Similarly, when we approach world problems, we like to reason from the general to the particular. When Eisenhower reportedly said at the time of the 1956 Suez Crisis that the U.S. would do whatever the UN majority thought just, he was acting on that belief, and in accordance with well-worn American patterns of thought. When we try, recurrently, to reduce foreign policy problems to formulas, we are illustrating the same tendency: "Communist aggression in Asia must be stopped."

A people prone above the norm to value ideas, abstractions, systems of ideas, are likely to take what they understand of the idea systems of other nations with the utter seriousness with which they take their own. Such a people are likely to undervalue the "sea change" that occurs in ideas transplanted in alien environments. And because their own idea system of "democracy" shares with communism pretensions of universality, they are prone to generalize on the largest and most abstract scale, seeing the world as engaged in a struggle "between two ways of life." (Even if they up the number to four or five, would it be adequate?) A weak historical sense will encourage this tendency further.

Coming back to the opening questions in this section, do we think that other peoples do share or can come to share American beliefs? And does it really matter? Asked another way the question becomes: do we think that peoples stand together against enemies because they share similar ideas and values, or because they fear similar foes? Or do we think that only those who think alike could have similar enemies? (If so, how do we explain Nazi-Soviet collaboration in 1939–1941 and Soviet-American collaboration in 1941–1945?) Should Portugal be expelled from NATO because of her authoritarian regime, and Spain excluded, even if they think their enemies are the same as those of the U.S., and on that ground alone?

If security problems are strictly classifiable along lines of categories of idea systems and values, a simple line could be drawn: Communists on this side, non-Communists on that. Is this workable? Apart from Castro's insults to the U.S. and the strategic location of Cuba off the

Florida coast, does it threaten U.S. security that the Cuban people today are made to say they are Communists? Or even if they were all sincere and happy in their Communist faith? Do we worry much about the fact that Albania is Communist?

The problem with mixing categories based on idea systems with categories based on national interests and security threats is that they do not match. Should a prime U.S. objective then be opposing communism, or should it be focused on achieving U.S. national interests and preserving American security? Which is the correct objective?

That the international Communist movement has run into the same dilemma does not mean that the question need not be faced. What can be concluded instead is that both communism and anticommunism are too simple as conceptions that will automatically advance the national interest and achieve national security. At the Communist Consultative Conference (March 1968) in Budapest (where 66 Communist parties were represented) the Czech delegate reaffirmed opposition to West Germany's claim on areas of Western Poland, while insisting that "there is still an honest role for maneuver in our policy." Vladimir Koucky, the Czech delegate and a Secretary of the Central Committee, urged "closer collaboration with socialist parties in Western Europe," arguing that such opportunities had "not been fully exploited." He particularly hoped to see overcome "the tendency toward an overly sectarian approach." At the same conference—at which the Romanian delegation walked out— the Romanians were criticized by the Hungarians for their refusal to put ideological conformity above national interest: for "sprouting phenomena of nationalism, the trend for isolation, the artificial confrontation of party independence with internationalism and the weakening of international solidarity." While the Hungarian speech had anti-Soviet barbs, too, it also contained this passage: "Unacceptable in principle and ineffective in practice is the striving of a Communist party, whether in power or fighting for power, to present [its] anti-Soviet attitude as a piece of evidence for [its] own independence."[2] (With appropriate substitutions, this is exactly how many Americans felt about de Gaulle's policies in 1968!)

One can respond to these observations by saying: "Yes, of course, now that there are divisions in the Communist movement, and wherever such divisions do exist, American foreign policy must be adjusted to take them into account." Such a reformed and elastic point of view will be a definite improvement over simple anticommunism as a foreign-policy objective, but it tends too much to assume that although the Communist movement is now polycentric, it used to be the reverse and the U.S. was perfectly justified earlier in treating it as a monolith. A careful study of communism shows that it has always been riddled with schisms. It is only

[2] Quoted from *The New York Times* (March 3, 1968).

that in the post-Stalin era, with the relaxation of terror, one can see more clearly that this is so. Granted the differences in the Communist world are now more evident than before. One may ask whether the doctrinaire policy of anticommunism really served U.S. interests in the period *before* the differences became public. Did not the U.S., exactly because it tended to treat the Communist movement as a solid bloc, help to keep it one? By espousing this view, did not the U.S. generally voluntarily restrict itself from efforts to exploit the diversive tendencies in the Communist world? (U.S. policy toward Tito is the one real exception.)

A major question in relation to the Viet-Nam War is appropriately raised here. While there is significant evidence that the war in 1967–1969 caused certain Sino-Soviet disagreements to be raised to a caustic pitch, did it not in its larger effects softpedal those differences? The Soviet need to show support for the Viet Cong—if only to preserve the Soviet revolutionary image—certainly led to parallel support actions for Ho Chi Minh by the Soviet Union and Communist China. When Chinese distrust of the Russians erupted, it was usually over whether the Soviets were engaged in an effort to help the U.S. find a way to disengage in Viet-Nam. By contrast the Chinese had no quarrel with the Soviets' sending aid, as long as it was massive. Did the U.S. weigh this loss in Sino-Soviet frictions against its gains in repulsing communism in Viet-Nam? Even more serious: did the U.S. properly weigh whether its interests were ultimately best served by a continuation of war in Viet-Nam? The vast destruction must weaken Viet-Nam's ability to resist Chinese domination. Do we care most whether Viet-Nam is Communist or whether it falls under Chinese control? Or do we assume that the one thing is exactly equal to the other?

Should the major U.S. policy objective be to contain communism anywhere and everywhere, relying heavily on direct and massive U.S. counterforce? Is it possible to do that in view of the example just given? And do we seriously believe that the only appropriate foreign policy strategy is one of organizing a "democratic bloc" to oppose a "Communist bloc"? Should not our major objective be a peaceful and secure world in which each nation, as long as it does not overtly threaten others, is allowed to develop as it sees fit? If this is our objective, the foreign policy strategy we have been following is not likely to achieve it—at least at reasonable costs.

Alternative Strategies for U.S. Policy

THE conventional American view of the world—that ideological belief indicates and delineates basic national interests—almost automatically results in a strategic conception of containment with special features. We will contain the enemy or potentially enemy states, *seen as a bloc*.

We shall do so by creating a direct counter-bloc, or counter-blocs; we shall do so even if we have to act and use force largely alone (because of the timidity or weakness or preoccupation of those who should aid us). In the older phase, we would build "positions of strength" at least equal to and hopefully surpassing that of the "Communist bloc." The alliance pattern the U.S. has evolved from this strategic conception is extensive but varied. Its stronger features include a viable Inter-American system, a still important NATO, and direct alliances with states such as South Korea, New Zealand, and Australia. Its weaker features include SEATO, which is so restricted in its Asian membership, and the security guarantee to Formosa. Thus its weaker features are in Asia, which is precisely where U.S. blood has been shed fairly frequently since 1941.

The U.S. has embraced these many alliances, and alliances are at the heart of the balance of power; therefore, the U.S., although in the habit of verbally condemning the balance of power as a security option, has nonetheless apparently become a foremost practitioner of the balance of power. Since bedrock "realists" normally espouse the balance of power alliance as far more effective for security than such loosely-organized alternatives as the United Nations, how could U.S. policy be considered unrealistic? After all, the UN has shown no great ability to solve the problems of Asia.

Here we arrive at a critical point. It is quite true that, of the three organizational forms or responses among which a great power can choose in seeking security in a multipower system (unilateralism, balance of power alliances, universal collective security), only alliances generally represent a realistic choice. It does not follow that, simply by choosing the correct power-organizational *option,* the proper consequences will automatically follow—any more than electing a candidate as President of the United States ensures that campaign pledges will be realized. Alliances take many forms and yield diverse results. The simple generalizations often made about the balance of power, imputing a "standard behavior" for nations in alliance and positing the inevitable formation of rival and opposed blocs, are too pat. Actually the formation of mutual opposition blocs represents only one form the balance can take—and not the most effective form at that. We said earlier that combination of those threatened is the essence of normal balance of power behavior. We did not say that it is inevitable for the disturber of the balance to have a bloc. It can happen that way, of course, but neither Napoleon nor Hitler was able to enlist great powers in support.

Woodrow Wilson's vigorous condemnation of bloc versus bloc alliances at the time of World War I had a certain justification. They *had* become entangling in the worst sense. Moreover, in the years just prior to World War I, the ineptitude of Germany (who had the crucial role to play) directly produced this worst (i.e., tension-enhancing) form of the balance. Kaiser Wilhelm brought a simple, two-bloc system into existence, with the one bloc arrayed against the other in direct opposition. Under these circumstances members of each bloc felt forced to support each other in crises, if only to preserve the alliance. The premium was on bloc cohesion rather than on the adjustment of problems or the lessening of tensions. Wilhelm, had he lived to see it, would have felt quite at home in the era of the Cold War.

It is ironic that this Wilhelminian balance is so often thought to be the archtype or sole model. Bismarck, as we saw earlier, created a very different, complex set of alliances and alignments, tied to Germany, and designed for one prime purpose: to *isolate* his major enemy (France). To accomplish this purpose Bismarck devised many ingenious arrangements, but the thrust of what he did in principle was to "take care" of certain essential interests of those nations who might have alternatively allied with France. He thus controlled the one alliance bloc existing among the great powers and kept the potential "French bloc" from coming into existence in the first place. When Wilhelm later refused to give Russia the same protection Bismarck gave her (assurance of German neutrality if Austria attacked Russia), she entered an alliance with France. That action created an anti-German bloc where none had existed before—a harbinger of Germany's defeat on the battlefield in World War I. This alliance of Russia with France, postponed so long as Germany would meet minimum Russian needs, was Russia's *second* choice.

Our excursion into nineteenth century European politics is to reaffirm a principle: there are always alternatives open to nations, and they may be induced to take second choices if their first choices are foreclosed. Various alliance systems are possible, producing quite discernibly different balances of power with drastically different results.

A nation never has only one set of interests, but many. Considerations supporting one choice are *counterbalanced* by factors arguing for its alternative. "Trade-offs" are inevitable. When any one choice is made because it seems best under the circumstances, something else is always temporarily suppressed. When France joined NATO, she suppressed her wish to have greater independence in handling her own problems. When she left the organized features of NATO (but not the alliance itself), she gained independence and lost certain support. When Romania publicly walked out on a Communist conference (1968), she risked retaliatory Soviet pressures, but she advertised she was her own master. How much Communist China keeps her quarrel with the Soviets in bounds, depends in part on how much U.S. power remains adjacent to her territory. When America takes on involvement in Viet-Nam, she diminishes the chance to exploit the common interest of the U.S. and the Soviets by lowering super power tensions. These new effects stem from alternative choices and may or may not be accurately gauged by those making the choices or observing the choices made. What is always true, however, is that the new choice, like the old choice, always has certain drawbacks: regardless of the course chosen certain counterbalancing interests must, as before, be suppressed.

From these observations follow two conclusions. Actual or potential alliances or blocs are always vulnerable to political attack, especially attacks focused on the suppressed counterbalancing national interests. A strategy which accepts an enemy bloc as inevitable or indissoluble, or assumes that ideology (or any other single factor) by itself assures bloc unity, has thrown away an important tactical card. While a nation may desire to erect an opposition bloc centered on itself, it is hardly warranted in denying itself opportunities to dismantle the enemy coalition, especially since the enemy coalition may well reject such tactical self-denial in its own maneuvers.

The second conclusion is that no nation should be considered a set-piece. It is open to blandishment, to inducement, to pressure. Whether it yields to these depends on how much these reach to the core of its suppressed counterbalancing interests. So the whole international system is *far more fluid* and the balance of power can take many more shapes than most Americans tend to believe. Not just any change is possible of course. There must be something to appeal to, to react to.

The balance of power in the 1930's illustrates these observations. It lacked organized coherence through much of the decade which led up to World War II; it was allowed to be far more fluid than was good for peace. For example, in 1934 Italy played a prime role in frustrating Hitler's first attempt to seize Austria. To Britain and France's satisfaction, Mussolini mobilized; and Hitler—whose rearmament program was still in its early stages—backed down. Yet by mid-1935 the anti-Hitler *de facto* coalition had come apart. Somewhat overcoming her distrust of communism, France entered (May 2, 1935) into a five-year alliance with the Soviet Union. For her part Great Britain (June 18, 1935) agreed to a naval rearmament program with Germany, which permitted Germany to set aside the provisions of the Versailles Treaty. Where France was attempting to contain Germany with Soviet help, Britain was simultaneously attempting to reconcile Germany through changes in the *status quo*. Not only did these efforts cancel each other out, but when Mussolini defied the League shortly thereafter and attacked Ethiopia, the League (and Britain and France) was forced to do *something* by way of sanctions against Italy; Italy for revenge joined the Hitler camp. Then in 1938, Britain and France appeased Hitler at Munich by sacrificing part of Czechoslovakia. Stalin had not been invited to Munich. Alarmed, he made a 1939 pact with Hitler to divide Poland. And, once World War II began, Britain and France attempted to aid the Finns against the Russians—an effort frustrated by Hitler's invasion of Scandinavia. But for that it would have resulted in Britain and France simultaneously fighting both Germany and the Soviet Union! The whole story is an object lesson in confusion. Critical to the problem was a joint agreement by Britain and France either to appease Germany in the West (and thus at least implicitly encourage a Nazi-Soviet war) or to arrange with also-threatened Russia for a common containment of Hitler. A choice was necessary but was not made.

An inconsistent policy among those concerned with restraining expansion (where there is more than one nation suspected of desiring expansion) can be very dangerous. It can induce those who would expand to set aside their own differences for a time. If differing assessments of the likelihood of Soviet or Chinese expansion moves are currently being made by non-Communist great powers, this can be highly dangerous and calls for a re-examination by all concerned. But there is a deeper point, and that is that the wish for expansion of any two powers is not only an inducement for them to use each other for a time, but also itself a potentially serious cause for friction between the two expanding powers—especially if they are neighbors or near-neighbors.

Today, for example, any great expansion of Soviet influence would also have serious negative connotations for the Chinese, and vice versa. Confronted with disarray by the other powers, China and Russia might cooperate for a time. Yet they also worry about each other. Thus, to refine more closely the Soviet attitude during the Viet-Nam War, they did not want a decisive upgrading of Chinese influence to result; they did want a struggle without dangerous escalation, which continued to confine both American and Chinese attention to this area remote from the Russian frontier.

In the meantime, since U.S. efforts in Viet-Nam appeared in Asian eyes generally to be morally ambivalent in involving great destruction in what must be considered at least in part a civil war, Japan, India, and Indonesia refrained from any effective part, citing their own weakness or whatever else would do. If China *was* engaged in a dangerous expansion via Viet-Nam, U.S. involvement protected these larger Asian nations and permitted their own noninvolvement. If, instead, American involvement in Viet-Nam was a tragic mistake that had little to do with any Chinese expansion (real or assumed), then the major Asian nations could not help by also becoming involved in the war. Either way the result is that the very large Asian nations which the U.S. presumably was protecting by the Viet-Nam War played no role. Neither were Sino-Soviet frictions basically intensified. (Serious Sino-Soviet border clashes only began *after* it was obvious that the U.S. was liquidating the Viet-Nam War.) One must conclude that this strategy leaves much to be desired.

If the U.S. bloc containment policy, in Asia especially, contains a serious strategic flaw, of what does that flaw consist? What alternative strategy might provide a more efficient use of the balance of power in U.S. interests, and thus better results?

A Better Alternative

THE U.S. strategy of bloc containment in Asia fails not so much on the grounds that the largely American counterforce cannot be made sufficiently available (although this is serious, too) as that the counterforce is largely furnished by the U.S. If the U.S. premise was correct, that our intervention in Viet-Nam was "saving" Asia, then why did Asia make so little effort to save itself? And if the U.S. were to get into war with China, would its power be sufficient considering that China has huge masses, is acquiring modern nuclear capabilities, and might under certain circumstances have Soviet tactical nuclear weapons made available to her? A consideration of these points might still yield the conclusion that the U.S. cannot afford to stand passively by no matter what happened in Asia. Yet a conclusion favoring action is by no means a conclusion that the bloc containment, force-direct counterforce strategy of the U.S., is appropriate to the problem.

A sober strategic judgment must turn on the response to two related questions. First, could U.S. strategy be altered so that the U.S. played a supporting rather than primary role? Second, if a supporting role was chosen, would it not necessitate a quite different assessment of the worth to the U.S. of maintaining land-force beachheads on the Asian mainland?

The idea of playing a supporting rather than primary role can be objected to on two grounds. First, it can be argued that no one else has the capacity or strength to play the primary role, so it becomes ours by default. But this is manifestly untrue. The Pacific phase of World War II was fought by the U.S. against a Japan who had overrun most of the area. Japan then held much of China and positions as far east as the Aleutians and as far south as New Guinea. Today, Japan has greater potential strength than then. Even India and Indonesia have far more potential than they have used so far. There is also the Soviet Union against whom Communist China has important territorial claims. Almost any one of these nations by itself could preoccupy China if it chose.

Second, it can be argued that, regardless of the capacity of Asian nations to play the primary role in Asian affairs, they lack the will now to step forward and play it, so it comes to the U.S. by default. This is a curious argument, for its essence is that Asian nations will not take actions that are in their own best interests and therefore the U.S. must save them from their own shortsightedness by taking up the burdens

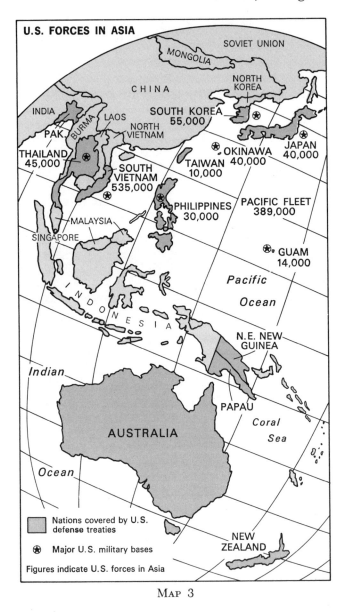

MAP 3

that they decline. Given this breathing space for reflection or for improvements in their military capacity, these Asian nations are then supposed to react by ultimately thanking us for our demonstration of how it should be done and relieving us in the front lines. The argument might be given some serious consideration if there were any evidence that U.S. actions in Asia are producing such results. But there is no evidence that this is so. Should we wait longer? How long? Should we continue to fight Viet-Nam wars until the Asian "awakening" comes?

Among reasons *not* usually advanced by the U.S. as justifying this primary role in Asia is that Americans—seeing a task to be done—are temperamentally impatient to step in and do it. But clearly there is some feeling that the large Asian nations may too slowly or never come really around to doing what they ought to do, and that the U.S. cannot allow "Asia to be lost." Yet national impatience will need to be balanced off against the blood-tax that it brings. Common sense suggests that if the large Asian nations cannot be brought to act to stabilize Asia, then the U.S. as an outsider will never accomplish it.

An entirely different perspective on the problem is given if one assumes that the major non-Communist Asian nations do have a prudent regard for their own security and are already acting in ways which, under the circumstances, they believe to be in their interests. Suppose that they consider the U.S. (for whatever reasons) to have plunged into an unwise military involvement in a remote corner of Southeast Asia, an involvement that could escalate into major war. Would they on the whole be grateful for the U.S. actions? Would they want themselves to escalate it by sending troops? Suppose that they considered the Viet-Nam War as a testing ground for whether Communist China or "communism generally" could expand by force. Would they be likely to choose to meet the test at that particular geographical point (Viet-Nam)? India would not feel directly threatened until or unless more of Southeast Asia fell under Chinese control, nor would Indonesia, and certainly not Japan. Because China in any case is already geographically adjacent to both India and Japan and is building a missile capability, the question of how much more threatened either would be if Viet-Nam were under Chinese control is a moot point. If it is only "communism generally" that is seen as expanding and not China in particular, no major non-Communist Asian nation is likely to feel that much is at issue.

On the whole the very point that gave strength to NATO (U.S. backing of the major West European nations' security) is what is conspicuously lacking in Asia. If China is believed to be to Asia what Russia is to Western Europe (i.e., the main serious threat), then the remedy ought to be U.S. backing of attempts by major Asian nations to build a common defense. For the U.S. to believe that the Viet-Nam effort was really worthwhile she must think of it as something like aid to Greece (1947), which was followed by the Western Union Alliance of Western Europe (1948) and by NATO (1949). Yet, to continue the analogy, it was not U.S. aid to Greece that brought Western Europe to unite and then also join NATO; rather, it was the fall of Czechoslovakia and the Soviet squeeze on Berlin. Really meaningful threats to Western Europe brought really meaningful responses by Western Europe.

To continue the analogy, if Greece had proved so vulnerable to revolt that it took more than a half-million U.S. troops merely to hold parts of it, one wonders whether—especially if Russia had not made the Czech and Berlin moves—Western Europe would have been encouraged by that example to unite.

Of course again, the ultimate argument for U.S. involvement is that (whether the U.S. is supported in Asia by the large non-Communist Asian nations or not) the U.S. must act as she has been acting—and even alone—in her own interests. This argument is simply not convincing, if only because China cannot destroy the Asian balance of power without first taking on one or more of the major non-Communist Asian powers. China can *alter* the balance short of such a drastic move, but she cannot *overturn* it. Should the U.S. try to prevent alteration which does not overturn? The answer would appear to be clearly *no*— or at least that the U.S. should not attempt this overly ambitious task by playing the primary role. Strategically the U.S. should *support* the large non-Communist Asian nations; it should not *supplant* them.

If the U.S. seeks to support rather than supplant, the whole question of U.S. beachheads on the Asian mainland changes focus. In the first place, any beachheads would not be "U.S." beachheads. Any military action taken on the Asian mainland with U.S. land forces would be supplementary to other significant land forces contributed by other large Asian powers. Even here it would be well to remember that the most flexibly effective U.S. power is in the sea and air forces. A U.S. contribution in an Asian war in which we supplemented other large nations would be or should be far more in air and sea power and logistical support. If the U.S. is the back-up power rather than the prime contestant she will concentrate on controlling the approaches to Asia rather than on holding Asian territory. An offshore strategy (except where direct support of U.S. supplemental land forces is needed) will be the normal requirement.

What of the example, then, of the Korean War? There the U.S. took quite contrary action to what has just been described. Indeed, many who have thought the Viet-Nam War in the real interests of the U.S. have argued that it is "like" Korea. Yet the U.N. never authorized a U.S. war in Viet-Nam, as it did in Korea. One can say that made no real difference since only 16 UN members exerted force in Korea, but it made a real difference. Consider that U.S. action in Viet-Nam was roundly condemned in the UN rather than largely supported. And 16 allies is far better than three or four (as in Viet-Nam). Other differences, however, between the two conflicts are significant. Korea is a true peninsula and susceptible to U.S. air, sea, and land power in a way which Viet-Nam never can be. Korea is of vital concern to Japan (who was happy to provide the "privileged sanctuary" near at hand from which the U.S.

forces were staged). The South Koreans also wanted their independence. In short, U.S. actions there had support and were feasible.

To sum up, the U.S. strategy of bloc containment (with its emphasis on force-counterforce) worked relatively well in Europe to prevent Soviet advances (although not to solve pressing problems like German reunification or exploit the fissures in the Soviet "bloc"). It worked well in stabilizing the balance, because the U.S. worked together with major European nations, sharing a similar conception of their vital interests. Even at its best this strategy was deficient, however, in exploiting the counterbalancing national interests *within* the opponent group because of American overvaluing of ideological considerations. The same bloc-containment strategy applied in Asia has suffered not only from the same deficiencies as in Europe (a failure to solve pressing problems such as the "China question" or to exploit the Sino-Soviet dispute) but has also had the added defects that it has been applied in a geographical area of limited concern to the major non-Communist Asian nations and has failed to associate those nations with it.

An alternative strategy, capable of gaining more widespread support and burden-sharing in Asia, is badly needed. Using this principle is impossible without taking an open-minded approach to who in the nature of things has a need to help restrain Chinese ambitions. Since this group obviously includes the Soviet Union, whose bond of communism with China (for whatever it is worth) is counterbalanced by Soviet concern over growing Chinese power, care should be taken not to place the Soviets in positions where, as in Viet-Nam, they feel compelled to soft-pedal differences with China. Viet-Nam on these grounds alone would have to be questioned as counterproductive to basic U.S. interests. The *objective* of U.S. strategy in Asia is properly the creation of conditions constraining any forceful Chinese expansion; and each of the major Asian nations (except naturally China) has a definite interest in seeing this condition accomplished. The alternative strategy argued for here is designed to isolate a major opponent by utilizing the counterbalancing interests of its potential major allies. It is an *opponent-isolating* or *limiting strategy*. It answers the question of what the U.S. should do only after first asking what we want accomplished and who could be made to do it.

An opponent-isolating strategy obviously is quite complex. China, for example, may not be successfully isolated from Soviet or other support under every circumstance. But that is not what is sought. What is sought (i.e., the objective) is to isolate the opponent from support for expansive purposes—and this could be obtained, since China cannot expand far in any direction without encroaching on the territory of one of her major neighbors. Here we see again why Viet-Nam was an inopportune occasion for the U.S. to make a test case. Since China had not injured her major neighbors by this move, neither were these neighbors disposed toward serious retaliation. (That South Viet-Nam would be worthwhile for the U.S. to defend simply because the *status quo* was being altered by other Vietnamese, or because communism was involved, might be argued by some—but consider the price in terms of what strategically have to be considered more major objectives.)

It is very difficult in principle for the U.S. in effect to isolate both the Soviet Union in Europe and Communist China in Asia from great power allies, because on the face of it this suggests that they will ally together. But if the isolation of the Soviets is accomplished as it has been (with U.S. and NATO forebearance from attempts to shrink the Soviet sphere by force), and if the expansion of China if it occurs would threaten Soviet interests too, it is possible to achieve this aim unless both Communist great powers can agree on supporting each other's expansion— a very dangerous but highly unlikely possibility. (What the Soviets eventually got from their agreement with Hitler to expand together into Poland was an assault by Germany without any assured Soviet allies.)

The opponent-isolating strategy assumes that seven features of the nation-state system are of fundamental importance. *First*, although Communist nations may allow their views of their own national interests to be shaped to some extent by ideology, if a clearcut choice must be made between tangible, immediate, and important national assets and the unity of the Communist movement, the former will outweigh the latter. *Second*, nations should not be considered as set-pieces but rather as responding to conflicting needs in a variety of ways in different periods of time. *Third*, the security goals of states are sought through alliances and alignments whose consummation necessitates the suppression of certain counterbalancing interests. *Fourth*, because situations change (no set-pieces) and because certain counterbalancing interests have always by a given course been suppressed, alliance blocs are always vulnerable to political attack. *Fifth*, great nations attempting to overthrow an existing *status quo* will ordinarily find difficulty in gaining support from other nations who might thereby be threatened. *Sixth*, expansive nations can therefore be isolated by adroit appeal to the interests of the others. *Seventh*, such appeal to be effective must take into proper account the counterbalancing interests of all the major nations whose roles can make a real difference in the outcome.

Since these seven features, if they are true descriptions of the nation-state system we live in, are not considered by American policy-makers generally as all true, it is apparent why we would follow a bloc-containment strategy in preference to an opponent-isolating strategy. Yet if these seven features are true, they make possible a more rewarding alternative strategy.

One important reason why Americans have tended toward the bloc-containment strategy is because of their conviction that there is indeed a "democratic bloc" and a "Communist bloc" (plus whatever else is left over). But in view of all the evidence, is this belief warranted? The second important reason is that Americans have (as indicated in the first pages of this book) been asking the wrong questions in the wrong order, in the process becoming confused as to what we want, who opposes, and how to succeed.

If the world and how it operates is different in important features from what are apparently generally-held American views, it is not only necessary to change strategies. It is also necessary to deal with major problems of American foreign policy on an altered tactical basis which would implement the new strategy. Looking forward, this is the task of the chapters that follow. Looking backward, this is the main moral to be drawn from the U.S. experience in the new age of American foreign policy, which we examined in Part Three.

CHAPTER 15

Military Problems

SINCE the U.S. set out as objectives after World War II to contain communism, oppose aggression, and preserve freedom in the world, choosing for this purpose a bloc-containment strategy involving simple and direct opposition with itself cast in the primary role, the commitments of the U.S. have been correspondingly wholesale in number and qualitatively very costly in terms of both dollars and blood. The Viet-Nam War is the best illustration. For the U.S. to have chosen to involve itself so heavily in Viet-Nam very strongly suggests an inability to discriminate between relatively meaningful and relatively meaningless military efforts.

Curiously enough, this ill-chosen war, although embarked upon for oversimple strategic purposes, was the first modern war fought by the U.S. under a sophisticated military doctrine: flexible response. By 1967–1968, many "hawkish" critics of the war were arguing that this very doctrine was at least partially responsible for U.S. military failure to break the enemy's will. They argued either that the doctrine was inappropriate or was misapplied. Of those who argued that it was misapplied, most objected to the gradual escalation of the war, especially as applied to the bombing of North Viet-Nam. To them, flexible response did not mean graduated escalation taking into account probable political consequences, but military means appropriate to the military problem. Those who defended the actions as taken argued that the perils of involving the large Communist nations (especially China) in the war necessitated "salami tactics" in escalation: one slice at a time.

Here was posed a fundamental problem of post-1945 U.S. foreign policy: how to relate the military factors and political factors in strategy together in a meaningful way. One thing was quite noticeable. Flexible response, whether misapplied in Viet-Nam or not, represented a sophisticated military doctrine far better adapted to U.S. problems than the crude "massive retaliation" concept of the pre-Kennedy years. Even if misapplied in Viet-Nam, the military *theory* side of the strategic equation had outpaced the political theory side, which was still bogged down in simple bloc-containment (with its emphasis on force-counterforce). Indeed, force-counterforce as the ultimate application of a bloc-containment political strategy has a family resemblance to massive retaliation as concept, whereas flexible response as military strategy more resembles an opponent-isolating political strategy. If flexible response is an involvement-limiting and damage-limiting approach, so, too, is opponent-isolating political strategy.

Sophistication, Game Theory, and Other Ideas or Models

THE "McNamara revolution" in the Pentagon attracted wide attention in the 1960's, inspiring many and varied reactions not only in the professional military establishment but also among scholars in the academic world. Among the many McNamara innovations was the installation of the "whiz kids"—a bevy of generally highly intelligent, academically highly trained personnel, particularly at the policy-making (assistant secretary) level. Consultants from the academic world were regularly in and out of the Pentagon to advise, and professional academic meetings of the social scientists in the 1960's frequently included panels on military problems. Indeed, the more stimulating discussions of military problems were often in the nonmilitary journals, and better books on strategy (with certain notable exceptions) were more frequently authored by those not in uniform.

These were on the whole healthy developments, reflecting widespread agreement in both governmental and academic circles that (1) political and military problems were interlocking, and (2) the unprecedented security problems of a nuclear-armed world needed to be properly worked out without delay. Not only was it essential to create an effective theory of deterrence as a guide to action; it was also vital to visualize in advance the kinds of conditions under which a nuclear war, if ever fought, would occur. There would be little or no opportunity to make proper plans for a full nuclear engagement, after the first buttons were pressed. To plan for "contingencies" (i.e., possible armed involvements), it was necessary to visualize the "scenarios" accurately in advance.

Plans had to be made which would necessarily make critical assumptions about the sequence of events in types of wars which have never occurred. (The dropping of the atomic bombs on Japan in 1945 gave only some limited clues to what was involved.) The sequence of events assumed would depend partially on calculations of physical damage but even more importantly on calculations of psychological effects. Would an enemy who in the first 24 or 48 hours of war lost a third of his population surrender for the reason that he could no longer physically continue to fight? Or after such appalling losses, would he instead take the attitude that surrender would render that fantastic sacrifice useless?

Would the destruction, if mutual, deprive one or both belligerents of a government able either to claim and enforce victory or offer surrender? If the destruction was fairly equal, would the two parties be able to decide who had "lost"? At the other end of the spectrum of possibilities, could and would nuclear powers fight one another and mutually and voluntarily refrain from the use of nuclear strategic weapons? Such formidable questions as these cried out for analysis and answers. Yet the answers largely had to rest on rational analyses of sometimes quite irrational situations. They had to turn heavily on assumptions about what reasonable men might be expected to do on the basis of a logical appraisal of a situation at a given stage of development. Hopefully, the appraisal would recognize that such decisions would inevitably be made under the stress of heavy emotion, with only partial information on all the factors to be considered, and with biases and attitudes influenced in each nation's case by a *varying* national environment and experience.

Each of these last three elements in the situation would inevitably introduce serious distortions from any abstract rational probability norm. Would, for example, Americans, Russians, Chinese, Frenchmen—all with diverse national experiences and contrasting temperamental inclinations —react in the same way to the same set of facts? Would each nation have a uniform capacity for accepting tragedy, and, if not, would the capacity be greater or lesser for those with more tragic experiences in their background? Abstract analyses would obviously be on sounder ground in visualizing the initial, prehostilities stage of a crisis. They might well lose reliability fast after that point. Whether they would or they would not is rather a crucial question.

The academic appraisal of these problems was conducted not only by individual scholars but by whole research institutes such as RAND, and it was encouraged with Pentagon research funds. The Pentagon's general appraisal of such problems tended to follow somewhat similar lines. Characteristic of much of these analyses was great emphasis on abstract rational calculation, with much less attention given to national variations. This emphasis, although natural, raises the question of reliability unless one assumes that objective conditions, if known, produce highly similar reactions and judgments, with little variation stemming from the nationality of the decision-maker. Is it warranted, for example, to assume that Asian nations, even as a group, make decisions in essentially the same ways as Americans do? (If one observes the way the Japanese went about making a decision to surrender in 1945, it is clear they do not.) The point is not that research along the lines of visualizing contingencies and their scenarios is not worthwhile, but rather that it may or may not reach reliable conclusions unless the three limitations to abstract assessment (emotional stress, imperfect knowledge, and national temperament) are accurately taken into account.

The analyses made of contingencies were highly influenced by such insights as modern "game theory." Where classical game theory was restricted to probability on the basis of pure chance, strategic game theory was specifically designed to probe conflict situations (i.e., involving more than one player).[1] By "players" we do not mean individuals but, rather, involved parties with distinct interests. In dual games, assuming a situation of diametrically opposed interests (which von Neumann and Morgenstern called zero-sum two-person games), what one party wins the other loses. In plural games, on the other hand, the possibility of both parties winning or losing, even if not equally, can be introduced and analyzed; for plural games are characterized by situations where the active interests are not diametrically in opposition.

Such an approach, especially coupled to computer analysis, had obvious utility in examining certain complex and concrete conflict situations. For example, in a zero-sum two-person game, one can explore the payoff for one nation of a strategy of massive saturation bombardment as against selective and spaced out bombardment, using either real or arbitrary loss factors, and comparing the figures to the losses one nation receives, while the other nation follows the same or a different strategy. In this kind of concrete military interchange, the nationality of the parties has little or no meaning.

The game theory approach lends itself in principle also to the analysis of complicated psychological interaction on the part of nations. But to yield accurate results the data used must itself be correct. If Soviet behavior, for example, is simulated by Americans, one must be sure that Americans play the game the way the Soviets would. Otherwise one goes astray. Since it is seldom possible in game theory as applied to American war gaming to ensure that this factor is correctly calculated, the results will be unreliable in exactly the proportion that nationality affects behavior. To use an example again: if the Soviets deploy for an amphibious assault somewhere in southern Africa, their replenishment and logistics problems in supporting that force are generally of the same nature as would be the case if American forces were deployed there. Where national variations in behavior are important, however, is in the more basic question of what kind of risks the Soviets would be prepared to accept to conduct such an operation, compared to Americans. It cannot be safely assumed that the risk limits at any point would be identical, especially since the Soviets have far less background experience in this type of operation. Tracing and establishing the problems involved in such a deployment through gaming has obvious value so long as this

[1] It was applied by John von Neumann and Oskar Morgenstern, who developed it, to competitive economic situations where conflicting interests, the interaction of rational decision and chance, and partial information are all present.

other factor is kept in mind. Deterrence analyses run into the same serious problem.

If abstract mathematical and computer-oriented strategic analyses assume a too simple model of the balance of power (in particular discounting other forms than a Wilhelmian or Cold War bloc versus bloc variation), the data input will again be distorted. American understanding of balance of power phenomena tends toward this simplistic model; therefore the danger of distortion is, in practice, quite real. It makes a great difference whether one assumes that the "domino effect" gives an advantage to a determined aggressor, or whether one assumes instead that aggression tends to foster its own opposition. It makes a great deal of difference whether one assumes that two opposing alliance blocs is the normal form of the balance of power. It makes a vital difference whether one correctly calculates the counterbalancing national interests involved.

Game theory and similar tools for analysis have provided valuable insights. Where they can be faulted is in their neglect of the lessons derivable from a more than casual study of balance of power theory and experience, which is at its best a kind of superior game theory in itself. Now, games must run according to rules, and rational considerations in crisis situations do impart a rule aspect (i.e., an assumption about a limited number of possible responses with probabilities for each); thus, the inclination to look to game theory was not wrong, but the failure to look harder at actual international behavior, and seek rigorous verification of the assumptions made, was disturbing. Too much of game theory analysis of international behavior was distinguished by its lack of reference to real nations in real situations; and its willingness to "simulate" foreign behavior in American terms. Most deterrence analysis ignored traditional balance of power phenomena altogether, assuming rather automatically that prenuclear knowledge was now obsolete.[2]

Since the prevailing American tendency is in any event not predisposed toward thorough historical appraisals of situations, and since the prevailing strategy of bloc containment with its emphasis on force-counterforce as applied to Asia has the drastic limitations noted in Chapter 14, it is unfortunate that so much, too, of contemporary deterrence theory is inclined toward downgrading what history can tell us. The result of each tendency interacting with the others is to encourage deterrence analyses based on logical abstractions that parallel if not reinforce our existing predisposition toward emotional-moral abstractions in our political doctrines. To return to the point made earlier about the greater sophistication of the military component of national strategy as com-

[2] See, as a notable exception, Glenn H. Snyder, "The Balance of Power and the Balance of Terror," in Paul Seabury (ed.), *Balance of Power* (San Francisco: Chandler Publishing Company, 1965).

pared with the political component, the greater sophistication in the military theory is offset by its high degree of abstraction. What this can mean in a Viet-Nam War is that the U.S. can be handicapped by all three main factors: (1) choosing formula objectives such as containing communism; and (2) choosing a political strategy of bloc containment in which the U.S. is miscast in the primary role; we also (3) apply military theories which undervalue the emotional stress, understanding of the situation, and national variabilities as they affect the outlook of our opponents. The military part of the strategy is more sophisticated than the political part, but still not sophisticated enough to do the job.

Whether contemporary military theory is in better shape for accurately predicting scenarios involving major powers with nuclear weapons is at least not proven.

Systems Analysis and Military Management

THE "McNamara revolution" is even better known for other features that also cause American military leaders concern. In the public press the picture is given currency that unimaginative "Colonel Blimp" types among the generals and admirals resist the whole trend of the last few years toward systems analysis and military management. This is not a very accurate impression. By and large the military leader of today recognizes the value of the techniques so associated with McNamara's name. Cost-effectiveness analysis of competing (duplicative) weapons systems is accepted in the military establishment today—with certain reservations. So, too, is the whole body of concepts called "military management" which seek to link program design and implementation to modern budget control techniques.

A rational evaluation of the military effectiveness which can be expected from alternative weapons systems "mixes" is a vast improvement in principle over the "political" system that once prevailed of each armed service trying to find financial support from adherents of its "position," or for its own peculiar "wonder weapon."

Actually, the earlier approach thrived for two reasons: (1) competition for scarce dollars unrestrained by (2) any rational administrative procedures for their allocation. Between the end of World War II in 1945 and the outbreak of the Korean War in 1950, the general approach to U.S. defense expenditures was negative. In much of this period the U.S. was demobilizing, cutting back. Despite the Cold War the mood was one of retrenchment. Scarcer dollars automatically reinstituted the psychological state of mind in the military which characterized the pre-World War II period when military budgets were also minimal. There was sharp competition for defense dollars, a competition waged essentially in political and psychological terms. The newly independent

Air Force, with its glamorous possession of a fleet of strategic nuclear bombers, seemed to many Congressmen to be the answer to the defense problem. Both the Army and Navy were much more sharply reduced. In view of the atomic bomb (the "absolute weapon"), what real need was there for a strong Army and Navy who presumably would play little part in any war (especially since such wars would presumably be strategic)? The Berlin Airlift (1948–1949), as a response to the Soviet blockade, put further emphasis on air power. The Army doggedly insisted that wars might still need to be fought on the ground; the Navy urged that control of the seas was still essential. Each service was fighting a rearguard action for survival.

The next event produced quite a change. The Korean War demonstrated clearly the continued need for strong land and sea forces; little by little missiles became the common property of all of the armed services (although the Air Force at first continued to have a monopoly of "strategic" weapons). With the further evolution of strategic thinking it began to be said (once the Soviets developed nuclear weapons) that a nuclear stalemate might make limited wars (i.e., wars in which land and sea forces played prominent roles) again feasible. By the time of the Kennedy Administration the Dulles doctrine of "massive retaliation" was in the discard, and a more energetic effort was being directed toward strengthening the Army and Navy. The Navy, which at one time was in despair about obtaining new carriers, received the nod to go ahead even with the development of a small, nuclear-powered task force. The Polaris system completed the process of giving the Navy a newly enhanced role in national defense by giving it a strategic missile function. The Army, concentrating on the further development of mobile forces, received encouragement, and created a large tactical air capability. By the time of the Viet-Nam War the need for a large and diversified army was no longer in dispute.

This healthy development (for history is filled with instances of military disaster following on the heels of an overreliance on a single weapons system) produced great psychological changes. Each service no longer had to argue for survival, and the stage was set for the competition for funds to move toward more nationally productive channels. Where new strategic thinking and joint organs had paved the way, a transformation in defense management could be and was initiated by Defense Secretary Robert McNamara.

Actually, cost-effectiveness, in the form of elimination of unnecessary duplication among the armed forces, was gaining ground as a technique before McNamara took office. McNamara's special contribution was to apply the new technique to validate the claims of competitive weapons systems, using data analysis to predict exactly what performance could be expected of alternative weapons systems for a certain level of expenditure. The question of what service operated them became only a secondary consideration.

As indicated earlier, the principle of approaching budget decision in this way was largely accepted by the armed forces after the initial resistance any new approach is likely to encounter in a bureaucracy. Also, as military men became adept at arguing their case with the same techniques used by the civilian analysts, and in the same format, the "civilian versus military" question became increasingly a false issue. Criticisms of systems analysis in the late 1960's were far more rational.

The problem with deriving weapon "mixes" from systems analysis comes in at the same point where general military theory runs into potential difficulties. To know what weapon mix one needs (let alone quantities) one needs to know the contingencies in which they will be used. If the actual wars fail to conform to the scenarios, one can be in trouble. Unless there is a generous allowance made for error, one can have too little of any one thing, and not enough range of things. The Viet-Nam war effort has demonstrated needs in riverine warfare which were not foreseen, or if foreseen, not acted upon beforehand. Other illustrations could be given—probably most illuminating is the contrast between the pilot training program and the actual needs that developed. Certainly the supply of pilots was grossly underestimated. The systems analysis approach, although highly desirable, is not foolproof by any means.[3] Some observers believe it has retarded too much the development of new weapons systems.

In a general analysis of American foreign policy such as this, it is not desirable to explore military management at any depth. Suffice it to say that orderly budget techniques, which more adequately place funds where command responsibility exists, is a highly overdue and desirable reform. The linking of budget commitments to the weapon mixture desired (as obtained from systems analysis), and the linking of both to the force levels foreseen as needed from the scenarios of contingencies for which the U.S. intends to be prepared, represent important advances in principle. Because the nature and number of the contingencies chosen determine the extent of the Defense Department budget request, it was also possible to conduct a rational debate over this question—something not true earlier. In view of congressional sentiment in 1969 for reductions in defense expenditures, it is well from the standpoint of national security that a reasonable way of reaching dollar-policy judgments is at hand. If the U.S. abandoned a bloc-containment strategy in favor of

---

[3] More complicated problems are also involved. For example, how should one analyze from a cost-effective standpoint a multipurpose, highly flexible weapon platform such as a destroyer? And when the *New Jersey* was built, who assumed its gunfire support role in Viet-Nam over twenty years later?

an opponent-limiting strategy, as suggested earlier, it could of course directly reduce the contingencies foreseen and thus also reduce expenditures. Perhaps the Nixon Doctrine was moving us in this direction.[4]

Effects of Advances in Military Technology

IT IS now necessary to grapple with a more elusive problem. Several times in the course of this book the caveat has been added that "unless one believes that modern weapons of mass destruction have altered this," something known from previous historical experience still prevails. If we can determine with somewhat more precision exactly what changes have resulted from the still continuing military-technological revolution, we may be better able before this chapter is over to make an assessment as to what war can be like and mean in a nuclear age.

Impressive as developments in weapons (in mass destruction capabilities) are, it will be well to look first at some associated changes. First, there are the great differences in the broad area of *communications*, with its profound effect upon warfare. Command and control systems depend upon rapid and secure communications and have been revolutionized from even the World War II era. It has become practical for the President to direct even tactical moves from the White House command center. Satellite systems for communication relay have overcome most of yesterday's atmospheric problems in reliable transmission. The rapidity of communications today attains or approaches a real-time basis; the "news" is no longer warmed over. Such advances allow quick reactions; in no way do they guarantee wise reactions.

Second of these changes is the advance in *mobility*. Popular descriptions of this feature tend as always to simplify the problem; however there can be no doubt that like communications the transport of men and matériel has been revolutionized. A whole division can be air-lifted in a short time to its destination to be "married up" with land-based pre-stationed equipment—as in West Germany. (But most of such equipment, it should be remembered, is normally sent there in the first place by sea.) Plans for a system of fast deployment logistics ships to be pre-stationed in or near troubled areas were well advanced in the U.S. in the late 1960's. Such ships would have the merit of lessening U.S. dependence on land bases (with all their political problems). Large transport planes would be used to rush the troops to the trouble area, where they would be supplied from this prepositioned floating stock. Closely connected is another development that has produced a new type of Marine assault ship. Establishing beachheads today on hostile territory can proceed

[4] In October 1969 the U.S. defense planning, after a nine-month review, was reduced to a capability for one major war at a time (instead of two), plus one brush-fire war under both plans. *The New York Times* (October 19, 1969).

through vertical envelopment, with a battalion landing-team moving in from its ship base by helicopters.

Third of these changes is in the general area of the application of *computer technology*. These applications range from inventory controls to fire control and target solution systems. These computers help men to make decisions in the foreshortened time-frames now available.

All three of these major developments are technological. Essentially they allow warfare and its associated decision-making to be speeded up. In a tactical sense they also allow for more accurate inputs. Combined with the well-known advances in destructive capability—symbolized most dramatically by missiles with nuclear warheads—they change both the tempo and scale of war and its character, from the standpoint of the degree of force which can be brought to bear in a given place within a given time. All of this is well accepted by both military and political commentators. What still remains in dispute is whether and where these changes have altered the conditions under which wars will continue to be used by technologically advanced nations as instruments of national policy, and the extent to which these changes have made traditional wisdom on warfare obsolete.

ICBM's, for example, today permit nations to launch devastating assaults from five and six thousand mile distances. Shorter-ranged, submarine-based Polaris or Poseidon-type missiles can be sent from the ocean depths some two to three thousand miles to their targets. Do these changes mean that nations who once were largely confined to fighting one another only where they could deploy forces in each other's geographical proximity will now choose to make wars on each other, even where their forces nearest to the enemy are still thousands of miles away? If, for example, as a result of some agreement to disengage in Europe, Soviet and American troops each evacuated their bases in Germany (thus breaking direct contact), would war be as likely or remain still likely? Suppose Soviet and U.S. troops were withdrawn entirely from the European continent outside the USSR because agreed solutions for central Europe had been reached. Under such circumstances, discounting for the moment the U.S.-Soviet frontier off the Aleutians, the two super powers would have no deployment anywhere near the other. Would they still be likely to have a war with each other?

Answering this question accurately is of utmost importance. Answering it means responding to the question of how much the coming of war turns *merely* or solely on capability, as distinguished from mutual policy attempts to dominate the same area. If the Soviets had withdrawn from Europe west of their own frontier and made now no threat to return even to the line once held, and barring direct physical confrontations elsewhere (as, for example, if the U.S. had mined the port of Haiphong), would a U.S.-Soviet war be likely to start at all? Obviously each would

remain ready to respond to an attack by the other, but would the likelihood of such an attack be at all great? The answer would appear to
be no. But, if that answer is correct, then the advances in warfare represented by long-range nuclear missiles change the character of a war if
fought, but they do not basically change the circumstances in which one
or the other nation might feel it necessary to fight. It is also worth
noting, conversely, that the advent of long-range weapons has not at all
convinced nations that the areas of approach to their own frontiers are
no longer of importance to control. Soviet sensitivity over Czechoslovakia
illustrates this point.

The argument above obviously ignores the sophisticated and profuse
literature on pre-emptive strikes and the like, but now that both sides
in a U.S.-Soviet confrontation have a guaranteed second-strike capability,
there is obviously less danger of temptation to resort to war to gain a
prior advantage or in the hope of escaping a reciprocal attack. No ABM
system under present circumstances is likely to be efficient enough to
allow a guaranteed defense, thus changing this strategic balance fundamentally—and certainly not if ABM deployment is reciprocal. Only a
radical breakthrough in technology which permitted submarine locations
at sea to be pin-pointed would seriously upset this balance.

The ABM debate in the U.S. in 1969 sometimes overlooked this last
point. A Soviet capability to destroy U.S. Minuteman missile complexes
on land is of limited utility so long as Poseidons deployed at sea remain
able to retaliate.

What of the proposition that today a war might be started between
the U.S. and Russia by a Chinese-initiated but unacknowledged attack?
If indeed it were true that the Chinese act would be undetectable—a
dubious assumption—then it is at least as likely that a U.S. response
would have to be directed against both Communist great powers, just
to be sure. But this whole approach is riddled with psychological and
practical implausibilities.

What of the idea sometimes advanced that there could be a three-
cornered exchange of missiles, with China, Russia, and the U.S. each
deliberately fighting the other two? Although this might seen plausible,
if it is, one ought to be able to point historically to prenuclear examples.
Missiles have nothing intrinsic about them that changes the logic of
such a situation. Yet what we find historically is that third states tend
either to opt for neutrality or choose one side or the other once a bilateral
great power antagonism has progressed to a stage where war is imminent. There are obviously good reasons for this kind of behavior.
The point here is not necessarily to indicate this logic but to show that
missiles do not change it.

Where, then, do we come out in an examination of this question? It
would seem to be true (granted the ultimate establishment of second-

strike forces by mutual potential enemies) that nuclear weapons in and of themselves do not make resort to war likely, and that the drastically increased range of such weapons does not increase in and of itself the tendency toward hostility where direct and continued physical contact between deployed forces is lacking. Where protected or invulnerable nuclear weapons are available on both sides, there is in fact a built-in tendency to refrain from provocation because of the certainty of unacceptable limits of destruction to one's own nation. Naturally, miscalculation through some form of nuclear blackmail could produce dangerous consequences. Naturally, too, a nuclear-backed antagonism between two states who are not each "invulnerable" is highly dangerous, but under conditions of relative stability of invulnerable forces the greatest effect is one of restraint.

The political conclusion to be drawn from an examination of the military aspects of the situation is that in a nuclear age it becomes more important to separate potentially belligerent nations from direct physical contact. While the UN has been applying this principle with some success to certain problems, it is apparent that U.S. policy has tended in the opposite direction, with massive troop deployments in both Europe and Asia. This is a point to which we shall return in the final chapter. Before finally leaving this point, however, note that the great freedom of the U.S. to refrain from direct physical contact with armed adversaries (assuming mutual withdrawals to accomplish this) is not matched by the built-in geographical circumstances of many other potentially hostile states. This is one reason why the relations of China and Russia, who share a long frontier, are likely to remain relatively rather tense even if they could agree on a demilitarized border zone.

Effects of Arms Control and Disarmament

THE issue of arms control or actual disarmament is naturally highly important in a world that has made great strides forward in destructive capabilities. Recent efforts in this area have focused on a Nuclear Test Ban Treaty (1963) and a Nuclear Non-Proliferation Treaty (with an agreed U.S.-Soviet draft text reached in 1968).

Despite French and Chinese refusal to accept the Nuclear Test Ban Treaty, and their insistence on continuing testing, there can be no doubt that the effort to prevent further pollution of the atmosphere is desirable for its own sake and as a means of reducing international tension. Testifying eloquently to this view is the enormous number of nations who have chosen to adhere to the treaty. Even if a cynic might point out that most nations are incapable of sponsoring nuclear explosions in their own right, there can be no reasonable doubt on this point.

The ultimate fate of the Non-Proliferation Treaty cannot be weighed at this time, but it poses certain other issues. Those nations who cannot in any case develop nuclear arsenals are, of course, in favor of it; so are those nations who have already attained nuclear arsenals. Those nations who are capable of doing so but so far have not done so feel more ambivalence. Japan, West Germany, and India are leading illustrations. Certain others (like Australia) are potential nuclear powers but feel that the U.S. nuclear arsenal would adequately protect them in case of need.

Even if the treaty is widely accepted, security considerations will determine whether and how long it continues to be accepted. Weighing strategic against political problems, West Germany on November 28, 1969, signed (but did not yet ratify) the treaty. Japan followed suit.

The German problem is quite complicated. Financial considerations reinforce the observations made in the preceding section to establish potentially important reasons for a U.S. cutback or elimination of a European deployment in conjunction with a Soviet pull-back. If this were to occur without quite well thought-out arrangements on European security, West Germany might wish to be free to maintain its own nuclear deterrent—although the Germans are well aware of the negative and potentially unsettling consequences of such an action. In Asia, the nuclear armaments of China pose a certain threat to Japan and India. Because India has refrained from alliances, this threat is more acute in her case; but Japan, too, has to consider what circumstances might result if the U.S. curtailed its Pacific commitments.

One thing is reasonably clear. The development of nuclear arsenals by any of these three powers would not constitute a direct threat to U.S. security. Directly adverse effects would be felt by either Russia or China. Any adverse effects on the U.S. would be indirect, in the form of heightened tensions. These effects would be also proportional in their intensity to the physical deployments maintained by the U.S. That is, the effects would be greater if the U.S. had deployments in Europe and Asia than if not, once such nations acquired their own arms.

The reason that Japanese nuclear weapons would pose no real threat to the U.S. (despite the experience of American-Japanese conflict in World War II) is that Japan's security priorities have to elevate China and Russia to higher places. In World War II, the Japanese could only choose to attack the U.S. because they were already in possession of much of China, and Russia was fully tied down by the German assault. Otherwise, Japan would not have dared. Similarly, Germany's unresolved problem is in the east and nowhere else. She would have no reason to fight elsewhere. The case of India is obvious enough without further comment.

These remarks are necessary to point out that the prevention of further nuclear proliferation may have disadvantages to the U.S. as well as advantages. In Asia today the U.S. role is greater than it ought to be, partly because the role of the Asian great powers is less than it ought to be. Not only is the U.S. attempting to fill a power vacuum, but as a non-Asian power it does so with certain handicaps it cannot overcome by willpower. Conversely, if India and Japan were to develop nuclear weapons, Asia might conceivably be more stable than it presently is. In Europe the development of French nuclear forces is generally considered by the U.S. as an adverse change, but it also frees the U.S. to consider a wider set of alternatives than before.

These remarks (if they contain the truth) are again a warning as to the defects of a purely abstract analysis of contemporary weapons-related situations. Mathematical probability assures us that any increase in the number of nuclear powers increases the danger of nuclear war. A more political and specific analysis leads to skepticism on this point, or even to the opposite conclusion. The greatest variable is the political environment in which these weapons changes might take place, rather than the weapons changes themselves. If Pakistan reached out for nuclear weapons because India had them, and if Pakistan could achieve such weapons (doubtful), this would produce a situation far more unstable than if Japan acquired such weapons when China already had them. Similarly, the U.S. and the world in general would be adversely affected by the acquisition of nuclear weapons by Israel and the United Arab Republic, especially because the tendency toward overt hostilities is already so pronounced in the area. What is true of some is not thereby true of all nations.

The Strategic Arms Limitations Talks (SALT), which began in Helsinki in 1969, involved all these complicated questions and more.

Effects of Military Developments on U.S. Policies

Ever since nuclear destructive capability was demonstrated (1945) to an astonished world, the presses have been flooded with scholarly and popular interpretations of the meaning of this development. Most such interpretations start out from the fact that the magnitude of destruction available had for the first time come near to or had reached totality and assumed that this fact in and of itself made all or most previous conclusions about warfare dubious or obsolete. Such an assumption was completely warranted as a starting point for inquiry. Any other assumption would have been highly dangerous.

Yet now that approximately a quarter century has passed, it is possible to see the issues more clearly. At the crux of the change that nuclear arms and associated technological changes represent is a revolution in destructive capability. The capability is of another and greater dimension entirely, and the time-frame within which the destruction can be accomplished is significantly shortened. What we cannot conclude from this observation is that wars will be initiated or concluded under radically different circumstances merely because of these technological changes. Obviously the sure knowledge of probable destruction will encourage a conservative evaluation of risks where those risks are clearly and immediately related to the likelihood of the destructive consequences. Neither the U.S. nor Soviet authorities, for example, will be at all anxious to initiate a direct nuclear exchange whose results for both are not even in doubt. To argue that any well-armed nation before 1945 went to war without giving it serious thought would be a very doubtful assertion. But now the results are both too serious and too obvious even to be debatable.

Yet if one concludes therefore that highly armed nations will refrain from a totality of policies or actions that involve the risk of war, one assumes far too much. If the U.S. were truly concerned primarily with avoiding risks that might lead to nuclear confrontation or exchange, it would never have followed the policy it did (1962) over Cuba or in 1965 and thereafter in Viet-Nam. One could say that the carefully controlled U.S. escalation in Viet-Nam stemmed precisely from a wish to avoid maximizing the dangerous possibilities, but one could never say that being in Viet-Nam reflected a wish to keep confrontation from becoming a possibility at all. One can say that U.S. actions were designed to show U.S. determination to limit enemy advances before they had reached proportions where a full nuclear response might be deemed the only alternative. This is merely a more sophisticated way of saying that nations try—in their opposition to opponents—to limit enemy gains at least cost. That is a very old principle of warfare, even if the setting is modern.

Risk-taking is more carefully calculated on both sides, but risks continue as before to be taken. Indeed few of the actions that led up to either world war were of a kind which were made in the knowledge of a full response (within the technological limitations of those days). That is, only the very last actions in a long chain of events that preceded both world wars were actions which initiated a full exchange (within the meaning of the term for those days). When the ultimate decisions for war were made, much of what had already happened made those decisions "inevitable."[5] Nothing in the present technological military revolution alters the pertinency of these considerations. Whereas Sunday supplements have dwelt dramatically on the last or button-pushing stage, this is a false abstraction from realistic experiences in our age as before. Wars today as before are a long time in the making; nations move as before relatively slowly toward deadlock. From a more optimistic point of view this means that there are also many places along the way where a new beginning could be made if the will exists.

[5] Ample evidence of the truth of this assertion can be found in my book, *The Relations of Nations.*

Over the long run nuclear arsenals will likely proliferate in the world for the very reasons that they had already spread to five nations by 1968. Each threatened nation, if it has the capability to create its own nuclear weapons, has only two fundamental options: to rely on the nuclear "umbrella" of an ally, or develop its own. Since the human and material costs of nuclear war are so large, an ally must have very convincing reasons to rely upon the nuclear arsenal of another nation for protection in lieu of developing its own. Only where the prospects of general and prolonged peace are very great will logic be on the side of rejecting maximum protection through nuclear arms under one's own national control. Unfortunately, the Cold War and other contemporary aspects of international rivalry and competition make the present world scene far removed from that kind of general stability. These considerations although serious are not automatically tragic. Much depends on whether political solutions can be found in Europe, Asia, and the Middle East that will lower the tension level and increase the likelihood of continued peaceful change. To express the problem most succinctly: the U.S. (by virtue both of its own desire to play a responsible role in world affairs and because of its possession of the greatest nuclear arsenal of any of the nations) has attempted a degree of responsibility in world affairs higher than is "natural" to the system. At the same time, the failure of all involved to make significant progress with such important issues as Germany's division and China's undefined role in Asia has raised tensions, despite U.S. good intentions. Yet the strains implicit in this broad American role have produced pressures both in the United States and abroad for changes which de Gaulle's position symbolized. So far the U.S. has chosen to try to continue to play a fully involved role and to discourage other nations from developing nuclear arsenals. A useful way of visualizing the problem of the next decades might be to turn greater attention to how the nuclear arsenals of other major powers (if they do develop) can fit into the overall world environment in a rational way. This implies greater roles for nations such as France and Japan and a less direct and comprehensive deterrent role for the United States. Although resort to violence has never arisen from sudden whim, but is rather the result of a steady deterioration of relations among states, in the contemporary nuclear environment the premium is even greater to find solutions to problems intimately affecting the overall tension level. It is to this problem that we shall devote the final chapter.

An Assessment

THE advent of nuclear weapons has revolutionized two dimensions of warfare: the scale of destructive capability and the time required to wreak such destruction. On the other hand there is little evidence that

other dimensions have been profoundly affected. Physical separation
between potential belligerents is today (as before) a potentially tension-
lessening factor. Major tensions among great powers today (as before)
do not spring suddenly into existence but are clustered around serious,
intractable, and prolonged issues—such as the future of Germany. Although the death and destruction that can follow the "button-pushing"
have changed so drastically in scale, there is no reason to suppose that
buttons will be pushed at sudden whim. Quite the reverse, and even
more so than before. As before, nations are not deterred from serious
risk-taking simply because the penalties for miscalculation are so drastically increased. Although the stakes of foreign policy in the contemporary international environment are raised, there is no great reason to
suppose that nuclear weapons have altered the general attitudes and
responses that nations have traditionally made to serious issues which
confront them.

Consequently, although the greater emphasis in much of the analysis
of nuclear-related problems has speculated upon the *differences* that
these weapons have brought to international relations, it seems even
more worthwhile to assess very carefully what they have *not* changed.
Especially is this important to a United States that has little tendency
to view problems in other than relatively shallow historical terms. Perspective is the critical factor. This is even more critical in a nation whose
foreign policy tends so much toward abstraction and whose strategic
analysis leans in the same direction. To counter this we must see our
military and political problems both more historically and more concretely. Otherwise we may find ourselves dealing with a world whose
real nature contrasts gravely with our conception of it.

CHAPTER 16

Socioeconomic Problems

Socioeconomic questions within the United States—questions involving race relations, urban ghettos, and rural poverty—have spillovers into the foreign relations of the United States in two senses. Not only does the world watch us to see how well we live up to our own professed standards, but also the actual presence of a black population in the United States gives us a greater interest in African problems than we otherwise would have. (And the ·African states account for about a third of all the states in the world.) To political stimuli which foster concern over the lot of the poorer and more dispossessed abroad are added other political motivations: fear of advances for communism into poverty-ridden nations, fear of ultimate recourse to revolution as a release to frustration.

Yet if none of these self-interested motives existed, U.S. foreign policy would still certainly have a large area of concern over the socioeconomic problems of a world where, in a real sense, the rich are growing richer and the poor are growing poorer. American generosity and American missionary zeal were well known to the outside world long before the U.S. became truly rich. Louis Kossuth's pleas for contributions to the cause of Hungary after the 1848 crisis did not go unheeded. Many similar pleas were answered—and long before Herbert Hoover's Belgian Relief program at the end of World War I and the CARE packages and Save-the-Children programs of a later day. This well-established humanitarian concern expresses itself today through many private programs and testifies to the interest of the American people in the welfare of foreign peoples; it arises partly from the fact that all the peoples of the world are represented in the present population mix of the United States. What is new in the American response in the new age of foreign policy is that the government itself has appropriated and administered large-scale relief, rehabilitation, and economic expansion programs.

Especially because American motives in giving aid are mixed, and the new age innovation of using tax money for these purposes causes the aid programs to take on much stronger political coloration, there has been much confusion and disagreement in the United States over the issue of the conditions under which official aid should be given. Views range from the one extreme that only friendly peoples should be helped to the other extreme that need alone should determine what is granted; views range from the one extreme that public aid money should be distributed solely by the U.S. government to the other extreme that all such monies should be given to the UN for distribution, so as to remove entirely any suspicion of U.S. motives. Before considering these controversies relating to the scope and method of U.S. public aid to foreign nations, it will help first to gain a closer insight into the range of wealth and poverty in the world, its causes, and the degree to which (especially rapid) change in these conditions can or cannot be brought about in view of world economic conditions and other factors. Because general world economic conditions and the U.S. position as it interacts with these conditions are basic to the problem, we must see these questions against that larger framework.

The Widening Gulf Between Rich and Poor

EVERYONE is aware of the enormous disparities in wealth and income that exist in today's world. These qualitative differences have existed in the modern era from the onset of the Industrial Revolution. But today the gulf is widening for two main reasons: unparallelled quantitative population growth in the newer and "underdeveloped" nations, and an enormous spurt forward in real incomes in the already industrialized nations. Not that either of these changes is uniform: India's population growth presses on any increases in food supplies more drastically than equivalent trends in Latin America; industrialized and rich nations like France and Britain complain of the "brain drain" to the U.S. and envy the more rapid computer-assisted spurt forward of American industrial production. Among industrialized nations, Japan's growth in GNP (gross national product) far exceeds that of Britain.

Modern medical techniques are applied today more and more universally and have consistently reduced the death toll from diseases that once ravaged unchecked. Thus, "natural" constraints on population growth have been removed. This accomplishment in the West coincided with industrialization and was followed more or less closely by generally declining birth rates coincident with urbanization. Yet in Asian nations such as India, still quite far from either real industrialization or urbanization on a Western scale, the control of disease has lowered the death rate while birth rates have continued very high.

Statistics dramatically illustrate what has been happening. In 1920, world population was 1,810 million. Twenty years later it reached 2,246 million. In 1960, it stood at about 3,336 million. The year 2000 estimate is for 5,965 million—an actual and anticipated growth of 3,719 million in 60 years, or about 165 per cent! In 2000, Asia alone should contain as many people as the whole world had in 1960; in other words the Asian 1960 population of 1,651 million is expected to *double* by the year 2000. In other areas of the world growth rates are anticipated which (comparing 1960 and 2000) will bring Africa from 273 million to 768; Europe from 425 million to 527; the USSR from 214 to 353; Latin America from 212 million to 624; and the U.S.-Canada population from 199 million to 354.[1] Thus Latin America's almost 200 per cent growth in only 40 years (and Africa's 181 per cent growth in the same period) are even greater than what can be expected in Asia—even though Asia's initially greater absolute numbers make that area's future problem of more critical concern. Besides which, both Africa and Latin America have far more latitude in utilization of resources (especially agricultural resources) than is true in the already crowded and frequently highly cultivated areas of Asia. Sending CARE packages will not do much about this problem. Not even the great agricultural surpluses of North America transported annually to Asia would represent a solution. One begins to see why birth control is so much discussed today.

These population changes are further exaggerating the already great differences in GNP that exist between nations, especially between the industrialized giants and the "underdeveloped" world. As Edwin O. Reischauer puts it:[2]

If we draw a rough line between the industrialized, modernized "North" and the unindustrialized, underdeveloped "South," we find more than two thirds of the people on the poorer side of the line but almost four fifths of the wealth on the richer side. Average per capita income is more than ten times as great in the more advanced nations as a whole than in the less advanced nations taken together, and discrepancies run higher than 50 to 1 between the richest nation, the United States, and the poorest ones.

Taking figures for important items in the GNP that relate to basic production, we gain an additional insight. The 1963 production of only six nations (the Soviet Union, France, the United Kingdom, West Germany, the United States, and Japan) accounted for all but 661.8 of the world's 1,929.0 millions of metric tons of coal produced, all but 856.3 of the 2,849.2 billions of kilowatt hours of electricity, all but 103.7 of the 386.6 millions of tons of steel, and all but 154.3 of 368.0 millions of tons of cement. Only in oil are the figures somewhat different, but even there these six nations produced all but 614.6 of the world's 1,303.5 million

[1] See Jean Bourgeois-Pichat, "Population Growth and Development," *International Conciliation* (January 1966), **556**:6.

[2] Edwin O. Reischauer, *Beyond Vietnam: The United States and Asia* (New York: Alfred A. Knopf, 1968), pp. 47–52.

barrels! The economic strength and wealth of the world is extremely concentrated.

It is within this context that one understands the implications of figures that tell us that between 1958 and 1965 the average population in the new sub-Sahara states of Africa rose 2.5 per cent annually, whereas food production went up generally only about 1.5 per cent. The combined contribution of these nations to the world production figures just recorded was infinitesimal. Such nations may dream of riches through industrialization, but their real and immediate problems center on raising enough food to keep alive. Only after that problem is solved, can these nations afford to progress much with the capital accumulation that forms the basis for industrialization.

Because the trade of the poorer and unindustrialized nations contains a high proportion of raw material exports necessary to the large GNP's of the industrialized states, these items will continue to be needed and can be effective sources of capital accumulation. But here another complication can be seen. Latin America, for example, is strong in raw material or commodity exports but is quite unbalanced from the point of view of diversity. The export earnings of these nations in 1964 *from a single commodity* varied from 16 per cent (Mexico, cotton) to 94 per cent (Bolivia, tin), but eight of the 20 states depended 50 per cent or more on only one export commodity. Considering the severe price fluctuations that occur in agricultural produce, a further element of instability is unveiled. Between 1955 and 1965, for example, the price of green coffee went as high as 90 and as low as 32 cents a pound, while cocoa varied from 58 to 13 cents. So even where surplus food production is possible, its economic rewards in terms of capital accumulation are unstable.

Examining figures based on Latin American trade with the United States illuminates yet another facet of the problem. Taking Latin American nations that (1966) both exported and imported merchandise with the United States in amounts exceeding $100 million, we find pronounced disparities between the degree to which that trade was quantitatively important to the U.S. and the Latin American nation involved.

What is striking in these figures is how relatively insignificant (quantitatively) the trade with these individual nations is for the U.S., and how very important it is to the Latin American nation involved. What makes this worse, from the Latin viewpoint, is that the net flow of money, despite U.S. aid, is out of Latin America and into the United States. In June 1969, 21 American states, meeting at Viña del Mar, Chile, stated their economic grievances against the U.S. Their Chilean spokesman said: "Private investments have meant, and mean today, for Latin America that the amounts that leave our continent are many times higher than those that are invested in it." The other side of this question is, of course, that U.S. investments have made possible the Latin economic progress in the first place.

Everything the U.S. does has a vital effect upon these states, but not normally vice versa. When the U.S. GNP growth (as in 1968) is estimated at a rate that includes a four per cent or more inflation, the effects on Brazil of changes in U.S. prices are much more significant than in the U.S. itself simply because so much of Brazil's trade is with the U.S. The reverse effects on the U.S. caused by Brazil's own greater inflation are not very noticeable.

To broaden the trade comparison further, let us take total trade percentage figures (as in the last four columns of Table 16–1) for three

TABLE 16–1

U.S.–LATIN AMERICAN TRADE (IN MILLIONS OF DOLLARS)

Country	Value of U.S. Exports to Country	Value of U.S. Imports from Country	Per Cent of Foreign Nation's Total Trade		Per Cent of U.S. Total Trade	
			Imports from U.S.	Exports to U.S.	Imports from Foreign Nation	Exports to Foreign Nation
Mexico	1,131	705	64.0	62.0	2.8	3.8
Brazil	565	603	39.0	33.0	2.4	1.9
Peru	303	297	39.2	39.8	1.2	1.0
Colombia	282	246	47.9	43.6	1.0	0.9
Chile	250	243	39.3	24.9	1.0	0.8
Argentina	239	146	22.8	7.7	0.6	0.8
Jamaica	114	132	36.2	36.3	0.5	0.4

SOURCE: Figures compiled from "International Trade: Gateway to Growth," U.S. Department of Commerce, 1967, tables on pp. 13 and 23. The figures showing the percentage of the country's total imports coming from the U.S. and what percentage of the country's total exports went to the U.S. are foreign-compiled and normally use a c.i.f. (cost, insurance, and freight) basis, whereas U.S. figures normally do not include ocean freight and marine insurance.

non-Latin nations selected at random. We find: Sweden 9.3, 6.8 versus 1.2 and 1.2; India 37.5, 19.3 versus 1.3 and 3.1; and Australia 22.0, 13.0 versus 1.5 and 2.1. Sweden is the most industrialized of these three and has the least unbalanced relationship to the U.S., while the figures for India and Australia roughly parallel the Latin American relationship—again with the same implications.

If we next look (in Table 16–2) at comparable figures restricted to the four largest importers from and exporters to the United States, we see a much different picture. For the nations in Table 16–2 the relation between the importance of the trade to the foreign nation and to the U.S. is much more equal (than with the earlier examples) and important enough to the U.S. to affect it significantly. Even here, however, the relationship is two to three times more important to the foreign nation. The fact is that the U.S. has only 7 per cent of the world's land area and only 6 per cent of the world's population but produces 33 per cent of the world's goods and services; and this fact has vital importance to all foreign nations, but with significantly varying effects.

TABLE 16–2

MAJOR U.S. TRADING PARTNERS (IN MILLIONS OF DOLLARS)

Country	Value of U.S. Exports to Country	Value of U.S. Imports from Country	Per Cent of Foreign Nation's Total Trade		Per Cent of U.S. Total Trade	
			Imports from U.S.	Exports to U.S.	Imports from Foreign Nation	Exports to Foreign Nation
Canada	6,487	6,106	72.3	59.8	24.1	21.7
Japan	2,312	2,948	27.9	30.4	11.6	7.7
United Kingdom	1,645	1,760	12.1	12.4	6.9	5.5
West Germany	1,559	1,789	12.6	8.9	7.1	5.2

SOURCE: *Ibid.*

In the 1960's, per capita income growth in the developing countries was only about 2.3 per cent a year as a result of an annual population growth of 2.4 per cent. But this composite figure concealed the fact that South Asia's per capita income growth rate was less than 1 per cent between 1960 and 1965, while in the same years Africa's figure was 1.4 per cent and Latin America's only 1.7 per cent. It is only the accelerated growth in the Middle East and southern Europe which, added in, makes the composite figure 2.3 per cent. Exports from the developing countries in 1966 rose about 7 per cent (or approximately at the rate of the five years previous), but the total exports of the industrialized nations rose more than 10 per cent.

Summing up this short survey of basic socioeconomic factors in the contemporary world, the disparities between the rich and poor nations are growing; population growth pressures in the underdeveloped areas are literally consuming much of the capital accumulation needed for industrializing (or at least broadening and diversifying the economic base); many nations are too heavily dependent on single commodity trade; and U.S. action (positive or negative) is the single largest factor affecting the world economic situation as a whole and many states individually.

Prospects for World Economic Development

MANY of the factors already considered, such as population growth, are obviously critical variables in the prospects for world economic development. Adequate liquidity in the financing of world trade and the provision or lack of provision of capital development funds to poorer nations are also critical; so are tariff arrangements among the trading nations. But before examining these technical factors it would be well to consider the even more fundamental question as to what kind of world economic development can be realistically sought and achieved, within what kinds of constraints, within what kind of a time-frame, and based on what kind of assumptions? How much industrialization should be sought or encouraged in the developing nations? More broadly, what do we think economic development should and can mean, and under what kinds of conditions do we think it can occur?

After they attained independence, many of the newer nations attempted to create the symbols of American wealth and power as a superstructure over an economic base completely inadequate to sustain it. Ghana's policies during Nkrumah's reign illustrate this. He established (among other things) a government-owned airline and a shipping line—bankrupting Ghana in the process. Sukarno followed similar showy policies and superimposed large expenditures for arms, which thwarted Indonesia's economic progress. Nasser did much the same and crippled United Arab Republic economic development by mortgaging Egyptian cotton for Soviet bloc arms. Examples could be multiplied of this groping for the symbols of economic or military strength,·so devastating in its effects to true economic progress in these countries. The nationalization of foreign-held assets that has usually accompanied these kinds of moves also caused great harm by discouraging foreign private investment. Many of the newer nations avoided these particular follies but went after symbols of another sort: erecting showy steel plants or industrial complexes whose produce could neither be utilized at home on any economic basis, nor compete in the export market. In short, many of these nations mistook the end result of wealth and power for its cause, and they attempted to achieve their goal by creating a sort of mock-up of what things would look like if the goal were once achieved. In the end this accomplished little and convinced few.

The competition between the U.S. and the Soviet Union for influence in these newer nations partly encouraged such recklessness, although it is noteworthy that even the Soviet economic aid program (which was always more oriented toward the "give them what they want" approach) has become somewhat more realistic in later years. More fundamentally, the Soviet example in how to industrialize also competed with the U.S. example for influence. Although it is not in fact true that the Communists industrialized Russia from no base through forced-draft moves, many of the newer nations believed it to be true. The U.S. example of a nation in which free competition allowed a great, steady and fairly even growth in *all* sectors of the economy, but over a fairly lengthy period, lacked some appeal simply because it took so long to arrive via that route.

The attempts of many of these newer nations to arrive at the results of wealth and power by creating the symbols of those results stemmed only in part from the immaturity of the leaders or the Soviet-American competition for world influence. In almost all cases, behind these naive moves there was a pent-up popular demand for quick progress.

Movies, television, and, even more, the cheap transistor radio, have literally changed the world by bringing hitherto remote peoples into contact with a knowledge of conditions in the world in areas with which these peoples before had no experience or contact. Thus, even in the older but underdeveloped nations of Latin America, popular pressures have increased substantially to bring about a higher standard of living. In the newer but underdeveloped nations these pressures have mounted within a political environment in which stability-enhancing factors have generally had much shallower roots. In Africa, for example, hauling down the old colonial flag and hoisting the new symbol of independence was equated with almost automatically leading to the satisfaction of the myriad desires blanketed under the label, "the revolution of rising expectations." In the Latin American nations with a long history of self-rule the cause and effect relationship had necessarily to be seen on a more sophisticated basis. The Latin American peasant knew that independence from Spain had not accomplished the miracle. But in Africa it seemed possible or at least plausible that once the French, the English, and the Belgians left all would quickly change.

These extravagant hopes were often encouraged by the leaders of the fight for independence and returned to plague those leaders in the days after independence was achieved. It is noticeable, for example, that Nkrumah began to complain a great deal about the residual "neo-colonialism," which (he asserted) still prevailed after nominal political independence had been achieved. By this term he meant the economic ties between the new nation and its former colonial master and the economic dependence the new nation still had on its former ruler. In the soberer new nations attempts were made to place these continuing relationships on a mutually satisfactory basis. This was the path chosen by most of the former French African colonies. But elsewhere nationalization was the remedy applied. These nations deal with the great industrial powers from a position of weakness (as the preceding section showed); therefore this remedy proved to have disadvantages.

Even more fundamental was the fact that the newer nations generally had only rudimentary political institutions. Apart from the lack of direct involvement of the masses in the political process and the fragmentation arising from tribal rivalries and a weakly developed sense of nationalism, the newer nations frequently lacked any organized political party opposition. One-party states were the rule. Optimistic political observers between 1945 and 1955 or 1960 often designated these states as "one-party democracies" or "tutelary democracies," but this hopeful label was very far from the actual facts.

The great majority of the 60 to 70 newer nations that achieved independence after World War II had no historic past as nations. This was not true of a few nations such as Egypt or Syria or Iraq, but by and large it was true—especially in Africa. The former Belgian Congo, for example, was a territory whose frontiers did not define the areas within which a Congolese "nation" existed. Rather, the Belgian Congo could be defined as that area of Central Africa not taken by Britain, France, and other colonial powers by the date the Belgians took over. Such states as Jordan and the Congo are synthetic concoctions whose frontiers are the result of the accidents of imperialism. Similarly, few of the many states once collectively known as French West Africa have any historic past or national meaning. To note this fact does not imply that "nation-building" in these areas is doomed to defeat or that no sense of modern nationalism will ever take hold. The point, rather, is that from almost any sober point of view, the coming of such states into independence could not conceivably be followed by immediate and sustained progress.

Indeed, given the lack of well-developed political institutions (themselves reflecting the lack of national cohesiveness and a national sense of purpose) and given the never-never land expectations that were associated with the end of colonialism, political and social unrest was bound to be expressed sooner or later in *coups*. A map of contemporary Africa on which one colors in the nations that have experienced military coups in the 1960's has only a few areas in white—and virtually none if one eliminates South Africa, Rhodesia, and the Spanish and Portuguese colonies!

Finally, because many of the newer nations are plagued with frontier disputes with their neighbors, it is quite likely that violence among the newer nations will be greater in coming decades.

These factors are all-important in setting limits to progress. Yet the problem of economic development in the undeveloped world is frequently taken up in an abstract frame of reference dominated by discussions of purely economic factors. Prospects for world economic development are directly affected by these political and psychological constraints, and they have important implications for the nature and extent of U.S. aid programs. Consider the 1967–1968 controversy in the American Congress over the size of U.S. arms shipments to Latin American states, at a time when the Alliance for Progress results have been disappointingly small. Should the U.S. react by telling these nations that they would do better to put their resources into more productive channels? More broadly, should the U.S. approach the aid programs on the basis of what America wants to give them or on the basis of what these nations want from the United States? As the other and newer underdeveloped countries approach a greater sense of nationalism, will they, too, up their armaments budgets?

Political and psychological constraints inevitably constitute very substantial barriers in the way of sustained economic and social progress in the world. Even if these noneconomic factors are somehow overcome, there are also substantial economic factors (even apart from more technical factors) that impede progress. What are these?

The United States is blessed with an extensive and rich territory and would probably have developed great riches under a variety of economic and political institutions. America chose a free, competitive economic system (under general governmental regulation) and a democratic political system. But even the Soviet Union (held back by excessive governmental controls and centralized planning systems, and with prolonged police state attributes) was able to make substantial economic progress. The point is that, given a large and naturally rich area and a reasonably large population, comparative wealth is attainable. Even regressive politico-economic institutions do not remove the oil from the ground or cause iron ore deposits to vanish; and given varied and plentiful resources, industrialization compounds the production of wealth. Given comparatively poor natural resources, a great deal can still be done—as Japan illustrates. But Japan has a skilled and literate work force and a configuration that permits her to exploit easy access to the oceans for shipping, for fishing, and for other uses. Many of the newer nations possess none of these wealth-producing factors in any abundance. Even if these states model their politico-economic institutions on the U.S. or Soviet pattern, they can not duplicate the benefits of the nations they imitate. They simply do not have the same resources and qualities.

Consequently, all can make progress, but they will all make very different kinds of progress; and even with the attainment (if it comes) of domestically stable institutions, the future of all cannot be equally bright in economic terms. Given equal political stability, the rich (those better endowed) will get still richer, while the poor will become poorer.

It would not be worth pointing this out were it not for the fact that much of the discussion of economic problems ignores these factors. Creation of expectations of great progress through industrialization all over the world is bound to bring frustration in its train. Even what progress can be made will inevitably be much slower than the demand for it, and again for two relatively simple reasons. First, as a nation's economy evolves, the parameters change for the optimum economic unit size. A steel industry of maximum efficiency for a highly developed economy could not be built from scratch in a semi-industrialized economy, because productive capacity would stand idle (i.e., more would be produced otherwise than could be consumed); but building a steel industry to meet a current demand (plus somewhat modest anticipation of the future) is uneconomic in the ultimate sense (i.e., it will not produce what is eventually needed). Industrializing nations have sought to meet this problem by periodic expansions of productive capacity over fairly lengthy periods of time—a process that naturally frequently ties up labor and resources in dismantling what has become obsolete to replace it with new capacity. Another reason why the most economic size cannot be built the first time around is that an unnecessarily large steel plant means an unnecessarily small something else. And here we reach the second and connected reason.

Economies are very complex. Consider the ordinary American telephone. It contains over 50 imported materials coming from over a score of countries, and the production of telephones in the U.S. on any significant scale implies whole hosts of other things, such as railroads, roads, and shipping. Or, an investment in printing presses implies a literate public; and a literate public implies schools, and so forth. In short, it is not possible realistically to move on a single sector front in upgrading an economy. Everything cries out to be done at once, and each is in competition with the rest. Sometimes it is possible to assign priorities to demands that are clearly keys to handling still other demands, but most demands must be met simultaneously. Although assured food production and a transportation network are more vital to progress than most things, even they are tied closely into a dependable supply of fertilizer, cement, and steel. Thus, to be effective, economic aid must take the economy as a whole into account. It must begin with key factors, expecting only slow overall progress. Initially, inevitably, it must be inefficient, often involving the import of materials that are needed but which cannot be produced effectively at the scene until the prior needs are met.

In a world crying out for quick progress, the progress will inevitably lag far behind hopes.

Technical Factors Affecting Development

INTERNATIONAL liquidity problems, adequate capital development funds, and tariff arrangements that foster world trade are three of the most important technical factors affecting world economic development. The U.S. happens to be the supplier of the major world currency, the prime source of capital development funds, and a major participant in world trade and, as such, has an important role to play in each of these areas.

The first technical factor affecting development is international liquidity, which is a dry but vital subject. The problem basically arises from the unevenness of trade among nations. If two nations bought and sold to each other equally valuable amounts of goods, each using no one else's services in transporting them, no problem would arise. Each debt balance would cancel the other. In the real world this is seldom if ever the case. In 1966, the U.S. imported $705 million worth of merchandise from Mexico, but exported $1,131 million. Mexico "owed" the U.S. the difference ($426 million). Mexico pays by dollars acquired in other ways: tourist income, dollar and dollar-convertible assets accumulated by trade surpluses with other nations, and dollars invested in Mexico by the U.S. government or U.S. businesses.

Convertibility of assets is thus the first key to a healthy and sustained growth in world trade. For convertibility to be both feasible and convenient, the comparative values of currencies must be known, they must be reasonably stable values, and there must be ease of exchange of one kind of asset into another. All of which is much easier to say than to do. Differing levels of economic growth, diverging degrees of inflation, and governmental manipulations of the currency supply, all continually change the comparative worth of national currencies. One nation through trading with others could nonetheless acquire and maintain stocks of a hundred or more different currencies; but for purposes both of efficiency and stability of values nations tend to convert such assets (if they can) into gold and the few national currencies that have the most ready acceptance by other nations as payments. Theoretically, Nigeria could purchase British machine tools and pay for them in Egyptian currency acquired by other trade. But in practice (for the reasons given) she will pay in American dollars or English pounds or—if there is no other way—in gold. The fairly universal tendency to use dollars and pounds is because of three factors: (1) widespread faith in the relative stability of these currencies; (2) the fact that U.S. and British trade is quite large scale (and thus dollars and pounds in fairly universal demand for settling accounts); and (3) the overwhelming importance of these currencies in international banking arrangements and banking facilities. In the case of the British pound there is also the historical factor that most of the former British colonies and dominions still maintain assets in British sterling. And, last but not least, the tendency to rely on dollars is tied to its guaranteed convertibility into gold.

In the 1950's, while Europe was struggling to rebuild itself, the problem was to find enough "pump-priming" dollars to pay for what was needed to resume production. In the 1960's, contrariwise, the problem of the "dollar gap" had not only been overcome but overdone. That is, far from a shortage of dollars there was a surplus—so great a surplus that if all dollars held abroad were simultaneously converted into gold, U.S. gold stocks would be exhausted. Of course, such an event was almost impossible short of total collapse of faith in the dollar, because supplies of dollars continued to be needed in foreign "cash drawers" for foreign-exchange purposes. For the U.S. this situation created worry, and a solution was not easy to find during the Viet-Nam War (which by itself enormously increased U.S. purchases abroad). The U.S. basically could reduce imports (difficult because of tariff-reduction agreements), expand exports (difficult because of competition abroad, especially from close U.S. allies), reduce private investment abroad, reduce troop-connected expenditures abroad, and/or reduce the U.S. monetary supply (by higher taxes and interest rates). In 1968, the "gold flow" continued to be a vexing problem, even though the market in private gold speculation was divorced and insulated from the pools of reserve gold supplies held by the major non-Communist central banks in arrangements that permitted drawing rights to cover temporary national reserve weaknesses. U.S. gold stocks declined by 9.6 billion dollars between 1958 and 1966 and went lower by 1.2 billion dollars in 1967. The 12.4 billion dollars left was something less than one third of the world monetary gold stock (as against U.S. holdings of two thirds in 1949).

Any manipulation of the dollar and pound thus not only had or would have serious domestic results on price structures at home but also involved foreign affairs directly by its monetary effects on other nations. When (November 18, 1967) the United Kingdom devalued the pound from $2.80 to $2.40 (a 14.3 per cent cut), its effect was to reduce foreign-held assets in pounds by the same per cent (in dollar terms). Speculation that the U.S. would also devalue next moved the price of gold up on the private gold market (which at that time could still buy gold supplies from the central bank) and forced the central banks to separate the two gold supplies from one another. If the U.S., by various measures, sought to resolve these problems by forcing too great a reduction in the supplies of dollars, it would remove dollars from world assets and inhibit world trade. If, for example, the U.S. government budget overall were in complete balance or ran a surplus for a number of years, dollar assets abroad would diminish steadily—provided American foreign investment and U.S. imports did not expand. Until lately, the U.S. budget format has traditionally ignored trust fund accounts (such as Social Security), which have taken in more dollars than they have paid out. The average citizen (knowing that the direct tax and revenue income of the government is far less than its direct expenditures) assumes that a deflationary trend in the supply of world dollar assets is far less likely than is actually so if the U.S. traditional budget items are in balance or more cash taken in than is paid out.

The major banking nations of the world (1967) reached agreement in principle to add a new facility attached to the International Monetary Fund (the instrument that permits them drawing rights on each other's currencies). This facility is an additional special drawing right coupled to a provision requiring repayment of only 30 per cent of a nation's first five year net use. The effect, if successful, will be to expand world reserves by the amount not repayable. It was hoped that this new agreement might aid international liquidity. In 1969 the agreement came into use. By the end of 1969 the price of gold on the "free market" had fallen to about the "official" price.

The second technical factor affecting development is adequate capital development funds. In part because of the difficulties in world financial markets just recounted, the overall assistance given by the wealthier nations had by 1967 increased very little over the 1960 level. Official and private long-term assistance was 9.17 billion dollars in 1961, 9.07 billion in 1964, 10.28 billion in 1965, and 9.87 billion in 1966. Aid from the United States, France, the United Kingdom, and West Germany showed no increase, comparing 1961 and 1966, while aid from smaller nations did increase. In composition, aid shifted further away from grants toward loans. Apart from completely individual national programs, the greatest sources of technical assistance aid were (1) the members of the Development Assistance Committee (DAC) of the Organization for Economic Cooperation and Development; (2) the multilateral organizations associated with the UN; and (3) the World Bank and such other banks as the Inter-American Development Bank.

Loans by members of the Development Assistance Committee (Western Europe, the United States, Japan, Canada, Australia, and Austria) were at 3.1 per cent in 1966 as compared to 3.6 per cent in 1965, whereas the World Bank rate went from 5.5 to 6.0 per cent in 1966. These figures illustrate the two types of loans available: "soft," for example, from the DAC, "hard" from the World Bank (most of whose transactions are more nearly like ordinary banking operations). But, regardless of source and rate, another significant set of figures was the accumulated debt service for past loans. Between 1962 and 1966, payments from developing nations for amortization and interest rose at an annual rate of 10 per cent, considerably above their rate of increased exports. The total developing country debt (which increased 16 per cent a year between 1962 and 1965) exceeded 41 billion dollars by the middle of 1966. India's debt service, for example, increased from 13 per cent in 1962 to 22 per cent in 1966, a period during which her exports increased only 14 per cent. If the ratio of increased debt service thus begins to consume most of the benefits deriving from increased exports, it will have many effects. One effect will be to lessen the amounts of money that can be borrowed in the future. Lengthening of repayment schedules is only a partial answer. Thus the problem of developmental aid turns not only on making money available to poorer nations but doing so on terms that they can afford—and even 3 per cent loans may be ultimately too expensive. For this reason the World Bank activities through its affiliate, the International Development Association (IDA), took on special significance. IDA was lending money at 0.75 per cent interest for 50-year terms to poorer nations with economically sound projects, but for IDA to take over a significant part of the job depended on more funds being put at its disposal.

The third technical factor affecting development is world trade. The general picture here in recent years has been toward continued expansion, 9 per cent in 1966, almost as much in 1965. World trade volume has been increasing faster than world production, with the industrial nations continuing to be more and more important customers to each other, accounting for almost half of total trade in 1966 (as compared with a bit more than a third in 1953). With the European Economic Community abolishing all internal barriers (July 1, 1968) and with the European Free Trade Area even before that point having reached a free trade status in industrial products, the further stimulus which the "Kennedy Round" agreements under the General Agreement on Tariffs and Trade (GATT) will contribute makes even greater trade almost certain. The "Kennedy Round" agreement (May 15, 1967) was the sixth (and most important) of the general tariff reduction agreements since World War II and involved almost half the nations of the world. About 40 billion dollars of trade (especially between industrial nations) was affected, and the tariff cuts agreed upon averaged about one third, the cuts to be spread over the period of January 1, 1968, to January 1, 1972. U.S. trade affected amounted to about $7.5 billion of imports and the same amount of exports. (U.S. total mechandise imports in 1966 amounted to $25.3 billion, and exports were $29.9 billion.) By 1972, the average European Economic Community external tariff was by agreement to be 7.5 per cent.

A final aspect of the world trade figures that has importance is the extent to which the leading exporters are or are not the leading world powers in an overall sense. Politics as well as economics counts heavily here. The 12 most important non-Communist exporting nations are in order (with 1966 figures in billions of dollars and including merchandise, insurance, and freight costs): United States, $30.4; West Germany, $20.1; United Kingdom, $14.6; France, $10.8; Canada, $9.9; Japan, $9.7; Italy, $8.0; Belgium-Luxembourg, $6.8; Netherlands, $6.7; Sweden, $4.2; Switzerland, $3.2; and Denmark, $2.4. For comparison, Soviet exports in 1966 were $8.8, not much more than Italy's. Total Eastern European exports were $20.9, compared to a Western European total of $86.3. EEC export trade ($29.4 total) went primarily to other Western industrialized nations ($19.1), secondly to less developed nations ($8.0), and only on a minor scale to Eastern Europe and the Soviet Union ($1.7, or $2.1 if the figure for West German exports to East Germany is included). One can see why the Eastern European nations are so interested in expanding trade with the West (and vice-versa). This possibility is the single largest stimulus readily and easily available for all concerned. Since West Germany is the key nation involved, this consideration aided Germany's political initiatives in 1969 toward Eastern Europe.

Implications for U.S. Policy

DISCUSSIONS in the U.S. press (1968) about domestic economic questions, although they focused largely on factors primarily due to the Viet-Nam War, had an important bearing as well on the U.S. foreign aid program. This war was the biggest cause of the budget deficits. It also influenced congressional attitudes toward a tax increase to absorb a significant part of the deficit. Congressional opinion remained fluid until mid-1968 primarily because some members of Congress were willing to increase taxes for war but not for poverty programs at home, while others took exactly the reverse attitude. Without the war there would still have been argument over domestic expenditures for the poverty program, but the sense of needing to decide between conflicting financial demands would have been far less acute. With the U.S. economy operating at a very high level, the danger of inflation preoccupied the alert public. Signs of further drain on the gold supply and setbacks in the balance of trade caused alarm precisely because there was so little agreement on what ought to be done. Yet, fiscal policy aside and over the longer run (once the war was finished), the U.S. economy was in substantially healthy shape and the world economic condition was highly satisfactory so far as the major industrialized nations were concerned. But because the argument in 1968 over allocating U.S. expenditures was so acute, the aid programs were being given an even closer and more hostile scrutiny by Congress than usual. The foreign aid approved in early 1970 was $1.8 billion (compared to the 1958–1967 average of $3.4).

These remarks point up that (the Viet-Nam connected disequilibrium aside) the U.S. could well afford almost any aid program it was likely to consider seriously. Of course, if involvements such as Viet-Nam became the rule rather than the exception, and if (like Viet-Nam) they involved very large expenditures in marginal situations, the U.S. might find itself restricted in its overall policies quite beyond the bounds of good sense or rational national interest. What was more likely was that Viet-Nam represented the extreme case of a marginally useful involvement and that its termination would be followed by a serious consideration of alternative foreign-policy strategies, which in turn would permit the U.S. to approach its overall policy commitments on a sounder basis. On this assumption, aid programs could be considered again more on their own merits as a part of U.S. policy.

If this proves true, what kind of foreign aid program would be of maximum value? At this point we come back to the policy objectives. What are they, what should they be?

To some extent, the motives behind the aid program have been negative. Aid was most often given to *prevent* something—to prevent Communist advances. Either it was assumed that a developing nation, in its frustration, would choose communism, or it was assumed that a nation, offered aid from both super powers, would fall under Communist influence (while remaining nominally non-Communist), if Western bids were rejected.

Actual experience indicates that the fears such motives express are largely unwarranted, at least in these simple terms. Communism is no cure-all for the problems of a developing nation. Most of these nations need to concentrate much more on improving agriculture than on anything else. Here the Soviet lure hardly exists, for it is in agriculture that the greatest possible gap exists between American success and Soviet failure. The gap is so great that it cannot be successfully hidden by any amount of Soviet propaganda. In the immediate post-colonial days, when new leaders like Nkrumah were trying to attain the symbols of a mature industrial society's wealth, Soviet aid in this nonagricultural category had great appeal, but this is no longer so true.

In "competitive bidding" between East and West (which leaders such as Nasser attempt to encourage) the situation is inherently unstable. That is, sooner or later either East or West irritably leaves the game, and the "victorious" side provides the aid. In the case of the United Arab Republic, the Soviets "won," but did this victory thereby transfer the UAR to the Soviet side? Not really. One might even argue that it induced the Soviets ultimately to something of an over-commitment in Middle Eastern politics. (Although it is more widely held that the Soviets have gained a great advantage in maximizing their influence in the Middle East, the inability or unwillingness of the Soviets to carry through with what it would take to satisfy Arab extremism suggests an ultimately limited Soviet success.) Even if this line of analysis is incorrect, it can be argued alternatively that Western financing of UAR projects would hardly have deterred Nasser in any real way from the policies he pursued, and indeed U.S. supplies of food (which *were* sent) probably had a greater—although still very limited—restraining influence.

The extreme case of Soviet "success" in becoming the supplier of aid is Castro's Cuba. Unless Cuba somehow gets its economic system to work, Soviet aid to Cuba (on the order of one million dollars a day) will continue to represent a drain on Soviet resources, which also causes irritation in Cuban-Soviet relations.

Aid extended as an inducement to alter foreign policy has had strictly limited success. Those who accept aid with strings of this kind attached are even more likely to resent the donor than they otherwise would!

Looked at more positively, there can be little question that (both for humanitarian and for practical economic and political reasons) the rich nations of the world simply cannot turn aside from the problem of the poor. This conclusion is, moreover, not really in dispute. What is in dispute is the scale of aid and its form. Encouraging is the development (noted earlier) of a flexible range of aid devices, so that loans, for example, can carry various rates of interest and be extended for economic purposes covering a range of risk.

It would seem desirable for the United States to encourage above all else cooperative regional development schemes in which a number of nations are associated. This device not only spreads the aid burden but also gives a sense of participation. It avoids, too, the bilateral lender-borrower relationship that injures or humbles foreign pride. Where direct political considerations make it desirable for the United States to support nations on a bilateral basis despite the drawbacks involved, the scale of aid and its form should be quite flexible. For here the financial soundness of the project is only of secondary importance. The danger in this method is centered on its potential abuse as a device whereby the United States may undergird an unpopular government, delay for a time its downfall, and suffer from the hatred with which a successor regime may then regard America.

There is another very important reason why the U.S. should limit carefully its bilateral foreign aid program. Experience in the 1960's in Latin America with the "Alliance for Progress" indicates clearly the dangers of associating the U.S. directly with economic progress (or its lack) in any particular nation. Although the U.S. attempted to ensure that its aid would be effective by tying it to developmental plans for individual states which involved land reforms, the vested interests in such nations have been slow to yield their power exactly at a time when the economic progress sparked has intensified popular demands. Behind overt official Latin dissatisfaction in 1969 with U.S. aid policies, cited earlier, are economic, social, and political phenomena. Industrialization or economic change of any sort is unsettling to established ways of life. (Consider what happened to English life during the Industrial Revolution. Consider Dickens' eloquent novels on the social injustices that accompanied this change in a notably humane and politically stable nation.) Economic change is likely to involve suffering, especially as inflation is hard to avoid, and people in masses are dislocated by the impersonal hand of technological change. Resentment is likely to be high— and seek a focus. Any foreign high-profile image will be a natural target. For all the rather unnecessary U.S. government worrying about the lures of communism for a poor people living in poverty, it did astonishingly little worrying about the effects of a too pronounced U.S. role in inducing economic and social change. Mere prudence dictates that U.S. aid accorded through truly multilateral instruments is likely to be better than almost any bilateral program.

Increased U.S. support for multilateral programs is highly desirable, especially if it is coupled with a deliberate total downgrading of political considerations in approaching world trade problems.

Such policies would reflect the judgment that economic development everywhere is a rational end to be encouraged by deliberate United States action, and that increases in world trade are beneficial regardless of the political views of the traders. United States lists of strategic materials barred from trade have been substantially overcautious and overlong; United States laws that do not extend most-favored-nation treatment to a number of the Eastern European nations are long overdue for reform.

In the economic expansion which more liberal policies can bring, loans are better instruments than grants, trade is better if it involves all who want to trade, and regional cooperation is generally better than bilateralism. In all of this the UN can play some part, but even here it is noticeable that its greatest progress in this field is in its regional groupings.

None of these policies separately nor all of them together can make all of the world rich, but they can develop it further and make it richer than it is. The United States with its great share of world resources carries a heavy responsibility in this sphere.

CHAPTER 17

Political Problems: I

APART from the question of a realistic relationship to the United Nations, all the major political problems facing the United States can best be assessed from a geographical area point of view rather than in functional terms. In this chapter and the next we shall look first at the United Nations, and then in turn survey each of the major geographical areas. In each case we shall (1) identify the existing problem, its nature, and the constraints involved, (2) show how the U.S. has so far handled the problem, and (3) suggest new approaches where these are indicated. Any such new approaches must themselves meet two tests: (1) survive assessment against the seven criteria for foreign policy success or failure listed in the second paragraph of Chapter 1; (2) conform to the standards of an opponent-isolating strategy described in Chapter 14.

The United Nations

THE United Nations above all else is a permanent diplomatic conference. It is more than that, but that is its essential nature. Like any institution that exists for many years, it acquires collective habits and corporate traditions, some of which may even take on greater strength than the actual words of its Charter. Since these customs were evolved in the first place because they proved useful for getting business done, they are self-imposed and not normally resented or rejected. Unless their usefulness declines because of changing conditions, they are retained and govern collective behavior by the membership. Of course a particular nation that light-heartedly and frequently accepts a given procedure may one day find itself restricted by it and want the procedure changed. It may or may not succeed, and it may or may not in the end refuse to honor the custom. The UN, for its part, may or may not seek to make it comply, depending on many things. In any case, the general thrust is clear. Long custom explains why a great power holding a permanent seat on the Security Council is not counted as casting a veto by abstaining in a vote, even though the Charter specifically requires an affirmative vote. Long custom explains the extra-Charter device of splitting into one-year lengths a two-year term for two candidates for nonpermanent Security Council seats, if the General Assembly deadlocks on this issue. The illustrations indicate the general nature of these customs: although largely concerned with permitting the UN to get its business done, these customs do not normally restrict the member's discretion or behavior on things where he really cares. Consequently, for all this institutional superstructure, the UN in the end remains what its members are willing to make of it. That is why it is above all else a permanent diplomatic conference.

If the UN is little more than its members, taken collectively, mean it to be, and has no real strength apart from the support of its decisions and recommendations by the members themselves, the resulting organization is neither inconsequential nor unimportant. Far from it. The very facts that it is more or less in continuing session, that it is fairly universal in its membership, and that its existence virtually automatically ensures a third party influence and presence in any dispute are of very great importance. Even from the standpoint alone of its always potential and frequently actual influence on the mitigation of tensions or the constructive settlement of disputes, the UN would justify its existence. When we add its great success in spurring and coordinating the work of its many technical and functionally-oriented specialized agencies, the clear plus on the constructive side cannot be denied. What the balance sheet adds up to is that the UN does certain things superlatively well (the work of the specialized agencies), certain things reasonably well (peaceful settlement of disputes), and certain things somewhat poorly (mitigation or resolution of great power tensions, prevention of the use of force by members, and prevention of aggression). That the box score runs in this fashion is in no way accidental, for the UN is most successful in handling collective business involving low risks and large returns and least successful in handling business involving the great powers— i.e., involving great risks with uncertain returns. This emphasis reflects very accurately the wishes, interests, and abilities of the members.

To understand the nature of the UN (and therefore the role it can play in the foreign policy of the U.S.) one must remember two things.

First is the fact that very few UN members have the military capability of sending a division of troops, an air squadron, or a group of destroyers to any great distance from their own territory—even if they possess such units. A tabulation (1967) of the armed forces of the 95 nations worth listing showed that 29 had an army greater than 100,000, 17 had more than 200,000, and only 12 had above 300,000 men. In that same year, only six nations had more than 25 destroyers in their fleet, there were 76 aircraft carriers in the whole world afloat (58 of them U.S.), and there were altogether 94 cruisers (40 of them U.S., 22 Soviet, leaving 28 for the rest of the world). In 1967, some 27 nations possessed an air force in excess of 200 planes, 15 exceeded 300 planes, and only 9 exceeded 500 planes. Of course, a nation with 100,000 troops that borders on a second nation on the UN's agenda could have a decisive influence on the success of any UN action against that second nation. If it were remote in location from that second nation, its armed force would hardly count at all (unless a larger nation transported and maintained the troops).

Second, one must remember that while Africa's vote in a UN of 126 members is a third of the total, there was only one nation on the African continent in 1967 that appeared in the above list as having forces in the 100,000 men or more category (the UAR with 140,600). The next largest army to the UAR's was Nigeria's, with 50,000 (excluding Biafra), and only four states in Africa besides these two had more than 20,000 men: Algeria (45,000), Morocco (42,000), Congo [Kinshasa] (30,000), and Ethiopia (32,000). Even South Africa's army totaled only 16,200 men. In short, voting power in the UN has little correlation with military power. Indeed it has little correlation with economic, financial, or any other kind of power.

Nations who possess so little power—meaning most members of the UN—have three basic choices open to them on UN issues involving the use of armed force: (1) they can vote to commit the forces of the great powers (assuming the veto permits this), (2) they can commit their own forces (but these hardly exist), or (3) they can generally endorse courses of action which avoid using forces in overt combat situations. That most UN members choose the third alternative is partly due to the freedom of the great powers to refrain from offering troops, and partly due to the great majority's genuine reluctance to assume any responsibility for encouraging enlargement of the dimensions of a conflict, even under the UN banner. This reluctance is tempered only in two situations: (1) in a case like Korea (1950) when aggression has undoubtedly occurred, where a permanent member of the Security Council is going to commit forces in any case, and where no great power is involved directly on the aggressor's side; and (2) where the issue is one in which the majority is highly involved emotionally (such as *apartheid* in South Africa).

These observations indicate that the organization is likely to give limited support to the U.S. in Korean-type cases (assuming that the U.S. itself wishes to fight again under such circumstances) and may, on the other hand, propose courses of action that could lead ultimately to a U.S. confrontation with a nation such as South Africa. The conclusion one reaches is that the U.S. must retain discretion to act or not act in sanctions matters and cannot assume that a UN vote for sanctions is always or necessarily in its best interests.

In contrast to sanctions activities is the dispatch of UN "nonfighting" units such as the UNEF and ONUC, which are primarily designed as agents of peaceful settlement. The issues raised by the UN use of such forces, drawn from smaller "third force" nations, are quite different. Here the main issues are the financing of such operations and the question of the proper use of such forces, so that they do not spill over into the questionable area of interference in the internal affairs of nations. Whether the UNEF on balance aided the settlement of the Arab-Israeli issue is a good question. One can argue that delaying or retarding renewed hostilities is desirable in and of itself, but this is a complex issue. The ONUC, when introduced wholly within the frontiers of a single nation (the Congo), soon found itself drifting from rescue activities to taking sides in a civil war. While one can argue that the UN action had value in preventing Cold War tensions from spreading into the heart of Africa, it is also apparent that the device can lead to abuses. Sufficient for the moment is to note that there are two sides to the issue of UN nonfighting forces, and it is clear that it is not in the interests of the U.S. to back such efforts indiscriminately.

Considering all of this, and particularly noting the different UN reactions on the issue of uses of armed force by great powers ("colonial" powers being judged somewhat more harshly than "noncolonial" powers such as the Soviet Union), it appears desirable for the U.S. to retain a general discretion of action.

Handling issues eventually comes down to voting. Of course, in voting three possibilities exist: an affirmative vote, a negative vote, and an abstention. The United States—like so many of the rest—has often under pressure voted affirmatively without the slightest intention of actually doing anything significant about the issue. It has often not abstained when it might have better done so, for it is difficult to see how either going through the motions of a meaningless vote, or committing U.S. prestige where U.S. interests are not meaningfully involved, does ultimate good either for the U.S. or the UN.

A UN with 126 members (as of 1969) is highly likely to put all or most of the issues in the world to a vote at one time or another. This feature is the obverse side of a great UN strength: that it is automatically virtually a third party in every dispute among the nations. Since any dispute is thus likely to get on the UN agenda, it is also likely to lead sooner or later to a vote. Votes on settlement of disputes are useful where they reflect some consensus by those less directly involved, which stands some chance of being at least grudgingly accepted by those nations directly involved. Where this is not so, it is better that quiet work behind the scenes go on, in an attempt to conciliate the dispute, rather than to record publicly irreconcilable viewpoints that will continue to be held, particularly where no real action is expected as a result of the vote, or where real action will run contrary to important great power interests.

A U.S. vote on a resolution should turn on a calculus of (1) the national interests of the U.S. affected, and (2) the degree of likelihood of making a positive contribution to the settlement of the issue. Where U.S. interests are neither directly involved nor the expectation held that real progress will be made, a U.S. affirmative vote merely involves the U.S. on a course of action that has difficulties. If the U.S. later draws back as the situation goes into a new stage, it will be accused of inconsistency. If the U.S. does not draw back, it will be going further down a questionable path.

In short, the very setting of the UN induces a tendency for everyone to take a stand on anyone else's affairs. The possibility of doing so easily translates into the probability of doing so. Yet the prudent rule is that although no nation will be allowed to do nothing, neither can any one nation reasonably do everything.

In general the U.S. in approaching the UN has too uncritically assumed that "strengthening" the UN is good in and of itself. We have tended to favor the UN involving itself in any number of directions, of backing it financially to the point where it can intervene beyond mere discussion in disputes, of encouraging its ability to deploy forces for various contingencies. Yet, while frequently such UN actions may accord with U.S. interests, it is certainly not always so. At the opposite extreme, avid critics of U.S. support of the UN have tended to assume that any or most actions by the UN are likely to affect U.S. interests adversely—which is even further from the truth. On balance, the U.S. must see the UN as an instrumentality that the various members use or attempt to use as their own interests dictate. We must be prepared to do the same.

The clearest clue as to what the U.S. should and should not support is to remember that the UN's positive potentialities are greatest where it assists the settlement or removal of tensions among or between nations, and its negative potentialities are greatest wherever (and for whatever reason) it intervenes in the internal affairs of any nation. It is questionable whether the U.S. should support UN actions that attempt to change institutions within a state, whatever the moral disapproval one may feel for how a given state conducts its own affairs. The UN sanctions effort against Rhodesia and possible actions against South Africa and the Portuguese colonies in Africa certainly fall in this category. The UN's inaction in the face of the great bloodshed of the Nigerian civil war makes a dramatic contrast. Rather than reflecting a new prudence on the part of the UN African members and a realization that encouraging UN meddling in internal affairs is dangerous, it probably reflected instead their greater indifference where whites are not shedding black blood,

SOUTHERN AFRICA: WHITE MINORITY RULE

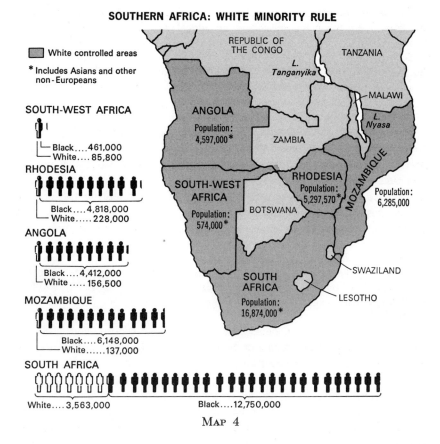

White controlled areas

* Includes Asians and other non-Europeans

SOUTH-WEST AFRICA

Black....461,000
White....85,800

RHODESIA

Black....4,818,000
White.....228,000

ANGOLA

Black....4,412,000
White.....156,500

MOZAMBIQUE

Black....6,148,000
White......137,000

SOUTH AFRICA

White....3,563,000   Black....12,750,000

REPUBLIC OF THE CONGO
TANZANIA
L. Tanganyika
MALAWI
ANGOLA
Population: 4,597,000*
ZAMBIA
L. Nyasa
MOZAMBIQUE
SOUTH-WEST AFRICA
Population: 574,000*
BOTSWANA
RHODESIA
Population: 5,297,570*
Population: 6,285,000
SWAZILAND
SOUTH AFRICA
Population: 16,874,000*
LESOTHO

Map 4

and their fears that Biafran success might jeopardize their own fragile unity. Inaction favored the federal forces, who won in early 1970.

However morally distasteful the internal affairs of white African states may be, they only constitute "threats to the peace, breaches of the peace, or acts of aggression" (to use the words of Chapter 7 of the UN Charter on sanctions and enforcement actions) in the minds of neighboring black African states. Until or unless some action *across* frontiers is initiated by a white-dominated state against a black-dominated state, no violation of the Charter has occurred.

That the U.S. has failed to sort this issue out is clear from the very words of the U.S. Ambassador to the UN. Of the Rhodesian sanctions issue (passed by the Security Council on December 16, 1966, with the U.S. voting affirmatively, banning exports of oil and oil products, asbestos, iron ore, chrome, pig iron, sugar, tobacco, copper, meat and products, hides and leather products) Ambassador Goldberg remarked, answering criticism that it was a dangerous precedent:

This argument overlooks a number of unique elements in the Rhodesian situation. Here we have witnessed an illegal seizure of power by a small minority bent on perpetuating the subjugation of the vast majority. Moreover, in this situation the sovereign authority with international responsibility for the territory [United Kingdom] has asked the United Nations to take measures which will permit the restoration of the full rights of the people of this territory under the Charter.[1]

Does this really answer the fundamental questions? Interestingly enough, after the General Assembly on October 27, 1966, terminated the 46-year old mandate of South Africa (as it had a right to do if it wished) and declared South West Africa "under the direct responsibility of the United Nations," and began to seek ways of implementing the changed status despite South Africa's opposition, Ambassador Goldberg took a different tack, as the African states pressed for forceful action:

. . . public opinion in my country, and indeed in many parts of the world, would not understand a policy which seems ready to resort to immediate coercion rather than explore the possibilities of peaceful progress. . . . What is needed now is not confrontation, but consultation.[2]

Finally we see a note of caution! In view of the record, had U.S. commitments in Southeast Asia not been so large, the U.S. might not even then have been quite so cautious.

One final observation. The UN, apart from all that has already been said, suffers from one grave weakness that limits its utility drastically: neither Germany nor Communist China is taking part in its debates. Thus, almost automatically, two of the three most important international problems in the world are handled, if at all, somewhere else. Only the Middle Eastern problem finds itself substantively on the UN's agenda.

Political Problems: Soviet Troops in Central Europe

THE major political problem faced by the U.S. in Europe is the extent to which the Soviet Union (through its continued politico-military presence in Central Europe) keeps Europe unstable and tensions unnaturally high. Following the Soviet invasion of Czechoslovakia on the night of August 20–21, 1968, with over 500,000 Warsaw Pact troops, tensions were higher than at any time since the Cuban Missile Crisis. By October 1, the invading troops had been reduced to about 450,000 Soviets and 80,000 Polish, but reports indicated the USSR intended to keep six to eight divisions permanently in Czechoslovakia. To this one must add something under a quarter-million Soviet troops in East Germany, where

[1] U.S. Department of State Press Release 304 (December 29, 1966), 6–7.
[2] USUN Press Release 49 (April 26, 1967).

they have now remained for about a quarter century. On the other side of Europe, NATO mans the line, including sizable U.S. contingents. While twenty-five years of this sort of thing has tended to reduce sensitivities on it, it is still true that it represents the most dangerous situation in the world. The threats of the Soviet Union to intervene unilaterally against West Germany under some obsolete provisions of the UN Charter added a further level of escalation to this tension in the months following the Czech occupation.

What can and should the U.S. do about all of this, what options exist, and how does each relate to this complex problem?

At the time of the founding of NATO it was widely believed in the United States that the Soviet Union either (1) had actual intentions of taking over all of Europe by force, or (2) would be in any event tempted to try it if Europe's defenses continued weak. The formation of NATO and its subsequent implementation under the "umbrella" of U.S. nuclear power, prevented such action although—as the record indicates —not without recurring trials of strength over Berlin. Stabilization had progressed so far by the mid-1960's that France had felt free to withdraw from most of the integrated features of NATO (although not from the alliance itself), and other NATO nations were revealing reluctance to fulfill their total obligations to NATO in terms of ready forces. The U.S., confronted by a gold drain, was eyeing a possible reduction in U.S. forces in Europe. Senate sentiment for drastic reductions was growing, and observers agreed that such a measure, if put to a vote in early 1968, would have passed.

To have reduced U.S. troop commitments in Europe without at least securing equivalent Soviet withdrawals would have been quite dangerous, despite this sentiment. Undoubtedly the idea stemmed from U.S. weariness, especially with the concurrent Viet-Nam War still being fought inconclusively, thus over-stretching U.S. military resources in being. It would have been highly ironical if the U.S. (after so much effort in Europe) had yielded to temptation and withdrawn most forces. It would have ensured, even more than de Gaulle's actions had, that any Soviet advance would need to be countered by quick escalation to nuclear levels. A much different military situation would arise if any attacking Soviet forces started from Polish or Soviet territory.

Indeed, although there was much to be said for mutual withdrawals from Central Europe of the troops of both sides, neither side could really afford the luxury of unilateral withdrawal. This leads us to ponder why the Soviets have remained in these forward positions in Central Europe and under what circumstances (if any) they could be induced to withdraw.

If there is truth in the assertion that the Soviets want to take Europe by force, the price is still clearly unacceptable to them. If the Soviets would be tempted in view of any weakness in Western defenses, such weaknesses have not really eventuated. The Soviets today have no means of advancing beyond the Iron Curtain without inviting full nuclear retaliation. Whether the Soviets are spurred by ideological fervor (which seems less convincing all the time) or by great power opportunism, the chances of advance at an acceptable price are not encouraging.

As one observes two decades of Soviet communications on Europe's problems, the striking thing is their emphasis on supposed tendencies in West Germany to "revanchism." While this emphasis is useful for propaganda purposes (to induce Eastern Europe to resist German overtures for trade and diplomatic relations), there is no good reason to doubt Soviet sincerity. The Soviet Union has never indicated that it believes a direct confrontation with the U.S. in Europe is likely except in connection with Germany. Although the great destructive capability of the U.S. would be an object of concern to the USSR even if all American and Soviet troops were today within their own frontiers, the friction has always turned on the German problem (and connected Eastern European issues) quite directly.

The basic Soviet fear is not of the U.S. but of the U.S. as the power reserve of Germany. Although Americans cannot quite find Soviet fears of Germany credible, it is because they visualize Germany as unable to act without U.S. support, with the U.S. retaining a meaningful veto. On the other hand, to the Soviets the picture is that German actions could automatically commit the U.S. because American forces are on German soil. Because the Soviet Union—confronting a West Germany without nuclear weapons and alone—could (as Khrushchev threatened) easily turn Germany into one vast cemetery, how can one otherwise explain Soviet fears? One could say it is mere propaganda. Yet no nation, after all, pretends over a lengthy period of time to believe something it does not believe at all. There are too many drawbacks to offset the advantages. There are only three plausible alternatives. Either the Soviets believe that West Germany would embark alone on aggression, believe that Germany would embroil the U.S. in its actions, or believe that the U.S. would incite Germany to aggression. They continually assert the second of these three propositions.

One must take Soviet fears in this context as real, whether justified or not. The Soviet homeland has known German invasion twice in 50 years, and the Soviets believe it could be tried again.

It is for these reasons that the recurrent postwar Western proposals for all of Germany to be reunited by free elections and allowed to join NATO have never sparked much Soviet interest. Look at the 1968 Soviet invasion of Czechoslovakia: this the Soviets have justified as due in large part to the advance of German influence there (and where it might lead); and here one can disbelieve the Soviets again. But if one accepts their contentions as sincere (even if wrong), one has to think again on the point as to why the Soviets although armed with nuclear weapons could still believe in the reality of a future German advance through Czechoslovakia to the Soviet frontier, especially since Germany at this time is without either nuclear weapons or U.S. support for any such move. Either the Soviets make it up as they go along, or the Soviet version of a scenario for how World War III would begin in Europe obviously contains elements that differ drastically from Western versions. For if Czechoslovakia had been invaded merely to keep Czech communism from going "soft," it seems consistent with Soviet behavior to assume that they would have felt that it was enough excuse for their actions to rest their case on the internal affairs aspect. Obviously, if they add charges about Germany which the rest of the world feels far-fetched, and if Eastern Europe is already convinced of Soviet "protection" in the event of a German assault, they only weaken an already weak case.

Why are these fears so prevalent, aside from the Soviet conviction that Germany would twist U.S. power to its own purposes?

Here we come directly to the weaknesses of the Soviet position in Eastern Europe, weaknesses that the invasion of Czechoslovakia does not deny but confirms.

Soviet Weaknesses

BEFORE Germany was unified (1871), Prussian forces were never locked in serious and continuing combat with Russian armies. Most Russian wars were against Turkey, the Prussians and Russians on the other hand cooperating along with Austria in despoiling and dividing Poland. In Napoleonic times France, not Germany, was the invader of Russia. Prussian and Russian forces combined to defeat the French emperor. In the Crimean War Russia's enemies were England and France. In the wars of German unification in the 1860's, Prussia fought Austria and then France—but not Russia. After 1871, German-Russian relations were frequently close. Not until after 1890 did Russia begin seriously to fear Germany, and then primarily as the potential supporter of Austria, whose Balkan role threatened Russian interests in the same area. Eventually, in World War I, Germany did fight Russia and defeat her. The abortive Treaty of Brest-Litovsk would have transferred Russian territories to Germany, but its results were set aside by Germany's defeat in the West. After the Soviet Union came into existence (1917), there was a Polish-Soviet war; and following that, defeated Germany and the weak Soviet Union cooperated with each other in both economic and military areas. Since Communist Russia had lost great territories on her western frontiers (as compared to Tsarist Russia) and was weak and isolated, such cooperation was not surprising. In those days, France dominated

Eastern Europe, entering into alliances with virtually the entire area—alliances directed both at Russia and Germany. How Germany under Hitler asserted her power and increased her influence in Eastern Europe (displacing France and potentially threatening the Soviet Union) is the story of the 1930's, leading up to the second German assault on Russia in the twentieth century. Although Stalin and Hitler had attempted to divide Eastern Europe (1939), including advances by both nations into Poland, in the end this uneasy alliance was terminated by the Nazis. As the tide of victory gradually turned against Hitler, the Soviet forces found themselves in possession of all of Eastern Europe and some parts of Germany.

This is exactly what is different about Russia's strategic position in terms of her western approaches from any previous time in modern history. Previously, she had divided influence with Germany (divisions of Poland) and competed for influence elsewhere in Eastern Europe with Austria, France, or Germany. Now France was virtually completely excluded, the Austrian Empire had fallen apart in World War I and no longer was a major contender, and Germany was divided and actually occupied in the East by Soviet troops. The Eastern European nations became "peoples' democracies," a way-station on the road to "true" socialism. Reactionary or at least hostile regimes from the Soviet standpoint were replaced by "friendly" governments.

What then is weak about this position, for on its face it appears the strongest achieved by Russia in modern times?

The Achilles' heel is that the Eastern European peoples (under communism or any other systems) have never wanted to be dominated by any great power, and there is only one practical path to avoiding it: introducing a direct counterweight. In turn, most of the potential direct counterweights have been eliminated, as may be seen even in our quick survey. The United States was confronted after Dulles' oratory about "liberation" by an actual opportunity in Hungary (1956) but chose to hold aloof. Austria is now a small state. Turkey no longer represents a challenge. France can indulge in speeches, but is too far away. Only Germany offers a possibility. If West Germany pursues an active policy in the area, she can threaten Soviet hegemony there—ultimately on a very serious scale. If, for example, West Germany enters into economic and diplomatic relations with Romania, she gains an opening wedge. If she can do the same with Czechoslovakia, she divides Eastern Europe into two groups and begins the isolation of and pressure on Poland and East Germany (who have almost as much to fear from a strong "real" Germany as the Soviet Union herself). This is, of course, exactly what was happening by the late summer of 1968.

East Germany's existence depends on two things: Soviet bayonets and a successful isolation of East Germans from the "real" Germany. The second factor was eroding rapidly. Even looking only at Romania one sees where things were going. In 1967, Romania had 640,000 visitors from the West, 400,000 of them West Germans. But because East Germans could also visit Romania and did so in large numbers, the Iron Curtain and Berlin Wall (which heretofore served to isolate East Germany) were being breached. What would things have been like if in 1968 or 1969 a million West Germans met a million East Germans in liberal but Communist Czechoslovakia—a nation bordering on both?

One can say that given Germany's limited power these are insignificant fears, but it is well to remember how rapidly Germany moved from weakness in the early 1930's to dominating all of Europe by the early 1940's. And Nazi Germany was not the ally of a nuclear-armed United States.

The point is not whether West Germany "intends revenge," or even whether the West German government consciously embarked on a policy of forcing a revamping of the *status quo* through economic and political means. The fact is that they did affect that *status quo*, and that they were able to do so because the Soviet Achilles' heel in Eastern Europe is real. Also, one can hardly blame the Germans for wanting to reunify their own country, and setting in motion these kinds of pressures would appear to be the only realistic path open to them apart from, say, an alliance with China (explicitly or implicitly) or, alternately, accepting some kind of neutral status that would produce a united Germany, evacuated of foreign troops.

Soviet interests are quite clear. Their preference, Soviet Option 1, has been generally to continue as is unless conditions change radically. This option has two disadvantages. First, it exposes the Soviets to the possibility of being drawn into war with the United States more or less by accident, simply because U.S. and Soviet troops are deployed only a few miles apart in Germany. Soviet fears on this score are probably low-level. Second, it risks war with the U.S., stemming from a popular revolt in East Germany into which West Germany might be drawn. The U.S. could not remain uninvolved because we are actually deployed there, and the U.S. could not afford to permit Soviet troops to take over West Germany, as the battle swayed across frontiers. Many views on this scenario exist, ranging from regarding it as likely to regarding it as completely far-fetched, but the Soviet assessment of this risk is probably intermediate.

Soviet Option 2 is to exploit opportunities for advances. This option is not inconsistent with Option 1 and has been attempted several times over West Berlin. *If* the Soviets saw a chance to force the West out of Western Germany and to control it or occupy it without major war, they undoubtedly would try. It is highly probable that they would attempt to establish a Communist system throughout Germany, but it is highly unlikely that the Soviets would cease worrying about Germany even under those circumstances. Yugoslavia is a Communist state, yet she is prepared to use force against an invading Soviet army. China is hostile. A liberal but Communist Czechoslovakia might have resorted to force defensively—and still might some time. In short, communism shared by states is not synonymous with shared friendship. But the Soviets are not likely to have a chance to implement Option 2.

Option 3 is to negotiate with the West to establish a neutral status for a single German state or for two German states. The second part of Option 3 has advantages for Russia but none for the West. It has no chance of being accepted by any foreseeable West German government. By contrast, the first part of Option 3 could, under certain conditions, be acceptable to all parties. Its great disadvantage for the Soviet Union is the certainty that communism would be uprooted in any united German state. Such a setback for communism would carry with it grave emotional and political implications. Thus the Soviets would not be likely to choose Option 3 unless there were compelling reasons.

Consequently, if the Soviets cannot advance, they prefer to stay where they are. For this reason most observers conclude that the reunification of Germany is unlikely, virtually regardless of the formula chosen.

The logic of this situation is that West Germany cannot expect to improve her prospects for achieving her national aims unless she alters the balance of pressures affecting Soviet decisions on Germany. If she merely behaves and is patient but does nothing, the results will be nil. Germany can either forego reunification or alter the objective conditions confronting the Soviet Union. She actually chose (1965–1968) to alter the objective conditions through a "peaceful rapprochement" with Eastern Europe. This in turn led to the Soviet occupation of Czechoslovakia.

Observing this event, many students of the question concluded that developments such as in Czechoslovakia between January and August 1968 cannot occur successfully any more because the Soviets will not tolerate them, and that the German problem was back again on dead center. This view was certainly correct for the moment. Yet the very occupation of Czechoslovakia turned the Czech feeling from one of friendship to the Soviets (in memory of previous support against the Nazis) to one of bitter distrust. The East Europeans could either resign themselves to a future under Soviet domination or try something else. That their hopes for greater freedom were frustrated in 1968 will, unless the lessons of history are no longer valid, lead to greater efforts later. The same result is likely to hold true for West Germany. Failure in one tactic is likely in time to lead to some other tactic. In view of the need of the Soviets to deal with a basically distrustful Eastern Europe and a hostile

China, there are in principle ample materials at hand for the Germans to work with if they choose.

Indeed, the rash of West German negotiations with the Soviets and with Eastern Europe, set into motion in late 1969, was probably itself the best proof that the situation remains more fluid than is generally believed.

In short, strategically speaking, the Soviet political position in Eurasia is very weak today. Not only is the Chinese threat growing, not only is the U.S. an enemy, not only is Eastern Europe unreliable, but Germany no longer is merely sitting still and accepting the "inevitable." In principle there is no more reason why the Germans will resign themselves to living under present conditions permanently than why the Soviets will want to undo their own security in Eastern Europe. Neither is likely to resign from the contest. It is only the balance of pressures on the Soviets that might be altered. Germany and China are the two principal fluid factors in that balance of pressures, with Eastern Europe the third.

The Crisis in NATO

THE second most important problem facing the U.S. in Europe is how to deal with changes in attitudes on the part of Europe's NATO members to defense problems. After 1958, when de Gaulle took power as President of the Fifth French Republic, the unity of NATO began to decline. The casual observer might believe this was cause and effect—a conclusion only partly true.

NATO's troubles in the last decades stem from three causes. First, at least until mid-1968 and the Soviet occupation of Czechoslovakia, it was increasingly believed in the West that the Soviets would refrain from any aggressive military moves against any areas in Western hands in Europe. After the Cuban Missile Crisis, the Soviets abandoned Khrushchev's "adventurism" and cooperated with the West in reaching certain disarmament agreements such as the Nuclear Test Ban Treaty and the Nuclear Non-Proliferation Treaty. Looked at coldly, these agreements did not really indicate necessarily any fundamental and permanent shifts in Soviet policy. That is, the Soviets could well co-sponsor both treaties and still be intent on military aggression—if they ever had been so intent. Their nuclear arsenal was advanced enough for a time, and certainly if potential Soviet enemies could be restricted from testing, the Soviets would remain ahead. Even more can one argue that the treaty to avoid the *spread* of nuclear weapons into new hands was decidedly compatible with a variety of strategic intents, including any plans for future aggression. Soviet cooperation in these disarmament measures, while they were easily understandable in terms of attempting to enhance Soviet security, could also be construed quite validly as efforts toward détente with the West. In any case, France and China refused to give up testing, and as 1969 drew to a close the treaty on nonproliferation was not yet ratified.

The second cause of NATO's troubles was an increasing ambivalence within NATO as to strategic military doctrine. Such ambivalence was not new, merely greater than before. Even in NATO's first years there had been an argument over the "forward strategy" question. Germany wanted its defense to commence on the line of the Iron Curtain rather than on the Rhine, since the latter strategy potentially entailed a nuclear devastation of the area in-between as Soviet troops advanced in it. To stop the Soviets on the Iron Curtain presupposed nuclear weapon use. Then later, as the Soviets achieved an equivalent nuclear arsenal, Europeans raised doubts as to whether the U.S. would be prepared to go "all out" in Europe at the price of devastation within the continental limits of the U.S. "Massive retaliation" cut both ways.

The U.S. answer, inspired by a number of factors, was to advance a new strategic concept: flexible response. Advances by Soviet forces would be met by whatever it took to hold them, with the U.S. matching escalation for escalation. Here French objections began to be raised, the French in the early 1960's arguing two alternative but related propositions. On the one hand the French doubted U.S. willingness to suffer devastation for Europe's defense, and on the other hand they saw flexible response as meaning that the U.S. might either shrink from escalation or resort to it too late to save Europe. The French wanted a "hand on the nuclear trigger" to ensure that the U.S. would not unilaterally retain discretion over the sole meaningful nuclear arsenal in NATO's hands. They wanted massive retaliation to continue in force so as to remove any Soviet temptation to make challenges too small or ambiguous to bring about escalation but of such a nature, if successful, as to tempt the Soviets to more "salami tactics."

Obviously these French views neither sit well with each other nor raise issues to which there are easy solutions. When the U.S. suggested a Multilateral Nuclear Force the argument continued. It ended with a French series of decisions to require NATO forces to withdraw from French soil (while France remained a member of the alliance as such) and to develop its own strategic nuclear striking force. Because there is no way for NATO members to really "share" a decision on resort to nuclear weapons, and because the French could logically hope to have a voice only if they also controlled their own nuclear force, these French decisions put an effective end to the debate. The fact that France was no longer available as a deployment and logistics rear area also in effect had the merit (from the French viewpoint) of requiring NATO in Germany to go rapidly to a full nuclear response if the Soviets advanced. The West could hardly well retreat in the compressed West German-

Benelux area. France could thus refrain from being involved automatically at the outset, could act only after the certainty that the U.S. was committed, and could retain full control over her own nuclear forces. Of course French troops continued to be deployed in Germany by West German consent, and one might argue that France in any event would also be automatically committed, but significantly these troops were located near the French frontier. One might also argue that the continued American troop deployment in forward positions on the Iron Curtain in Germany should have convinced the French that the U.S. really was committed, but we have also seen that American sentiment for drastic cut-backs in these forces had been growing. One might even argue that the French, without saying so, were lessening their automatic commitment if Soviet fears about Germany proved correct. If one approaches all of these arguments in the expectation that they will all make sense on their own merits, they simply will not. What they represent in aggregate is the rationalized fear of being caught up in a nuclear war. With Germany between her and the Soviets, France is really saying that she hopes to use this circumstance in her own interests and with a minimum automatic commitment.

The third cause of NATO's troubles is that West Germany has been restive. Ambivalences here are even greater than in the French case. In Adenauer's time and until the early 1960's, the Germans accepted Acheson's "position of strength" concept with little question. Membership in NATO protected West Germany and gave her backing in seeking reunification. The Berlin Wall shook this assumption. When Germany's "grand coalition" was formed (December 1, 1966), and the opposition Social Democrats entered into the government with the Christian Democrats, it permitted those elements from both parties who sought to have a more active policy toward Eastern Europe to achieve majority representation within government councils. Of this policy, which quickly led to diplomatic relations with Romania, Chancellor Kurt Georg Kiesinger said to the Bundestag (January 18, 1968): "It is the aim of this government to relax and remove tensions from our relations with the Eastern European countries and with the Soviet Union. This is not aimed against anyone, also not against the Russians." But it cannot help but be against the Russians, in the sense that any improvement for Germany as a member of NATO represents a drawback to the Soviets. We saw how this culminated at the end of the first phase in the new German initiatives in Czechoslovakia's occupation by the Soviets (August 1968). We saw how it led to the beginning of the second phase at the end of 1969.

The sources of the basic ambivalence in Germany are clear enough. NATO membership has given protection but not reunification, and the Soviet forces are actually on German soil and in neighboring Czechoslovakia. This is not reassuring. France seems to be going her own way and indisposed to take risks of any sort for German interests. Although verbally reassuring Germany, the U.S. has made détente overtures to the Soviets and has been contemplating large troop withdrawals from German soil. A German nuclear force is a tempting proposition but fraught with danger. The U.S. might pull out, the Soviets might intervene, Eastern Europe would be worried, and so on; and the "revanchist" image painted by Soviet propaganda would take on more reality. Should West Germany then resign herself to her situation with its overwhelming insecurity features, with her protection forever in foreign hands?

In these circumstances there is bound to be increasing discussion in West Germany of other options, either to change the balance of pressures on the Soviets, or attempt to gain troop withdrawals by both sides. If the latter were done (even assuming Soviet agreement) could Germany rely for protection on the United States once American troops were no longer in Germany? Could a Germany without allies defend itself with conventional weapons?

At this point one can see the real troubles in NATO, obscured as they have been by American preoccupation with de Gaulle's irritating tactics. For all members of NATO except Germany, the prime goal has been to prevent a Soviet advance. German national interests also require a Soviet retreat—an interest and conviction shared mostly only verbally by the rest. As long as NATO could be believed to be a way of inducing Soviet withdrawal, no real problem existed. The point is not that NATO (and the U.S.) would not be far better off if the Soviets withdrew from Central Europe; it is rather that NATO generally can afford to live with a Soviet Central European presence far better than the Germans can; for the Germans it represents permanent dismemberment.

If the Germans can bring themselves to accept the present situation indefinitely, there is no real problem provided the Soviets do not try to advance. But will Germans be so accepting? They see a United States anxious for a détente with the Soviets while Germany is still divided; they see a United States anxious to "bring the boys home." At the same time they see a Soviet Union whose political position has weakened and on whom real pressures could be brought to bear by a policy that would be highly risky.

It seems clear that the United States will have to make up its mind. A case can be made for a détente with the Soviets that keeps Europe divided, but one wonders how much real merit it has. It turns on accepting a Soviet forward deployment but eliminating U.S.-Soviet adjacent deployments in Germany, through mutual withdrawals from the two German states. Looked at candidly, it sounds like a formula for inviting hostilities between the two Germanies.

From a deeper point of view, how can the U.S. have a meaningful détente with the Soviets unless they each become convinced that they are unlikely to have hostilities with each other if war breaks out in Europe (or possibly elsewhere)? How could this miracle come about? Certainly no amount of verbal gestures can alter the deadly threat the U.S. is to the Soviet Union and vice versa. In short, the hostile posture of the two super powers stems from the objective reality that they can and might destroy one another. Only three kinds of actions can alter or mitigate these tensions: thoroughgoing and effective mutual strategic disarmament, solution of major outstanding quarrels between them, or a change in the pressures on one or the other which would effectively detract from its ability to constitute a meaningful threat because of preoccupation with other enemies. We have already looked at the first of these three; now let us look at the other two as they affect and are affected by Europe.

The U.S. cannot resolve Central European tension by concessions over German interests that are not freely accepted by the Germans, for the Germans are in a position ultimately to take matters in their own hands. Unless the U.S. sought an alliance with its Soviet enemy to restrain its present ally, this option is not real. Seeking to do away with tension in this way is suicidal. Suppose, alternately, the U.S. encouraged a situation where overt pressures on the Soviets were increased by German initiatives, obviously designed for that purpose? Certainly that would be a dangerous game.

This leaves only one realistic option for the United States (other than a continuation as is): to seek a general settlement of European security interests that is acceptable to Germany, while meeting Soviet needs. Neither the Soviet Union nor West Germany might be willing to agree to a neutral (but armed) united Germany from which all foreign troops are withdrawn, yet it is only by some such means that this dangerous problem can be resolved. A united Germany would still constitute a Soviet enemy (as the Soviets well know), but it would not be an enemy with a grievance, automatically backed by the nuclear arsenal of the United States. These would be important differences. One can say, in the wake of the "lightning" occupation of Czechoslovakia by the Soviets (actually several months in the making!), that the U.S. could not afford the risk; but occupying Czechoslovakia (already in the Soviet orbit, and small) is not the same as occupying Germany. Such a neutral, united, armed Germany could be guaranteed within its existing frontiers. If *it* committed aggression, it would have no automatic support from anyone. Even under these circumstances, if the U.S. still decided to support her (rather unlikely), Germany would hardly gamble on this possibility with no real grievance to motivate taking risks of this kind.

What is wrong with this idea? It has cropped up in negotiations over more than two decades but has never been advanced by the U.S. First, West Germany has never supported it, although that may change as the alternatives become clearer to the Germans. Second, the Soviets—although advancing this as a solution in earlier years—may have been insincere then, or be against it now. Insincerity could be tested by proposing to create suitable safeguards. More important is whether the Soviets would feel that they were better off through adopting this option. This will depend on the interaction of two main potential developments in the time ahead: what the Germans do, and how Eastern Europe reacts to the new Soviet determination to hold what they have through Red Army troops. A bold German action would arouse Eastern European anxieties and would not be attempted by a rational Germany, unless the total change in the balance of pressures on Russia would make the Eastern European reactions less important to the Germans. (An example could be *de facto* Sino-German coordinated pressures.) As to Eastern European reactions to Soviet deployments on their soil, it is highly likely that these will continue to be very negative and important enough for the Soviets to weigh whether the advantages will outweigh the disadvantages. The Soviet calculus will turn on two things. One is whether Germany will accept some form of the *status quo*, which would have a chance of enduring without a need for Soviet deployments. The other is whether deployments in Eastern Europe will in the long run prevent pro-Soviet attitudes there from becoming sufficiently strong and reliable. Military occupations, after all, are a means to an end, and not an end in itself. The Soviets want security in the area of their western approaches. Those who might argue that only bayonets will achieve this have to recognize that post-Stalinist foreign policy in the area on the whole rejected that proposition and sought to create real bonds of friendship within the European "socialist commonwealth" (to use the recent Soviet term).

A third argument against this idea (of seeking a settlement of European security interests that is acceptable to Germany, while meeting Soviet needs) is that a large nation located in the center of Europe and flanked by areas with contrasting ideologies could never be neutral. If this is true, it hardly squares with the opposing view that Germany will rest content with permanent division. If Germany is inclined to upset any distribution of power that may prevail at a given time in Europe, she can of course do so, and she is likely to do so if she has reason; but a neutral and united Germany whose security was safeguarded within an all-European security arrangement would have far less cause to "rock the boat" than she presently and prospectively has. Unless one wants to argue that powerful nations can pursue only policies designed to change a *status quo*, one must accept the proposition that it is possible to create conditions where a powerful nation stands for a stable *status quo*. If one wants to argue that Germany would lack the wisdom to do so, one must also argue that Germany now presumably lacks wisdom. If so, is it not dangerous to be allied with her?

When one examines the arguments and cuts through the ambivalences and ambiguities, one finds that the U.S. has really been opting for the *status quo* and hoping that the problems would continue to be manageable. As the very restrained German initiatives in Eastern Europe between 1965 and 1968 clearly show, the policy has turned on two further assumptions: that the Germans will not "rock the boat" in any meaningful fashion, and that the Germans will continue to accept a policy that deprives them of assurance of any real security other than by accepting permanent division—if then.

Chancellor Kurt Georg Kiesinger, addressing the German Bundestag in the first State of the Nation Speech delivered by a West German Chancellor (March 11, 1968) said:

> Strong as our ties in the Atlantic Alliance are, friendly as our relations with the United States are, we may not seek our own future, and, we believe also, the future of a united West Europe in the firm structure of a North Atlantic imperium.
>
> Such a solution would transform the demarcation line that divides Germany and Europe into a permanent border wall. Such a solution could also increase the danger of a world conflict in a dramatic way.

Kiesinger emphasized he was talking about the "situation of the nation in divided Germany," saying that "self-determination cannot be permanently denied the German people." He added: "Compared with 1933 the entire German population has grown by 11 million, but it lives and works in an area shrunken by about 44,000 square miles and torn apart therein by the international political development after the war." Only, said the Chancellor, in the context of normalizing relations with Communist Europe could the national division be overcome. (Of course, these remarks were made before the Soviet occupation of Czechoslovakia. Even so they indicated German restiveness.) The new Social Democratic government under Chancellor Willy Brandt, which took office in October 1969, did so with the avowed intent of exploring a further rapprochement with Communist Europe.

If a more tranquil situation in Europe could be brought about by a solution to Germany's dilemma, the problems that have weakened NATO would in many ways be resolved at the same time. If the Soviets could be induced to return to their own frontiers and American troops were also withdrawn, Europe would cease to be divided down the middle and could play a role much better suited to its own needs and desires. At the same time, the danger of a Soviet-American clash would be substantially reduced. Whether a Western European alliance grouping existed, and whether an Eastern European grouping also existed, and what the relationship of the super powers to these groupings would be, could surely be worked out within the confines of this general approach. The long-range objective of the U.S. in Europe is not to preserve Germany in NATO but to decrease the likelihood of war through encouraging an end to Soviet forces in Central Europe.

CHAPTER 18

Political Problems: II

L ET US now look at the major political problems confronting the United States in the world outside Europe: in Asia, the Middle East, Africa, and Latin America. As before we shall want to (1) identify the existing problem and its nature and constraints; (2) show how the U.S. has so far handled the problem; and (3) suggest new approaches where these are indicated. Again, we shall want to judge any new approaches against the standards of (1) the seven criteria for foreign policy success or failure, and (2) the requirements of an opponent-isolating strategy.

Asian Developments

ASIA has already received much attention in this book, from the standpoint of the extent and wisdom of U.S. postwar involvements. We want to sketch in here the main features of an Asia in flux, complete a survey of how the U.S. has handled the problem, and enlarge upon new approaches by the U.S. that meet the tests just mentioned.

The extent of change in Asia so far in this century is difficult to portray because of its very enormity. It helps to remember the major features of Asia when this century began, and the main developments since.

In 1900, Japan was just setting out to test herself in military conflict and build an empire. In 1900, she had not yet fought Russia, the United States, and Great Britain. Although she had defeated China in a small war, not until the 1930's would she embark on the second and third rounds of this protracted war. From these modest beginnings, by World War II she came to control most of Asia, fighting all of the nations mentioned and in addition absorbing temporarily all of the Dutch and French Far Eastern empires. Defeated in 1945, she lost all she had taken, even being forced to transfer outlying islands such as Okinawa into foreign hands. Dedicated to regaining influence in peaceful ways, Japan maintained only a modest military establishment. Yet by 1968, she had become the third industrial nation in all the world—and increasingly restless.

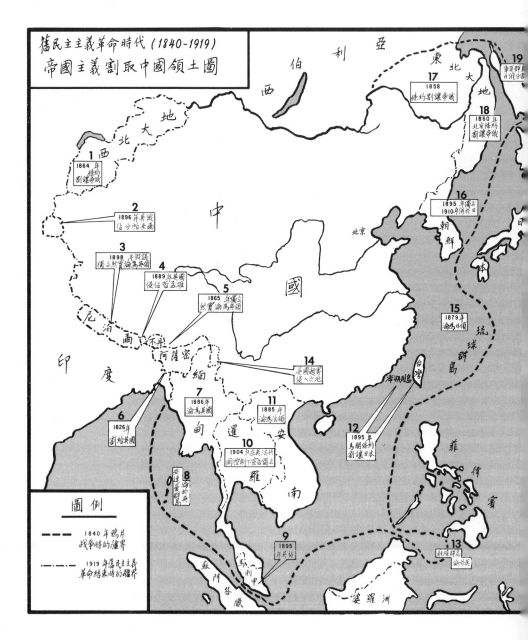

舊民主主義革命時代 (1840-1919)
帝國主義割取中國領土圖

亞
西 伯 利 東 北 大
地
西 北 大 地

19
（庫頁群島
日俄分割）

17
1858
條約割讓帝俄

18
1860年
北京條約
割讓帝俄

1
1864年
條約
割讓帝俄

中 國

北京

16
1895年獨立
1910年併吞日

2
1896年英俄
佔分帕米爾

朝
鮮

日

3
1898年租議
獨立於實淪為英轄

4
1889年英國
侵佔哲孟雄

5
1865年立
於實淪為英轄

15
1879年
淪為日領

尼
泊
爾

不
丹

阿薩密

14
英國越界
侵入之地

琉
球
群
島

印
度

緬

7
1886年
淪為英國

台灣
澎湖列島

甸

11
1885年
淪為法領

安

12
1895年
馬關條約
割讓日本

6
1826年
割給英國

暹

10
1904年在英法共
同控制下宣告獨立

羅

南

菲

8
淪於英

律

賓

9
1895
年英坊

蘇
門
答
臘

馬
剌
甲

婆 羅 洲

13
新嘉群島
淪於英

圖 例

- - - - 1840年鴉片
戰爭時的疆界

—·—·— 1919年舊民主主義
革命結束時的疆界

Indonesia, Malaysia, India, Pakistan, and such smaller units as Cambodia, Burma, and the Philippines—all of whom played independent roles in 1970—were under Western domination in 1900. China was already rapidly passing into foreign hands, its long coast and adjacent hinterland carved into a succession of spheres of influence held by the British, the French, the Japanese, the Germans, and the Russians. Foremost among those seeking to carve her up were the Russians (who by 1858 had actually incorporated major sections of Chinese territory within their own frontiers and until 1904–1905 maintained a strong position in Manchuria). Had Japan in succeeding decades not sought to

---

MAP 5. A CHINESE VIEW OF CHINA

The map is reprinted from a Chinese textbook entitled, "*A Brief History of Modern China,* 1954." The legend in the bottom left in the map reads: *Dash Line:* Borders at the time of the Opium War, 1840; *Dash-and-Dot Line:* Borders on the conclusion of the era of the old Democratic Revolution, 1919. Basic translation of the text inside the map:

"1 The Great North-West [covering huge segments of the present-day Soviet Republics of Kazakhastan, Kirghizia and Tajikistan] was seized by Imperialist Russia under the Treaty of Chuguchak, 1864.

"2 The Pamirs was secretly divided between Britain and Russia in 1896.

"3 Nepal went under the British after 'Independence' in 1898.

"4 Che-Man-Hsiung [i.e., present-day Sikkim] was occupied by Britain in 1889.

"5 Pu-tan [i.e., the whole of Bhutan] went under Britain after 'Independence' in 1865.

"6 Ah-sa-mi [i.e., the whole of Assam, NEFA and Nagaland] was given to Britain by Burma in 1826.

"7 Burma became a part of British Empire in 1886.

"8 The Andaman Islands went under Britain.

"9 Ma-la-chia [i.e., Malaya and Singapore] went under Britain, 1895.

"10 Hsien-Lo [i.e., the whole of Thailand] was declared 'Independent' under joint Anglo-French control in 1904.

"11 Annam [covering the present-day North and South Vietnam, Laos and Cambodia] was captured by the French in 1885.

"12 Taiwan and P'enghu Islands were relinquished to Japan in accordance with the Treaty of Shimonoseki, 1895.

"13 Su-Lu Island was 'occupied by the British.'

"14 The Region where the British crossed the border and committed aggression.

"15 Liu-Chiu [i.e., Ryukyu Islands] went under Japan in 1879.

"16 Ch'ao-Hsien [i.e., Korea] 'independent' in 1895; to Japan, 1910.

"17 and 18 The Great North-East [covering a huge area of the Soviet Far East] was given Russia under the Treaties of Aigun (1858) and Peking (1860).

"19 K'u-Ye [i.e., Sakhalin] was 'divided between Japan and Russia.' "

displace the others, embarking upon a drive to control all of China by itself, China might have suffered the fate of Poland in the eighteenth century.

China's role in these events is pathetic. Plunged into further weakness by 1900 (through civil war which lasted 50 years) and struggling simultaneously to resist foreign encroachments, China survived to attain a new unity (1949) under the Communists. The area of Peking-controlled China includes most of the traditional continental spaces but does not include the very large areas detached by Russia in the north and those smaller areas detached by Britain in the south. By the 1960's, China was again in great disorder as Mao pushed his "cultural revolution," a sort of "communism revisited" or second stage of what went before. Fought over so long and struggling toward a redemption of her ancient prestige via modern nuclear weapons, China found herself precariously confronting two nuclear powers (the United States and the Soviet Union) against whom she felt real grievances, and who seemed to China in tacit alliance against Chinese ambitions. Tied to the U.S. was Japan, who so long had waged bitter war against China.

In these successive scenes as the decades flashed by, the United States played a changing role: now as champion of a hard-pressed China (at first in words but later in deeds), later as a new enemy, attempting to frustrate the unification of ancient Chinese territories and to prevent a final end to the struggle with the Nationalists. Still later, America appeared as antagonist to China in Korea and a threat in Indo-China. Looked at through Chinese eyes, the United States in the postwar period passed from a friendly role (in helping to end French rule in Indo-China and Dutch rule in Indonesia) to an enemy role of armed presence in Indo-China combined with a far-flung deployment around China on the sea and on island bases that dominate the areas from which the former colonial powers have been expelled.

This Asia in ferment, confronted by the persistent presence of Westerners bent on remaking Asia to their own specifications, has on the whole a great wish to be left alone. We see this in recent times in India's aversion to any military commitments, in the strong minority views in Japan that seek to sever the links to the United States, in China's xenophobia, and in Indonesia's erratic behavior under Sukarno. Other evidences could be cited, such as the independent course of Burma and Cambodia. America's presence is looked at with ambivalence, some of these nations fearing what may indeed happen if the U.S. forces one day sail away, but even then having a strong wish to be free from the white foreigner. This Asia has never had the chance in modern times to try to regulate her own affairs. Therefore one cannot predict with any absolute certainty what Asia would be like with the Western white man removed.

If the Westerner were not still there, changes would undoubtedly occur faster than they have already occurred despite a Western presence. Undoubtedly the greatest change would be a very determined attempt by China to dominate its approaches and to redraw further certain of its frontiers. Yet China could not proceed very far with such a policy without soon coming up against determined opposition from neighbors, either ones having great power (the Soviet Union and Japan) or ones presenting more of a problem to conquer (India and Indonesia) than would be worth risking in view of the temptation to China's other neighbors once her back was turned. The only really "soft area" where China has small and weak neighbors is Southeast Asia. Geopolitically, this area is the approach zone to either India and/or Indonesia (for to think of a real full-scale Sino-Indian war over the Himalayas strains credulity). This is the very area (plus the Korean approaches to Japan) that the United States chose to defend in the postwar era and, interestingly enough, against challenges not really directly mounted by China.

What is clear is that the United States role in these affairs has been increasing steadily in magnitude. We have come lately to play the foremost role in resisting violent change. What is not so clear is whether change so long delayed because of Western influence in a day of Chinese weakness can be further delayed primarily by non-Asian power in a day of increasing Chinese strength. What is also not clear is why the United States has chosen to make itself the main champion of the *status quo*. By what stages did the United States come to assume this strenuous role? What influenced that role to take the shape it did?

The U.S. Role in Asia

UNTIL this century U.S. involvement in Asian affairs was slight. Perry's visit to Japan (1853) was no token of a lasting involvement. Only with the taking of the Philippines did the U.S. acquire a meaningful political presence. The "Open Door" notes indicated a U.S. wish for equal commercial access to a Chinese market being cut up and constrained by European "spheres of influence" carved from a weak and impotent China, but not much more. True, by the time of Japan's occupation of Manchuria (1931), the U.S. had registered vehement opposition in the form of the Stimson Doctrine—nonrecognition of territorial changes wrought by force; but the U.S. still did not go beyond verbal condemnation of China's dismemberment. No real temptation to intervene forcibly existed; nor were American armed forces of a size to make it possible. Only in the late 1930's did the U.S. seriously begin to contemplate the eventuality that war with Japan might be unavoidable. Although the U.S. long continued feeding Japan's war machine (to delay an open rupture) she also began to extend aid to China. The outbreak of World War II, the Fall of France, and the occupation of Indo-China by Japanese forces increased tension drastically. Although the U.S. demanded that Japan terminate its program of expansion, it is not clear that the U.S. would have gone to war with Japan except in response to a clear attack on U.S. territories. Yet the American demands led Japan to a decision that war with the U.S. was going to be necessary. Having already a heavy involvement with China and an undeclared war on the Manchurian border with the Soviets, the Japanese might have chosen not to attack the United States had they been unable to make a deal with the Soviet Union. But (April 1941) Japan signed a five-year nonaggression pact with Russia (who thereby sought to avoid a two-front war in the event of a Nazi attack). This event led directly to Pearl Harbor. Whether the U.S. could have countered the Soviet-Japanese pact (once made) is highly questionable. In the long run Russia could no more (in fact, less) accept Japanese domination of China than the U.S. could, but Russia's move had turned Japan loose in the Pacific Ocean areas, and thus Russia had neatly forced the U.S. to act in what were also Soviet interests. Japan, seeing a once-in-a-lifetime opportunity to seize the Dutch East Indies, Malaya, and all the rest of the South Pacific, could not now be stopped except with U.S. force.

As a consequence of World War II, Japan, ironically, lost China at a time when she had fairly well finally subdued her. Japan was disarmed and occupied; and even after she regained control over her own affairs, she continued to play an extremely modest role in Asia. Meanwhile, China was convulsed in civil war, which by 1949 had been resolved on the mainland by a Communist Chinese victory.

No result for China could have more severely jolted the United States. From a balance-of-power standpoint it appeared that a solid Communist bloc had now been brought into existence from the middle of Germany to the shores of the Pacific. The bitterness was further enhanced when Chinese troops entered Korea (1950) to keep North Korea from passing into an American sphere of influence. Responding with hostility, the U.S. now allied herself with Chiang's Nationalist government on Formosa and effectively banned Communist China from a seat in the UN. No diplomatic relations were established, although a form of discussion in Warsaw was carried on intermittently. Even after the Sino-Soviet split became fully apparent, the U.S. pursued its course of opposition to Chinese interests and (1965) intervened again on the periphery of Chinese territory in Viet-Nam. Thus any chances to improve relations continued to be lost.

Yet, analytically speaking, it is apparent that Russia—who (April 1941) succeeded in passing its Asian burden to the United States— is today largely relieved of its full share of concern over China precisely because the U.S. continues to look at China as a potentially dangerous enemy who must be countered primarily through U.S. actions. It is difficult to see why this state of affairs should be encouraged by the U.S. In the case of Japan (1941), the Japanese possessed formidable seapower which had been unused in the war against China, and she had a pressing need for raw material resources that were available in the Indies. The U.S. was forced in her own interests to counter an attempt by Japan to dominate the Western Pacific, even if it could be argued that Russia inevitably would have had to dispute Japan's conquest of China. If China now embarked on a Pacific Ocean expansion à la Japan, the U.S. would be forced to counter it in the same way. This eventually may happen, but it is certainly far down on China's list of projects. She must first at least redress her more obvious grievances against such territorial neighbors who (in the years of her weakness) annexed Chinese territories. Indeed, the maps of the rival Chinese governments on the mainland and on Formosa agree that some 500,000 square miles of what is conventionally considered as part of the Soviet Union really belong to China.

In short, China's main substantive grievance is against Russia, not against the United States. A lack of diplomatic relations with the U.S. is not a Chinese cause for war, nor is the U.S. policy of keeping Peking out of the UN a substantive question in a meaningful sense. As prestige issues, of course they have meaning—but only when viewed in conjunction with U.S. support of Taiwan's pretensions to return to Peking and U.S. military intervention around China's periphery. It is highly unfortunate that a necessary U.S. intervention in Korea (1950) begat a whole series of moves, including SEATO, which cumulatively gave Peking a feeling of U.S.-led encirclement—highly unfortunate because Russia can only escape her full "natural" burden arising out of her long-disputed joint frontier with China because of these U.S. pressures.

The argument reduces to these essentials: much of Sino-American tension arises out of secondary issues in terms of U.S. security, for the U.S. in no way would be less secure if she established diplomatic relations with Communist China, allowed that China a seat in the UN, and formally disassociated herself from Taiwan's revisionist claims. Nor would the U.S. be less secure if American forces were withdrawn in an "honorable" way entirely from the Asian mainland, except in South Korea (i.e., the approach zone to a sensitive and important area: Japan). The reason these actions would not endanger U.S. security is that (excluding a direct but senseless missile attack) China cannot seriously threaten the U.S., except through an expansion into the Western Pacific, which she cannot well do in view of her built-in tensions with the Soviet Union. Because of this China simply does not dare to get seriously involved in prolonged active quarrels with other major Asian nations whom she must in any event challenge if she wants to expand. How could she expand other than through full-scale war with other major Asian nations, except into North Korea or Southeast Asia? Otherwise she must find herself confronting Japan, India, Pakistan, and Indonesia, because it is their territories she would be trying to absorb. None of these nations could be expected to be supine in the face of a direct Chinese attack.

Three objections to this course of action for the U.S. have not as yet been considered. *The first objection:* It can be argued that China could take Southeast Asia (or at least Cambodia, Laos, Thailand, Viet-Nam, and possibly Malaysia) without necessarily finding herself at war with any of the major Asian nations, which at this point would not have been directly attacked in their own territories. True. But if the U.S. were not at the moment allied to Thailand and had not been engaged in a war in Viet-Nam, it would be difficult at the outset to advance a cogent argument as to why the U.S. should feel threatened by such Chinese action—especially if no major Asian nation reacted in kind. Moreover, the other major Asian nations would not be likely to be indifferent to such a development. Indeed it would more likely have a chastening effect on their policies, conceivably bringing into existence an Asian defense arrangement of major nations that might seek logistical backing from the U.S. This would be a vast improvement over a SEATO which is composed of some *minor* Asian powers plus the United States (and other nominal members). Even so, this scenario of an unopposed Chinese triumph in Southeast Asia has an Alice-in-Wonderland character: it is only somewhat believable. This scenario is only given here because it represents the greatest "disaster" imaginable with the major Asian nations not thereby induced to protect themselves.

The second objection (to this course of action): China will not rest until she liquidates her civil war by gaining control of Formosa. This may well be, although one can think of many solutions for Formosa that Peking might accept, which would leave Formosa independent. What Peking *cannot* tolerate on Formosa is a rival government for all China. There is no reason why she should place recovery of Formosa as a piece of territory ahead of her much greater concerns on the Soviet frontier.

The third objection: The picture here painted of U.S. security interests so far in Asia is at variance with the actual U.S. policy and commitments there. This is a valid concern. It is also an accurate indication of how far we have strayed. Even as this is written, the Paris peace talks on Viet-Nam are taking place. Obviously at some date and on some terms these talks will end and the U.S. will evacuate South Viet-Nam. Then Thailand will be left. Could not Thailand be induced to look elsewhere for allies? It is not completely unreasonable to think that she could find Asian neighbors willing to make common accord with her in their own interests. Even under SEATO, presumably France, Great Britain, and Pakistan have just as great an obligation to defend Thailand (or South Viet-Nam) as the United States does. Yet we know from the Viet-Nam War how SEATO obligations work themselves out. If the bonds to Thailand cannot be severed by the U.S. without destroying Thai security, they may have to be kept; but it seems highly unwise for the U.S. to continue a direct commitment to defense on the Asian mainland unless there is absolutely no other alternative. (Obviously the Thais themselves had mixed feelings about the situation.[1])

Rearrangements and retrenchments in U.S. security commitments in Asia could not be accomplished either easily or overnight. Changes would have to occur with due regard for "face," "honor," and such other important intangibles. Yet if no attempt is made to change our course, we are in for more of the same if not worse than we encountered in Viet-Nam. What is important, then, is to chart a new direction. On December 17, 1969, a Senate-House conference committee attached to the defense appropriations bill a prohibition against using U.S. ground combat troops in Thailand or Laos, without the consent of Congress.

In view of the extravagant involvement of the U.S. in Asian affairs in most of the years since World War II, the implications of this new direction may appear to be coterminous with withdrawal, with a "neo-isolationism." This is not meant at all. What is desirable is rather a general return of the U.S. to its pre-1950 involvement in Asia or—more precisely—to its strategy of dominating the Western Pacific, while remaining *offshore*. It would be highly unwise for the U.S. to abandon an active role in Asia, just as this analysis argues that (the special case of Korea aside) it is wrong for the U.S. to accept continental *onshore* involvements and commitments. To the extent that China may attempt expansion into the Western Pacific, she should be countered by U.S. power—presumably assisted by Japan. This is not a likely threat, because China has greater immediate involvements and interests to worry about on the Asian continent. Here, whether Russia likes the role or not, history and geography have cast her in the role of prime container of China in the north. Should China move south or southwest, India, Pakistan, and Indonesia are cast by fate to play the leading roles. In every case except a direct Chinese thrust into the Pacific area, the U.S. does not have (and should not have) the leading role.

When one has made a very sober assessment of the U.S. position in Asia, it is difficult to see why it should essentially go beyond maintaining an offshore presence, with direct alliance links with Japan, and possibly others on a back-up basis. In this conception the U.S. could offer

[1] Foreign Minister Thanat Khoman of Thailand (February 13, 1969) said of 48,000 U.S. troops there: "If after the fighting is over [in Viet-Nam], there is not a compelling reason for the troops to stay, then they will have to leave." He went on to say that the people of Thailand were "not too happy about the presence of foreign troops on Thai soil." *The New York Times* (February 14, 1969).

support if other major nations are constrained to fight in self-defense to repulse threats from a major continental nation. Any such guarantees would be extended to *onshore* areas only when, as a minimum, as with India, they are units that are large enough to be capable of effectively tying down much enemy power. The minimum defense posture envisaged would permit the U.S. to dominate the Pacific Ocean, have defensive links with offshore friendly nations, and maintain only a watching brief (with no commitments) to Asian continental nations. The U.S. could then in conjunction with other Asian major nations supplement if necessary the self-defense actions of continental nations endangered by aggressive moves by other continental nations.

Applying these principles to the concrete case, one reaches the following conclusions: (1) China and Russia have no opportunity to allay their mutual tensions by dividing up a weak nation on their mutual frontier—for there are none between them; (2) China's main territorial grievance is against Russia, consequently Russia might connive in diverting Chinese attention elsewhere, but she would have to act if China concentrated forces in her own direction; (3) if China moved elsewhere she would soon encounter either Japan, Indonesia, or India, (each of whom would have to protect her own interests). And there is no reason why Russia should aid China in that event.

Such a strategic system is one in which China has no real opportunity to find a great power ally actively disposed to aid her aggression. She is self-isolated by the nature of the problem, for what great power will be willing to fight for China's expansion? By the same token China's continental expansion must be stopped in the first place by some major continental nation, because any real expansion there involves China's aggression on some major continental nation. The U.S. role can essentially be restricted to guarding the offshore areas, with a flexible option to supplement self-defense action by a major onshore nation.

The U.S. can be threatened by China today in a realistic sense only if the U.S. puts itself on land, within Chinese reach. As China gathers future strength she may conceivably be tempted to assault the U.S. by missiles. This is unlikely, but it could conceivably happen. But neither the present onshore strategy nor the offshore strategy proposed for the U.S. would significantly affect the Chinese achievement of an intercontinental missile capacity nor directly influence whether and when it might be used. Such a capacity is purely an internal event and is not affected by whether China expands or does not expand; therefore both of the U.S. strategies discussed here are irrelevant to that contingency. Only an assured U.S. second-strike capability can influence Chinese judgment on that point. As to the balance of power in Asia, it is certainly in the U.S. interest to prevent the entire continent of Asia from passing under the control of a single power. It is even more immediately in the vital interests of those Asian nations who would first need to be conquered in order for this dire result to come to pass. Because the U.S. is geographically based far away from Asia, she has an option in this respect and a latitude of choice on how to respond, which geography denies those who live there. Why deny ourselves these advantages?

The Middle East

THE Soviet Union and the United States, neither of them Middle Eastern powers by right of geography, today both play an important role in the region's affairs. In mid-1967, when the "third round" of Israeli-Arab hostility played itself out in one of the shortest wars in modern times, the U.S. and the Soviet Union for the first time used the "hot line," and agreed precariously to stay aloof from direct involvement in the fighting. With peace uneasily restored, by 1968 the U.S. Sixth Fleet and the new Soviet Mediterranean Fleet eyed each other warily. The Soviets continued to supply large quantities of munitions to Arabs bent on revenge, and the U.S. supplied arms to an Israel bent on survival. How curious in a sense that this state of affairs was the direct result of President Nasser's own policy decisions. For Nasser as child cut his teeth on anticolonial slogans and as man set out to free the Arab lands from foreign influence.

U.S. formal commitments in the Middle East are less substantial than in the parts of the world we have already surveyed. Greece and Turkey belong to NATO; then there is CENTO with which the U.S. "associates" itself. There are some somewhat dusty formulas and doctrines left over from earlier years—including the Truman and Eisenhower doctrines— but that is about the extent of our formal commitments here. No Arab state has any formal defense link with the U.S., nor with Russia (although the Soviet presence in the United Arab Republic keeps increasing in size and activity).

Yet that is far from the whole of it, for the American people have a very real emotional connection to Israel and feel a basic sense of responsibility for its continued survival. Many commentators attribute this feeling to the Jewish minority in the U.S., and unquestionably that minority plays a role in influencing American policy. But the American feeling is much deeper and more widespread than that, and any analysis that does not take that into account will go seriously astray. What the American people feel toward Israel can best be described as a collective guilt complex. Having failed to support the League (which "led" to Hitler's successful aggression after Munich), the American people feel a need to make amends for what is seen as their "sin of omission," which allowed Hitler an opportunity to slaughter the greater part of Europe's Jews. Overwhelmingly impressed in retrospect by the great error of appeasement at Munich, and aware that the U.S. sat it out until Hitler

ISRAEL AFTER THE "THIRD ROUND"

MAP 6

made war on *us,* many people feel strongly that the few who escaped Hitler's wrath cannot now be allowed in their turn to be slaughtered by the Arabs. Whether the U.S. should indulge itself in this sentimental approach or not, there is no realistic chance that it would change its basically emotional attitude on the question, short of some act of geno-cide or equivalent horror perpetrated by the Israelis. It is a fundamental fact, not likely to change. (Indeed there are only two other deeply senti-mental, nation-centered notions which are of equal importance in U.S.

foreign policy outside the Americas: the fond "kinship" with Britain, and the odd love-hate relationship with China—whom we saved and who then turned against us.) It goes so deep that it is largely irrelevant whether it makes sense. Only those who believe policy can be formulated in disregard of emotion (for which view this book offers only occasional support) will ignore the very realistic implications of these feelings. They mean that the U.S. would intervene to prevent Israel's destruction.

Probably the great majority of U.S. Foreign Service Officers charged with Arab affairs and academic scholars of Middle Eastern affairs wish this were not so, although far fewer would dispute that it is so. They point to the area, its enormous Arab and small Jewish population, its strategic waterway and large geographical area in Arab hands, its enormous petroleum resources under Arab control, and conclude that the U.S. would do well to be on the Arab side. But the U.S. will not be on the Arab side unless a firm peace with Israel—*de facto* or *de jure*—is concluded by the Arab states. That is why a long course of events had led by 1968–1969 to Soviet pilots overflying U.S. fleet units in the Mediterranean in Soviet-built planes flying from UAR bases with UAR markings.

The point is that Nasser's assessment of U.S. policy toward Israel is basically correct in that he calls her a "Western outpost" in the Arab heartland, even an "imperialist outpost." She is a Western outpost in the basic sense alluded to above. Nasser thus finds himself caught in the difficult position of trying to fight fire with fire, by using Soviet foreigners against Western foreigners. This is a highly dangerous game; but its alternative is to accept Israel's existence and come to terms with it—an alternative as deeply emotion-laden as the U.S. reaction toward the object of Nasser's hatred.

Watching the pendulum of Soviet influence in the area swing ever more sharply toward the increase side, the U.S. reaction is one of anxiety. Yet the cards in Soviet hands to play are not very strong. They know that the Soviet Union is flanked in Europe by a restless Germany and in Asia by a bitter China (with American nuclear might poised, as it were, all around); and Russia seeks to outflank the threats nearer to home by expanding into the vacuum in the Middle East. Seeking the rewards that a true world maritime power may hope to claim as its due, the Soviets by their efforts have created a new and important threat of rivalry with the West.

Yet Soviet access to the Mediterranean is restricted by the Straits at the Bosporus and Dardenelles. One may compare this to the Western access at Gibraltar, but the comparison is not equal. For the Straits are controlled by Turkey and the approach from either north or south leaves little open sea to hide in, whereas Gilbraltar is controlled by Britain with the wide ocean on one side and a large sea area on the other. The Soviets depend on continued Arab willingness to have them present—a willingness strongly tempered by basic Arab distrust of all foreign powers. If it were not for the American emotional feeling already mentioned, and assuming Arab success against the Israelis, the Soviets would doubtless find their reward at that point by being eased out of their Arab foothold (unless by then they were too deeply intrenched). The U.S. does, however, have to be reckoned with; thus the irony is that unless they continue to be careful the Soviets may find themselves drawn into hostilities with the United States. Whether such a result would be more tragically irrelevant to real Soviet interests or real American interests would be a moot but academic point.

Finally, by meddling in Middle Eastern affairs, the Soviets run the risks attendant upon any great power meddling: they cannot long be actively involved without incurring substantial enmity either for what they do or what they do not do. The U.S. involvement, via NATO, runs this risk far less, for it is not so complete an involvement and there are less cross-currents among its friends and allies in the Western Mediterranean than there are potentially or actually among the Arab states. The Arab states presently are obviously divided into the "progressive socialist" and the "conservative monarchies," but are much more fundamentally divided than that—or would be if the Israeli issue were once settled. If Spain and Britain are at odds over Gibraltar (as they are), it is still true that they and other Western nations in the area have had several centuries to adjust to each other's existence. The Arab states, on the contrary, have never truly faced inter-Arab problems because of the Israeli distraction. They have many internal problems as well, which have been put to one side because of that distraction—in some cases, perhaps, gratefully.

It would be false to give the impression that all Arab states have been affected by the Israeli question in fundamentally the same way. Jordan, Syria, and the UAR are directly and obviously affected. Although sharing a common frontier with Israel, Lebanon has normally had little or no "war fever" over the issue, partly because Lebanon is half-Christian in population, but also because Lebanon is too busy profiting from its financial and trade activities to waste its substance. Farther away from Israel, Iraq (primarily because of cross-connections of this issue with internal unrest) has continued to take an active interest in the problem, and in recent years has even stationed part of its army in Jordan. Saudi Arabia is internally highly conservative and opposed to many of its "socialist" Arab neighbors' policies but has lent diplomatic and financial support to anti-Israeli activities. Yet Saudi Arabia's prime attention has been diverted nearer to home toward Yemen, where until mid-1967 and the "third round," the UAR was supporting with troops a republican Yemeni government, attempting to defeat the royalist regime friendly to the Saudis. Still farther away and under moderate leadership, Tunisia has tried on several occasions to urge accepting Israel's existence; whereas Algeria, even farther away, but under "socialist" leadership, has equaled the UAR's vehemence.

The "third round" was initiated in mid-May by Nasser's demand for the UNEF to be removed from its positions on the Sinai border and his decision (May 22) to close the Straits of Tiran to Israeli shipping; and this brought humiliating defeat to the Arab forces. Israel mobilized immediately but could not sustain full mobilization long; the logic of events took over, and (June 5) in a preemptive attack Israeli air power destroyed the UAR air force. Israeli forces in less than six days managed to take the whole Sinai Peninsula, all of Jordan's west bank territories, and the hill positions in Syria overlooking Israel. In the ensuing debates in the UN the U.S. made clear its position that these territories should be restored to Arab hands but linked this development to the achievement of a stable peace settlement. The Soviet Union for its part emphasized withdrawal. In the sequel the Swedish diplomat, Gunnar Jarring, sought as UN mediator to find some way to settlement. As 1969 ended, there had been some slight signs of progress, including rumors that Jordan might accept a separate peace. The Soviets had rearmed Syria and the UAR. Seeking a more impartial image, the U.S. announced a new peace plan for the area, less tolerant of the Israeli position.

What would come of it all was uncertain; where the U.S. interest lay was, on the other hand, very clear: to promote a stable peace. In the Middle East the U.S. policy was much less open to criticism than in the Far East, for in the Middle East the U.S. was not actually intervening with its own forces but rather attempting to encourage the states in the area to resolve their own problems. Although the U.S. announced herself on the first morning of the "third round" as neutral in "thought, word, and deed," the UAR subsequently accused the U.S. of having given intelligence information to Israel—a charge that the UAR later had, in effect, to withdraw. While it is argued above that the U.S. will not tolerate Nasser's proclaimed ambition of May 1967 ("Our objective will be to destroy Israel."), this means only that the U.S. will not tolerate what would amount to control of the Middle East passing into UAR hands. Short of this, many things are possible. It is certainly not unreasonable for the U.S. to favor a settlement that would permit Israeli shipping to pass unhindered through both the Straits of Tiran and through the Suez Canal.

With the impasse continuing, the Suez Canal remained blocked. The Israeli government dug in its forces on the Sinai side of the Canal and indicated its intention to keep the Canal closed until its ships were permitted to use it. Losses in canal revenue to Egypt exerted little economic pressure on Nasser (because Kuwait and Saudi Arabia were making up

Nasser's loss). Soviet frustrations over being unable to use the Canal to put naval forces directly into the Persian Gulf constituted a form of political pressure. Humiliation over a continued Israeli occupation of UAR territories added a psychological pressure. These pressures clearly existed; what was not clear was the UAR policy consequences to which they would lead. The choice was peace or a fourth round. In the meantime, the U.S. had little option but to reequip the Israeli air force to balance the actions of the Soviet Union. Meanwhile, too, Israeli was apparently trying to find formulas that would return the bulk of the occupied areas without undermining Israeli security in the process.

Africa and Latin America

AFRICA and Latin America in some ways pose identical or similar policy problems for the U.S.; in some ways the problems are quite dissimilar. Both areas contain largely "underdeveloped" countries; neither is of great concern to the U.S. unless it passes under unfriendly control. This is even essentially true of the Caribbean area of Latin America, in which the U.S. has time and again indicated its direct concern and interest. The U.S. interest there is not so much to control the area but to prevent its control by others: a position stated as early as the Monroe Doctrine. All over Africa, as all over Latin America, the winds of change are blowing strongly. The U.S. problem is how to keep such change as will occur consonant with her own interests.

Strategically, of course, Africa is no more of an entity than is Latin America. Africa divides into the northern (Moslem) tier of states, facing toward and concerned with the Mediterranean, or with the Middle East. In the center of the continent is "Black Africa," divided into many small states shaped arbitrarily for the most part in their frontiers and composition by the accidents of former colonial control. In the south are black areas under Portuguese control, as well as Rhodesia and South Africa. These three regions (although on a single continent) represent three entirely distinct problems with distinct strategic implications for the United States. Latin America can similarly be divided for strategic purposes into three regions: the Caribbean area, the north-central area dominated by Brazil, and the southern area. Each of the two continents by virtue of geographical shape has a north nearer the zones of direct super power interest and confrontation and a south somewhat remote from those zones. The northern regions have been affected far more by the Cold War. It is no accident that communism has gained a foothold in Cuba first and has threatened to become installed elsewhere in the Caribbean crescent, rather than further south. It is no accident that Algeria has received massive arms aid from the Soviet Union and that the most "leftist" areas have been in the northern parts of Africa. Only the rather unusual accident of events threatened to put the Soviet Union and the United States into a competition for control in the Congo. This does not mean that super power competition could not be extended southward in both continents; it merely means that the northern areas are of greater interest to both super powers.

Certain factors differ in nature from Africa to Latin America but are similar in effects and could nonetheless push the southern areas in each case nearer the status of active super power competition. The great ferment of socioeconomic change in Latin America with its soaring population could produce a species of Communist government that would give the U.S. concern. In the southern parts of Africa the great unresolved racial issue could bring about a situation involving the U.S. and the Soviets far more significantly than at present.

Progress and Reform in Latin America

IN Latin America today—apart from what the future may bring—the United States faces the problem of Castro's Cuba (and its ramifications extending to the Dominican Republic, Venezuela, and other places). Cuba for long was dominated by a domestic tyranny of the right, now succeeded by a form of tyranny of the left. True, these tyrannies have not been completely similar in their effects. In Batista's day, no one paid much attention to such simple but important matters as bathing beaches and recreation facilities for the poor and dispossessed. Castro does. On the other hand, the general standard of living is worse now than ever before, as Castro's policies have cost him Cuba's natural markets for sugar and tobacco. It is true that Castro has given individual Cubans pride in their ability to defy the U.S., and that he broke the U.S. stranglehold on the Cuban economy (whose benefits to most Cubans were somewhat minimal), but he has done so at the cost of dependence on alien Russia. One control of one sort has been substituted for another control of a different sort. Arbitrary police measures, rump trials, and executions are even worse under Castro; and Castro has attempted to export his brand of violence. The United States has generally responded with a policy of isolating Cuba, and there appear to be no better alternatives.

Behind all the fine words of the "Alliance for Progress," there is a rather ugly reality: there are millions of dispossessed in Latin America who have little stake in the *status quo*. In many of the countries where real economic progress has been made the opportunity for the masses to share potentially in the fruits of progress exists. In these countries the severe material pressures confronting large numbers of people are not further compounded by a political structure reserving power for an elite group. Mexico, Brazil, Venezuela, even Argentina fall into this

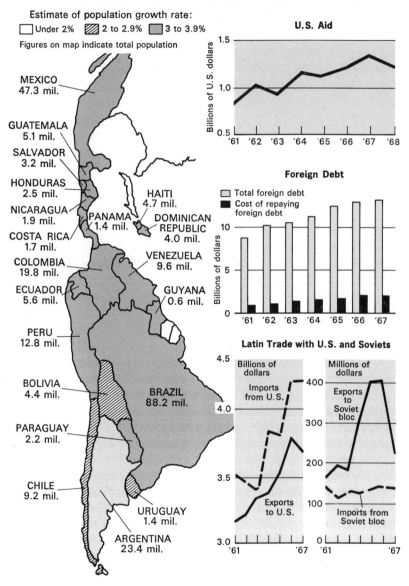

LATIN AMERICA: A CONTINENT IN TRANSITION

Estimate of population growth rate:

☐ Under 2%   ▨ 2 to 2.9%   ■ 3 to 3.9%

Figures on map indicate total population

MEXICO
47.3 mil.

GUATEMALA
5.1 mil.

SALVADOR
3.2 mil.

HONDURAS
2.5 mil.

NICARAGUA
1.9 mil.

PANAMA
1.4 mil.

COSTA RICA
1.7 mil.

COLOMBIA
19.8 mil.

ECUADOR
5.6 mil.

PERU
12.8 mil.

BOLIVIA
4.4 mil.

PARAGUAY
2.2 mil.

CHILE
9.2 mil.

HAITI
4.7 mil.

DOMINICAN
REPUBLIC
4.0 mil.

VENEZUELA
9.6 mil.

GUYANA
0.6 mil.

BRAZIL
88.2 mil.

URUGUAY
1.4 mil.

ARGENTINA
23.4 mil.

U.S. Aid

Billions of U.S. dollars
1.5
1.0
0.5
'61 '62 '63 '64 '65 '66 '67 '68

Foreign Debt

☐ Total foreign debt
■ Cost of repaying foreign debt

Billions of dollars
10
5
0
'61 '62 '63 '64 '65 '66 '67

Latin Trade with U.S. and Soviets

Billions of dollars
4.5
4.0
3.5
3.0
'61   '67

Imports from U.S.

Exports to U.S.

Millions of dollars
400
300
200
100
0
'61   '67

Exports to Soviet bloc

Imports from Soviet bloc

MAP 7

category. (It would be false to separate these nations on the grounds that some are and some are not dominated by military regimes.) But in many other Latin American states there is neither sufficient economic progress nor a reasonable opportunity for popular will to prevail. Some of these states in turn have authoritarian regimes that rule oppressively; in others there is benevolent paternalism. It is a very mixed picture, with more often than not a crying need for land reform existing.

These observations are not intended to imply that the "Alliance for Progress" is not an excellent concept, built as it is on the proposition that U.S. aid makes most sense when coupled with domestic self-help. Even so, nothing the U.S. has done or is likely to contemplate doing will avoid the likelihood of violent change in the years ahead in Latin America. The "Dominican situation" will reappear: the dilemma for the U.S. turns on the simple fact that Communists will be on the side of change and will be a part of any movement for reform.

What was most important about the U.S. intervention in the Dominican Crisis (1965) is that it identified the U.S. in many Latin eyes with a determination to preserve the *status quo*. If the young reformer in Latin America becomes convinced that joining forces with communism is the only path to effective change, the U.S. can expect more Communist nations in Latin America. The U.S. intervention in the Dominican Republic may have averted communism there (although it is not clear that it would have turned out that way at all), but it did so through an action which would have been obviously illegal if the Latin American states had not rescued us from the stain of a unilateral action. It is highly significant that later efforts of the U.S. to create a permanent Latin American "peace force" were greeted by an obvious lack of enthusiasm. The greater number of those states who (because of their own lack of adequate reform measures) may as individual nations later call on the U.S. to repeat its Dominican action refused to sanction this effort.

When one considers the unanimity with which the OAS supported the U.S. (1962) over the Cuban Missile Crisis (with its clear external security overtones), the grudging support in 1965 (where the issue was essentially domestic), and the subsequent lack of support for a permanent force (which might be used for either), the picture is reasonably clear. Where the U.S. is directly threatened by a Soviet military presence, the U.S. can expect Latin support. In other cases it would do well to act if at all only after the majority of the Latin states make it quite clear that they favor action. The point here is similar to the one made about our actions in the Far East, where we ourselves have taken initiatives that we believed to be in the majority interest, and then have had to beat the bushes to have the majority come out and support us.

A simple policy of nonintervention under any and all circumstances is unrealistic for both the U.S. and Latin America. There can be crises, as in Cuba (1962), which threaten the Western Hemisphere too directly to be countenanced. Yet a policy of unilateral intervention by the U.S. has such obvious negative features as to be unfeasible. The moral of the story is that the U.S. must curb its impatience and obtain genuine support before acting in anything but desperate circumstances— very conservatively interpreted.

The Latin American states today are governed in many instances directly by military men. In virtually every Latin state the attitude of the military is crucial to the continuance in power of the government. In most Latin states the military are either the sole really efficient arm of government or one of the few efficient instruments at its command. In many states the military is also an efficient source of progress through civic action: building bridges and roads, teaching, aiding the sick, and inoculating against disease. It is for this reason that one cannot generalize that military rule or military influence in government in Latin America should be opposed by the United States. In some Latin states a semblance of constitutional government exists today *because* the armed forces have intervened and prevented civil coups. No generalization for U.S. policy here would be appropriate except a pragmatic one, judging the merits of the particular case. But the observation permits another one, connected to it: that the U.S. would be well advised to recognize any government effectively in power, whether it sympathizes with that government or not. Otherwise the U.S. is in the intolerable position of making decisions on the merit of the regimes.

Finally, in terms of Latin America, it is clear that the desire of their armed forces for American military equipment, if heeded, has a generally adverse effect for U.S. goals by potentially sparking a minor arms race but even more by diverting scarce resources from economic progress. Yet if Latin nations persist in their quest for arms, and if other sources of supply are open to them, and they show willingness to take advantage of those sources, it does not redound to U.S. interests to deny supplies. The most that can probably be done is to attempt to prevent the creation of overwhelmingly greater power in the hands of two rivals. In addition, the U.S. economic aid program can quite properly be adjusted to take account of Latin failures in reform or progress which clearly are caused by the diversion of resources to arms. Beyond that, there is little the U.S. can do.

Clearly what this adds up to is a policy that does not attempt except very sparingly to tell Latin Americans how to run their own affairs.

The African Dilemma

Equally difficult for the U.S. is the great unresolved racial issue in the southern parts of Africa. Partly this is a purely colonial issue: Portuguese

Africa does not have self-rule and independence. Partly it is an issue of the internal distribution of power: in both Rhodesia and South Africa white self-governing Africans keep black Africans from power in their own countries. To the Black African states these two issues appear to be one issue, but they are so only in the sense that in neither case does the black majority rule. Otherwise there is a great deal of difference, for Rhodesia and South Africa control their own affairs, whereas Portuguese Africa is ruled from Lisbon. In both sets of cases the situation is complicated by the fact that many of the whites in this area are native-born. This is like the problem of the French in Algeria, some of whom had lived there since the 1830's. But it is also unlike the Algerian problem in that the Afrikaners (descendents of the Boers) have no homeland to return to. They are no longer "Dutch" in the sense that the Algerian whites remained "French." Their settlements go back to 1652, and today's Afrikaners are descended for the most part from immigrants who were in South Africa by 1707. To require these people today to "return" to Holland would be a bit more farfetched than to suggest that the descendants of early American settlers "return" today to England. Also, most of the large black population there today is not originally native to the area but was initially imported from other areas of Africa as slaves. Quite a complicated problem results.

The continued existence of Portuguese Africa long after most colonialism had been dismantled in the world demonstrates how much colonialism's demise stemmed from the wish of the colonial power to give independence, rather than from the effectiveness of the local pressures for freedom. Portugal is weaker by far than France and Britain and still hangs on to her colonies long after other powers have left. Partly this results from Portugal's isolation from the mainstreams of Western modern thought, isolation from the effects of industrialization, and so forth. Portugal also continues to consider these colonies important (again perhaps a reflection of lack of industrialization and growth at home) in economic terms. Despite African efforts, the U.S. feels the need for bases in the Azores, shies away from pressuring its NATO ally, and has tried as much as possible to avoid the issue—which would seem to be a correct policy. Here one can say that a problem exists, and no doubt it will ultimately be solved by Portuguese withdrawal; but it is not America's problem.

Rhodesia and South Africa, as independent but white-dominated states, are another issue. There is also an important difference between them in that Rhodesia's white population dates back only to the last part of the nineteenth century. This means that from the standpoint of abstract justice one might argue that the Rhodesians could be "sent home" if they do not choose to give power to the black majority. Yet, Rhodesia and South Africa are both neighbors and subjected to the same pressures from most of Black Africa; therefore in a practical sense they will be likely to stand or fall together. It is hard to envisage South Africa permitting Rhodesian resistance to collapse, simply holding aloof. But this means that the UN economic sanctions against Rhodesia either ultimately will fail to bring Rhodesia to heel or will need to be extended to South Africa. On November 7, 1968, the General Assembly (86–9, with 19 abstentions) voted to strengthen sanctions against Rhodesia and extend them to include Portugal and South Africa. The U.S. voted against this measure. Severe economic measures against South Africa would also be disastrous to Britain's solvency because of financial links; and South Africa is the most important producer of gold in the world and has considerable economic importance to the West. Moreover, since the South Africans have no place to go, in the end they would doubtless fight.

Here (as indicated in Chapter 17) the U.S. has again been cautious (which would seem to be the correct policy). A factor in the U.S. handling of this situation is, of course, that the U.S. has a large black population. Yet the sense of identification of the U.S. black citizens with African problems is nothing like the Jewish minority's identification with Israel. More important, the "Munich complex" does not exist in this case. Much of black American sympathy for Black Africa is a somewhat tenuous reverse side of the coin of a wish to demonstrate ancient cultural roots and provoke further progress in advancing black interests within the United States. Pressures from U.S. Negroes on the U.S. government over Africa are therefore partially deflected in other directions.

Even if this were not so, a cautious, rather neutral U.S. policy would seem best. It is difficult to believe that a policy of U.S. involvement against South Africa could lead to anything other than an eventual bloody affair in which large numbers of Black Africans would be killed. Although the U.S. cannot prevent the Black African states from waging war on South Africa if they acquire the necessary armaments to attempt it, certainly it would be very foolish of the U.S. to do it for them.

Where all these thoughts lead will be made clear in our next and last chapter.

PART FIVE

Conclusions

CHAPTER 19

One Foot in the Future

THE problems confronting U.S. foreign policy (surveyed in Part Four) are formidable. They lend themselves neither to agreed nor easy answers. Indeed, some of the conclusions reached in the last four chapters will be uncongenial to almost anyone. Conservatives may applaud the view that Latin American military regimes are not *ipso facto* retrogressive, that the military frequently plays a large part in Latin American progress; but they will not be likely to applaud the skepticism shown over U.S. intervention in the Dominican Republic. They will be likely to agree that it is not the duty of the U.S. to carry the "black man's burden" in Africa but look askance at the proposition that U.S. policy in Southeast Asia is counterproductive to U.S. interests. They will probably greet with approval the signs of Soviet difficulties shown but be skeptical as to whether the Communist "monolith" is not "still" in existence.

Liberals, on the other hand, although they may agree that the interventions in Viet-Nam and in the Dominican affair were probably mistakes, may recoil from the thought that the economic well-being of the U.S. cannot be replicated all over the world. The skepticism shown over the prospects for stability in the developing world may be greeted equally negatively. The coolness of the observations about the UN, especially the negative view over intervention in Africa against the white minority, may not be very acceptable.

If these guesses are accurate, they point to the two subquestions at the heart of the great question of *how* to make U.S. foreign policy succeed: (1) where and how and with whom to commit American resources; (2) where and how and with whom to make commitments of support. Some would prefer that we do little or nothing outside our own frontiers, but these probably represent the smallest group in the contemporary American "interested and aware public." A larger group, whose ranks appear to be thinning today, argue instead that American defeats and failures stem largely from faltering application of sound propositions: that the U.S. is too important to play a role less involved than its power can support, that our difficulties stem from a lack of resolution in fully carrying out our principles. This group, who essentially want the U.S. to police the world, are not dismayed (although disappointed) if the U.S. finds itself committed with little or minor support from other nations. What counts for them is the "rightness" of what we are doing. They are likely in most cases to approve of the three formulas that bulked so large in the new age of American foreign policy after 1945: oppose aggression, contain communism, support freedom. They are likely to think of the implementation of these formulas primarily via U.S. armed strength, and through a bloc-containment, direct power application, forward deployment strategy. Many of them would criticize American policy only where we have not fought to win. Indeed, part of the erosion in this group, to augment the ranks of the first group, is a result of the Viet-Nam War experience: the conclusion being reached that it is better not to fight than to fight "with one hand tied."

Obviously, this is too simple an analysis of feeling or attitude as it stands, for among the "globalists" are also a great (even predominant) number who both approve the formulas and yet accept the limitations on their application as legitimate and necessary. Former Secretary of State Rusk's letter, quoted in Chapters 1 and 14, shows his concurrence with the formulas. Yet clearly he also concurred with the policy of restraint in Viet-Nam which kept the U.S. from mining the harbor of Haiphong, inundating North Viet-Nam by destroying the dikes through bombing, or "taking the enemy out" through the use of nuclear weapons. But other terminology to describe these differences of feeling and attitude is even less helpful, for the "hawks" are by no means all globalists and the "doves" are by no stretch of the imagination all neo-isolationists.

It is meaningful to typify American approaches to U.S. policy problems in terms of how far to be involved, where to be involved, or with whom to be involved. But the really critical differences turn on *how* to be involved (i.e., what strategy to use).

An Overview of the Argument

THE United States in its first decades faced a difficult but quite obvious foreign policy problem: to survive, to buy time, to expand as opportunity presented itself, and conversely to seek Europe's withdrawal from the periphery of American frontiers. All of these objectives were achieved through a strategy that took realistic advantage of the workings of the balance of power. Immersed in mid-century with continental development and civil war, the U.S. for some decades had little foreign policy involvements at all—and scrupulously held aloof from extra-American adventures. By the turn of the nineteenth century, the U.S. had grown great in power but, until the Spanish-American War, modest in commitment. With the taking of the Philippines, all that began to change. The

U.S. became a Pacific power and shortly thereafter intervened decisively in Europe to restore the balance of power. Having retreated for a time into "isolationism," the U.S. shortly found itself again playing a world role that bit by bit took on increased dimensions. With enormous power at its disposal, the U.S. found difficulty choosing what not to do. From a temporary intervention in Europe came a prolonged American armed presence; from an offshore role in Asia, she moved to two limited but onshore wars. By the late 1960's the rationale for these extensive commitments was under attack. The questions asked had a central thrust: granted that a super power, especially in a nuclear age, has to be involved and concerned with world affairs, and has to play a meaningful role, by what standards did one realistically assess the nature and extent of the necessary commitments? What were the objectives, what alternative grand strategies could achieve those objectives (and at what cost)? The answers given to those questions varied most importantly with how the nature of international relations was perceived.

Even the first step of defining objectives properly depended critically on a realistic understanding of the world environment in which U.S. foreign policy must function. If the U.S. chose after 1945 to oppose aggression, contain communism, and defend freedom, it did so with serious misconceptions.

It was widely believed that aggressions form a chain reaction, ultimately threatening U.S. security, and that history showed therefore that it was better to face the threat when it first appeared. As Dean Rusk said, World War II "could have been prevented" if "the world community" had acted at the time of the Manchurian and Ethiopian crises, and then later in Central Europe. There is no convincing historical evidence for this view. Indeed the evidence points instead to the critical failure of Britain and France to come to terms with the Soviet Union if they wished to constrain Hitler. That evidence has no tangible link to Manchuria or Ethiopia. Believed as an abstract principle, though, it led logically to a U.S. policy opposing aggression *per se*, with little thought as to its real relevance to U.S. interests.

It was widely believed that communism was a monolithic force, defying and overcoming the traditional force of nationalism. From this assumption it followed that Communist nations constituted a hostile and indissoluble bloc. China and Russia, China and North Korea, China and North Viet-Nam, all were the same enemy acting out of the same interests. Any Communist enemy thus represented all, and a hostile move by one was considered a hostile move by all. The historical evidence, of course, indicates that this is a great oversimplification, that Communist China is no puppet of the Soviet Union, nor are North Korea and North Viet-Nam puppets of either.

It was widely believed that the defense of freedom abroad was in

U.S. interests, although in practice the U.S. interpreted the principle to be at stake largely only when Communist subversion or attack was involved. It was assumed that "free nations" have a sufficient importance to each other that they have by that fact of freedom a common vital interest. The historical evidence indicates that the forces that produce alliances against a common foe have little to do with whether the parties are all or equally "free," and that other less grave conflicts of interest equally defy the standard of free-unfree.

The objectives defined in the Truman Doctrine and many other post-war policy statements of the U.S. thus failed to measure up to a critical comparison with the historical evidence. Given the unusual nature of the American experience, it could be expected that the U.S. might under-value certain forces at work in international affairs and therefore make generalized judgments on weak historical grounds. A realistic under-standing of balance of power phenomena was especially lacking—and that gap in itself was critical. For example, in approaching Asian prob-lems after World War II, the U.S. by its policy indicated a belief that its active intervention would, could, or should make all the difference, but failed to muster significant support for that policy. The less Asian support we received, the greater became our own commitment. (Com-pare Korea and Viet-Nam.) Nor was our political system, with its tendency toward center consensus and "bipartisanship," well adapted to posing strategic alternatives—especially in a nation not given to much historical speculation. Compounding these weaknesses was the tendency toward abstract analysis of strategic questions in terms undervaluing national behavioral differences, within a nuclear environment frame-work believed to make much of traditional knowledge obsolete. With ICBM's making feasible strikes at enormous distances, it could easily be assumed that geography had lost its former meaning—which was only partly true.

On the positive side, American foreign policy had substantial success in Europe after 1947, because the actual conduct of the U.S., even if carried out in the name of these three formulas, correlated quite well in general outline with elementary considerations of national prudence. The Soviet overextension into the heart of Europe was dangerous and had to be contained. Any temptation to aggression had to be removed. The freedom of the major Western European powers had to be pre-served. All this was necessary purely to keep the balance of power from turning against the U.S. These three formulas were not inconsistent with balance of power principles, even though they did not make best use of balance of power wisdom in that they consistently treated all the European Communist states (except Yugoslavia) as a solid bloc. By this failure to capitalize on the divergencies among the European Communist states, and their friction with the Soviets, the U.S. unnecessarily threw away an important card. Worse, the U.S. assumed a Sino-Soviet unity, which influenced us to follow an Asian policy with quite apparent defects.

Following these formulas in Europe led to the elaboration of instruments admirably suited to the job: the Marshall Plan and the North Atlantic Pact. Through these devices the great strength of Western Europe was effectively revived and coordinated, successfully putting a limit to any further Soviet expansions. This coalition held against Khrushchev's intense battering. From a politico-military defensive point of view the NATO strategy passed the test. Where it could be faulted was in its tendency to bypass the unsuitability of the *status quo,* with its division of Europe on an arbitrary line drawn through the middle of Germany. For both U.S. and Soviet troops to continue for a quarter century or more to be deployed immediately opposite each other in Europe was not only a sign of the tension and distrust continuing between them but of the mutual danger that they confronted by their failure to agree on some alternative. However important it was to keep the Soviets from advancing, it was even more important to induce them to retreat.

The defensive success of these formulas as executed through these instrumentalities raised American hopes that the same formulas could be exported to Asia with similar results. But SEATO, unlike NATO, never gained major Asian nation support. Consequently the U.S. played a disproportionate role and carried the major burden. Once U.S. deployments began with the Korean War and then the Viet-Nam War to also move onshore, the U.S. found itself holding beachheads on the periphery of Chinese frontiers with a consequent deflection of Chinese Communist anxieties away from the Soviet Union. From a defensive point of view, holding South Korea could be considered appropriate insofar as it guarded the approaches to Japan; but the occupation of South Vietnamese territory had a much less clear strategic purpose, coupled with clear disadvantages. The major defects in this U.S. Asian strategy were its extensive and fairly unilateral military involvement in forward onshore positions, its lack of Asian great power support, and its mitigation of Sino-Soviet tensions.

Where the disadvantages in both the Europe and Asian strategies came to a similar focus is that they each involved the U.S. in carrying the burden of advanced military deployment positions, thus ensuring great expense and risks.

The question then becomes whether other arrangements, other strategies, could reduce these disadvantages and risks without themselves creating greater negative consequences for the U.S. The answer to that question turns essentially on whether the U.S. can take greater advantage of the seven basic features of the nation-state system described in

Chapter 14, and in the light of the perspective thus gained, ask the strategic questions of Chapter 1 in the correct order. Obviously, the U.S. must be completely clear first on what it wants to see done, then on who can or will oppose or assist, and only then arrive at the conclusion as to how to succeed at minimum cost.

The U.S. should have as its strategic objectives a roll-back of Soviet influence in Europe, the prevention of Chinese hegemony in Asia, and the establishment of a viable degree of political-military stability—all at minimum cost and risk.

The argument in this book is that these objectives can be realized— if at all—only at great costs and risks by a strategic foreign policy of bloc containment, and that what is needed instead is an opponent-isolating strategy. It has been further argued that who can or will oppose or assist U.S. strategic objectives cannot properly be answered on ideological grounds. The essential clues to behavior in the world system are to be found in the seven principles of Chapter 14. Behind the workings of these principles is the influence of location and its subtle effects on counterbalancing interests. Let us look in turn at the implications of *geographical location* on behavior and its cross-connections to the concept of *counterbalancing national interests.*

Reality and Image: Geography and Strategy

THINKING through the politico-military meaning of geographical fact in the contemporary world is difficult. There is a shortage of thought on this question, which is so fundamental; and "geopolitics," by reason of some of its past excesses, has earned a dubious reputation. Scholars concerned with defense issues have predominantly turned their attention to modern management procedures in the Department of Defense, to the psychology of crisis management, to theories of nuclear deterrence, to speculation on the probable nature of nuclear war. These are all meaningful questions, provided these analyses are adequately correlated with the contemporary implications of geographic fact and the actual behavior of nations in the present nuclear environment. Missiles launched anywhere in the world can reach targets, no matter how far distant, in forty minutes; therefore there is an inevitable tendency to regard all states as immediate neighbors of each other. People tend to assume that the older body of conclusions about the interfaces of geography and foreign policy are either no longer valid or only marginally so, but this assumption has not been examined rigorously, either through logical analysis or through correlation with actual state behavior. What we need to know is which, if any, of the geopolitical generalizations of yesteryear are no longer valid, or if all such generalizations no longer apply.

These are difficult questions to pose since they cut across popular folklore. One strains patience when one says: "Yes, the world has shrunk, but in what ways has it not?" Capsules flying in space, missiles plowing through the stratosphere, airplanes cutting cross-country through the air, all seem in principle immune from earlier geographical constraints. We forget that the bulk of trade and communication is still carried by sea and follows well-established ocean routes, that most air traffic does not bind the continents across the poles. We forget that the bulk of the world's population is in the northern hemispheres, that all the world's great cities are in the temperate zone, that the straits scattered around the world remain critical points. Yet all these things are still all true—and have important consequences.

From the existence of a U.S. ICBM capability sufficient to destroy Russia twice or more, one might logically argue that the U.S. has no rational need for allies or for foreign bases. The same observation applies in reverse to the Soviet Union. If war came, and it involved a mutual all-out nuclear launching, any additional damage resulting from the missile launchings of allies and any aid that allies could render would presumably be superfluous. Why have allies or foreign bases? Yet neither super power acts as if it thought allies and bases superfluous.

It can be argued that each believes that the inevitable mutual destruction will prevent war from becoming nuclear (at least in the all-out strategic sense), and thus conventional armies and forces will be used, and allies and foreign bases will be needed. Wars will be fought in conditions of restraint, with less than the arsenals available and therefore (by implication) for less than total victory. If this is true, deploying troops on foreign soil is also a very effective deterrence, preventing the enemy from taking that territory without war (and its possible all-out escalation). Precisely because of the "balance of terror," it may be critical to eliminate power vacuums (i.e., areas which, since not occupied by one's forces, could be taken without automatically starting war by inflicting damage and death on one's nationals). In that case the premium is on leaving no area neutral or vacant between the potential belligerents. They are "safest" when they are dug in opposite one another along every conceivable front, at every conceivable point.

How does this conclusion square with actual American and Soviet behavior? Up to a point, quite well. Consider the Iron Curtain in Germany. But in other respects, not well. Consider Swiss neutrality, Austrian neutrality—perhaps one ought to include Yugoslavian "neutrality." And Sweden is outside NATO, as Finland is outside the Warsaw Pact. Curiously enough, from this viewpoint, neither is being coerced to join the one pact or the other. Can some areas be left unoccupied, then? But if Sweden and Finland might be called peripheral, what of Switzerland

and Austria, plus Yugoslavia? And is Finland, the gateway to Leningrad, peripheral?

What do these facts mean? Do we conclude that in some cases opposing troops must be deployed to keep the enemy constrained, and in other cases nations are permitted to opt for neutrality and their word is accepted as sufficient? Do we conclude that one side or the other would like to change this by occupation of the neutrals, but cannot do so without starting a war? (Yet Austria was actually occupied and divided for ten years after the war before it was mutually evacuated.) Or do we conclude that only certain areas are considered so important that they cannot be evacuated (i.e., Germany)? Is this why it was possible for the U.S. and USSR to reach agreement on Austria but not on Germany? Is control of some geographical areas critical, and the occupation of such areas and their continued division (where it exists) the only safe policy?

Actual U.S. and Soviet behavior over Germany strongly indicates that they consider it a crucial area. Since American-Soviet behavior in other areas like Austria has not been consistent with the "frontal confrontation is safest" hypothesis, they evidently believe that some areas are critical to their security under present circumstances (and what happens in those areas is of prime importance and concern), while just as clearly they are willing to exclude certain other areas from competition. They choose to compete in some places but not in all places. Equivalent geographically related value judgments are reflected respectively in U.S. concern over France's "defection" from NATO, and Soviet concern over Czechoslovakia's wish to find her own way. What cannot be deduced from Soviet-American behavior is whether they consider that keeping critical areas like Germany occupied and divided is necessary under present circumstances, or under all circumstances.

While all these examples concern Europe, the principle is the same elsewhere. Modern nuclear arsenals have evidently not changed the fundamental value perceived in having allies and bases, although it may have modified the way these values would be counted. Geographical considerations are still highly important today, meaning not terrain and area for its own sake, but position and location linked with the policy inclinations of those who hold important positions or strategic locations. Actual Soviet behavior indicates that they would feel far less secure, even with a full nuclear capability, if they were to withdraw into their own frontiers and dissolve their pacts, while the U.S. did not. Whether each super power could afford to withdraw from Germany if the other would, and what effects this would have, is another question. The United States and the Soviet Union in Europe are like two swordsmen whose sword-arms are for the moment locked together, and each of whom also fears being knifed in the back by a third contender in Asia. It is difficult to step back and dangerous not to.

This is the point where counterbalancing interests come in. Are the two super powers each safer by being deployed closer together or not? Does confrontation actually increase the risk of violence or lessen it? What can be done, if they draw further apart, to prevent a dangerous power vacuum? Are two enemies, each with a nuclear arsenal, more deterred from war if each is deprived of the foreign bases such allies provide? What will important third states in other geographically important areas be doing which affect one's interests under each variation of deployment—from confrontation all the way to withdrawal?

Reality and Image: Counterbalancing Interests

ONE of the seven principles laid down in Chapter 14 is that no nation is a set-piece but rather responds to conflicting needs in a variety of ways in different periods of time. No relationship among nations in a multilateral environment can be purely or exclusively bilateral. Even if both the Soviet Union and the United States act on the correct assumption that, given their nuclear strike capability and the serious divergence of their respective national interests, each must fear and regard the other as a potential prime enemy, neither can ignore third party considerations.

Nations have a whole spectrum of interests and fears whose importance to them varies with time and circumstances. The options open to them are limited by the past history of those interests and fears, by where those nations are located, and (especially) by the policies of other nations involved. Any option taken reflects the subordination of other options (of counterbalancing interests), but those counterbalancing interests do not disappear; they are simply submerged. Under changed conditions, under circumstances where policy changes are made by other states, the submerged options can be re-evaluated and new choices made. How much the decisions of any one state create or inhibit flexibility for others in choosing or rejecting options varies enormously, but certainly the choices made by the U.S. have very great effects upon both Soviet and Chinese behavior.

If two potential enemies of the U.S. are also potential enemies of each other, and each of the three has anxieties about the other two, which set of anxieties proves decisive has a great deal to do both with geography and with the foreign policy strategy followed by the other two. The three-way antagonism is fixed, as it were, in its general nature, but which way the teams are formed reflects what goals are set and how the game is played. If we choose, for example, to make ourselves prominent in China's immediate vicinity, we influence both Chinese and Russian behavior in a meaningful fashion. For the basic question each nation asks itself in choosing and rechoosing options is: who (which state, or which states) constitutes at this time the gravest threat? Given full nuclear arsenals, the threat is not eliminated by distance, but, on the other hand, a lack of "distance" makes the full nuclear arsenal more meaningful and converts a potential threat into a perceived menace. Confrontation deployments tend to raise tensions steeply.

Nations who do not share frontiers have many more deployment options open to them than merely confrontation; therefore the common-sense observation that one cannot choose one's enemy or enemies needs careful qualification. Besides, before "choosing enemies," there are always third states and their policies to consider. In the same way, the common-sense observation that the essential need of a threatened state is to collect allies is not quite true as stated. It may be equally or more important to deny your potential enemy allies or to dissolve his coalition (through appeal to counterbalancing interests).

For these reasons, the common-sense observation that the best way to do a job is to do it yourself is in serious need of qualification. Others may not only have to do it if you do not, but will not do it if you do it for them. In Western Europe, whether the U.S. actually makes alliances or not, the U.S. has "natural" allies in the form of those states who would suffer (or do suffer) from Soviet expansion; just as in Asia the U.S. has "natural" allies in those states who would suffer (or do suffer) from Chinese expansion. This means that in principle China can be made to help restrain Russia in Europe and in Asia, while Russia can be made to help restrain China. But since the Sino-Soviet bilateral relationship occurs in a multilateral world, other considerations can and do offset that bilateral relationship under certain circumstances. In particular, a large and continued U.S. onshore involvement in Asia can offset the Sino-Soviet hostility.

The availability of allies to a would-be expansive state can be a crucial variable in the results. If China has nuclear arms but has no foreign bases or allies she by that fact is much restricted in what she can do. (Essentially this is the actual case unless one includes North Korea, North Viet-Nam, and Soviet Russia—all dubious or qualified from this viewpoint.) Consider the geopolitical impact if Russia were really with her, or what it would mean if Japan, or India, or Indonesia were to be allied to China. The whole balance of power in Asia would be altered. It makes a great difference whether China does or does not have allies. Without allies she might still bring destruction to others, but at the price of destruction to herself. With allies she would automatically attain a larger "presence" and influence, to "be" where she presently is not, with further unsettling effects. An alliance between China and *any* other major Asian nation would have important policy effects in Asia, quite apart from specific Chinese actions, purely because of the "position" change—with lesser effects if the allies are smaller powers.

It follows that the direct route for the U.S. to Chinese containment in Asia is by keeping other major Asian nations out of alliances with China, rather than by onshore beachhead periphery involvement. Since there are no compelling reasons for any major Asian nation to actively support China, this result is certainly attainable.

The "beachhead" concept in the U.S. forward deployment in Asia followed in the 1960's makes quite different assumptions. It assumes that U.S. counterforce is directly required onshore to keep Southeast Asia, as a power vacuum, from passing into Chinese hands. This confrontation deployment would have worse effects on the tension level except that the Chinese do not maintain troop units in either North Korea or North Vietnam. If, on the other hand, a Chinese armed presence in Southeast Asia were introduced, because it would escalate her "position" effect, China would become a greater threat to Indonesia, India, Burma, and Thailand. Therefore, if China advanced, important Asian opposition to it would automatically be present which the U.S., upon request, could support. From any point of view except the fear that Chinese advances would meet no opposition in Asia, the conclusion that an offshore, opponent-isolating strategy makes sense for the U.S. in Asia is difficult to refute. It makes the most effective use of the interaction of location and counterbalancing interests.

We have looked first at Asia because U.S. deployments there can be more easily altered without serious risks to important positions, whereas in Europe a U.S. pullback without an equivalent Soviet withdrawal might be very dangerous. If any such change of strategy by the U.S. in Asia came about, it would drastically increase overall pressures upon the Soviet Union, something the Russians understand very well—and fear.

For 25 years, the Soviets have been able to maintain an overextended presence in Europe involving limited risks because they have had little to fear from the Chinese so long as the U.S. obligingly distracted their attention toward Korea, Taiwan, and South Viet-Nam. This comfortable state of affairs would come to an end. (Even without actual U.S. onshore withdrawal from Viet-Nam, but merely with its presumed approach, serious Sino-Soviet border clashes occurred.)

Ideally the U.S. objective in Europe is to induce a Soviet withdrawal that at the same time is consistent with legitimate Soviet security concerns. The objective is to lessen their "position" at a price acceptable to them.

Strategically speaking, the Soviet interest in keeping Germany divided and East Europe under control is essentially defensive. It does away with a power vacuum that the West might and probably would fill. At least this is true now, for Soviet risk-taking over Germany has failed to show that any reasonable grounds for successful Soviet advances exist. The Eastern European nations really, even collectively, represent very little military power; therefore their real importance to the Soviets is by way of a "position," a protected buffer zone on their western approaches. They represent a position from which Germany can be pressured and through which Germany can be kept at a distance. The real crux of the situation revolves around Germany.

Germany's problem if she wants reunification is to induce a Soviet withdrawal. Within limits, Germany can count on much Eastern European sentiment in favor of this goal. These cards existed in Germany's hand before the 1960's; they simply were not used. The politico-economic challenge to the Soviets these cards represent will almost inevitably be played in the time ahead. Only the tactics are in doubt. Thus pressures on the Soviets will increase on the western flank, too. Holding German territory on a confrontation basis, as the Soviets so long have done, will be more costly—at least in political terms. What the Soviets will need to weigh is whether the U.S. may somehow tire of its European deployment and pull out at no cost to the Soviets, and whether it is riskier to have a united Germany free to pursue its own policies but unbacked by an American commitment, or to dig in and hold the line as pressures increase in every direction. The Soviets, if they stay on German soil, must weigh in the back of their minds the ultimate fact that Germans may one day be at least as willing to die to regain German soil as the Soviets may be to retain it. The specter of a Sino-German alliance, hovering over the horizon, must permeate the whole Soviet perspective.

In these circumstances the U.S., weighing its policy, ought to be willing to withdraw its troops from Germany (and even, under suitable circumstances, from Western Europe), provided the Soviets do so as well. A united neutral Germany would still have the "natural" support of NATO against any aggressive Soviet move. If in this way Soviet troops returned to their own frontiers and U.S. troops were withdrawn from Europe, the tension in Europe would diminish greatly. Thus an offshore U.S. deployment for Europe, if coupled with Soviet redeployments to Soviet soil, would isolate the Soviets from their presently threatening "position," and would isolate them (even if the Warsaw Pact continued nominally in effect) from meaningful alliances. This opponent-isolating strategy on the part of the U.S. would simultaneously take care of legitimate Soviet security needs and yet permit a much needed revamping of the *status quo*. Since accelerating Soviet tensions with China, *if obvious*, might influence the Soviets to dig in doggedly in Europe, the time available for the U.S. and Russia to reconsider this problem may be shorter than they assume.

The Strategic Implications

WE have seen that the main variables of strategy are location and counterbalancing interests, with their complex interactions. Depending on where a nation is located, its options increase or decrease; and which option it exercises influences drastically the counterbalancing calculus of interests by other states. That is why, in particular, it seems unwarranted for the U.S. in effect to throw away the flexibility it has by virtue of its location. Geography permits the U.S. wide options, since it means that great power centers, such as Russia and China, who constitute potential threats to U.S. interests cannot, other than through a simple but meaningless missile exchange from one remote area to another remote area, execute that potential threat except by first bringing the interests of other and nearer major powers into jeopardy. It means that while the U.S. potentially can put geopolitical distance between itself and both China and Russia, they cannot put distance between themselves. It is on these most basic facts that the security system of the U.S. should be built. In its continental base and deployed at sea the U.S. should maintain an invulnerable, second-strike capability. Offshore in Asia it should support the opposition of major Asian powers to a radical change in the balance of power. Onshore in Europe (or offshore if disengagement becomes feasible) it should support the opposition of major European nations to any radical change in the balance of power there. For the other nations of the world, more remote by location from a Chinese or Soviet threat, and indeed to a large extent insured against such threats because the threats are relatively meaningless unless in conjunction with radical alterations in the balance of power in Asia or Europe, it should support their freedom to find their own way to progress. This is *how* the U.S. should conceptualize its strategy, restraining its opponents by denying them allies and positions that would increase the threat, but doing so by supporting major Asian and European nations who in the nature of things have to be even more concerned with the problem. It has the great merit of maximizing Sino-Soviet preoccupation with each other. It also answers how far to be involved, and where, and with whom.

To implement an opponent-isolating strategy would not be easy, especially after a quarter century of bloc containment. In Europe, as we saw, the difficulty is primarily with Germany. Yet if Germany could be evacuated by both sides, the European-connected tension between the U.S. and the Soviets could be lowered. Correspondingly, the Soviet attention on China could be expected to increase without the distraction of an active German problem. Especially without a hold on Germany, the Soviet Union has no "position" in Europe to foment a tension which is just as dangerous to her as to us. With a neutral German state the Soviets could relax their hold on Eastern Europe, nearer the model of 1956 and de-stalinization, even withdrawing troops again as then. Russia, like China, would then be without major allies or threatening "positions" —which is exactly what an opponent-isolating strategy intends. This would be brought about for China primarily by the U.S. shifting from onshore positioning. It would be brought about for Russia primarily through disengagement in Europe because there are real benefits implicit in such agreements for Soviet interests too. From this point of view, Soviet efforts to increase their offshore fleet presence in Asia are not necessarily contrary to U.S. interests.

What would this shift imply for the U.S. strategically in the other areas of the world? Here we come to problems in which the confrontation between U.S. and Chinese interests is minimal, and the confrontation between U.S. and Soviet interests is largely peripheral—a generalization least true of the Middle East. For Africa south of the Sahara, and for Latin America, Chinese influence is extremely limited and the Soviets (at least since the Congo affair) have shown themselves unable or unwilling to make serious direct attempts to gain usable "positions." Indeed there is evidence that the Soviets have sought to curb certain activities of Castro in Latin America. Soviet caution in these regions has partly to do with the difficulty of bringing communism to essentially unindustrialized areas. Part of the caution springs also from Soviet unwillingness to spread limited resources too thinly around the world. They would have great difficulties holding such far-flung positions in a way contributing to Soviet interests. The very instability of much of Africa, for example, suggests that in the wake of a new coup any large investment of effort may vanish. It is noticeable that the greatest non-European extension of Soviet influence since 1945 (Cuba apart) is in the Middle East, where latent or active Arab antagonism toward the West gives a basis, strongly reinforced by the Israeli issue, on which the Soviets can build a more than passing position. Although the tremendous Soviet effort to make the USSR a world maritime power may in the years ahead give the Soviets both more interest in and capability for manipulation in these areas, what happens there remains essentially secondary in the world balance of power.

The U.S. position in Latin America and Africa ought in principle to continue to be one of supporting the efforts of these states to handle their own affairs and look to the achievement of their own interests primarily through their own efforts. The U.S. ought to attempt to inhibit any Soviet presence in these areas, but it can only do so practically if it responds to requests for help rather than attempting to generate calls for assistance—or intervening and then looking around for support. Only in the Middle East would it seem desirable to go further (for reasons given earlier). Here a Soviet presence exists and can only be countered effectively by destroying the basis on which that support has thrived: Arab-Israeli confrontation. Since the U.S. in fact cannot accomplish the elimination of the Israeli problem by agreeing in effect to the elimination of Israel, the only available option is to work for Arab-Israeli peace through mutual agreement. This end may not be obtainable, but there is no other realistic option.

Such U.S. policies for the major areas of the world add up to an answer to the questions posed at the beginning of this chapter: how far to be involved, where to be involved, and with whom to be involved. The emphasis in the strategy of bloc containment on direct U.S. troop commitments, sometimes with major allied support as in NATO, but sometimes without as in SEATO, should be changed. U.S. troop commitments make most sense as a supplement to the efforts of major allies, and they are likely to make little sense under other conditions. The objective is, after all, not to involve the U.S. but to contain potential enemies and maneuver them into positions where they are not more threatened but still become less able themselves to threaten. For the U.S. to thrust itself forward (asking only to be pointed in the direction of the enemy) reveals more courage, energy, and optimism than it reveals a careful and conservative evaluation of how to do the job at least cost in blood and treasure. The simple answer to how to contain an enemy or potential enemy is to do it ourselves. But a more sophisticated appraisal of alternative routes to the same objective should lead to an understanding of how others can be brought to do much more of what needs doing.

The keys to this more sophisticated understanding do not involve magic or farfetched formulas. Indeed, the remedies proposed here for our troubles largely come down to saying: start from the way the world is and actually operates, and go on from there. Our fall-shorts in performance are directly traceable to misconceptions about fundamental phenomena in international relations, to our tendency to ignore the real world. These tendencies, in turn, can easily be linked to their main reflections that include an underdeveloped sense of history, undervaluation of the effects of geography, and pronounced abstractionism in political doctrine and strategic thought. In a computer-oriented society we might say that our outputs reflect in their defects the inadequacies of our inputs. And, in turn, our undervaluing of history and geography and our uncertain feel for how nations react in such basic stress-strain situations as the balance of power can be traced to the uniquenesses of the American experience (analyzed in Part One). Having largely "discovered" world politics after prolonged isolation, we went in 1945 and after to full participation. Convinced that our lack of involvement had been all wrong, we took the approach that full involvement was correct. Having in this way finally taken the potentially unlimited implicit commitments of the Truman Doctrine about as far as they could conceivably be taken (a Viet-Nam War or any similar marginal onshore Asian involvement), we ultimately find ourselves frustrated. We have attempted too much in at least questionable places and at astounding costs. From an academic standpoint the greatest value of the Viet-Nam War may lie precisely in giving us a dramatic case study in where the strategy of bloc containment, with its emphasis on simple force-counterforce, can lead.

There would appear to be little doubt that the American people will ultimately choose in the years ahead to turn away from extreme marginal involvements such as Viet-Nam. While it may take more than one war of this type, the odds are that one is enough to induce a change. That change can be either toward doing enough, and in the right way, or doing little or nothing (which could be disastrous). If the American people conclude that "Viet-Nam Wars" should be avoided but do not really realize why the strategy which led to it was faulty, they may well be tempted to vent their frustration through an equally faulty neo-isolationism. There is a mean between these extremes, and it consists in choosing effectively between doing everything and doing nothing. The key to that effective choice rests on understanding what other nations, because of their own interests in the world as it is, can or must do "for" us.

Bibliography

ACHESON, DEAN G. *Power and Diplomacy*. Cambridge: Harvard University Press, 1958.

————. *Present at the Creation*. New York: Norton, 1969.

ALMOND, GABRIEL A. *The American People and Foreign Policy*. New York: Praeger, 1960.

AMME, CARL H., JR. *Nato Without France*. Stanford: Hoover Institution on War, Revolution, and Peace, 1967.

BADER, WILLIAM B. *The United States and the Spread of Nuclear Weapons*. New York: Pegasus, 1968.

BAILEY, THOMAS A. *Diplomatic History of the American People*. (6th ed.) New York: Appleton-Century-Crofts, 1958.

BALL, GEORGE W. *The Discipline of Power*. Boston: Little, Brown, 1968.

BARNETT, A. DOAK. *Communist China and Asia*. New York: Vintage Books, 1960.

BARTLETT, RUHL J. (ed.) *The Record of American Diplomacy*. New York: Knopf, 1948.

BEAL, JOHN R. *John Foster Dulles*. New York: Harper, 1956.

BEARD, CHARLES A. *The Idea of National Interest*. New York: Macmillan, 1934.

BEAUFRE, ANDRÉ. *NATO and Europe*. New York: Knopf, 1966.

BEMIS, SAMUEL FLAGG. *A Diplomatic History of the United States*. (4th ed.) New York: Holt, 1955.

BERLINER, JOSEPH S. *Soviet Economic Aid*. New York: Praeger, 1959.

BLACK, EUGENE R. *The Diplomacy of Economic Development*. Cambridge: Harvard University Press, 1960.

BLOOMFIELD, LINCOLN P. *The United Nations and U.S. Foreign Policy*. Boston: Little, Brown, 1960.

————, et al. *International Military Forces*. Boston: Little, Brown, 1964.

BLUM, ROBERT. *The United States and China in World Affairs*. New York: McGraw-Hill, 1966.

BÖLLING, KLAUS, *Republic in Suspense*. New York: Praeger, 1964.

BORMKE, ADAM (ed.). *The Communist States at the Crossroads*. New York: Praeger, 1965.

————, and UREN, PHILIP E. (eds.). *The Communist States and the West*. New York: Praeger, 1967.

BRODIE, BERNARD. *Strategy in the Missile Age.* Princeton: Princeton University Press, 1959.

BRZEZINSKI, ZBIGNIEW. *Alternative to Partition.* New York: McGraw-Hill, 1965.

———. *Ideology and Power in Soviet Politics.* (rev. ed.). New York: Praeger, 1967.

———. *The Soviet Bloc.* (rev. ed.). Cambridge: Harvard University Press, 1967.

BUCHAN, ALASTAIR. *NATO in the 1960's.* (rev. ed.). New York: Praeger, 1963.

———. *War in Modern Society.* New York: Harper and Row, 1968.

BULL, HEDLEY. *The Control of the Arms Race.* (2nd ed.). New York: Praeger, 1965.

BUNDY, MCGEORGE. "The End of Either/Or," *Foreign Affairs,* **45,** No. 2 (January 1967).

——— (ed.). *The Pattern of Responsibility.* Boston: Houghton Mifflin, 1952. (A compilation of Acheson's speeches and congressional testimony.)

BURKE, FRED G. *Africa's Quest for Order.* Englewood Cliffs, N.J.: Prentice-Hall, 1964.

BYRNES, JAMES F. *Speaking Frankly.* New York: Harper and Row, 1947.

CARR, EDWARD H. *The Twenty Years' Crisis, 1919–1939.* New York: Harper and Row, 1964.

CATER, DOUGLASS, JR. *The Fourth Branch of Government.* Boston: Houghton Mifflin, 1959.

CHEEVER, DANIEL S. and HAVILAND, H. FIELD, JR. *American Foreign Policy and the Separation of Powers.* Cambridge: Harvard University Press, 1952.

CHILDS, J. RIVES. *American Foreign Service.* New York: Holt, 1948.

CHURCHILL, WINSTON S. *Triumph and Tragedy.* Boston: Houghton Mifflin, 1953.

CLARK, KEITH C., and LEGERE, LAURENCE J. *The President and the Management of National Security.* New York: Praeger, 1969.

CLAUDE, INIS L., JR. *Power and International Relations.* New York: Random House, 1962.

———. *Swords into Plowshares, The Problems and Progress of International Organization.* (3rd ed.). New York: Random House, 1964.

COHEN, BERNARD C. *The Political Process and Foreign Policy; The Making of the Japanese Peace Treaty.* Princeton: Princeton University Press, 1963.

———. *The Press and Foreign Policy.* Princeton: Princeton University Press, 1963.

COOK, THOMAS I., and MOOS, MALCOLM. *Power Through Purpose; The Realism of Idealism as a Basis for Foreign Policy.* Baltimore: Johns Hopkins University Press, 1954.

CORWIN, EDWARD S. *The President: Office and Powers, 1787–1957.* (4th ed.). New York: New York University Press, 1957.

COTTRELL, ALVIN J., and DOUGHERTY, JAMES E. *The Politics of the Atlantic Alliance.* New York: Praeger, 1964.

CRABB, CECIL V. *Bipartisan Foreign Policy: Myth or Reality?* Evanston: Row, Peterson, 1957.

———. *The Elephants and the Grass.* New York: Praeger, 1965. (An analysis of the foreign policy of nonaligned nations.)

CREMEANS, CHARLES D. *The Arabs and the World.* New York: Praeger, 1963.

DALLIN, DAVID J., *Soviet Foreign Policy After Stalin.* Philadelphia: Lippincott, 1961.

DAVIES, JOHN PATON, JR. *Foreign and Other Affairs.* New York: W. W. Norton, 1964.

DAVISON, W. PHILLIPS. *The Berlin Blockade.* Princeton: Princeton University Press, 1958.

DE CONDE, ALEXANDER. *The American Secretary of State: An Interpretation.* New York: Praeger, 1962.

DINERSTEIN, H. S. *War and the Soviet Union.* (rev. ed.). New York: Praeger, 1962.

DRAPER, THEODORE. *Abuse of Power.* New York: Viking, 1967. (A critique of U.S. interventionism.)

———. *Castroism, Theory and Practice.* New York: Praeger, 1965.

———. *Castro's Revolution.* New York: Praeger, 1962.

DULLES, ALLEN W. *The Craft of Intelligence.* New York: Harper and Row, 1963.

DULLES, JOHN FOSTER. *War or Peace.* (Reissue). New York: Macmillan, 1957.

DUTT, VIDYA PRAKASH. *China and the World.* New York: Praeger, 1966.

EDEN, ANTHONY. *Full Circle.* Boston: Houghton Mifflin, 1960.

EISENHOWER, DWIGHT D. *Mandate for Change.* New York: New American Library, 1965.

———. *Waging Peace.* New York: Doubleday, 1965.

ELDER, ROBERT E. *The Policy Machine; the Department of State and American Foreign Policy.* Syracuse: Syracuse University Press, 1960.

EMERSON, RUPERT. *From Empire to Nation.* Boston: Beacon Press, 1962.

ENTHOVEN, ALAIN C. "Systems Analysis and Decision Making." *Military Review,* **43**, No. 1 (January 1963).

EPSTEIN, LEON D. *Britain—Uneasy Ally.* Chicago: University of Chicago Press, 1954.

FALL, BERNARD B. *The Two Vietnams.* (2nd rev. ed.). New York: Praeger, 1966.

FARNSWORTH, DAVID N. *The Senate Committee on Foreign Relations.* Urbana: University of Illinois Press, 1961.

FEIS, HERBERT. *Between War and Peace: The Potsdam Conference.* Princeton: Princeton University Press, 1960.

———. *China Tangle.* New York: Atheneum, 1965. (U.S. policy toward China during World War II.)

———. *Churchill, Roosevelt, Stalin.* Princeton: Princeton University Press, 1957.

———. *Foreign Aid and Foreign Policy.* New York: St. Martin's Press, 1964.

———. *Japan Subdued: The Atomic Bomb and the End of the War in the Pacific.* Princeton: Princeton University Press, 1961.

FLOYD, DAVID. *Mao Against Khrushchev.* New York: Praeger, 1964.

FULBRIGHT, J. WILLIAM. *The Arrogance of Power.* New York: Vintage Books, 1966.

————. *Old Myths and New Realities.* New York: Vintage Books, 1964.

FURNISS, EDGAR S. *France, Troubled Ally.* New York: Praeger, 1960.

————. "A Personal Evaluation," in Furniss, Edgar S. (ed.). *The Western Alliance.* Columbus: Ohio State University Press, 1965.

GALBRAITH, JOHN KENNETH. *Ambassador's Journal.* Boston: Houghton Mifflin, 1969.

GALLOIS, PIERRE M. "U.S. Strategy and the Defense of Europe." *Orbis,* 7, No. 2 (Summer 1963).

GARDNER, RICHARD N. *In Pursuit of World Order, U.S. Foreign Policy and International Organizations.* New York: Praeger, 1964.

GARTHOFF, RAYMOND L. *Soviet Strategy in the Nuclear Age.* (rev. ed.). New York: Praeger, 1962.

GEHLEN, MICHAEL P. *The Politics of Coexistence.* Bloomington: Indiana University Press, 1967.

GOLDSCHMIDT, WALTER (ed.). *The United States and Africa.* New York: Praeger, 1963.

GRAEBNER, NORMAN A. *Cold War Diplomacy, 1945–1960.* Princeton: Van Nostrand, 1962.

————. *The New Isolationism.* New York: Ronald Press, 1956.

————. (ed.). *An Uncertain Tradition: American Secretaries of State in the Twentieth Century.* New York: McGraw-Hill, 1961.

GROSSER, ALFRED, *The Federal Republic of Germany.* New York: Praeger, 1964.

————. *French Foreign Policy Under De Gaulle.* Boston: Little, Brown, 1967.

GURTOV, MELVIN. *The First Vietnam Crisis.* New York: Columbia University Press, 1967. (Covers the Eisenhower administration's decision not to intervene.)

HAAS, ERNST B. *The Uniting of Europe.* Stanford: Stanford University Press, 1958.

HALLE, LOUIS J. *The Cold War as History.* New York: Harper and Row, 1967.

HALPERIN, MORTON H. *Limited War in the Nuclear Age.* New York: Wiley, 1963.

HAMMER, ELLEN J., *The Struggle for Indochina, 1940–1955.* Stanford: Stanford University Press, 1966.

HANRIEDER, WOLFRAM F. *West German Foreign Policy, 1949–1963.* Stanford: Stanford University Press, 1967.

HARTMANN, FREDERICK H. *Germany Between East and West.* Englewood Cliffs, N.J.: Spectrum Books, 1965.

————. *The Relations of Nations.* (3rd ed.). New York: Macmillan, 1967.

HARTZ, LOUIS, *The Liberal Tradition in America.* New York: Harvest Books, 1955.

HAUSER, PHILIP M. (ed.): *Population and World Politics.* New York: Free Press of Glencoe, 1964.

HAVILAND, H. FIELD, JR. *The Formulation and Administration of United States Foreign Policy.* Washington: Brookings Institution, 1960.

HEILBRONER, ROBERT L. *The Great Ascent.* New York: Harper and Row, 1963. (Prospects for economic development in underdeveloped countries.)

HILSMAN, ROGER, *Strategic Intelligence and National Decisions.* New York: Free Press of Glencoe, 1956.

————. *To Move A Nation.* Garden City: Doubleday, 1967.

HITCH, CHARLES, and McKEAN, ROLAND N. *The Economics of Defense in the Nuclear Age.* Cambridge: Harvard University Press, 1960.

HOFFMANN, STANLEY. *Gulliver's Troubles; or, the Setting of American Foreign Policy.* New York: McGraw-Hill, 1968.

HOFSTADTER, RICHARD. *The Paranoid Style in American Politics.* New York: Vintage Books, 1967.

HOLBORN, HAJO, *The Political Collapse of Europe.* New York: Knopf, 1951.

HOLT, ROBERT T., and VAN DE VELDE, ROBERT W. *Strategic Psychological Operations and American Foreign Policy.* Chicago: University of Chicago Press, 1960.

HULL, CORDELL. *The Memoirs of Cordell Hull.* (2 vols.). New York: Macmillan, 1948.

HUNTINGTON, SAMUEL P. *The Soldier and the State: The Theory and Politics of Civil-Military Relations.* Cambridge: Harvard University Press, 1957.

IONESCU, GHITA. *The Break Up of the Soviet Empire in Eastern Europe.* Baltimore: Penguin Books, 1965.

JONES, JOSEPH M. *The Fifteen Weeks, February 21–June 5, 1947.* New York: Viking Press, 1955. (The Truman Doctrine decision.)

JORDAN, AMOS A. *Foreign Aid and the Defense of Southeast Asia.* New York: Praeger, 1962.

KAHN, HERMAN. *On Escalation: Metaphors and Scenarios.* New York: Praeger, 1965.

————. *Thinking About the Unthinkable.* New York: Avon, 1964.

KAPLAN, JACOB J. *The Challenge of Foreign Aid.* New York: Praeger, 1967.

KAUFMANN, WILLIAM W. (ed.). *Military Policy and National Security.* Princeton: Princeton University Press, 1956.

KAUTSKY, JOHN H. *Political Change in Underdeveloped Countries.* New York: Wiley, 1962.

KENNAN, GEORGE F. *American Diplomacy, 1900–1950.* New York: Mentor Books, 1952.

————. *Memoirs.* Boston: Little, Brown, 1967.

————. *On Dealing with the Communist World.* New York: Harper and Row, 1964.

————. *The Realities of American Foreign Policy.* Princeton: Princeton University Press, 1955.

————. *Russia and the West under Lenin and Stalin.* Boston: Little, Brown, 1960.

KIRK, GEORGE E. *A Short History of the Middle East.* (7th rev. ed.). New York: Praeger, 1964.

KISSINGER, HENRY A. *The Troubled Partnership.* New York: McGraw-Hill, 1965.

————. *The Necessity for Choice.* New York: Anchor Books, 1961.

KITZINGER, U. W. *The Politics and Economics of European Integration.* New York: Praeger, 1963.

KNORR, KLAUS (ed.). *NATO and American Strategy*. Princeton: Princeton University Press, 1959.

LACOUTURE, JEAN. *Vietnam:Between Two Truces*. New York: Vintage Books, 1966.

LANGER, WILLIAM L., and GLEASON, S. EVERETT. *The Challenge to Isolation and the Undeclared War*. New York: Harper and Row, 1952; 1953.

LARSON, DAVID L. (ed.). *The "Cuban Crisis" of 1962*. Boston: Houghton Mifflin, 1963.

LEFEVER, ERNEST W. *Crisis in the Congo, A UN Force in Action*. Washington: Brookings Institution, 1965.

―――. *Ethics and United States Foreign Policy*. New York: Meridian Books, 1961.

LEGAULT, ALBERT. *Deterrence and the Atlantic Community*. Ontario: Canadian Institute of International Affairs, 1966.

LEVINE, ROBERT A. *The Arms Debate*. Cambridge: Harvard University Press, 1963.

LIPPMANN, WALTER. *The Public Philosophy*. Boston: Little, Brown, 1955.

LISKA, GEORGE. *Imperial America*. Baltimore: Johns Hopkins University Press, 1967.

―――. *The New Statecraft; Foreign Aid in American Foreign Policy*. Chicago: University of Chicago Press, 1959.

LONDON, KURT. *How Foreign Policy Is Made*. Princeton: Van Nostrand, 1949.

LOWENTHAL, RICHARD. *World Communism: The Disintegration of a Secular Faith*. New York: Oxford University Press, 1966.

LUARD, EVAN (ed.). *The Cold War, A Reappraisal*. New York: Praeger, 1964.

MARTIN, LAURENCE W. (ed.). *Neutralism and Nonalignment*. New York: Praeger, 1962.

MASLAND, JOHN W., and RADWAY, LAURENCE I. *Soldiers and Scholars: Military Education and National Policy*. Princeton: Princeton University Press, 1957.

MASON, EDWARD S. *Foreign Aid and Foreign Policy*. New York: Harper and Row, 1964.

MAY, ERNEST R. (ed.). *The Ultimate Decision: The President as Commander-in-Chief*. New York: George Braziller, 1960.

MEHNERT, KLAUS. *Peking and Moscow*. New York: New American Library, 1964.

MILLIS, WALTER, MANSFIELD, HARVEY C., and STEIN, HAROLD. *Arms and the State: Civil-Military Elements in National Policy*. New York: Twentieth Century Fund, 1958.

MILLIS, WALTER (ed.). *The Forrestal Diaries*. New York: Viking, 1951.

MCCAMY, JAMES L. *The Administration of American Foreign Affairs*. New York: Knopf, 1950.

―――. *Conduct of the New Diplomacy*. New York: Harper and Row, 1964.

MCGOVERN, WILLIAM M. *Strategic Intelligence and the Shape of Tomorrow*. Chicago: Henry Regnery, 1961.

MCNAMARA, ROBERT S. *The Essence of Security*. New York: Harper and Row, 1968.

McNeill, William H. *America, Britain, and Russia, 1941–1946.* London: Oxford University Press, 1953.

Montgomery, John D. *Foreign Aid in International Relations.* Englewood Cliffs, N.J.: Prentice-Hall, 1967.

Morgenthau, Hans J. *A New Foreign Policy for the United States.* New York: Praeger, 1968.

————. *In Defense of the National Interest: A Critical Examination of American Foreign Policy.* New York: Knopf, 1951.

————. "A Political Theory of Foreign Aid." *The American Political Science Review,* 56, No. 2 (June 1962).

————. *The Purpose of American Politics.* New York: Knopf, 1960.

Morison, Samuel Eliot. *The Oxford History of the American People.* New York: Oxford University Press, 1965.

Mosely, Philip E. *The Kremlin and World Politics.* New York: Vintage Books, 1960.

Mosher, Frederick C. *Program Budgeting: Theory and Practice with Particular Reference to the U.S. Department of the Army.* Chicago: Public Administration Service, 1954.

Muller, Kurt. *The Foreign Aid Program of the Soviet Bloc and Communist China.* New York: Walker and Company, 1964.

Neustadt, Richard E. *Presidential Power: The Politics of Leadership.* New York: Wiley, 1960.

Nicholas, H. G. *The United Nations as a Political Institution.* (2nd ed.) Fairlawn, N.J.: Oxford University Press, 1962.

Niebuhr, Reinhold. *The Children of Light and the Children of Darkness.* New York: Scribner, 1944.

————. *The Irony of American History.* New York: Scribner, 1954.

Northedge, F. S. *British Foreign Policy.* New York: Praeger, 1962.

O'Connor, Raymond G. (ed.). *American Defense Policy in Perspective.* New York: Wiley, 1965.

Organski, A. F. K. *The Stages of Political Development.* New York: Knopf, 1965.

Osgood, Robert E. *Ideals and Self-interest in America's Foreign Relations.* Chicago: University of Chicago Press, 1953.

————. *Limited War.* Chicago: University of Chicago Press, 1957.

————. *NATO: The Entangling Alliance.* Chicago: University of Chicago Press, 1962.

Perkins, Dexter, *The American Approach to Foreign Policy.* Cambridge: Harvard University Press, 1952.

Planck, Charles R. *The Changing Status of German Reunification in Western Diplomacy, 1955–1966.* Baltimore: Johns Hopkins University Press, 1967.

Plischke, Elmer. *Summit Diplomacy: Personal Diplomacy of the President of the United States.* College Park, Md.: University of Maryland Press, 1958.

Pratt, Julius W. *A History of United States Foreign Policy.* Englewood Cliffs, N.J.: Prentice-Hall, 1955.

Ransom, Harry H. *Central Intelligence and National Security.* Cambridge: Harvard University Press, 1958.

RASKIN, MARCUS G., and FALL, BERNARD B. (eds.). *The Vietnam Reader.* (rev. ed.) New York: Vintage Books, 1968.

RAUSCHENBUSH, STEPHEN. *The Challenge to the Alliance for Progress.* Washington: Public Affairs Institute, 1962.

REES, DAVID. *Korea: The Limited War.* New York: St. Martin's Press, 1964.

REISCHAUER, EDWIN O. *Beyond Vietnam: The United States and Asia.* New York: Knopf, 1968.

REITZEL, WILLIAM A., KAPLAN, MORTON A., and COBLENTZ, CONSTANCE G. *United States Foreign Policy, 1945–1955.* Washington: Brookings Institution, 1956.

ROBINSON, JAMES A. *Congress and Foreign Policy–Making.* Homewood, Ill.: Dorsey Press, 1962.

ROSECRANCE, RICHARD N. (ed.). *The Dispersion of Nuclear Weapons.* New York: Columbia University Press, 1964.

ROSENAU, JAMES N. (ed.). *International Politics and Foreign Policy.* (rev. ed.) New York: Free Press of Glencoe, 1969.

———. *Public Opinion and Foreign Policy.* New York: Random House, 1961.

ROSSITER, CLINTON. *The American Presidency.* New York: Harcourt, Brace and World, 1956.

ROSTOW, WALT W. *The Stages of Economic Growth.* New York: Cambridge University Press, 1960.

———. *The United States in the World Arena.* New York: Harper, 1960.

RUSK, DEAN. "Our Foreign Policy Commitments to Assure a Peaceful Future." *The Department of State Bulletin,* **56,** No. 1456 (May 22, 1967).

SAPIN, BURTON M. *The Making of United States Foreign Policy.* Washington, D.C.: Brookings, 1966.

SCHELLING, THOMAS C., and HALPERIN, MORTON H. *Strategy and Arms Control.* New York: Twentieth Century Fund, 1961.

SCHILLING, WARNER R., HAMMOND, PAUL Y., and SNYDER, GLENN H. *Strategy, Politics and Defense.* New York: Columbia University Press, 1962.

SCHLESINGER, ARTHUR M., JR. *The Bitter Heritage.* New York: Crest Books, 1967. (Contrasts the Kennedy and Johnson policies on Viet-Nam.)

———. *A Thousand Days.* New York: Crest Books, 1967.

SCOTT, ANDREW M., and DAWSON, RAYMOND H. *Readings in the Making of American Foreign Policy.* New York: Macmillan, 1965.

SHANKS, MICHAEL, and LAMBERT, JOHN. *The Common Market Today—and Tomorrow.* New York: Praeger, 1962.

SHERWOOD, ROBERT E. *Roosevelt and Hopkins: An Intimate History.* New York: Harper and Row, 1948.

SHULMAN, MARSHALL D. *Beyond the Cold War.* New Haven: Yale University Press, 1966.

SNELL, JOHN L. *Illusion and Necessity: The Diplomacy of Global War, 1939–1945.* Boston: Houghton Mifflin, 1963.

SNYDER, RICHARD C., BRUCK, H. W., and SAPIN, BURTON (eds.). *Foreign Policy Decision Making: An Approach to the Study of International Politics.* New York: Free Press of Glencoe, 1962.

SOKOLOVSKY, V. D. (ed.). *Military Strategy: Soviet Doctrine and Concepts.* New York: Praeger, 1963.

SORENSON, THEODORE C. *Decision Making in the White House*. New York: Columbia University Press, 1963.

————. *Kennedy*. New York: Bantam Books, 1966.

SPANIER, JOHN W. *The Truman-MacArthur Controversy and the Korean War*. (rev. ed.) New York: W. W. Norton, 1965.

SPEIER, HANS, and DAVISON, W. PHILLIPS (eds.). *West German Leadership and Foreign Policy*. Evanston, Ill.: Row, Peterson, 1957.

SPROUT, HAROLD and MARGARET. *The Rise of American Naval Power, 1776–1918*. Princeton: Princeton University Press, 1944.

STALEY, EUGENE. *The Future of Underdeveloped Countries*. (rev. ed.) New York: Praeger, 1961.

STEIN, HAROLD (ed.). *American Civil-Military Decisions: A Book of Case Studies*. University, Ala.: University of Alabama Press, 1963.

STEINER, ZARA S. *Present Problems of the Foreign Service*. Princeton: Center of International Studies, 1961.

————. *The State Department and the Foreign Service: The Wriston Report—Four Years Later*. Princeton: Center of International Studies, 1958.

STILLMAN, EDMUND, and PFAFF, WILLIAM. *Power and Impotence: The Failure of America's Foreign Policy*. New York: Random House, 1966.

STIMSON, HENRY L., and BUNDY, McGEORGE. *On Active Service in Peace and War*. New York: Harper and Row, 1948.

STOESSINGER, JOHN, *et. al. Financing the United Nations System*. Washington: Brookings Institution, 1966.

STRAUSZ-HUPÉ, ROBERT, *et al. Protracted Conflict*. New York: Harper Colophon Books, 1959.

STUART, GRAHAM, H. *American Diplomatic and Consular Practice*. (2nd ed.) New York: Appleton-Century-Crofts, 1952.

————. *The Department of State*. New York: Macmillan, 1949.

SZULC, TAD, and MEYER, KARL E. *The Cuban Invasion: The Chronicle of a Disaster*. New York: Ballantine and Praeger, 1962.

TANNENBAUM, FRANK. *The American Tradition in Foreign Policy*. Norman: University of Oklahoma Press, 1955.

TAYLOR, MAXWELL D. *Responsibility and Response*. New York: Harper and Row, 1967.

————. *The Uncertain Trumpet*. New York: Harper and Row, 1959.

THAYER, CHARLES W., *Diplomat*. New York: Harper and Row, 1959.

THOMPSON, KENNETH W. *Political Realism and the Crisis of World Politics*. Princeton: Princeton University Press, 1960.

THOMSON, CHARLES A., and LAVES, WALTER H. C. *Cultural Relations and U.S. Foreign Policy*. Bloomington: Indiana University Press, 1963.

TRUMAN, HARRY S. *Memoirs*. (2 vols.) New York: New American Library, 1965.

TSOU, TANG. *America's Failure in China, 1941–50*. (2 vols.) Chicago: Phoenix Books, 1963.

TUCKER, ROBERT C. "Russia, the West, and World Wonder." *World Politics*, 11, No. 1 (October 1959).

TURNER, GORDON, and CHALLENER, RICHARD (eds.). *American Strategy in the Nuclear Age*. New York: Praeger, 1960.

ULAM, ADAM B. *The Unfinished Revolution.* New York: Vintage Books, 1960.

U.S. DEPARTMENT OF STATE. *Foreign Relations of the United States: The Conference of Berlin (The Potsdam Conference).* (2 vols.) Washington: 1960.

————. *Foreign Relations of the United States: The Conferences at Malta and Yalta, 1945.* Washington: 1955.

UNITED STATES SENATE. *Subcommittee on National Policy Machinery and Subcommittee on National Security Staffing and Operations of the Senate (Jackson) Committee on Government Operations.* Hearings and materials, 1961– —.

VON DER MEHDEN, FRED. *Politics of the Developing Nations.* Englewood Cliffs, N.J.: Spectrum Books, 1964.

WALKER, RICHARD L. *China Under Communism.* New Haven: Yale University Press, 1955.

WALLERSTEIN, IMMANUEL. *Africa: The Politics of Independence.* New York: Vintage Books, 1961.

WALTZ, KENNETH N. *Foreign Policy and Democratic Politics.* Boston: Little, Brown, 1967. (Compares effectiveness of American and British political systems in foreign policy.)

WARD, BARBARA. *The Rich Nations and the Poor Nations.* New York: W. W. Norton, 1962.

WESTERFIELD, H. BRADFORD. *Foreign Policy and Party Politics: Pearl Harbor to Korea.* New Haven: Yale University Press, 1955.

WHITE, THEODORE H. *Fire in the Ashes.* New York: Sloan, 1953. (Europe's recovery after 1945.)

WILLIAMS, WILLIAM APPLEMAN. *The Tragedy of American Diplomacy.* Cleveland and New York: World Publishing Company, 1959.

WINT, GUY, and CALVOCORESSI, PETER. *Middle East Crisis.* Baltimore: Penguin Books, 1957.

WISE, DAVID, and ROSS, THOMAS B. *The U-2 Affair.* New York: Random House, 1962.

WOHLSTETTER, ALBERT. "The Delicate Balance of Terror." *Foreign Affairs,* **37,** No. 2 (January 1959).

WOHLSTETTER, ROBERTA. *Pearl Harbor: Warning and Decision.* Stanford: Stanford University Press, 1962.

WOLF, CHARLES. *Foreign Aid: Theory and Practice in Southern Asia.* Princeton: Princeton University Press, 1960.

WOLFERS, ARNOLD (ed.). *Changing East-West Relations and the Unity of the West.* Baltimore: Johns Hopkins University Press, 1964.

WRISTON, HENRY M. *Diplomacy in a Democracy.* New York: Harper and Row, 1956.

ZAGORIA, DONALD S. *The Sino-Soviet Conflict.* New York: Atheneum, 1962.

Index

Acheson, Dean
  anecdote of, on "machinery" of government, 135, 136
  comments on, by Senator Butler, 190
  disagreement with Kennan of, 126, 127
  discusses Nationalist Chinese collapse, 189
  espouses aid to Europe, 132, 133
  German reaction to "position of strength" concept of, 333
  value to Truman, 84
Adams, John Q., 29t., 99, 142, 143
Adams-Onis Treaty, 143
Adenauer, Konrad, 187, 203, 225
Africa
  and Congo Crisis, 230–33
  partition of, 34
  percentage of total states in world, 299
  "revolution of rising expectations" in, 306
  tribalism vs. nationalism, 307
  UN strength of, compared to armed strength of, 320
  and white vs. black issue, 358–60
Agency for International Development (AID), 87, 91
Alabama Claims, 174
Alaska, 35, 174
Albania, 241
Algeria, 210, 251, 320, 353
Alliance for Progress, 14, 308, 316, 355, 357
Allied Control Council in Berlin, 182
American
  attitudes, 46–63
  deterrence theory, tendency toward abstract in, 5
  handicaps in formulating policy, 12–18
  historical experience, unusual nature of, 3, 27–37
  humanitarian concern, 299, 300

American [cont.]
  impatience and inclination toward direct action, linked to strategic approach, 9
  mobility, 54, 55
  nationalism and national character, 4, 5
  political analysis, tendency toward two extremes, 5
American Legion, 111, 112
American Revolution, 24, 25, 27
Americans for Democratic Action, 111, 112
Anglo-Japanese Alliance, 157, 159
Antimissile system (ABM), 104, 113, 292
Aqaba, Gulf of, 112
Armed forces of the world, figures on, 319, 320
Arms Control and Disarmament Agency, 95
Arms embargo
  enactment of, 114
  repeal of, 114, 166
Army War College, established, 73
Aron, Raymond, 173
Aswan Dam, 211, 212
Atlantic Charter, 168
Australia, 38, 198, 199, 294, 303
Austria, 33, 205, 328, 370

Baghdad Pact, 211
Balance of power
  2nd counterbalancing national interests, 10, 272, 273, 279, 280
  theory, 264–67
  U.S. distaste for, 4, 16, 143n.
Bay of Pigs incident, 69, 79, 135, 223
Belgium, 34, 231, 232, 254
Beneš, Eduard, 181, 182
Beria, Lavrenti P., 201, 204, 205

389

Berlin
    access question, 76, 77, 170, 183–86,
        218–21
    blockade, 182, 183, 186, 187
    Foreign Ministers Conference, 197,
        202
    second crisis over, begins, 217–19
    Wall, 224, 225
Biafra, 320, 323
Bill of Rights, 41, 42
Bipartisanship, 127
Bismarck, Otto von, 16, 32–34, 272
Blaine, James G., 144
Bliss, Tasker, 73
Bohlen, Charles E., 88
Bourgeois-Pichat, Jean, 301n.
Boxer rebellion, 148
Brandt, Willy, 250, 337
Brazil, 303, 354, 355
Brest-Litovsk, Treaty of, 154, 327
Brezhnev, Leonid I., 247
Briand-Kellogg Pact, 162
Brogan, Dennis W., 188, 189
Brzezinski, Zbigniew, 238n.
Buchanan, James, 29t.
Buenos Aires Conference, 164
Bulganin, Nikolai, 201, 205–207, 209,
        213, 217
Bundy, McGeorge, 79, 80
Butler, Hugh, 190

Caffery, Jefferson, 100
Cairo Conference, 169
Cambodia, 198, 199
"Camp David formula," 221, 223
Canada, 38, 197
Canning, George, 27, 143
Castro, Fidel, 226, 230, 355
Central Intelligence Agency, established,
        77
Chamberlain, Neville, 17
Chamoun, President of Lebanon in 1958,
        213
Chiang Kai-shek, 132, 169, 188, 195, 196
Chief of Naval Operations, concept, 73
Chile, 302, 303t.
China
    and Chiang Kai-shek, 132, 169, 188,
        195, 196
    collapse of Nationalist rule, 187–89
    humiliation of, 57
    Nationalist government's treaty with
        U.S., terms of, 196, 197
    population size, on Formosa, 12n.
    spheres-of-interest leases, 34
China, Communist
    armed clash with India, 242
    attitude on Soviet occupation of
        Czechoslovakia, 250

China, Communist [cont.]
    frontier clashes with Soviet Union,
        246, 249
    "Great Leap Forward," 241, 245
    and Hungarian uprising, 240
    and Khrushchev's revisionism, 240–43
    motives for ending Indo–Chinese War,
        195, 196
    polemics with Soviets, 240–46, 249,
        250
    and Seventh Fleet, 189, 195
    U.S. policy toward, alteration in, 133
China Lobby, 132
Chou En-lai, 242
Churchill, Winston, 167–69, 176, 177
Clark, Keith C., 6n.
Clark Memorandum, 162
Clay, Lucius, 184–86
Clayton–Bulwer Treaty, 35
Cleveland, Grover, 144, 146
Code-breaking, 74
Colonial imperialism of 19th century, 34
Commager, Henry Steele, 260
Committee to Defend America by Aiding
        the Allies, 116
Common Market, United Kingdom ap-
        plication to, 106
Communism, as U.S. election issue, 129
Congo, 34, 125, 320
Congo Crisis, 230–233
Congress
    and communism as election issue, 129
    differences with President, 107, 120,
        121, 124
    influences on members of, 107, 108
    length of Senate debates on foreign
        policy, 123n., 127
    opinion splits within, 107
    Senate Foreign Relations Committee
        hearings, 101, 122–24
    and use of U.S. combat troops in
        Thailand and Laos, 347
Constitution, American, powers of Presi-
        dent and Congress under, 119–22,
        124, 125, 126
Contingency plans, 107, 283, 289, 290
Coolidge, Calvin, 71
Cost-effectiveness, 287–89
Council for Mutual Economic Assistance
        (COMECON), 249
Council of National Defense, 74, 75
Counterbalancing interests
    principle of, 10, 272, 273, 279, 280
    used by Bismarck, 33
Counterinsurgency, Special Group for, 80
"Country Team" concept, 92, 93
Crimean War, 26
Cuba, 148, 164. 223, 226–30, 268, 269,
        355, 357, 358

Cuban Missile Crisis 98, 112, 225–30, 357
Curzon Line, 169
Czechoslovakia, 17, 166, 180, 181, 249, 250, 269, 324–30, 335

Davies, John Paton, 215
Davison, W. Phillips, 108, 109
Dawes Plan, 161
Defense, Department of
    civilian-military differences of opinion in, 108
    contingency plans of, for Thailand, 107
    creation of Secretary of Defense position, 73
    establishment of Department, 77
    establishment of Deputy Secretary position, 77
    liaison and coordination with State, 93, 94
    Office of International Security Affairs, 94
    relation of U.S. budget to contingency plans, 289, 290
Defense Analyses, Institute for, 6
De Gaulle, Charles, 13, 106, 173, 174, 250–55, 331, 334
Deutscher, Isaac, 239n.
Development Assistance Committee, Organization for Economic Cooperation and Development, 312
Dien Bien Phu, 122, 197, 198
Dillon, Douglas, 222
Disarmament, naval, 158, 159, 162
Dominican Republic, 35, 53, 149, 162, 355, 357, 363
Dubcek, Alexander, 250
Dulles, John Foster
    comments on Khrushchev's denunciation of Potsdam, 218, 219
    discusses Nasser with Eden, 212
    "massive retaliation" doctrine of, 135
    moves to end Korean War, 195, 196
    promises support to "captive" Europe, 200, 201
    proposes intervention in Indo-China, 198, 214
    speech on Communist China, 133
    State Department reductions under, 215
    withdraws support for Aswan Dam, 211, 212
Dunkirk, 167

Eden, Anthony
    and Aswan Dam, 211
    and formula for Germany joining NATO, 202

Eden, Anthony [*cont.*]
    German election formula of, referenced by Communist bloc, 203
    gives Dulles no encouragement on Indo–China, 198
    and reaction to Nasser's canal seizure, 212
    represents Britain at summit, 205, 206
Egypt. *See* United Arab Republic
Eisenhower, Dwight D.
    announces Eisenhower Doctrine, 130
    army career, 72
    attitude on *1956* Middle East crisis, 212–14
    and "Camp David formula," 221
    conception of Presidency, 52, 134
    decision not to take Berlin, 176
    and Defense Department, 80
    first year actions as President, 195, 196
    at Geneva summit meeting, 205–207
    increases U.S. Asian commitments, 196–99
    on intervention in Eastern Europe, 201
    and McCarthy, 129
    and National Security Council, 79
    and Operations Coordinating Board, 4
    at Paris summit meeting, 222
    policy on Berlin access, 220
    Truman comments on, 131, 132
    and Viet–Nam, 70
Eisenhower Doctrine, 130, 135
Ernbick, Stanley D., 75
English Constitution, 47, 48
Ethiopia, 165, 191, 231, 320
European Defense Community, 201, 202
European Economic Community, external tariff, 313
European wars before *1815*, 31
"Excomm" device, in national security affairs, 69, 79, 80

Faure, Edgar, 205, 206
First Opium War, 26
Foreign aid, by U.S., 314
Foreign ministers conferences, West with Russia
    Berlin, 197, 202, 207
    Geneva (on Far East), 197, 198
    Geneva (*1959*, on Germany), 220, 221
    Paris, 207
Foreign policy
    American handicaps in approaching, 12–18
    critical nature of conceptualization in, 9
    seven tests of success for, 8
Foreign Service, of the U.S. *See also* State Department
    competing services established, 90

Foreign Service [*cont.*]
    growth of, 85*t*.
    Martin Report on, 86, 88
    recruitment sources of, 87, 88
    and Rogers Act, 72, 89
    "Wristonization" of, 89
Formosa, 12*n*., 169, 190. *See also* China
Four–Power Treaty, 159
Fourteen Points, the, 153, 154
France
    alliance with Soviet Union, *1935*, 273
    and the Americas, 34, 143
    casualties in World War I, 153
    and de Gaulle's concepts, 250–55
    demand for Rhineland buffer by, 155
    Fifth Republic, 13, 250
    force de frappe, 252, 253
    and Indo-Chinese War, 197, 198
    postwar problems of, 251, 252
    and Suez War, 210–13, 251
Frankel, Max, 70
Fulbright, J. William, 101, 121–25, 260

Game theory, 285, 286
Gavin, James E., 260
General Agreement on Tariffs and Trade,
    313
Geneva Far Eastern Conference, 197,
    198
Geneva Foreign Ministers Meeting of
    1959, 220, 221
Germany
    Adenauer, Chancellor of, 187, 203, 225
    admission to NATO, 202, 205
    armistice with, World War I, 154
    Berlin Foreign Ministers Conference,
        197, 202
    Bonn Agreement, 201, 202
    Brandt, Chancellor of, 250, 337
    East German refugee figures, 224
    East German uprising, 201
    formation of West German govern-
        ment, begun, 182
    "Grand Coalition," 249, 333
    Iron Curtain intensified, 202
    Kiesinger, Chancellor of, 249, 333, 337
    negotiations with Eastern Europe, 328,
        330, 331, 333, 337
    and Nuclear Non-Proliferation Treaty,
        294
    Paris Agreements, 202, 203, 205
    Potsdam reparations issue, 182, 183
    rearmament in East Germany, 201
    rearmament under Hitler, 273
    representation at Geneva Foreign Min-
        isters Meeting, 220
    and Soviet troops in Central Europe,
        324–31
    submarine warfare of, 151, 153

Germany [*cont.*]
    trade with U.S., 304
    unification of, 31, 32
    weak position of East Germany in,
        328, 329
    and World War I losses, 155
    and World War I reparations, 161
    weak position of East Germany in,
        328, 329
    and Zimmerman Note, 151
Gero, Erno, 210
Ghana, 305
Gibraltar, 351, 352
Gluck, Maxwell H., 101, 102
Gold
    free market price, 312
    special drawing rights ("paper gold"),
        312
    world monetary stocks, 311
Goldberg, Arthur J., 12, 323, 324
Gomulka, Wladyslaw, 209
Goodell, Charles E., 116*n*.
Gore, Albert, 123, 124
Government officials, influences on
    opinions of, 109
Great Britain. *See* United Kingdom
Great White Fleet, 149
Greece, 126, 177, 180
Greenland, 167
Gromyko, Andrei A., 217, 221, 227, 228
Guevara, Ché, 226

Haiti, 150, 164
Harding, Warren G., 156
Hartmann, Frederick H., 32*n*.
Hawaii, 35, 144
Hay, John, 147, 148
Hay–Pauncefote Treaty, 35
Hilsman, Roger, 133, 226, 227
Hiroshima, 169
Hiss, Alger, 129
Hitler, Adolf, 24, 166, 169, 266
Hoover, Herbert, 162, 164, 299
Hoover moratorium, 162
"Hot line," 98
Hull, Cordell, 75–77, 164
Hungarian uprising, 135, 210
Hungary, 177–79, 209, 210, 240, 249
Hussein, King of Jordan, 213

Iceland, 167
Immigration into U.S., figures on, 39
India
    contributor to ONUC, 233
    debts and loans to, 312
    as member of Indo–China commis-
        sion, 197
    Soviet arms aid to, 242
    Soviet policy on, 246
    trade figures of, 303

Indo–China War. *See also* Viet–Nam War
  French and Dien Bien Phu, 197, 198
  terms of settlement of, 197, 198
Indonesia, 21, 305, 342
Industrializing, problems in, 308, 309
Institute of Defense Analyses study, 6
Inter-American Development Bank, 312
Inter-American system established, 35. *See also* Latin America
Interdepartmental Regional Groups (IRGs), 81–83
International liquidity, 310–12
International Monetary Fund, 312
Iran, 211
Iraq, 211
Israel
  and Gulf of Aqaba, interference with free access to, 112
  second war with United Arab Republic, 210, 212, 213
  and Straits of Tiran, 353
  "third round" with Arabs, 352–54
Italy, 34, 155, 168, 169, 273

Japan
  disproportion between present power and policy, 21
  Emperor of, allowed to retain throne, 169
  factors in high standard of living of, 308
  and Manchuria, 150, 162, 163, 165
  and Nuclear Non-Proliferation Treaty, 294
  Root–Takahira Agreement, 150
  Taft–Katsura Memorandum, 150
  tension with U.S. over immigration, 149
  trade with U.S., 304
  and war with Russia in *1904*, 31
  and Washington Conference, 74, 158–60
  and World War I gains, 155
Jarring, Gunnar, 353
Jefferson, Thomas, 27, 29*t.*, 142
Johnson, Louis, 93, 94
Johnson, Lyndon B.
  announces Viet–Nam bombing limitation, 68
  announces will not run again, 69
  attitude on Indo–China War in *1950*'s, 198
  clashes with Senator Fulbright, 121
  decision to use force in Viet–Nam, 70
  decision-making style on national security affairs, 132
  effort to tie State Department to foreign affairs coordination, 102

Johnson, Lyndon B. [*cont.*]
  issues NSAM *341*, 81
  trip to Berlin as Vice-President, 225
  "Tuesday lunch" device of, 80
  view of State Department efficiency of, 84
Joint Chiefs of Staff
  origins, 76
  statutory arrangements on, 77
  varying viewpoints within, 108
Jordan, 213
Jupiter missiles, in Turkey, 229

Kádár, János, 210
Kasavubu, Joseph, 213–33
Katzenbach, Nicholas deB., 122–24
Kennan, George F.
  analyses Soviet behavior and U.S. policy attitude swing, 192
  comments on passing of monolithic Communist power, 260
  containment theory of, 178
  disengagement theory of, 127
  heads Policy Planning Staff, 77
  leaves State Department, 215
  part in Berlin access question, 185
Kennedy, John F.
  abolishes Operations Coordinating Board, 4
  as author, cites pressures on Senators, 107, 108
  Bay of Pigs incident, 69, 79, 135, 223
  concept for handling national security affairs of, 79–81
  consolidates ambassadorial authority, 92
  and Cuban Missile Crisis, 226–30
  during the "McCarthy era," 190
  improvises "Excomm," 69
  opinion on State Department of, 84
  and second Berlin crisis, 223
  tendency to handle foreign affairs detail, 102, 132
  Vienna meeting with Khrushchev of, 223
Kennedy, Robert, 80, 230
Key, Francis Scott, 25
Khrushchev, Nikita S.
  and "Camp David formula," 221, 223
  and Congo Crisis, 231
  consolidates power, 209
  delivers "secret speech" on Stalin, 208, 209
  denounces Potsdam Agreement, 218, 219
  falls from power, 246
  at Geneva summit conference, 205
  intensifies second Berlin crisis, 223–25
  at Paris summit meeting, 222

Khrushchev, Nikita S. [*cont.*]
    political style of, 216, 217
    reveals Beria–Malenkov divergent for-
        eign policy, 204, 205
    revisionism on inevitability of war
        doctrine, 239, 240
Kiesinger, Kurt, 249, 333, 337
Kissinger, Henry, 82, 134
Knowland, William, 198
Korea
    American public opinion on war in,
        115, 116
    armistice negotiations, 191
    earlier division of, 18
    treaty with U.S., terms of, 196
    U.S. response to aggression in, 19
Korean War
    effects on U.S. force composition, 288
    events of, 189–91
    as factor in shaping U.S. Asian poli-
        cies, 20
    moral issue in, compared to Viet–Nam
        War, 62
    swings in U.S. opinion on, 115, 116
    U.S. troop strength involved in, 19
Kosygin, Aleksei, 247
Kuwait, 353

Lansing–Ishii Agreement, 157
Laos, 197, 347
Latin America
    and "Alliance for Progress," 14, 308,
        316, 355, 357
    and attitude on hemispheric security,
        53, 164, 357
    and Buenos Aires Conference, 164
    and Cuba, 228, 357
    dependence on single commodity sales,
        302
    and Dominican Republic, 357
    and military rule, 358
    and Montevideo Conference, 164
    and U.S. arms shipments, 308
League of Nations
    Lytton Report on Manchurian crisis,
        163
    and Manchurian crisis, 162
    Senate attitude toward acceptance of,
        156
    weakening of, by Covenant interpreta-
        tion, 68
    Wilson's concept of, 61, 155
Lebanon, 130, 135, 213, 214, 352
Legere, Laurance J., 6n.
Lemnitzer, Lyman L., 253n.
Lend–Lease, 114, 167, 174
Lenin, V. I. 208, 236–38
Lima, Declaration of, 164
Lincoln, Abraham, 117

Livingston, Robert R., 142
Lodge, Henry Cabot, Jr., 100
Lodge, Henry Cabot, Sr., 156
London Economic Conference, 164
Loyalists, 25
Ludlow Amendment, 115
Lumumba, Patrice, 231, 232
Lytton Report of League, 163

MacArthur, Douglas, 116, 129, 190
McCamy, James L., 87, 88, 108
McCarthy, Joseph, 43, 84, 128–30, 190
McGroarty, John Steven, 108
McKinley, William, 145–47, 153
McNamara, Robert S., 80, 134, 283, 287,
    288
Madison, James, 29t.
Mahan, Alfred Thayer, 74
Maine, U.S.S., 145
Malenkov, Georgi, 201, 203–205, 208,
    209
Manchuria, 150, 162, 163, 165
Mansfield, Mike, 124, 260
Mao Tse-tung, 241, 245, 246, 248, 249
Marshall, George C., 75, 77, 129, 180,
    187
Marshall Plan, 62, 127, 180, 181
Marx, Karl, 40
Maximilian, Archduke, of Austria, 28, 34
May, Ernest R., 74, 75
Mendès-France, Pierre, 197, 201, 251
Mexican War, 36
Mexico, 28, 34–36, 150, 151, 162, 164,
    310
Mikoyan, Anastas I., 220, 230
"Military-industrial complex," 105
Millis, Walter, 73n., 75n.
"Mini-states," 12
Mobutu, Joseph, 232, 233
Mollet, Guy, 212
Molotov, Vyacheslav, 180, 201–205, 209
Monroe, James, 27, 29t., 143
Monroe Doctrine
    British suggest joint sponsorship of, 27
    British support of, 28
    originates with policy toward Russia,
        143
    redefined in joint terms, 162
    Roosevelt corollary to, 35, 149, 162
    strategic significance of, 141
Montevideo Conference, 164
Morgenstern, Oskar, 285
Morgenthau plan, 175
Morison, Samuel Eliot, 39, 190n.
Morocco, 149, 320
Moscow Conference of 1957, 241, 245
Moscow Conference of 1960, 241
Multilateral Nuclear Force (MLF), 252,
    253, 332

Munich Conference and Agreement, 17, 166, 175, 273
Mussolini, Benito, 273

Nagasaki, 169
Nagy, Imre, 210
Napoleon III, 28, 34n.
Nasser, Gamal Abdel
    arms deal of, with Soviets, 211, 305
    assessment of U.S. Israeli policy by, 351
    expropriates Suez Canal Company, 212
    initiates "third round" with Israel, 353
    and Middle East events leading to U.S. landing in Lebanon, 213
    negotiates Aswan Dam project, 211
    policy of, increases foreign influences in Middle East, 349
    receives economic support from Kuwait and Saudi Arabia, 353, 354
National Security Act
    of 1947, approved, 77
    later amendments to, 77
National Security Council system
    "Ecomm" device of Kennedy, 69, 79, 80
    Interdepartmental Groups, 82
    National Security Action Memo 341, 80, 81, 84
    operation under different Presidents, 77–82
    Review Group, 82
    Senior Interdepartmental Group (SIG), 81–83, 96, 132
    Under Secretaries Committee, 82, 96
National security policy, discussion of definition of, 6
National security policy planning, discussion of definition of, 6
National Security Resources Board, 77
Naval War College, established, 73
Nehru, Jawaharlal, 196, 242, 246
Neumann, John von, 285
Neustadt, Richard E., 131n.
Neutrality Acts, 114, 115, 166, 167
New Zealand, 38, 198, 199
Nicaragua, 150, 162
Nigeria, 320, 322, 323
Nine-Power Treaty of 1922, 159
Nixon, Richard M.
    approach to national security organization, 80–83
    confirms "country team" concept, 92
    Doctrine, 290
    moves to disengage in Viet–Nam, 135
    newspaper reaction to speech of, 69, 70
    politico-military options review, ordered by, 7, 290n.

Nixon, Richard M. [*cont.*]
    TV press conference, questions put, 104
North Atlantic Pact, 37, 187
North Atlantic Treaty Organization (NATO)
    causes of difficulties in, 331–335
    failures of members to reach force-level goals, 325
    Franco–American differences on strategy in, 332, 333
    German gains and losses through membership in, 333–38
    strategic effects on of French withdrawal from organized features of, 253n.
    Vandenberg Resolution on, 127
Nuclear Multilateral Force (MLF), 252, 253, 332
Nuclear Non-Proliferation Treaty, 293–95, 331, 332
Nuclear Test Ban Treaty, 243, 244, 293, 331

Okinawa, 71, 169
Olney, Richard, 144, 145
Open Door principle, 35, 147, 148, 157, 158, 162, 164
Operations Coordinating Board (OCB), 4, 78, 79
Organization of American States, 53, 228, 357
Organization for Economic Cooperation and Development, 312
Organization for European Economic Cooperation, 180
Ostend Manifesto, 35

Pakistan, 199
Panama, 35, 148, 149
Panay incident, 165
Peace Corps, 95
Pearl Harbor, 168
Pendleton Act, 72
Percy, Charles H., 124
Perry, Commodore, visit to Japan, 35
Peru, 6, 303t.
Philippines, 35, 146, 147, 160, 199
Platt Amendment, 148, 164
Poland
    and Curzon Line as eastern frontier, 169
    division of, in 1939, 166, 328
    interest in Marshall Plan of, 180
    member of Indo–China commission, 197
    Potsdam provisions on, 169, 170
    reaction in 1967 to West German diplomatic initiatives, 249

Poland [*cont.*]
   and Soviet deployment issue in *1939*,
      175
   Soviet postwar tactics in, 176, 177
   under Gomulka government, negotia-
      tions with Soviets, 209
   war with Soviets, 327
   Yalta provisions on, 169, 170
Polaris missiles, 288, 291
Political process in U.S.
   center consensus, 194, 195
   effect on strategic choice, 195
Polk, James K., 143n.
Population of world, figures on, 300, 301
Portuguese colonies in Africa, 359
Poseidon missiles, 291, 292
Potsdam Conference, 169, 170
Powers, Gary, 222
President, of U.S.
   as Commander-in-Chief, 119, 121
   constraints on action by, 67–70,
      131–35·
   and Supreme Court view of powers
      of, 120
Presidential news conferences, 104
Pressure groups, 110–12
Prisoner-of-war issue
   in Indo–China War, 197
   in Korean War, 191
Production, world figures on, 301, 302
Public opinion data, 109n., 115–17

Quemoy–Matsu (Taiwan Straits) crisis,
   132, 241, 245

Radford, Arthur W., 198
Reischauer, Edwin O., 260, 261, 301
Rhodesia, 49, 307, 323, 324, 359, 360
Robinson, James A., 119, 120, 127n.
Rockefeller, Nelson A., 11, 134
Rogers Act, 72, 89
Romania, 177, 178, 249, 269, 328, 329
Roosevelt, Franklin D.
   approach to administrative problems
      of, 132
   death, 176
   establishes diplomatic courier service,
      99
   good neighbor policy of, 164
   master of public relations, 69
   and Neutrality Acts, 114, 165, 166
   plan for occupation of Berlin, 185
   "quarantine the aggressors" speech,
      115, 133, 166
   reorganizes Foreign Service, 90
   tendency to by-pass State Department,
      102
   at wartime conferences, 169
   wartime mistakes of, 176

Roosevelt, Theodore, 72, 149–50, 153
Root, Elihu, 73
Root–Takahira Agreement, 150
Rostow, Walt W., 80
Rubottom, Roy R., Jr., 29n.
Rush-Bagot Agreement, 143
Rusk, Dean
   essential differences with critics, 263
   as member of "Tuesday lunch," 80
   no intimate of Kennedy when ap-
      pointed, 134
   serves two Presidents, 84
   speculates on future decline in use of
      force, 22, 57
   time spent as negotiator, 88
   on Viet–Nam War, 21, 22, 261, 262
Russian territory on North American
   continent,, 35, 142
Russo-Japanese War, 31

Samoa, 35, 144, 148
Santo Domingo, 35. *See also* Dominican
   Republic
Sapin, Burton M., 90n., 94n.
Saudi Arabia, 352, 353
Save America First Movement, 116
Security
   assessment of influence of missiles on,
      266, 267, 369
   structural-organizational patterns of,
      264
   varying reactions to problem of, 265
Senate, of the U.S.
   approves treaty with Korea, 196
   approves treaty with Nationalist China,
      196, 197
   approves treaty with SEATO, 199
   approves Washington Conference
      treaties, with stipulation, 159
   debates on foreign policy, length of,
      123n., 127
   Foreign Relations Committee of, 101,
      122–24, 259, 260
   rejects Treaty of Versailles, 156
   and World Court, 161
Seward, William H., 29
Smith, Walter Bedell, 100
Snyder, Glenn H., 286n.
Sokolovsky, Marshal, 182, 183
Sorensen, Theodore, 80, 84, 134, 230n.
South Africa, 49, 191, 307, 324, 359,
   360
South West Africa, 324
Southeast Asia Collective Defense Treaty
   (SEATO)
   Dulles as proponent of, 135
   establishment of, 197, 198
   Manila protocol, 198, 199
   Rusk's views on, 261

SEATO [*cont.*]
Senate ratification of, 199
strengths and weaknesses of, 199, 200, 346, 367
terms of, 198, 199
Soviet Union
aid policies, 315, 316
arms aid to Arabs, 211, 353
arms to Cuba, 226–30
Berlin free city proposal by, 219
creates Warsaw Pact, 205
develops H-bomb, 201
evolution of U.S. views on, 192, 193
frontier clashes with China, 246, 249
German policy of, at Geneva summit meeting, 206, 207
and Hungarian revolt, 210
and India, 242, 246
Molotov defines democratic election in Germany for, 202
occupation of Czechoslovakia by, 324, 326, 327
polemics with Communist China, 241–46
policy in 1956 Middle East crisis, 213
proposal in 1955 for German elections, 203
reaction to Munich Conference, 175
role in Middle East, 349–52
separate peace treaty with East Germany by, 225
strengths and weaknesses of deployment in Central Europe of, 327–31
and Warsaw interparliamentary conference, 203, 204
Spain, 27, 143, 145, 146
Spanish-American War, 36, 145, 146
Special Assistant for National Security Affairs, 79, 80, 82
Sputnik, 216, 217
Stalin, Joseph, 170, 188, 200, 208, 209, 237–39, 242
Standing Liaison Committee, 75, 76
State Department
ambassadorial salaries, 101
Bureau of Politico-Military Affairs, 94
and coordination, 78–83
Counselor, 96
and "Country Team" concept, 92, 93
courier service, 99
embassies abroad, range in size of, 99
Foreign Service, 72, 85–90
liaison and coordination with Defense, 93, 94
Operations Center, 98
organization of, 95, 96
Planning and Coordination Staff, 96, 97
Policy Planning Council, 96

State Department [*cont.*]
Policy Planning Staff, 77
Stevenson, Adlai, 229
Stimson, Henry L., 74, 162–64
Stimson Doctrine, 162
Strategic Arms Limitation Talks (SALT), 295
Strategic concept, three questions leading to, 9, 10, 259
Strategy of bloc containment, flaws in, 274–79
Strategy of isolating opponent, advantages of, 279–81
Suez Canal, 212, 213, 353, 354
Sukarno, 21, 305
Supreme Court, and powers of President, 120
Sweden, 303
Systems analysis in Pentagon, 287–90

Taft, William H., 72
Taft-Katsura, Memorandum, 150
Teheran Conference, 76, 169
Thailand, 107, 198, 200, 346, 347
Tiran, Straits of, 353
Tito, Marshal, 209
Tonkin, Gulf of, Resolution, 122–24
Truman, Harry
action at outset of Korean War by, 189
announces Truman Doctrine, 126, 177
attitude toward national security organization by, 78
circumstances at outset of tenure of, 134, 176, 177
observations on Eisenhower by, 131, 132
orders U.S. withdrawal from Soviet Zone, 176
quality of his Secretaries of State, 84
recalls General MacArthur, 116
Truman Doctrine, 126–28, 177, 178, 180
Tshombe, Moise, 231–33
"Tuesday lunch," 80
Tunisia, 353
Turkey, 126, 177, 180, 211, 229

U-2 incident, 222
Unilateralism, as basic security option, 264
United Arab Republic
arms deal of, with Soviets, 211, 305
and Aswan Dam project, 211
and crisis of 1956, 210–14
expropriates Suez Canal Company, 212
and Lebanon, 213
and Nasser's views and policies, 349, 351
receives economic support from Kuwait and Saudi Arabia, 353, 354

United Arab Republic [*cont.*]
  and "third round" with Israel, 352, 353
  and Yemen, 352
United Kingdom
  application for Common Market membership, 106
  attitude on Far Eastern security, 198
  Churchill speaks for, 169, 176, 177
  concessions to Hitler, 273
  devaluation of pound in *1967*, 311
  Eden speaks for, 198, 202, 205, 206, 211, 212
  Middle East policy of, 210–13
  "special relationship" with U.S., 252
  trade with U.S., 304
United Nations
  Afro-Asians in, 49
  American attitudes toward, 49, 50
  basic choices for members on issues involving force, 320
  Congo Force (ONUC), 231, 233, 321
  considerations affecting U.S. votes in, 321–24
  effects of custom on, 318, 319
  Emergency Force (UNEF), 213, 321
  essential nature of, 318
  Latin American attitudes toward, 50
  and Middle East, after "third round," 353
  sanctions against Rhodesia, 323, 324, 360
  and South West Africa, 324
  Unified Command in Korea, 191
  U.S. budget contribution to, 11
  U.S. support of, in Korean crisis, 19, 189–91
United States
  aid program, 314–17
  armed forces sent to France in World War I, 154
  armed forces, strength of at time of Spanish-American War, 145
  Arms Control and Disarmament Agency, 95
  Army, strength of in nineteenth century, 30*t.*
  attention to areas of world, uneven, 4
  attitude toward World Court, 161
  Bill of Rights, 41, 42
  considerations affecting votes in UN, 321, 322
  Constitution, 13, 41, 48
  continental expansion of, 27
  contingency plans for Thailand, Senate concern over, 107
  Council of National Defense, 74, 75
  and Dominican Republic, 357

United States [*cont.*]
  earlier long–range trends in foreign policy of 141–43
  effects of geographic isolation on, 23–26
  elections, communism as issue in, 129
  entry into World War I, 151
  and fall of China, 189
  foreign policy, reversal in after *1945*, 18, 19
  "gold flow" problems of, 311
  government personnel abroad, 90
  immigration figures, 39
  Information Agency (USIA), 87, 91, 92, 99
  intelligence agencies, before World War II, 68, 74
  Intelligence Board, 95
  and Latin America, 14, 53, 164, 228, 308, 316, 355, 357, 358
  and military in Latin America, 358
  national security system, 69, 77–84, 96, 132
  Navy, Chief of Naval Operations concept, 73
  options in dealing with German problem, 334–38
  a perspective on role of in Asia, 343–49
  political process, center consensus feature of, 194
  political process, effect on strategic choice of, 195
  relations with Japan, 149, 150, 168, 343–45, 347
  relations with Soviet Union, attitude swings in, 174, 175, 177–79, 192
  Supreme Court, 120
  trade figures, 302–04, 310, 313
  trade with Latin America, 303
  treaty with Korea, terms of, 196
  treaty with Nationalist China, terms of, 196, 197
  treaty with SEATO, terms of, 198, 199
U Thant, 229

Van Buren, Martin, 29*t.*
Vandenberg, Arthur H., 127
Vandenberg Resolution, 127
Venezuela, 35, 144, 145, 149
Verba, Sidney, 109*n.*, 117*n.*
Versailles Conference, 154–56, 158
Versailles Treaty, 155, 156
Viet-Nam
  and Asian attitudes and policies toward U.S. actions in, 274–77
  and Manila protocol, 198, 199
  division at 17th parallel, 197, 198

Viet-Nam [*cont.*]
    liberal dissatisfaction with war in, 112
    military and political theory on, compared, 282, 283
    moral and strategic issues in war in, 62
    North Viet-Nam PT attack on U.S. forces off, 122
    public opinion data on war in, 109*n.*, 116*n.*, 117*n.*
    Rusk's rationale for war in, 261, 262
    and television coverage of war in, 113
    and U.S. Civil Rights movement, relation to war in, 111
    War as watershed of postwar U.S. policy, 19–22
Vincent, John Carter, 215

War of *1812*, 16, 25
Warsaw Pact, created, 205
Washington, George, 27, 29*t.*
Washington, Treaty of, 35, 174
Washington Disarmament Conference, 158–60
Welles, Sumner, 75
Wilhelm, Kaiser, 145, 272
Wilson, Woodrow
    degree of realism of, 37, 61

Wilson, Woodrow [*cont.*]
    evolution of attitude toward World War I, 151
    explains League proposal, 37
    Fourteen Points of, 16, 153, 154
    international reform and action program of, 16
    policy in Asia and Latin America, 150
    views on causes of World War I, 36
    and wording of League Covenant, 68
Winant, John G., 185
World armed forces, figures on, 319, 320
World Bank, 211, 312, 313
World Court, 161
World population, figures on, 300, 301
World production, figures on, 301, 302
World trade, figures on, 313
World War II, military turning-point in, 168, 169

Yalta Conference, 169, 170, 178
Yarborough, Ralph W., 124
Yemen, 352
Yugoslavia, 241, 249, 330

Zhukov, Marshal, 209, 216
Zimmermann Note, 151
Zorin, Soviet UN ambassador, 229